Growth Dynamics in New Markets

GROWTH DYNAMICS IN NEW MARKETS

Improving Decision Making through Simulation Model-based Management

MARTIN F.G. SCHAFFERNICHT & STEFAN N. GROESSER

Facultad de Economía y Negocios, Universidad de Talca, Chile

School of Engineering, Bern University of Applied Sciences and Institute of Management,

University of St Gallen, Switzerland

WILEY

This edition first published 2018
© 2018 John Wiley & Sons Ltd

The right of Martin F.G. Schaffernicht and Stefan N. Groesser to be identified as the authors of this work has been asserted in accordance with law.

Registered Offices
John Wiley & Sons, Inc., 111 River Street, Hoboken, NJ 07030, USA
John Wiley & Sons Ltd, The Atrium, Southern Gate, Chichester, West Sussex, PO19 8SQ, UK

Editorial Office
9600 Garsington Road, Oxford, OX4 2DQ, UK

For details of our global editorial offices, customer services, and more information about Wiley products visit us at www.wiley.com.

Wiley also publishes its books in a variety of electronic formats and by print-on-demand. Some content that appears in standard print versions of this book may not be available in other formats.

Library of Congress Cataloging-in-Publication Data

Names: Schaffernicht, Martin F. G., 1961– author. | Groesser, Stefan N., 1978– author.
Title: Growth dynamics in new markets : improving decision making through simulation model-based management / by Martin F.G. Schaffernicht, Facultad de Economia y Negocios, Universidad de Talca, Chile, Stefan N. Groesser, School of Engineering, Bern University of Applied Sciences and Institute of Management, University of St. Gallen, Switzerland.
Description: Hoboken, NJ : Wiley, [2018] | Includes index. | Identifiers: LCCN 2017052554 (print) | LCCN 2017054563 (ebook) | ISBN 9781119118220 (pdf) | ISBN 9781119127413 (epub) | ISBN 9781119118237 (cloth)
Subjects: LCSH: Decision making. | Management. | Marketing. | Strategic planning.
Classification: LCC HD30.23 (ebook) | LCC HD30.23 .S294 2018 (print) | DDC 658.8/02–dc23
LC record available at https://lccn.loc.gov/2017052554

Cover design: Wiley
Cover image: © Leontura/Gettyimages

Set in 12/15pt Times New Roman by SPi Global, Pondicherry, India

Printed and bound by CPI Group (UK) Ltd, Croydon, CR0 4YY

10 9 8 7 6 5 4 3 2 1

CONTENTS

RELAXING ASSUMPTIONS AND ADDING RELEVANT ASPECTS OF REALITY 377

SYSTEM DYNAMICS: A METHODOLOGY FOR MODEL-BASED MANAGEMENT 405

PREFACE

Invitation to explore

We are inviting you on a journey to explore the different elements of introducing a product into a new market. You will assume the role of a manager responsible for successful product introduction while a competitor strives to do the same. Your potential customers are free to choose either of the products. How should you make your decisions given that you have a direct competitor acting simultaneously? Which strategies can improve your decision making in such a dynamic situation?

Remember, not only managers have goals, make plans, decide, and execute. This is what individuals do irrespective of their profession. What follows are a few general remarks to set the stage.

Making plans requires the ability to know where you currently are, where you want to go, and how to get from here to there. Maps or diagrams are helpful tools. There are many well-known examples of maps. For instance, explorers developed maps to navigate through a geographical area or topological space.

The map in Figure 0.1 dates back to the year 1630. It was created to help navigators cross the Atlantic Ocean ('Mar del Norte') to the Pacific Ocean via the Strait of Magellan. At this time, ships sailed from Europe to the New World, and since navigators always looked in the upward direction, it was useful for them to draw a map and position East at the top.

'To navigate' stems from the two Latin words 'nāvis' (ship) and 'āgis' (drive); it literally means to steer or drive a ship. However, that what we want to steer is not always a ship, and not all the maps are geographical ones. Architects

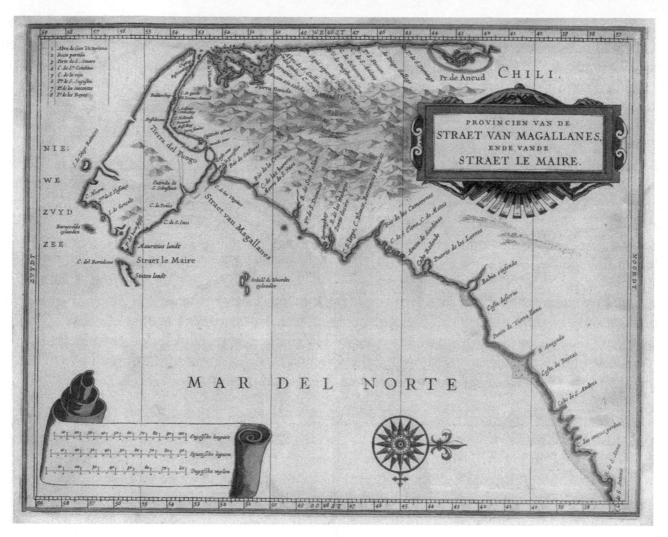

Figure 0.1 A navigation map of the Strait of Magellan (Princeton University Library, 2016)

and planners design maps of buildings or bridges. Systems engineers map information systems with databases and computer programs. Both architectural and information systems maps are construction plans for artificial, man-made objects. Organizational consultants map, revise, and design business processes and organizational structures, thereby planning how different organizational members interact to carry out their work. In these cases, the maps represent structures, i.e. elements that are essentially static.

However, business managers are often confronted with situations, with or without a map, that defy their ability to anticipate what will happen. Imagine you are a corporate strategist. You must develop a plan for long-term success and, thereby, need to anticipate the potential actions of your suppliers, competitors, and customers who have also developed their own plans based on their own goals and expectations about your actions. Such structurally interdependent situations are 'dynamic systems'. A dynamic system consists of several interrelated components with different actors. The components and actors react to one another and have different reasons for influencing and altering the system.

One example of a dynamic system is the strategic planning of football (soccer) matches. The map in Figure 0.2 illustrates the movements a soccer team can perform when the opposing team's defence players attack a player. The teams have opposing goals and the actions of one team decrease the level of goal achievement of the other team. Further, each team plans and decides its moves considering the respective previous and expected moves of the opposing team. Therefore, the soccer-planning map not only illustrates structural elements but also considers past or expected moves.

Managers are faced with even more dynamic situations: the 'game' they are in is not as well defined as football. Competitors, customers, and other actors are free to decide on their course of action. Let us assume there is a company: NewTel. It is about to introduce mobile phones – a durable consumer good typically used for 9–18 months – to a new market in the presence of one rival of approximately the same size. You are a top manager at NewTel and face the challenge of taking the necessary decisions to lead the product introduction to a success. Uncovering and developing a new market in parallel to your rival is the dynamic challenge at hand: both you and your competitor will strive to capture customers from the same population as quickly as possible. The customers,

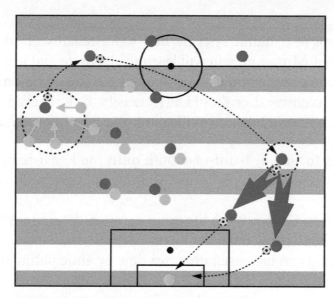

Figure 0.2 A map for switching sides and keeping control of the ball in soccer

of course, are influenced by the actions of both companies in the market. The interdependency between you and your competitor in this limited market leads to a highly complex situation, where your decisions may easily generate undesired effects and dynamics.

Which factors should you include in your management map to successfully 'navigate' NewTel? How do you determine these factors? How will this map help you to make successful decisions? Since many of those factors will be changing, and at different speeds, you will need to know why and how quickly they are changing and how you can influence them through the decisions you take. What you need are tools for mapping and planning in dynamic systems. You need an approach to determine the relevant factors in messy situations, map their dynamic relationships and show immediate, as well as delayed, effects to determine their impact over time on the relevant outcome of interest. The simulation model-based management approach will support you in this regard.

What will you learn?

You will learn how to develop maps of dynamic systems, how to formulate candidate decision policies, and how to evaluate them based on simulations. Moreover, you will learn to elaborate and use your own computer simulations to find out what decisions you could and should make (content of the decision), when you should make them (timing of the decision), and how intensive they should be (intensity of the decision). When reaching the end of the book, you will have an intuitive understanding and skills to master dynamic business challenges such as:

1. **Self-limiting growth**: dynamics fuelled by word-of-mouth diffusion is self-reinforcing and displays exponential growth until the shrinking population of potential customers limits growth. Overall customer growth follows an S-shaped behaviour.
2. **Obsolescence speeds re-purchases**: the product's life cycle duration determines the relationship between current customers and new sales to potential customers.
3. **Sell earlier, not more**: advertising can increase purchases now by anticipating future purchases. It is recognized that a decrease in purchases will follow.
4. **Sources of revenue**: revenues depend on new purchases from customers who pay the sales price and current customers who pay the subscription rate. With a limited population, higher revenues from sales cannot be sustained without losing revenues from subscriptions, and vice versa. Your business model must state how you balance these two revenue streams.
5. **Customer net value**: advertising can require more financial resources than the value of the additional sales.
6. **Double-action of prices**: an increase in prices leads to higher revenues from sales and revenues from subscription, but it also reduces the new sales and, therefore, the number of current customers paying the subscription, which in turn decreases revenues.
7. **Relative attractivity**: in rivalry situations, customers make decisions about purchasing and switching according to the price and the amount of advertising the company displays in comparison to its competitors.
8. **Options for rivalry**: companies can compete for potential customers or each other's current customers. The levers used for each type of rivalry are different.

9. **Competition versus cooperation**: competing by lowering prices can lead to acquiring more new customers, but it also decreases the revenue per sale and monthly subscription, thereby reducing the market value. Moreover, it is likely to trigger a price war.

Each chapter guides you through applicable content and questions enabling you to develop these insights yourself. You will first arrive at answers and then elaborate on them while going deeper and deeper into the subject. Methodological concepts such as variables, causal links, and feedback loops will become your normal language, and you will develop and experiment with simulation models. These simulation models will allow you to qualify your answers and to pose new questions. In summary, the book prepares you to approach dynamic management problems in a systematic and consistent way. Moreover, you can use simulation models to reflect upon the dynamics of business and make better grounded decisions. At the end of this journey, you will be able to develop dynamic maps and use simulation models to reflect upon the dynamics of business for designing successful business policies. Such models serve the purpose of designing decision policies. When management relies on such policies, we refer to it as model-based management (Schwaninger, 2010). This book is designed to help build several skills that belong or relate to the system dynamics competency framework (Schaffernicht and Groesser, 2016).

What are the components of the book?

The book consists of three components.

The printed text. This is the thread in your learning journey. It successively introduces you to management challenges at the company NewTel. In addition, it introduces concepts and examples of possible dynamics, poses relevant questions, guides you through model conceptualization, allows you to develop hypotheses, to test your findings through simulations, and to interpret the simulation results for decision making.

Simulation models. Each chapter is augmented by one or more simulation models. They are available from the companion website. In this cascade of simulation models, each new model builds on the previous ones. The models help you to explore the dynamics resulting from your decision. Each simulation model is explained in a video tutorial.

Business simulator 'SellPhone'. SellPhone allows you to gain first-hand experience in your role as a manager of NewTel. You can get a feeling for how complex your task is. After you have mastered the content chapters in the printed text, SellPhone allows to you to double-check your learning to see how successful you have been at leading your business.

What is the structure of the book?

The book has nine chapters. Chapter 1 introduces you to the telecommunication case. It provides relevant contextual information and identifies the goals and decision variables you have at your disposal to achieve the goals at NewTel. SellPhone is used to provide first-hand experience in managing NewTel. You will address the following questions: What are the relevant factors in this case? How do the factors interact with the decisions made during the simulation? The following chapters will also address these questions. In Chapter 2, you will explore the dynamics of diffusion by word-of-mouth. We will introduce the mapping method. Three simulation models enrich the text of this chapter. Chapter 3 adds a limited product life cycle duration to the basic situation and explores its implications for the diffusion dynamics. Chapter 4 considers the effects of advertising spend on the acquisition of customers. You will discover the fundamental effect of advertising and discover what effect advertising has on purchases and the accumulation of customers. Chapter 5 introduces financial resources to the situation through a limited life cycle duration and advertising spending. You will explore the implications of purchasing price and subscription rate for revenues, and how the changes in the life cycle duration and in advertising spend impact profits. All aspects discussed so far are integrated into one systemic simulation model about NewTel. Chapter 6 helps you to systematically optimize your decisions for NewTel. It concludes the analysis of your company, since now you have the know-how to ideally introduce your product into the new market. However, what about your direct competitor? Your strategy needs to consider your rival in your environment. How can you optimize NewTel's success under these circumstances? Chapter 7 introduces your rival company RivTel. You will become familiar with two types of rivalry. The first deals with competing for potential customers and the second deals with competing for each other's current customers. The simulation models help you to clarify the interdependencies and guide you to design superior policies. To follow, you are again invited to SellPhone to demonstrate what you have learned about managing a business in highly complex environments. Chapter 8 discusses the simplifying assumptions made in the case models. Possible modifications of the assumptions are discussed and a set of scenarios provided. Chapter 9 reviews the methodology used in the book and generalizes the case of NewTel to other management challenges.

Within the book, a number of icons are used.

The more active you are, the more you will learn. Throughout the journey, new questions arise. If you reflect on them and develop your own answer before you continue reading, your mind will be best prepared for the upcoming content. Therefore, throughout the book we will frequently ask questions or suggest specific activities for you to 'Do It Yourself' (DIY). These places are marked with the icon shown to the left. For many DIYs, there are worksheets you can download from the companion website; they guide you through the steps you are asked to do on your own. You will also find a discussion of each DIY on this website.

In many stages of our analysis, specific concepts and tools are useful. Each time these occur, there is a 'Toolbox' marked with the icon shown to the left. Here you will find an explanation of concepts and tools.

At the end of each chapter, you are invited to assess your understanding and ability to use the new concepts and tools by answering a set of questions.

This book provides you with an introduction to the management of products and services in new markets using a simulation modelling-based approach to management. Of course, these initial learning steps can be deepened. Going further requires additional learning engagement from you. For this, we have provided additional challenges; the icon to the left signals them.

In many places in the book, **systems insights** (SI) and **management insights** (MI) about the dynamics and structure of the business case can be gained. These SI and MI are relevant because they can be transferred to similar cases you encounter in your work. We also identify a series of **principles** (P) of dynamic systems that are not bound to the business case but which are fundamental concepts and relationships valid and applicable in any dynamic situation. Whenever appropriate, we have inserted **Guidelines** (G) as practical recommendations to help you develop good practices as a business modeller.

Who is the book for and how to use it?

Individual learners. If you are an undergraduate student (sophomore, senior; major as well as non-major) or a graduate student (master, executive MBA, Ph.D.) in business administration, strategic management, management science, business engineering, industrial engineering, marketing, decision making, economics, public policy, or public management, you will benefit from this book.

The book can also serve as a self-directed learning journey supported by e-learning components: an online simulator, video tutorials and worksheets for the DIYs. It is self-contained and does not require other technical training or theoretical knowledge. Therefore, you can familiarize yourself with the approach, develop intuitive insights concerning the principles of diffusion for durable products, and you will enable yourself to work with specialized consultants.

The book invites you to be active. While you progress through each chapter, we strongly recommend that you replicate the simulation models and experiments and continue to perform your own experiments. As a guideline, you will find video tutorials for each experiment on the companion website. We encourage you to develop the book's models on your own. Moreover, at the end of each of each chapter, you will find questions and further challenges for self-study.

Lecturers. If you are interested in lecturing in business administration, strategic management, management science, business engineering, industrial engineering, marketing, decision making, economics, public policy, or public management with a new and engaging approach, the book is beneficial to you. You can implement the material in undergraduate or graduate courses immediately. The book is purposefully short but is a comprehensive story on growth dynamics in business under rivalry conditions in new markets. Our approach offers a pragmatic and systematic method for studying management challenges and prepares your students for future courses in dynamic systems. Moreover, the book offers value by introducing a visual mapping approach that enables interdisciplinary thinking. The book has the potential to motivate students to follow-up with more detailed studies on their own. The material accompanying the book requires no further preparation. It can be used directly off the shelf. We suggest using the book in one of the following ways:

- For undergraduate students, it belongs to a business or strategy module and requires eight contact sessions (each 45 minutes). The lecturer guides students through each chapter. For Chapters 2–7 there are two possibilities. Firstly, you can have the students read each chapter, reproduce the small simulation models and perform the simulation experiments before the class session. Time in class is used for resolving questions and discussing challenging aspects. Or, secondly, you can introduce each chapter and reproduce the short simulation models; the students then experiment with the models in their self-study time.
- In a generalist MBA course, the book should be used in eight contact lessons. As in case-based work, students read each chapter before the session and try to reproduce the simulation experiments with the pre-developed models. The contact session is dedicated to resolving questions and reproducing a project-like discussion where the lecturer guides the learners through the steps – from raising a question to a simulation model and towards simulation experiments. Students should be able to interpret the results in a plenary discussion.
- In master's courses with students who already have experience in system dynamics, the book can be studied in a reduced number of sessions. After the SellPhone game, students are challenged to develop their own model to design a strategy and decision policy. Each modelling attempt is debriefed in a plenary session in which the lecturer discusses the content of the respective chapter. After two iterations, there should be an additional session where discussion centres on the diverse simplifying assumptions and how to relax them.

If you are a lecturer, and you have questions, ask us: martin@utalca.cl and stefan.groesser@bfh.ch (www.stefan-groesser.com).

Before you start

We hope that you will gain as many dynamic insights while studying the book as we had while writing it. Moreover, we hope that the book helps you to train your disciplined, systemic, and dynamic thinking skills. Enjoy the time you spend developing hypotheses, formulating simulation models, and experimenting with them to solidify your understanding of management challenges and to develop your decision-making capabilities in dynamic systems.

References

Princeton University Library. 2016. The Strait of Magellan: 250 Years of Maps (1520–1787). http://libweb5.princeton.edu/visual_materials/maps/websites/pacific/magellan-strait/magellan-strait-maps.html (last accessed 23 October 2017).

Schwaninger, M. 2010. Model-based management (MBM): a vital prerequisite for organizational viability. *Kybernetes*, **39**(9/10), 1419–1428. https://doi.org/10.1108/03684921011081105.

Schaffernicht, M. and Groesser, S. 2016. A competence development framework for learning and teaching system dynamics. *System Dynamics Review*, **32**(1), 52–81. doi: 10.1002/sdr.1550.

ACKNOWLEDGMENTS

This book would not have come into existence without the contribution of many people. Over the past years, several generations of MBA students at the Universidad de Talca, Chile, and those following the European Master in System Dynamics programme at various institutions have worked their way through previous versions of what is now in your hands. Conversations about management books using simulation modelling with Kim Warren and George Richardson reinforced the idea that such a book has an important role to play in management education. We would like to thank many people from Wiley for their vital support in developing this book. We wish to thank Graham Winch.

And most importantly, we thank our partners. Thank you, Paula, for your patience while I (Martin) was sitting in front of the screen and for your encouragement. And thank you, Saskia and Finn, that you have given me (Stefan) the time to work on this book.

ABOUT THE COMPANION WEBSITE

This book is accompanied by a companion website:

http://www.wiley.com/go/Schaffernicht/growth-dynamics

The website includes:

• simulation models;

• an online simulator;

• worksheet formats for working through the DIYs;

• discussion of the DIYs, questions, and challenges.

Scan this QR code to visit the companion website

INTRODUCING A DURABLE PRODUCT IN A NEW MARKET

1.1 Introduction

This chapter introduces your challenge as a responsible manager at the telecommunication company NewTel. You have to introduce a durable product in the new market 'Plutonia'. You will use the SellPhone-Simulator (described later in the chapter) that provides you with first-hand experience in dealing with your new situation. You are faced with difficult questions as the unfolding sequence of decisions that are required to manage your company unravels in a highly dynamic market with the major competitor RivTel. One hint: to manage is to convert information into decisions. In this sense, a manager is a decision maker; we will use both terms interchangeably. This book will help you to answer these questions systematically, so that you are better equipped to develop a successful strategy. After completion of the first chapter, you will have covered the following learning outcomes:

- You will have become acquainted with your decision task and the SellPhone-Simulator.
- You will know the concepts 'policy' and 'variable', which are fundamental concepts that will accompany you throughout the book.

Growth Dynamics in New Markets: Improving Decision Making through Simulation Model-based Management,
First Edition. Martin F.G. Schaffernicht and Stefan N. Groesser.
© 2018 John Wiley & Sons Ltd. Published 2018 by John Wiley & Sons Ltd.
Companion website: www.wiley.com/go/Schaffernicht/growth-dynamics

- Your first attempt at growing NewTel in Plutonia will have yielded expected, and also unexpected, outcomes that require consistent explanations.
- You will have practiced the use of 'behaviour-over-time graphs' displaying the behaviours and trends of variables over time, to identify important aspects of how these variables develop.
- You will have generated questions about the factors that drive customer growth, and you will need the answers to manage NewTel's market introduction successfully.

1.2 Your briefing for the business challenge in Plutonia

It is late afternoon on a Wednesday in July. You are sitting on a plane from Boston to Frankfurt on your way to the NewTel headquarters. You have been with the company for eight months. NewTel is a major telecommunication company that is about to introduce mobile telecommunication in Plutonia, a country where this type of service does not exist yet. Your task is to manage the company's strategy for introducing your product and service into the country. The objective by which your superior will assess you is the *Accumulated profits* at the end of the first year of introduction. The market potential is estimated to be one million persons. As a first initiative, your predecessor in Plutonia distributed 5000 mobile phones to individuals for free, but then suddenly left NewTel. The free phones came with a subscription contract for nine months, which was not free: the subscription fee was initially set at $20. Also, an initial sales price for the mobile phone of $50 has been suggested to you. This is all the information you have now. No other plans exist to advance the business. Therefore, you have been appointed to take over immediately.

The market analysis available to you shows that you will have one major competitor – RivTel. The competitor is also preparing to sell mobile phone products and service bundles in Plutonia. Your market analysis team has provided you with further information informing you that the final customer can only differentiate the product and service bundles by the *sales price* of the product, the amount of the monthly *subscription rate* and the *life cycle duration* of the bundle. Hence, other factors such as quality, designs, or services are not differentiating factors for the final customers in Plutonia. However, you can also influence *Potential customers* by means of your monthly *advertising spending*.

Moreover, since Plutonia (Figure 1.1) is grateful that you are attempting to enter and, thus, develop its market, the government is willing to provide an infrastructure (e.g. telecommunication network) and other means needed (e.g. technical standards and legal regulations), so that you can concentrate on introducing the telecommunication service.

While looking out of the window as the flight enters the European area over Great Britain, you reflect on your situation: Once you have introduced the product-service bundle, how much profit would be a good result at the end of the year? What initiative should you launch to achieve good results? When should you launch it and how intensely? How will your decisions be influenced knowing that RivTel is on Plutonia's doorstep?

Figure 1.1 Map of Plutonia

Many questions are waiting to be answered. To reiterate, NewTel currently has 5000 customers in Plutonia. Your research shows that one million individuals could be interested in subscribing to a mobile telecommunication bundle. Your revenue will come from two sources. Firstly, from the sales price that new customers must pay for the initial purchase of the mobile phone and, secondly, from the monthly *subscription rate* they have to pay for the duration of the contract. The current legal situation in Plutonia, which you cannot alter, is that both the duration of the contract and the life cycle duration of the phone need to be identical. This current length is nine months; it can become shorter or longer if you decide to change it. NewTel does not produce the phones but purchases them from a long-term business partner: Samuria Technologies from Neptunia sells them to you at a fixed price of $40, which will remain the same for the next few years because NewTel recently successfully renegotiated a supplier contract with Samuria. Moreover, NewTel incurs operating costs for using the telecommunication network and government services of Plutonia, i.e. costs for routing the calls and for using the required technical equipment. These costs amount to an average of $10 per month for each customer. NewTel can influence the operating costs by process improvement spending to fund cost reduction projects.

RivTel, your rival, has the same objective of maximizing *Accumulated profits* at the end of the first year. Your opponent manager at RivTel – whom you do not know yet – must make the same type of decisions. The decisions each of you make concentrate on the following variables: the mobile phone *sales price*, the monthly *subscription rate*, the *life cycle duration* of the mobile phone bundle, the monthly *advertising spending*, and the monthly *process improvement spending*.

Toolbox 1.1:
Variables, units of measure, and behaviour modes

Companies or markets are dynamic: their components and elements change over time. A variable represents relevant components and elements and is something that may change its value over time.

Relevance: why do we need variables?

Variables are relevant for the process of structuring and understanding challenging situations. In such situations, we need to think about what the situation consists of and what the options are. When reflecting on a situation, we describe the thoughts in words. Some factors are relevant because of their behaviour and their presumed influence on one another. For example, in the case of a bakery business, if one wants to understand how *revenue* is generated over a period, for instance one month, important variables might include the number of *customers purchasing* during that month, the *prices* of the products purchased, and the number of *products purchased by each customer*. One must decide which factor is relevant enough to be considered as a variable.

It is also essential that each variable in a model has a corresponding entity in reality. If a variable is only there to avoid formulation problems or erroneous model behaviours, but the modeller cannot tell which real entity is represented by the variable, then the model loses contact with the real situation it is supposed to portray. Ensuring that each variable is linked to a real entity is part of the permanent validation effort.

Endogeneity: input, output or computed?

We need variables to decompose a problem and represent its relevant aspects. If a variable is relevant depends on the model purpose and problem to be solved. This indicates that a model boundary must be defined that delimits relevant, i.e. to be considered, from non-relevant content, i.e. to be left out of a model. However, in the real situation such boundaries do not exist. Therefore, the variables inside the model boundary, for which equations will be developed, are not independent from the outside world. For this reason, we use input variables that contain estimated or approximated data instead of equations. These input variables will influence inner or endogenous variables in the model. The word 'endogenous' contains two ancient roots; 'endo' means 'inside', and is the opposite of 'exo' ('outside'), and 'genous' means 'generated'. Endogenous variables are computed by the equations inside the model's boundary. Input variables are exogenous and nothing in the model influences them. Output variables, even though they are computed in the model, are also exogenous because they do not influence anything inside the model.

Definition: what is a variable?

When defining a variable, its attributes must be specified: name, unit of measure, and range of values.

Name: The name of a variable is substantive and should reveal the variable's meaning. For example, product price is a transparent and valid name for a variable, as involved parties can easily understand what element of the system under study is meant.

Units of measure: Each variable needs a 'unit of measure' or 'unit'. Being clear about units helps to ensure that the variables and the relationships between them are meaningful. Unit consistency, sometimes called dimensional consistency, means that the equations describing the relationships between the variables do not attempt to compare apples with oranges. Unit consistency also helps to ensure a conceptually sound model formulation, which is an important part of model validation.

For instance, the variable *temperature* can be measured in degrees Celsius, Kelvin, or Fahrenheit. Another example, *currency reserves* of the American Central Bank are measured in US Dollars ($). A bakery's *customers* are measured in numbers of individuals and the *price of bread* might be expressed in Euro/kg. In cases, such as *customers* or *workers*, sometimes we make a difference between plural and singular: the baker may have 150 *customers* (individuals), monitors weekly *sales* ($/week) and wants to know the weekly *sales per customer* ($/week/individual). Different modelling software packages, which we start using shortly, have different ways to deal with the difference between singular and plural in units. To avoid unnecessary complications, we use only singular in the following equations, but follow the rules of grammar in the written text. The units are indicated in square brackets.

Value range: Often, only a limited range of values makes sense for the variable in the context under study. For instance, the numbers of customers can only be positive. By specifying the minimum and maximum value of a variable, it becomes easier to recognize flaws in one's reasoning by realizing that an unreasonable value has been generated.

Behaviour: variables vary over time – but how?

It is important, but not sufficient, to know the current value of a variable at a given point in time. For a dynamic analysis, it is essential to know how the variable is changing over time. Considering the past, the rate of change of a variable and the fact that its rate or the direction of change are changing themselves is decisive to figure out how it might behave in the future, given that other elements in the system remain unchanged. Taking these dynamic features into account allows one to make hypotheses about causes for development over time and how one could possibly influence it to our favour.

For example, for the central bank to decide on its monetary policy, it needs to know if the inflation rate is stable or not. Moreover, the bank needs to know if the behaviour of the inflation rate has responded as expected after taking monetary action. And virtually any company will not only need to know how many customers it has at the end of the current month – but it also needs to know if the customer stock is growing or shrinking and if this is occurring with an increasing or decreasing slope.

There are many different such behaviours and they are categorized in behaviour modes (Table 1.1); they can be organized in three 'atomic' behaviour modes and several composed behaviour modes (Ford, 1999). The former behaviour patterns are called atomic behaviour modes because they cannot

Table 1.1 Atomic behaviour modes

Description: the variable …	Behaviour mode
… keeps the same value over time or grows or decreases linearly	Linear behaviour
… grows or decreases at an accelerating slope	Exponential behaviour
… grows or decreases at a diminishing slope	Goal-seeking behaviour

be decomposed in simpler elements of behaviour. More complex behaviour modes, such as oscillation or S-shaped growth, can be decomposed into phases of atomic behaviour modes.

To gain an overview of the development of variables over time, graphs that show the behaviour of the variables are best to use. Such graphs are behaviour-over-time graphs (or BOTG in short). The horizontal axis represents time and the vertical axis displays the variable's values in the respective unit of measure; for instance *Accumulated profits* measured in $. In the book, we use the word 'graph' as a synonym for BOTG. Figure 1.2 illustrates graphs for the most common behaviour modes.

The first three examples in Figure 1.2 show atomic behaviour modes that cannot be decomposed further. When the amount of change per time period is constant, the behaviour is linear. A special case of this behaviour mode is 'steady state': this is when a variable has stabilized at one value and neither increases nor decreases. Another term used for steady state is equilibrium. Exponential behaviour is accelerating growth or decline. Goal-seeking behaviour is a slowing growth or decline, steadily approaching a long-term value. The second three behaviour modes are more complex but can be decomposed in phases that correspond to atomic modes. S-shaped growth is then a sequence of exponential growth followed by goal-seeking growth. Oscillation is a longer sequence of exponential and goal-seeking phases. Overshoot and collapse can be decomposed into exponential growth, then goal-seeking growth, and eventually exponential decline.

In this book, variables appear in *italics*. This helps you to remember that regardless of the form in which a variable appears – in text, diagram, or equation – it is always the same variable. In the equations, the unit of measure of the variable will appear in brackets. For example, *Current customers* [individual]. The behaviour of the variables, i.e. the type of changes that occur in a variable, will be described in <u>underlined</u> words. This notation helps to get acquainted with the fact that *structure* (i.e, variables and causal links) is not the same as the <u>behaviour</u> of this *structure*.

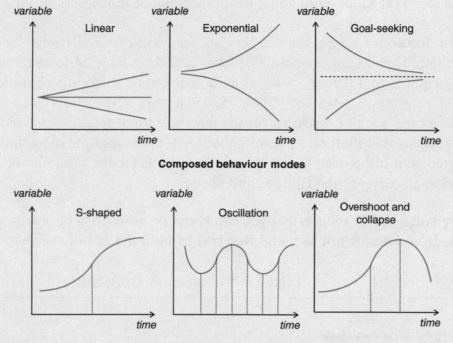

Figure 1.2 Graphs of the three atomic and three composed behaviour modes

Behaviour: reference mode versus simulated behaviour

We can partially test a model and its quality if we compare the simulated behaviour of variables to empirical data available of their behaviour over time. The term 'reference mode' refers to the empirical data. The data available may not always be statistically robust or detailed. However, if this is the case, one can attempt to obtain estimates from experts and then convert them into approximate behaviour patterns to estimate inflection points, extreme values, and value ranges. This reference mode often builds the starting point of an analysis. Most often, the behaviour of the reference mode is not fully understandable and requires further analysis.

Variables are important. Every time you reason about NewTel or something else, you use variables – explicitly or implicitly. Table 1.2 summarizes the variables you can change, i.e. the decision variables, their current values, and units of measure as well as the minimum and maximum values of the variables.

You must make your decisions once per month. You can set the *sales price* between $0 and $70. We use the $ symbol to represent US Dollars. There is only one mobile phone model available. Moreover, there is only one type of service contract, i.e. a subscription, and the service contract is acquired as an additive bundle with the mobile phone. The monthly *subscription rate* can vary between $0 and $30. Changes in the *subscription rate* are applied to all *Current customers* at the same time, i.e. all *Current customers* pay the current monthly *subscription rate*. This rate is part of the contract and legally solid in Plutonia. The initial *life cycle duration* of the subscription-and-phone-bundle is nine months. You can change it in between 6 and 18 months. Just as for the *subscription rate*, changes of the *life cycle duration* are applied to all current subscriptions and phones.

You have a monthly budget of $1 million that you can spend on *advertising* or *process improvements*. You are free to allocate the budget. If you decide not to spend that budget until the end of the year, it remains in the accounts of

Table 1.2 Your decision variables

Variable	Definition of the variable	Unit of measure	Initial	Min	Max
Sales price	Amount paid by each customer when purchasing a mobile phone.	$	50	0	70
Subscription rate	Monthly amount paid by each *current customer* for the life cycle duration of the contract.	$/ month	20	0	30
Life cycle duration	Number of months that a phone is used.	month	9	6	18
Advertising spending	Monthly amount spent by NewTel for advertising. All advertisement channels have the same effectiveness.	$/ month	0	0	1 M
Process improvement spending	Monthly amount spent by NewTel to improve the cost efficiency of processes. This yields a reduction of operating costs.	$/ month	0	0	1 M

NewTel and, thus, will be part of the *Accumulated profits*. However, if you choose to spend some or your entire budget, the amounts spent will be costs, and they will reduce your *monthly profits* of that month. Naturally you would spend the budget only if you believe that the effects of spending it will compensate for the costs and bring a net increase of the *Accumulated profits* at the end of the year. Money spent for *advertising* provides messages on TV, radio, or social media (for details see Chapter 4). When investing in *process improvements*, e.g. improvement of equipment and personnel, the impact gained depends on the amount spent and the size of your internal service infrastructure (more details on this in Chapter 5). The *operation costs* can be reduced by up to 1% per month. In the case of NewTel, we make assumptions to provide learning experiences about market dynamics and the diffusion of new product-service bundles when facing a major competitor. Chapter 8 discusses and relaxes several of those assumptions.

There are no other financial restrictions imposed on you; you could make losses during the months of the year. You will not go bankrupt since the parent company ensures your liquidity. This said, you are responsible for achieving superior *Accumulated profits* at the end of 12 months.

At the beginning of your year-long mission in Plutonia, you find yourself with specific initial values for each of the five decision variables. You could just stick to these initial values, but you could change them as well. As the responsible decision maker for NewTel, you have sufficient autonomy to interpret the information you receive and make decisions based on them. Of course, not all policies yield satisfying results. To maximize the *Accumulated profits* over 12 months, you must define policies that lead to the appropriate values for NewTel's *sales price, subscription rate, life cycle duration, advertising spending, process improvement spending* in the dynamic market situation you are in. At the microlevel, you must search a set of five specific policies for NewTel.

As mentioned in Toolbox 1.2, policies can be routinized or implicit, and making them explicit can be difficult. Therefore, we start with two introductory scenarios, which are introduced in Sections 1.3 and 1.4. For each of them, you are invited to simulate the scenario yourself. In the first, you will follow a simple policy; in the second, we will examine the fictitious reasoning of two decision makers following implicit policies. Thereafter, each scenario will be debriefed to uncover the relevant business structure.

Toolbox 1.2:
Policies and models

Organizations must be successful or at least follow a viable course of action in their interactions with changing environments. To measure success, it must be stated firstly what the goals are. Then, a strategy is needed, meaning a general guideline about what success is. Carrying out a strategy requires the ability to sense relevant conditions and changes and to use that information to decide about the best actions. Thus, organizations design and use explicit or implicit decision rules that prescribe how input information is transformed into decisions. Such rules are called 'policies'. A policy is a course or principle of action adopted or proposed by an organization or individual (Oxford Dictionaries, 2016). Policies define what should be done when certain circumstances exist. The circumstances are represented by variables and their specific values or behaviours. The goodness of an organization's policies determines the quality and success of the organization.

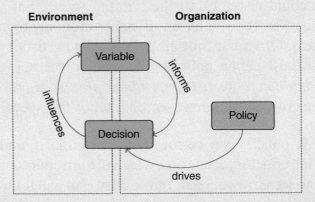

Figure 1.3 A decision is driven by a policy and informed by the behaviour or variables

A policy specifies which variables are to be monitored and which decisions will be taken in response to observing certain conditions or changes in those variables (Figure 1.3).

Figure 1.3 shows that there is a policy which influences variables via decisions. This become clear in our central bank example. Central banks are usually responsible for maintaining the value of their respective country's currency. They define an upper *limit for the inflation rate*, and if the observed *inflation rate* <u>rises above</u> this threshold then the central bank <u>intervenes</u> and sets the *interest rate* such that *inflation rate* <u>falls</u> below the limit hence keeping the currency's value stable. Of course, a central bank cannot fulfil this goal by simply changing one variable: there are many other factors involved. This suggests that the term 'policy' exists at two levels: specific (or single) policy and comprehensive (or combined) policy. A specific policy is a decision rule that sets the values of one specific variable. And a comprehensive policy consists of several single policies, i.e. a set of single policies, and, thereby, sets the values of several variables. For the latter, the monetary policy of a national bank involves different variables, such as the *interest rate*, the *inflation rate,* and the *unemployment rate*.

In the areas of government and business, a policy is a rule that allows organizational actors to select and interpret relevant information and decide on a course of action. The term policy should not be mixed up with business processes or procedures. Since the 1960s, the term 'policy' has gradually been replaced by other words, e.g. business policy by strategy. In this book, we use the term 'policy'.

Routinized or deliberate? Policies can be implicit or explicit. When activities are carried out intuitively because they have been routinized by repetitive execution, individuals do not usually need an explicitly stated policy, for instance answering phone calls or e-mail messages. A policy is explicit when it has been articulated and expressed in documents or verbal statements. For instance, when new situations are encountered, i.e. when there is no experience that guides decision making, a policy is often designed explicitly by discussion and reflection.

How are policies adjusted? Policies are adjusted in an iterative way, which can take the form of evolution or deliberate design. Trial and error can lead to increasingly more successful policies over time. One example is when young children learn to walk; another example is when an investment banker learns under which circumstances to sell or to buy a stock. This is an evolutionary process. Trial and error require time, and errors incur costs. When the cost of these errors becomes serious, policies are often deliberately designed. In the design process, candidate policies are specified and subjected to tests before implementation (Sterman, 2001). This can help avoid catastrophic costs and diminish the total amount of time needed to arrive at a satisfying policy. Another difference between evolutionary and deliberate policy designs is that an evolutionary process is not built, in principle, to explicate the policy and the underlying causal structure. In consequence, one does not know why a policy works or fails. In a world where things change over time, making policies explicit is insightful: policies can adjust when they are outdated. To adjust an explicit policy is easier and faster than to make an implicit policy explicit and then correct it.

What is a model in the context of policies? A typical dictionary definition of model is 'a representation, generally in miniature, to show the construction or appearance of something'. Per this definition, a model is an object in lieu of another object or entity. It is smaller than the object it represents, which means that a certain number of features of the original object are not included in the model. Car builders and aircraft builders develop and test models of their vehicles to avoid design flaws. They run crash tests and use wind channels. In the realm of business and government, there are no wind channels or crash test dummies to test policies. But we can run simulation model tests. Thus, the reason for learning to develop simulation models in this book is that modelling is explicating causal relations in the system under study and by means of simulation you can test different policies. We use simulation models to advance the development and implementation of policies. For this purpose, the models developed in the book will be specific to the context under study.

Guideline 1 (G 1): Account only for the necessary complexity
A model should be as simple as possible and as complex as necessary. Policies and the decision-making logic should be modelled in sufficient detail.

1.3 Managing NewTel's new business in the simplest scenario: business as usual

The first scenario is 'Business as Usual' (BAU). Business as usual assumes the decision variables keep their default values for all months. 'Stick to the established values of the decision variables, no matter what happens' is a simple policy prescribing 'a course or principle of action adopted'. This policy means that for each of the five decision variables, the same policy is in place. This has the advantage of saving you the time figuring out more sophisticated policies, which might consider changes in a variable you want to monitor or decisions taken by your competitor in the previous month. Despite its simplicity, it is not an unreasonable scenario: you would be right to assume that your predecessor must have put some reasoning into the current values of the decision variables, and you should know the *Accumulated profits* you could expect if both companies decide to keep these values over the entire year. The results produced by this scenario will later be used for benchmarking with other scenarios.

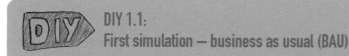

DIY 1.1:
First simulation – business as usual (BAU)

Go and have a try at managing NewTel in the 'SellPhone simulation' (for accessing the simulator and for a tutorial about how to use it, visit the book's companion website). You can use the simulation in one-player or two-player mode. In the one-player version, the computer manages RivTel. In the two-player mode, you play against a colleague.

Use the simulation to work through the BAU scenario. In this scenario, the values of the decision variables remain constant, just stay on the control panel and click on the button 'next month'. After each click, observe the graph beneath the buttons: it shows how the *total population* of one million individuals is distributed between *Potential customers* (yellow), your *Current customers* (green) and *RivTel's customers* (maroon) at the end of each month. To advance 12 months in the simulation, you have to click the button 'next month' 12 times. When the year is over, the button will be displayed in grey.

Click on the 'Decisions NewTel' option and you arrive at a view where you can inspect how different variables have developed over time. The view contains different sheets showing variables related to customers and another one showing information concerning financial flows. Also, inspect the corresponding information concerning RivTel (on the page 'Decisions RivTel').

Prepare to describe important features of what happened during the simulation to a colleague by telephone (no visual contact, therefore words are the only way to transmit information). You will need to identify the variable you refer to and the important aspects of its behaviour: Does it increase or decrease? Is the slope constant or does it decrease or increase? Can you identify specific behaviour modes? Write the information you would like to give to your colleague on a piece of paper. Use the worksheet at the end of the chapter.

Assume that your predecessor had good reasons to set the current *sales price, subscription rate, life cycle duration,* and financial resources spent on *advertising* and *process improvements* at the values as they currently are in the SellPhone simulation. Let us also assume that these values are also reasonable decision values for RivTel. How successful would you be in 12 months, if you followed the course defined by your predecessor?

Figure 1.4 shows the graph of *Potential customers* and the *Current customers* of each company.

Let us now examine the BAU scenario. At the beginning, 990 000 *Potential customers* had not bought a mobile phone yet. NewTel and RivTel have 5000 *Current customers* each. This situation quickly changes. *Potential customers* dramatically decline until they stabilize at around 113 000 towards the end of the year. This means that after little more than half of the year, nearly every Plutonian has acquired a mobile phone bundle either from NewTel or RivTel. Note that not all individuals in the *population* are using the services of one of the companies, and this has not changed over the last six months of the year. This is an important aspect of the customers' behaviour: there is always a certain fraction of the *population* who are not *Current customers*. You may wonder why this is the case. Chapter 4 explains the reasons.

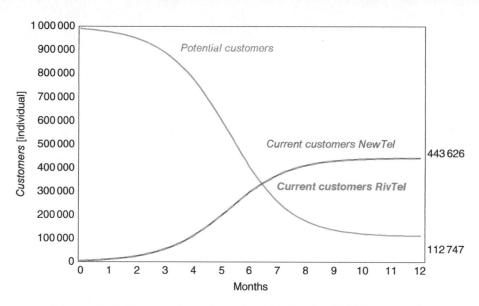

Figure 1.4 Dynamics of customers in the BAU scenario

In the simulation, both companies make the same decisions. Hence, both companies have equal *customer market shares* and equal *monthly profits* during and at the end of the simulation. The *monthly profits* <u>grow</u> exponentially until the end of the first quarter and then peak at approximately $6 million. Then, they slightly <u>decrease</u> and <u>stabilize</u> at approximately $5.24 million per month (Figure 1.5):

Monthly profits <u>grow</u> with a shape similar to the behaviour of *Current customers* and <u>stabilize</u> slightly under $5 million. Detecting this behaviour leads to the discovery of a relevant aspect of the system's behaviour: Plutonia's mobile telecommunication market has developed through different phases. An initial phase of exponential growth is followed by a phase of stability. You may wonder why this is the case and think about factors that determine the difference between the peak in *monthly profits* and the lower and stable *monthly profits* achieved in the remaining months of the year. Chapter 5 provides the details.

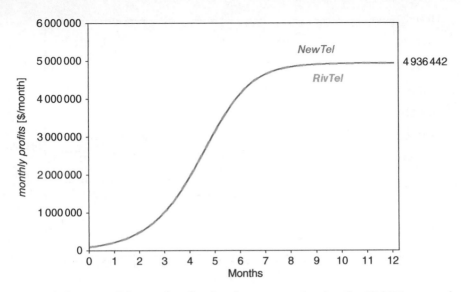

Figure 1.5 *Monthly profits* for both companies in the BAU scenario

Monthly profits accumulate over 12 months. We can differentiate the behaviour of *Accumulated profits* (Figure 1.6) in phases, too. The first phase lasts from the beginning until month 6 and shows an increasing slope of *Accumulated profits*. Afterwards *Accumulated profits* grow in a linear way until the end of the year. Note that the transition from the first to the second phase occurs at the same time when the level of *monthly profits* reaches its local peak and the transition to the third phase initiates a phase of stability which lasts until the end of the simulation. The *Accumulated profits* at the end of the 12 months amount to $37.7 million for both companies.

1.4 A competitive scenario: compete for customers

In some business areas, performing *better than* direct competitors is a desirable objective. And you with NewTel want to be better than RivTel. To manage this, you can choose relative performance objectives. For instance, *customer market share*, i.e. the company's share of all *Current customers* in the market, or *revenue share*, i.e. the company's share of the *total revenues* from mobile phones sold and used each month.

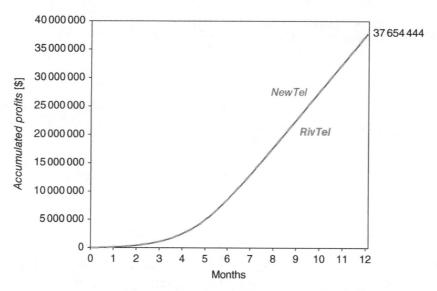

Figure 1.6 *Accumulated profits* for both companies in the BAU scenario

Try to outperform your competitor in the SellPhone simulation by winning more customers than RivTel.

In the simulator's interface, you can see the number of *Current customers* NewTel and *Current customers* of RivTel at the end of the month.

For this challenge, use only the *sales price* and the *subscription rate* to gain an advantage over RivTel. You are free to set the *sales price* and the *subscription rate* as best you can to achieve the objective. The value ranges for the variables are: *sales price* between $0 and $70, and *subscription rate* between $0 and $30 per month (Table 1.1). For each month, you need to decide the value for each of the two variables.

On a sheet of paper, write down what the purpose of each decision each month is. For instance, if you decide to <u>lower</u> the *sales price* and <u>maintain</u> the *subscription rate* at its current level, what effect are you trying to achieve by doing so?

When you reach the end of the year, use the data from the graphs or the tables to analyse the development of NewTel's and RivTel's *Current customers*. For each month, assess if the decisions taken by both companies in the previous month resulted in <u>winning</u> more *new customers*. How many *Current customers* does each company have at the end of the simulation?

Then, turn your attention to *monthly profits*. Were the companies' monthly decisions followed by a <u>rise</u> or a <u>fall</u> in their respective *monthly profits*? What was your *Accumulated profit* at the end of the year? Was it better than RivTel's? Was it higher than the *Accumulated profits* achieved in the BAU scenario? Use the worksheet at the end of the chapter.

Let us analyse a sequence of possible competitive moves between NewTel and RivTel in the CFC scenario. For simplicity, in the scenario you only use the *sales price* and the *subscription rate* to influence the *new customers* and hence your *customer market share*. Obviously, in both companies the monthly decisions are taken without knowing what the other company has decided. Each company's pricing decisions become visible for the respective competitor in the month after the decision: if you want to know RivTel's prices, all you need to do is look at its website – and, of course, they look at yours. The following description narrates the typical reasoning and decisions of a competitive situation between a symbolic NewTel and RivTel. In DIY 1.2, you have written down your own reasoning. As you read the following paragraphs, compare the reasoning described to your own, paying attention to similarities and differences.

The competition begins...

At the beginning of month 1, NewTel thinks: 'We start with an important discount on the *sales price* to attract *new customers* and maybe get ahead of RivTel'. Decision: *Sales price* <u>reduced</u> to $20. At the same time, RivTel's reasoning is: 'We start with a strong discount on the *sales price* to attract *new customers*'. Their decision: *Sales price* <u>reduced</u> to $30. Both decisions are implemented.

When preparing for month 2, NewTel's thoughts are: 'reports from the end of month 1 tell us we now have 27 246 *Current customers*, this has worked well: we are ahead of RivTel.' Decision: 'We follow the same course and keep everything as it is'. RivTel perceives the current situation in the following way: 'We now have 25 249 *Current customers*. Not bad. But NewTel made a larger <u>discount</u> on its *sales price* and it has attracted more *new customers*.' Its decision reveals a competitive attitude: 'We will respond: match their *sales price* and <u>lower</u> the *subscription rate* to $15 per month: *Sales price* <u>reduced</u> to $20 and *subscription rate* <u>reduced</u> to $15'.

When month 2 is over and the decisions for month 3 must be made, both decision makers look at what they perceive to be the current situation. NewTel: 'Our *Current customers* <u>increased</u> to 127 585 and we believe we are still ahead of RivTel despite their <u>discount</u> on the *subscription rate*. Again, we follow the same course'. And RivTel: 'Our *Current customers* <u>increased</u> to 109 706 – we need to continue the discount for at least one more month. No changes made.'

Again, one month later, NewTel's decision maker reflects over their course of action: 'Currently, we have 268 147 *customers*. Market research believes RivTel has outpaced us. We need to turn this around and send a message to RivTel'. The new decisions: '*Sales price* <u>reduced</u> to $0 and *subscription rate* <u>reduced</u> to $15'. In parallel to this, RivTel decides not to move: 'We <u>increased</u> *customer* count to 378 908. Market research believes we are well ahead of NewTel. We will <u>keep</u> to the current values and expect to dominate the market soon. No changes made.'

For month 5, neither company decides to change anything. NewTel: 'Our *customers* count has <u>hardly increased</u> (278 317); we need to <u>keep</u> the current *prices* <u>as low as they are</u>. No changes made'. And RivTel: 'As of the end of month 4, we have 613 788 *customers*. One more month and we can <u>raise</u> *prices* again. No changes made'.

Later, NewTel prepares for month 6 '*Customers* were at 370 878. An encouraging development. We can <u>increase</u> the *sales price*'; *sales price* <u>raised</u> to $20. RivTel's reasoning is: 'NewTel's discounts have made us <u>lose</u> many *customers*, we <u>fell</u> to 567 087. We need to protect our *market share*; therefore, we will <u>reduce</u> our *subscription rate*: *subscription rate* to $10.'

For month 7, NewTel keeps to its current prices: 'Reports show a good tendency (442 685 *customers*). We need to advance, thus no changes'. The same for RivTel: 'We kept <u>losing</u> *customers* (reports state 501 002), but are still ahead of NewTel. No changes made'.

But by the end of month 7, NewTel revises its decision: '*Customer* count is <u>down</u> to 291 105. RivTel's discounts have hurt us. We will not let them get away with this': *Sales price* <u>reduced</u> to $0, *subscription rate* <u>reduced</u> to $10. At the same time, RivTel has its thoughts: 'Reports suggest we are back on track (653 252 *customers* as of the end of month 7). We can <u>raise</u> the *subscription rate* a bit: *Subscription rate* <u>increased</u> to $15.'

Here is what NewTel's decision maker thinks about the upcoming month 8: 'We kept <u>losing</u> *customers*, now arriving at 191 301. But we <u>cannot</u> <u>reduce</u> *prices* anymore. No changes made'. His opponent at RivTel thinks: 'The trend has shifted, we <u>won</u> back *customers* (753 133). Let us keep to the current values to consolidate: no changes made.'

By now three-quarters of the year are over, and both decision makers are getting ready for the tenth month. NewTel: '*Customer* count is back <u>up</u> to 454 884 for the end of month 9. We should <u>raise</u> *prices* a bit, but try to stay attractive': *Sales price* <u>increased</u> to $20; *Subscription rate* <u>increased</u> to $20. RivTel: 'NewTel's discount attack has cost us many *customers*; we are back <u>down</u> to 489 560. This must be turned around: *sales prices* <u>reduced</u> to $0!'

For month 11, NewTel analyses: '*Customer* count has continued to <u>increase</u>, now counting 626 219. Let us consolidate the position: no changes'. In its own way, RivTel arrives at a similar decision: '*Customers* have <u>dropped</u> to 318 226, but we cannot make any substantial discounts. Let us keep fighting with the current values'.

Now, both companies are getting ready for the final month of the year. NewTel is considering its latest developments: '*Customers* started to <u>decrease</u> again (now 381 122). Should we try to send a peace signal to RivTel? We will not <u>reduce</u> *prices* this time'. RivTel's reasoning is somewhat different, unbeknown to NewTel of course: '*Customers* are <u>up</u> to 563 322. Good trend, but we will keep *prices* down a little longer'.

Closing a year of severe competitive action, NewTel concludes, 'We have <u>dropped</u> to 231 954 *customers*, have a very low *market share*, and RivTel has not responded to our collaborative signal'. In its local headquarters, RivTel is reasoning: 'We now dominate the market with 712 490 *customers*. Now we can respond to NewTel's signal of last month'.

We as external and omniscient observers have a chance to detect a pattern here, and maybe feel that it is bad luck for both companies that RivTel's decision to respond to NewTel's 'signal of collaboration' appears to have come too late. Anyway, we now have sufficient data and insights to analyse what has happened during the 12 months. The reasoning behind each of the companies was focused on winning *customers*, and the *sales price* and *subscription rate* were used to change the stock of *Current customers* and, occasionally, to send a competitive or cooperative signal to the other company. A narrative in the form of a free text contains much information but does not make it particularly easy to detect patterns of behaviour. As a complementary kind of representation, a graph helps to focus on the relevant behaviours. Figure 1.7 provides an overview of the sequence.

Let us now analyse what is happening in the graphs. During the first month, the vast majority of Plutonians still are *Potential customers*. The initial <u>discounts</u> of NewTel are somewhat larger than RivTel's and, therefore, NewTel gains a small advantage in number of *Current customers*. The graph of *Current customers* seems to suggest that the benefit in absolute numbers is not significant, but you should keep in mind that for the decisions taken in month 2, RivTel had only the reports from month 1. RivTel detects that NewTel's *sales price* <u>discount</u> was larger and that NewTel's customer uptake (*new customers*) seems to be <u>quicker</u>. Therefore, RivTel <u>reduces</u> both *sales price* and *subscription rate*. And, indeed, until the end of month 4, RivTel appears to be winning the race for *customers*.

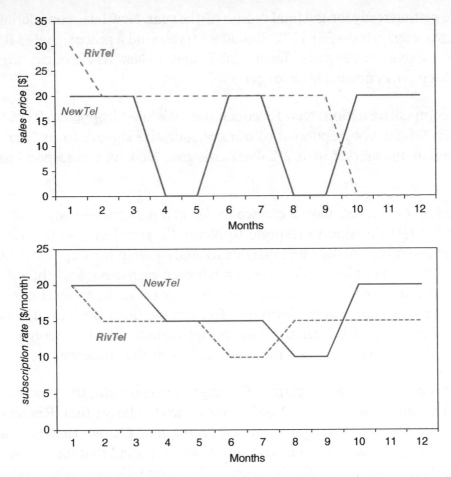

Figure 1.7 Changes to *sales price*, *subscription rate*, and the behaviour of *customers* in the CFC scenario

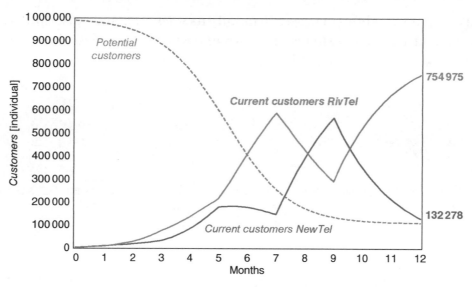

Figure 1.7 (Continued)

NewTel attributes the relative slowness of its *Current customers* <u>growth</u> to RivTel's <u>discounts</u>; as a reaction, it reinforces its own <u>discounts,</u> which results in <u>winning</u> more *Current customers* and pushes RivTel to <u>lose</u> *Current customers* until the end of month 6. Then, it is RivTel's turn to <u>lower</u> its own *prices* and <u>expand</u> its *customer* base, inflicting a <u>larger loss</u> in *customers* to NewTel until the end of month 8. NewTel counterattacks by <u>cutting</u> its *sales price* and, by the end of month 10, the *customers* base of NewTel quickly <u>increases</u> – again at the expense of RivTel. During the last months, RivTel strikes back and <u>wins</u> back most *customers*. A classical price war has unfolded.

Clearly, both NewTel and RivTel have taken decisions driven by similar policies and these policies are different from the one in the BAU scenario. Each company observes its own *new customers* and *Current customers* as well as the respective competitor's *sales price* and *subscription rate*. Based on the behaviour of these variables and the respective policies, each company modifies or ceases to modify its *sales price* and *subscription rate*. We can tentatively state that their policies were 'if our *new customers* or *Current customers* grow less than the one of the competitor, then set our *prices* a little lower than the competitor price.'

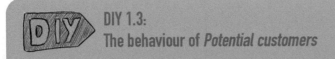

DIY 1.3:
The behaviour of *Potential customers*

Note that the behaviour of *Potential customers* has not changed between the BAU scenario (Figure 1.4) and the CFC scenario (Figure 1.7). Why?

At the end of the twelve months, NewTel serves a little more than 230 000 *customers* and RivTel more than twice this number, with more than 770 000 *customers*. And at the end of month 12, RivTel wins in terms of *customer market share*. The competition for *customers* has sometimes favoured NewTel, and at other times RivTel. Since month 6, almost the entire *population* had been using a mobile phone from either NewTel or RivTel. Therefore, a growth in *Current customers* of one company almost always meant a loss in *Current customer* of the other company. Competing for *customers* had adverse consequences on *profits* (Figure 1.8).

Figure 1.8 displays the unfolding of *Accumulated profits* of both companies over the 12 months. During the first 3–4 months, losses increased quickly (that is, *profits* decreased); this was due to massively reducing *sales prices* and *subscription rates* while the costs of buying the devices and serving *customers* remained unchanged. Starting at month 4, losses decreased, then increased and decreased again. Note that losses are negative *profits*; if losses decrease, that means that your *profits* are negative, but less than before. Your *profits* increase, even if it is only in a relative manner. When RivTel has many *customers* (months 4–6), their losses decrease, but after deciding to lower the *subscription rate* to a monthly $10 (equalling the monthly *Service costs*, which amount to $10 per *Current*

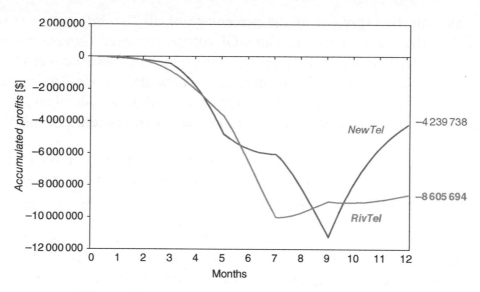

Figure 1.8 Development of *Accumulated profits*

customer), the situation worsens again. NewTel's profit took a dive when it decided to <u>reduce</u> the *sales price* to an extreme $0 and the *subscription rate* to $10 at month 8, but then losses were <u>reduced</u> when in month 10 both *prices* were <u>raised back</u> to $20.

1.5 Outcomes of both scenarios in terms of key performance indicators

Since your objectives, as well as RivTel's, are to achieve the highest possible *Accumulated profits* at the end of the year, it is likely that both of you use *Accumulated profits* as a 'key performance indicator' (KPI). The term 'performance' refers to how well an activity is carried out as compared to a standard or predefined level of accomplishment. Naturally, this means KPIs convey the information that should give you a clear idea of how well the organization is performing. In your case, *Accumulated profits* is one of them; however, it is not necessarily the only one. In the CFC scenario, the fictitious managers of NewTel and RivTel also considered their respective market share. *Market share* can be expressed as the percentage of all *Current customers* who are your *Current customers*; this then is called the *customer market share*. Of course, you need *Current customers* to gain *revenues from sales* and *revenues from subscriptions*; the fact that you have a high *customer market share* would then indicate that you fulfil at least one necessary condition for building up *Accumulated profits*. Additionally, your *profit market share* indicates the percentage of your *Accumulated profits* relative to all *Accumulated profits*. This will allow you to better understand whether a given amount of *Accumulated profits* is a strong result or not.

How do these three KPIs look for each of the two scenarios? At the end of the year, NewTel achieved *Accumulated profits* of $75 106 and RivTel had negative *Accumulated profits.* In fact, its losses amounted to $2 718 392. As far as *customer market share* and *profit market share* are concerned, Table 1.3 summarizes the values for the two scenarios.

In the BAU scenario, neither company outperforms the other. Both complete the first year with a *customer market share* of 47%, since 6% of the *population* does not use a mobile phone at the end of the year. The *profit share* for each company is 50%, which corresponds to about $38 million for each company. In the CFC scenario, RivTel is the clear winner when considering the *customer market share* as a performance indicator. When considering the *Accumulated profit*, both companies performed poorly: RivTel incurs losses of almost $3 million and NewTel barely gets away without any losses. Of course, when comparing the absolute *Accumulated profits*, NewTel has performed better than RivTel. However, each of the companies significantly lost compared to the $53 million profit in the BAU scenario.

Table 1.3 Key performance indicators for both scenarios

Key Performance Indicator (KPI)	Business as Usual (BAU)		Compete for Customers (CFC)	
	NewTel	RivTel	NewTel	RivTel
Customer market share [dimensionless]	47	47	23	71
Profit market share [dimensionless]	50	50	n.a.	n.a.
Accumulated profits [million $]	37.7	37.7	0.08	−2.72

You will be evaluated for *Accumulated profit* after 12 months and, in the CFC scenario, NewTel's *Accumulated profits* were below the BAU results. But then again, to make profits, you needed to acquire *customers*; when RivTel outpaced you by <u>lowering</u> prices, did you also not have the right to compete for *customers* by <u>lowering</u> prices? Was it wrong that you paid attention to *customer* market share as an indicator of your current situation?

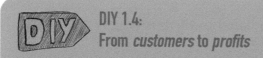

DIY 1.4:
From *customers* to *profits*

Specify the ways in which *Current customers* have an influence on *profits*. Draw a diagram using variables, e.g. *Current customers, customer market share,* and *monthly profits*. Use arrows to represent the relationships between the variables. Use the worksheet at the end of the chapter.

In retrospect, you might wonder: When is your performance good? Is it good when your performance is better than RivTel's performance or when it is the best result you can achieve? When comparing the results from Table 1.3, you suspect that NewTel's board will not regard your performance as good only because it is higher than RivTel's performance. How much *Accumulated profit* could it be then? Was $38 million a strong performance or could it be even higher?

Since RivTel's decisions influence what happens in the market, you cannot determine how much *profit* is possible without considering RivTel's goals and policies. In such a setting: What policy should you implement to achieve the best result? Since you are trying to improve the *Accumulated profits* for NewTel, you could ask yourself the following questions:

- In which ways are the *sales price* and the *subscription rate* connected to *Current customers* and *monthly profits*. How do *Current customers* influence *monthly profits*? <u>Reducing</u> the *sales price* influenced *Current customers* and *monthly profits* changed in response to it. But how exactly are these variables linked?

- What will the results be when I <u>increase</u> or <u>decrease</u> the *sales price* compared to when I <u>increase</u> or <u>decrease</u> the *subscription rate*?
- How can I capture *customers* quickly without *advertising spending*?
- What happens to *monthly profits* if I spend money for *advertising*?
- What would be the impact if I <u>change</u> the *life cycle duration* of the mobile phones?

In principle, you ask yourself: How are the elements and decision variables related to the business system?

Your airplane is approaching Frankfurt and these questions on your mind make it clear that you need to understand the complexities of your business system. Since you are responsible for succeeding, you tell yourself that you must uncover the structures and behaviour of the business system or you need to leave NewTel.

1.6 Chapter summary
In the chapter, you made two attempts to steer NewTel through twelve months after the product introduction while RivTel strives to do the same. An initial simulation with the SellPhone simulation showed that under the given circumstances, each company could expect to make around $38 million *Accumulated profits*. We have also seen that competing for customers by <u>reducing</u> *prices* may be successful at attracting *customers*, but it substantially <u>reduces</u> *Accumulated profits* over the twelve months. We have concluded that with no more than this information, important questions arise and need to be answered before deciding on policies for NewTel.

1.7 Questions and challenges

Questions
1. Define 'variable'.
2. Why is it important to define the variables' units of measure?
3. What is a behaviour-over-time graph? For what is it used?
4. What atomic behaviour modes are discussed in this chapter?

5. Explain how the composed behaviour modes can be decomposed into atomic behaviour modes.
6. What is a policy? What types of policies can you name?
7. What problems can arise when a model is too simple or too complex?
8. What are NewTel's key performance indicators? Why is it important to define and used key performance indicators?
9. How can you be satisfied that your performance as manager is sufficient?
10. How are the decision variables related to one another?
11. How can different scenarios be defined?

Challenges

Based on your annotations from DIY 1.2, formulate policies for setting the *sales price* and the *subscription rate* for NewTel. As an example, this can be a phrase like 'If the competitor has won more *new customers* than I did, then I will <u>lower</u> the *sales price*'. Now assume that RivTel would apply the same policy and use the SellPhone simulation to play through the 12 months. What was your performance regarding *Accumulated profits* and of *customer market share* this time, as compared to the BAU and the CFC scenarios?

You can use worksheet 1.5 from the companion website for that challenge to write down your policies, produce the graphs and write up the essentials of your scenario comparison.

References

Ford, N. 1999. A behavioral approach to feedback loop dominance analysis. *System Dynamics Review*, **15**(1): 3–36.
Sterman, J.D. 2001. System dynamics modeling: tools for learning in a complex world. *California Management Review*, **43**(4): 8–24.
Oxford Dictionaries. 2016. Policy. http://www.oxforddictionaries.com/definition/english/policy (last accessed 1 November 2017).

Worksheet DIY 1.1:
First simulation - business as usual (BAU)

Identify the two most relevant variables and write their names on top of the vertical axes of the graphs. Next identify their respective units of measure and indicate them next to "Unit of measure" on the vertical axes. Then identify the range of observed values and inscribe them in "Max" and "Min" for each graph. Eventually, draw the variables' respective behaviours in the graphs.

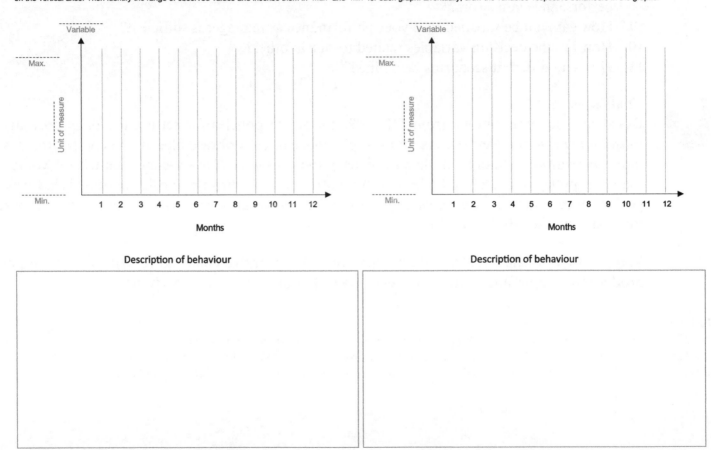

Worksheet DIY 1.2:
Second simulation – compete for customers (CFC) (Sheet 1 of 3)

Month	Decisions				What effect do you want to achieve with each decisión?	Consequences			
	sales price		*subscription rate*			*Current customers*		*monthly profits*	
	NewTel	RivTel	NewTel	RivTel		NewTel	RivTel	NewTel	RivTel
1						○↗ ○↘	○↗ ○↘	○↗ ○↘	○↗ ○↘
2						○↗ ○↘	○↗ ○↘	○↗ ○↘	○↗ ○↘
3						○↗ ○↘	○↗ ○↘	○↗ ○↘	○↗ ○↘
4						○↗ ○↘	○↗ ○↘	○↗ ○↘	○↗ ○↘
5						○↗ ○↘	○↗ ○↘	○↗ ○↘	○↗ ○↘
6						○↗ ○↘	○↗ ○↘	○↗ ○↘	○↗ ○↘
7						○↗ ○↘	○↗ ○↘	○↗ ○↘	○↗ ○↘
8						○↗ ○↘	○↗ ○↘	○↗ ○↘	○↗ ○↘
9						○↗ ○↘	○↗ ○↘	○↗ ○↘	○↗ ○↘
10						○↗ ○↘	○↗ ○↘	○↗ ○↘	○↗ ○↘
11						○↗ ○↘	○↗ ○↘	○↗ ○↘	○↗ ○↘
12						○↗ ○↘	○↗ ○↘	○↗ ○↘	○↗ ○↘

Final values   CFC   ....

BAU   ....

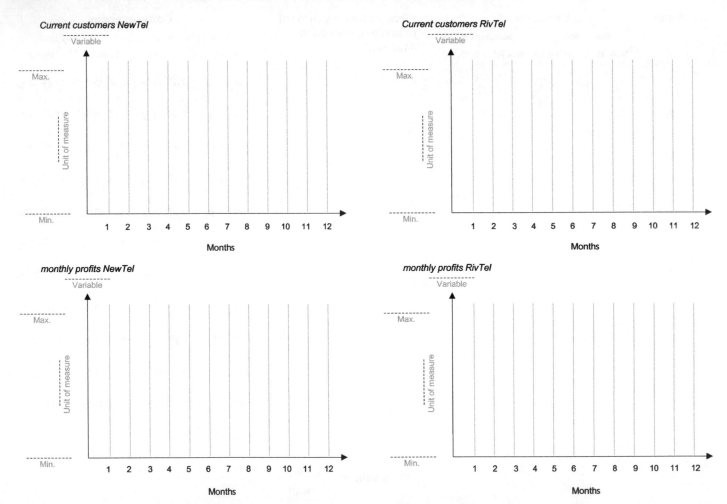

Current customers NewTel

Variable

Max.

Unit of measure

Min.

1 2 3 4 5 6 7 8 9 10 11 12

Months

Current customers RivTel

Variable

Max.

Unit of measure

Min.

1 2 3 4 5 6 7 8 9 10 11 12

Months

monthly profits NewTel

Variable

Max.

Unit of measure

Min.

1 2 3 4 5 6 7 8 9 10 11 12

Months

monthly profits RivTel

Variable

Max.

Unit of measure

Min.

1 2 3 4 5 6 7 8 9 10 11 12

Months

Worksheet DIY 1.2:
Second simulation – compete for customers (CFC) (Sheet 3 of 3)

For each month, assess if the decisions taken by both companies in the previous month resulted in winning more *new customers*. How many *Current customers* does each company have at the end of the simulation? Were the companies' monthly decisions followed by a rise or a fall of their respective *monthly profits*? What was your *Accumulated profit* at the end of the year? Was it better than RivTel's? Was it higher than the *Accumulated profits* achieved in the BAU scenario?

Worksheet DIY 1.4:
From *customers* to *profits*

A cause-effect relationship between two variables v_1 and v_2 is represented by an arrow from v_1 to v_2: $v_1 \xrightarrow{+/-} v_2$ A causal link has a polarity: positive or negative.

For positive cause-effect relationships, use $\xrightarrow{+}$, for negative cause-effect relationships, use $\xrightarrow{-}$

Sometimes causal relationships are circular: $v_1 \rightleftarrows v_2$ Do not hesitate to draw such relationships if you perceive they exist.

CAPTURING CUSTOMER DYNAMICS DRIVEN BY DIFFUSION

2.1 Introduction

In this chapter, you will work out the fundamental causal structure of your business case. The core is the mechanism of product and service diffusion in the customer *population* in Plutonia. You will investigate the relevant factors underlying this diffusion as well as the relationships between them. The steps you undertake to formulate and analyse the diffusion of the service in the business environment will provide you with a new perspective on the system's general dynamics.

In particular, you will learn that the diffusion of your telecommunication service is propelled mainly by word-of-mouth diffusion dynamics, i.e. *Current customers* of your mobile phone service are seen by *Potential customers* or they talk about your services to their peers and, thereby, promote your offering. You will discover how several factors influence the speed of this word-of-mouth diffusion.

Customers are – together with other factors – an important resource for your business. In this book, they are represented as a resource stock that will change according to the decisions you take over time. You will also

Growth Dynamics in New Markets: Improving Decision Making through Simulation Model-based Management,
First Edition. Martin F.G. Schaffernicht and Stefan N. Groesser.
© 2018 John Wiley & Sons Ltd. Published 2018 by John Wiley & Sons Ltd.
Companion website: www.wiley.com/go/Schaffernicht/growth-dynamics

develop a first simulation model with the fundamental causal structure of word-of-mouth dynamics and perform simulation experiments to explore possible behaviours of this resource stock. This all will support you in making decisions that are grounded in information about likely behaviours driven by the system's structure.

2.2 Diffusion: a regular dynamic in social systems

2.2.1 'Going viral'

Diffusion is defined as the process of spreading something more widely. Words such as spreading, propagating, or broadcasting have a similar meaning. Something that is diffused spreads relatively homogenously and can, therefore, give the negative connotation of becoming weaker or more diluted. However, the process of diffusion is important in many sciences including physics, chemistry, biology, and the social sciences. We will explore some examples that illustrate its relevance for your mission in Plutonia.

Unless you live on a desert island, you meet and talk to other people every day, be it at work, in the streets, or at home. Occasionally, the ensuing conversations will have marketing effects. For example, if you watch videos on YouTube, you will have noticed that some videos have an explosively increasing number of *views* – users who watch them – or *likes*, signalling that people 'like' them; how many of us have not seen or at least heard of 'Charlie bit my finger' (HDCYT, 2007). When there is an exponential <u>growth</u> in *views*, *likes*, or *downloads*, this is referred to as a 'viral' video. Some videos are specifically designed to 'go viral', for instance 'Gangnam Style' (PSY, 2012).

The expression 'going viral' is mainly associated to internet videos but the term has its origins in the field of virology: if some individuals are *infected* and carry a transferable virus, then a given percentage of uninfected (*susceptible*) people they meet will be infected and the likelihood of triggering an epidemic is very high. During such an epidemic, the number of *infected* individuals <u>increases</u> in an accelerated manner for some time. After a while, the virus stops infecting new people since the number of *susceptible* individuals has diminished. For instance, between the years 2008 and 2009, the number of *influenza cases reported* by the Centers for Disease Control <u>went up</u> from 300 to 600 weekly cases within as little as three weeks, then <u>up</u> to 3000 four weeks later, only to <u>decline</u> as quickly as it had risen (CDC, 2009). During the same season in a different country, in Denmark, *cases* <u>went up</u> from

10 (per 100 000 inhabitants per week) to 20, to 100, 200, and 300 in less than 10 weeks. Again, the number <u>dropped</u> to the normal number in less than three weeks (Influenzanet, 2009). The medicine and the internet are not the only places where virus-like behaviour can be found.

What about diffusion in an economic system? You might recall news about financial and economic crises, when *panic* <u>spreads</u> amongst traders at a stock exchange or amongst bank account holders. Such crises are likely to explode, and usually stock exchanges or the withdrawal of money will be suspended or restricted. Over the past 100 years, several such banking crises have occurred, some of which have spread globally, e.g. in 1929 or in 2008. One recent crisis took place in Greece around 2015. And as *fear* of a 'Grexit' from the European Union <u>spread</u> throughout the system, the *total deposits* in Greek banks <u>declined</u> from €250 billion to around €150 billion (Cox and Copeland, 2015). Finally, *banks* in Greece were <u>closed</u> and ATM *transactions* were <u>limited</u> to €60 per individual per day. And when, on 23 June 2016, a majority of participating *voters* in Great Britain voted in favour of 'Brexit', the *value of the British Pound* <u>dipped</u> notably (Bloomberg, 2016).

In the following sections, you will discover how 'virus-like' behaviour works for NewTel's mobile phones in Plutonia. Your services may not take on Gangnam style proportions but word about your services will spread throughout Plutonia's *population* as people interact with each other. To avoid unnecessary complexity, we will keep RivTel out of the discussion until the causal structure underlying customer dynamics and their relationship to profits has been established and analysed.

2.2.2 A Story about selling mobile phones

Again, your goal is to achieve the highest possible *Accumulated profits* over the first 12 months in Plutonia. One thing you will need is enough *new customers* and *Current customers*: The former pay the *sales price* and the latter pay the monthly *subscription rate*. What is the situation when you start? Your predecessor at NewTel kick-started the market entry by providing 5000 mobile phones to Plutonians for free. Hence, you take over the driving seat with an initial stock of 5000 *Current customers*. This also means that 995 000 individuals are not currently using the mobile phone service of NewTel, but they could and should be: they are *Potential customers*. Since your goal is to make the highest possible profits until the end of the year, you need *Potential customers* to buy your mobile phone bundle and become *Current customers*. Therefore, the numbers of *Potential customers* and *Current customers* will change over time.

What factors does the speed of the conversion from *Potential customers* to *Current customers* depend on? How will your decision variables influence them? You need to know the answers to these questions. And to do this, you need to understand what 'causal links' are.

Toolbox 2.1:
Causal links

In Chapter 1, the concept of a variable was defined. The analysis of problem descriptions allows you to identify relevant variables involved. However, the variables would be meaningless if they were not related to one another.

These relationships between the variables need to be accounted for. Synthesizing, i.e. to form by combining parts or elements, is the complement of analysing. We use causal links to connect the variables and, thereby, transform a set of isolated variables into a model. A causal link asserts that a change in one variable has consequence for other variables. Since changes in *variables* mean that *variables* increase or decrease, this can be restated more precisely: when the value of *variable B* increases or decreases as result of an increasing or decreasing value of *variable A*, this is represented as a 'causal link'. Such links appear in various forms. In our descriptive language we use phrases such as 'a fall in A causes a fall in B, 'when A goes up, B goes down', etc. In equations, they appear as mathematic operations; in causal diagrams, they are depicted as thin arrows. Consider the following example:

'When the *interest rate* decreases, the bank will pay less *interest* to your savings account. The *interest payments* made by the bank to your savings account increase the account's *balance*. The higher your account's *balance* is, the <u>greater</u> the *interest payment* the bank will make.' Of course, this is usually true if there is a positive interest rate. However, there are cases when an *interest rate* can go negative, as in the context of the Euro-zone still struggling to overcome the 2008 financial crisis and shaken anew by Great Britain decision to leave the EU in June 2016 (Ewing, 2016; Moore, 2016; Randow and Kennedy, 2016)

Figure 2.1 shows a causal diagram with the variables and the relationships mentioned in the above example:

Clearly, the causal link from *interest payment* to *bank balance* represents the phrase '[…] *interest payments* […] <u>increase</u> […] *bank balance*', and the plus sign at the arrowhead of this causal link represents this. Furthermore, the first phrase of the text is represented in the causal link from *interest rate* to *interest payment*, while the last phrase is expressed by the causal link from *bank balance* to *interest payment*.

The following equations provide the same information represented differently:

$$interest\ payment\ \big[\$/\text{month}\big] = bank\ balance\big[\$\big]\ *\ interest\ rate\big[\%/\text{month}\big]$$

$$bank\ balance\big[\$\big] = bank balance\ \big[\$\big] + interest\ payment\ \big[\$/\text{month}\big]\ *\ \textbf{TIMESTEP}\ \big[\text{month}\big]$$

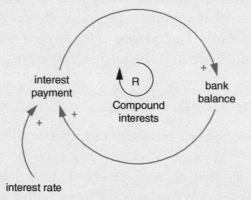

Figure 2.1 Example of causal links between variables

The equation for *interest payments* contains both causal links pointing at the variable in the diagram: the mathematic operator 'multiplication' guarantees that an <u>increase</u> in either the *interest rate* or the *bank balance* yields an <u>increase</u> in the *interest payment*. The 'addition' operator in the equation for *bank balance* also assures that *interest payments* add to the *bank balance*, as indicated by the causal link.

The text describing this example describes the interdependency between the *bank balance* and the *interest payment*. This interdependency is also shown in the equations: in the first one, *interest payment* is on the left side and *bank balance* on the right, whereas in the second equation it is the other way around. Such blocks of interdependent variables are called 'feedback loops'; the diagram contains a symbol ↻ to explicitly show this feedback loop. The letter 'R', denotes a reinforcing feedback loop. Such a feedback loop exists when there is a closed chain of causal links: the bank's *interest payment* has a positive influence on the *bank's balance*, which, in turn, affects the next *interest payment*, also with positive polarity. Therefore, the <u>increased</u> *bank balance* leads to <u>higher</u> *interest payments* and further <u>increases</u> the *bank balance*, so that the effect of this feedback loop is self-reinforcing. Feedback loops are important for complex systems and will are discussed in more detail in Section 2.2.2.

Coming back to causal links, note that the diagram and the equations do not directly state what happens: they represent the causal structure and, therefore, tell how an initial change in one of the variables will influence other variables. Therefore, the diagram is more general than the text. The text only states the consequences if a <u>decrease</u> in the *interest rate* occurs, but the diagram and the equation express also what would happen if the *interest rate* <u>increases</u>.

This is relevant as the model must be able to describe both, that is, the initial development of relevant variables from the text (the problem), and the consequences of interventions in that situation (the solution).

Usually, textual descriptions of problems or opportunities refer to the behaviour of certain variables rather than the underlying causal structure. It is then the task of the analyst to discover the variables and the causal links implied by such descriptions and formulate underlying causal structure in a model. This process of 'discovering' is often termed 'abstraction' because behaviour and other aspects are removed (*to remove* is the original meaning of the verb *to abstract*) from the description until only the causal structure is left.

Table 2.1 Initial situation and your goal for *Current customers*

Month	Potential customers	Current customers
(initial)	995 000	5000
(later)	as few as possible	as many as possible

If your objective is to maximize *Accumulated profits* over a twelve-month period and you need *Current customers* to achieve *monthly profits*, then logically you also have an intermediate goal of winning *Current customers*. Table 2.1 illustrates your initial situation and your intermediate goal in terms of *Current customers*. You know how many *Potential customers* and *Current customers* exist in Plutonia. You also know that you have to change these numbers in your favour in the coming months. But you do not know how many months such a change will take.

Is it possible that the interest in mobile phones can spread from individual to individual like a virus, a banking crisis, or a YouTube video? Let us see. The people of the island Plutonia are social animals; they meet at work and during leisure activities. When the free mobile phones were distributed to 5000 *Potential customers*, this was done randomly to assure that these *Current customers* did not form clusters but were spread homogeneously throughout the *total population* of 1 000 000 individuals. Further, marketing studies suggest that each Plutonian meets 100 other Plutonians, on average, per month; these could be friends or colleagues. This is an important fact and is represented as:

$$contact\,rate\left[1\,/\,\text{month}\right]=100 \tag{2.1}$$

Contact rate is assumed to be an average value that is constant for the time being. This assumption helps to avoid unnecessary complexity. Chapter 8 discusses how to relax this assumption. You can also see that the unit of measure is practical.

A value of, for instance, '100' is not sufficiently clear. One then would ask: 100 of what? In the case of *contact rate*, the unit of measure is 'individuals per month per individual'. This means that each *Current customer* meets 100 individuals per month. As discussed in the methodology and Toolbox 1.1 in Chapter 1, it is important that you pay attention to the units of measure; being explicit about them helps to develop conceptual and cognitive clarity (Weick, 1989).

DIY 2.1:
Determine the *contact rate* of the first month

Perform this calculation yourself. Given the situation of 5000 *Current customers*, how many encounters will they have throughout the first month?

The answer is 500 000 encounters. Why? Each of the 5000 *Current customers* has 100 *encounters per month*. The unit of measure is individuals per month.

How many of these 500 000 encounters will take place with *Potential customers*?

One way to produce the answer is to consider that the *population* consists of 1 000 000 individuals and is made of the two groups: *Potential customers*, i.e. individuals who do not own a mobile phone, and *Current customers*, i.e. the current users of your mobile phones. To diffuse mobile phones, only encounters taking place between a *Current customer* and a *Potential customer* are relevant. When two *Current customers* meet, neither of them will consider purchasing a mobile phone as they both already have one. In an encounter between two *Potential customers*, no one shows the phone being used and spreads the word. For *Current customers*, the percentage of encounters with *Potential customers* depends on the *potential customers fraction* in the *population*:

$$potential\ customers\ fraction[\text{dimensionless}] = Potential\ customers[\text{individual}] / population[\text{individual}] \qquad (2.2)$$

995 000 *Potential customers* and a *population* of 1 000 000 individuals yield a *potential customers fraction* of 99.5%. This means that, on average, 99.5% of the 500 000 (i.e. 497 500) encounters in the first month occur between a *Current customer* and a *Potential customer*. The remaining 2500 encounters occur between two *Current customers*.

When a *Current customer* meets a *Potential customer*, the latter can see how the former uses his/her new mobile phone or may even demonstrate its function. This triggers the desire to own a mobile phone; this is called the 'word-of-mouth' (WoM) effect. How strong is this influence? Not everybody decides to buy a mobile phone at first demonstration. A conservative assumption would be that only one out of one hundred encounters between a *Potential customer* and a *Current customer* results in a *Potential customer* deciding to buy a mobile phone. This is the *conversion fraction*.

$$conversion\ fraction[\text{dimensionless}]=0.01 \tag{2.3}$$

DIY 2.2:
Determine the *new customers* of the first month

> Now try to determine the number of *Potential customers* who will buy a mobile phone in the first month, considering the initial number of *Current customers*, the *contact rate*, the *conversion fraction*, and the *potential customers fraction*.

When a *potential customer* buys a mobile phone and signs a contract for the *life cycle duration* of the phone, his or her status changes to *Current customer*. In the first month, 4975 *Potential customers* buy a new phone. The number of *Current customers* therefore changes from 5000 at the beginning of the first month to 9975 at the beginning of the second month. At the same time, the number of *Potential customers* will decrease to 990 025 because the *new customers* leave the stock of *Potential customers*. This logic is also valid for month 2, and for every other month after that. Table 2.2 shows the values for each month:

Table 2.2 Development of customers over 12 months

Month	Potential customers	Current customers	current customers encounters	potential customers fraction	new customers
0	995 000	5000	500 000	0.995	4975
1	990 025	9975	997 500	0.990	9875
2	980 150	19 850	1 985 000	0.980	19 456
3	960 694	39 306	3 930 600	0.961	37 761
4	922 933	77 067	7 706 700	0.923	71 128
5	851 805	148 195	14 819 500	0.853	126 233
6	725 572	274 428	27 442 800	0.726	199 117
7	526 455	473 545	47 354 500	0.527	249 300
8	277 155	722 845	72 284 500	0.277	200 340
9	76 815	923 185	92 318 500	0.077	70 914
10	5901	994 099	99 409 900	0.006	5866
11	35	999 965	99 996 500	0	35
12	0	1 000 000	100 000 000	0	0

The number of *Current customers* increases quickly until month 7 and then grows at a slower rate. By the end of the year, every individual in the *population* on Plutonia has a mobile phone. Also, the number of *new customers* rises quickly until month 7 and after that the rate of growth declines rapidly. The value of *current customers encounters* almost doubles every month until month 7. The *potential customers fraction* decreases, slowly at first, but with an increasing downward slope; between months 5 and 9, it freefalls from 85% to less than 10%.

Although Table 2.2 details the numbers with considerable accuracy, it cannot clearly reveal the trends of a variable's behaviour over time. This becomes more evident when using a graph (Figure 2.2).

Figure 2.2 shows the behaviour of *new customers* as a solid line and *Current customers* as dotted line. In the beginning, both values are low when compared to 1 000 000, so they appear to be almost 0. Then, they both

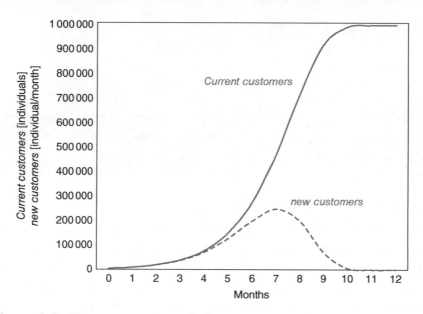

Figure 2.2 *New customers* and *Current customers* over 12 months

increase for about half of the 12 months and their growth accelerates over time. However, the value of *new customers* reaches a peak when *Current customers* reach the value of 500 000 individuals. In the following months, *new customers* is still positive but quickly declines to 0. Note that each month for which *new customers* is greater than 0, a certain number of individuals is added to the *Current customers*. Therefore, as long as *new customers* is larger than 0, *Current customers* continue to grow at a slower pace. Towards the end of the 12-month period, the stock of *Current customers* reaches 1 000 000, which means that the entire *population* has now bought a NewTel mobile phone. Overall, the graph of *Current customers* shows an S-shape curve. This shape is characteristic of product or service diffusion and is often called 'S-shaped growth'. Rogers (2013) wrote a standard and highly accessible publication on diffusion of innovations.

DIY 2.3:
Market saturation

Search for 'market saturation' on Wikipedia. Compare the behaviour shown there to the behaviour of *new customers* and *Current customers* in the figures above. What are the similarities? What are the differences? Use the worksheet at the end of the chapter.

2.2.3 Diffusion is based on a network of variables and causal relationships

The previous sections have shown that the word-of-mouth dynamics help to grow NewTel's *Current customers* in two different phases: initially, growth accelerates and then slows down. *New customers* will increase each month during the first phase and then decrease towards 0. The resulting S-shape curve of *Current customers* is characteristic and is defined as S-shaped growth. However, up to now it is not clear why the growth has occurred this way. What are the reasons for this growth behaviour? Could the S-shaped growth behaviour be faster and steadier? Could there be a different growth path? What factors influence the growth rate? To make reliable decisions for NewTel, a deeper understanding of the situation is warranted.

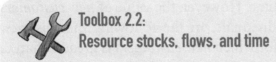

Toolbox 2.2:
Resource stocks, flows, and time

By now, you have calculated a set of variables and assigned a specific value for each month. For purposes of storing and representing the series of values that each variable has in each month, we now consider each variable as a vector that has a specific name and which has as many values as there are months in the analysis: 12 in the current case. Table 2.2 shows the variables in columns and the monthly values in rows.

Resource stocks: Some entities of a system are tangible and can, therefore, be counted at any given moment in time. For example, supermarkets can only sell their products if they are in stock, so they take inventory of their *Products in stock* regularly to monitor *availability*. In places where consumers can order supermarket items online, the burden of having sufficient stock may be shifted from supermarket to suppliers; a product that is not available cannot be delivered. A fuel gauge in a car (or any other motorized vehicle) that continuously monitors how much *Fuel* is left in the tank is another example. *Fuel* and *Products in stock* are both system entities that can be counted and are required to perform certain actions. We call them resources and represent them by stock variables. We say that such resources accumulate in a stock because if an additional unit of the resource becomes part of the stock, it will stay there until it moves out of the stock.

Principle 1 (P 1): Resource stocks
Resource stocks accumulate the individual units entering over time, until they leave.

If it is necessary to know the number of units in the stock, all inflows to or outflows from the stock must be stopped so that no change occurs. Imagine how the inventory is taken when the supermarket is closed. Or, when clerks count the cash in the cash register at the end of a business day. And going back to our car example, when you check the fuel before going on a long trip.

Counting the number of units in a stock is important because these quantities change over time. *Bank account balances* change each time money is *deposited* or *withdrawn*. Soccer teams <u>hire</u> and <u>fire</u> *Players* between seasons. *Fuel* in the tank of a vehicle is <u>filled</u> at the petrol station and <u>burns</u> while the vehicle is moving. Resources that accumulate into stocks can be interpreted as opening balances or closing balances for a given period. At the opening of each period a certain quantity of each resource is available. Then, the closing balance of the first period is the initial balance of the second period and so forth.

The initial letter of the names of variables representing stocks is capitalized in this book to distinguish them from other types of variables.

Flow: Between any two counting moments, units can enter or leave a stock. We say they flow into or flow out of a stock. The variables that represent such in- and outflows are flow variables or flow rates. An inflow adds to a stock, whereas an outflow subtracts from a stock. If you add up all inflows and subtract all outflows, you can compute the net flow; since the net flow may be positive or negative, it is a bidirectional flow, with an arrowhead at each one of its ends. A flow is always defined over a period of time, i.e. the time that passes between establishing the opening balance and the closing balance of the stock.

If you want to know the size of the net change of a stock over a given period of time, you can compare the quantity of a stock at the beginning and the end of this period. For instance, when clerks count the *Cash* in the cash register at the end of a business day, the difference between end-of-day and beginning balance represents the total change of cash or *cash flow* of that day. You can measure the *fuel consumption* of your car in a similar way, by checking the amount of *Fuel* in the car tank before and after a trip. If your car has a gauge indicating the total number of kilometres (or miles) your car has been driven: each time the wheel turns around 360 degrees, a given distance is added to the *Total distance driven*.

> **Principle 2 (P 2): Flow rates**
> **Flow rates increase resources if they are inflows, or deplete resources if they are outflows. All flows into and out of a stock can be expressed as net flow.**

Time: Since each variable can, in principle, have a different value at each instant, these values are stored as a vector with one row for each value. Since each row stores the value measured at a given time, the row numbers correspond to the respective time indices. The example of a bank account in Table 2.3 illustrates this. Time is measured in months; the amounts of money in dollars:

Since *Bank balance* is a stock, its time indices refer to moments. Moment 0 is the balance at the opening, and the indices 1 through 3 refer to the closing balances of the respective months. This

Table 2.3 How stock and flow variables are stored

Time (Months)	Bank balance ($)	Time (Months)	deposits ($/month)	withdrawals ($/month)
0	5000	0,1	3000	4000
1	4000	1,2	3000	3000
2	4000	2,3	5000	2000
3	7000			

means that month 1 is the amount of time transcoding between the indices 0 and 1. The *deposits* and the *withdrawals* are flows, and their time indices indicate the beginning and the ending of each respective month. For instance, during the first month, *withdrawals* exceed *deposits* by $1000 and, therefore, the *bank balance* <u>declines</u> from $5000 to $4000. During the second month, *deposits* and *withdrawals* are equal and the *Bank balance* at the end of that month <u>remains</u> the same as at the beginning of that month. In the third month, *deposits* exceed *withdrawals* by $3000 and, accordingly, the *Bank balance* <u>increases</u> to $7000 by the end of that month.

Since stocks refer to specific points in time, the time index of a stock is always a number, for example: $MyStock_3$ represents the value of *MyStock* at time 3. Flow variables have time indices consisting of two numbers, representing the opening and closing of the period of time they refer to: $myFlow_{2,3}$ describes the variable *myFlow* between the times 2 and 3. In the case of a store selling only juice and operating hour wise, one could say that $Juice_{10}$ is the stock at 10:00 a.m. and $Juice_{11}$ the amount of juice at 11:00 a.m. The flow *juice sold*$_{10,11}$ would represent the sales of juice between the hours 10:00 a.m. to 11:00 a.m.

Let us use *m* as in 'month' as time index, where *m* stands for 'beginning of a month', and *n* for 'beginning of the following month'. Stocks start at the opening balance and change according to the respective flow rates. Flows have a composite time index *m,n* (with $n > m$). The initial value of stocks is defined externally.

Consider now what is already known about the structure of your management challenge at NewTel regarding variables and causal links. The known variables appear in the headings of Table 2.2: *Potential customers*, *Current customers*, *current customers encounters*, *potential customers fraction* and *new customers*. Three aspects of the situation are assumed to be constant: the *population* remains stable at 1 000 000 individuals and each individual encounters 100 other individuals per month. When a *Potential customer* encounters a *Current customer*, the likelihood that the *Potential customer* becomes a *new customer* is always 1%. You also know that the initial values of stocks at $m = 0$ are: 995 000 *Potential customers*$_0$ and 5000 *Current customers*$_0$. The values of each variables over time are stored in the respective rows of the table: indeed, each variable is a vector.

During each month ($m = 1$ to 12), a certain number of individuals will become *new customers*$_{m,n}$, leaving the stock of *Potential customers*$_m$ and becoming part of the stock of *Current customers*$_m$. In other words, *Potential customers*$_n$ will be *Potential customers*$_m$ minus *new customers*$_{m,n}$, and *Current customers*$_n$ will be *Current customers*$_m$ plus *new customers*$_{m,n}$. The monthly value of *new customers*$_{m,n}$ depends on the *current customers encounters*$_{m,n}$, the *potential customers fraction*$_m$ and the *conversion fraction*. The *potential customers fraction*$_m$ is calculated by:

$$potential\ customers\ fraction_m\ [\text{dimensionless}] = Potential\ customers_m\ [\text{individual}] / population\ [\text{individual}] \qquad (2.4)$$

If the relationships between the variables explained are accurate, then they must be able to reproduce the S-shaped growth of *Current customers* shown in Figure 2.2. Therefore, simulating the behaviour of the equations by calculating the 12 months is an effective way to check if your conceptual understanding of the situation is sufficient. As we mentioned before, the initial values of *Potential customers* and *Current customers* are defined. Each month is calculated in the same way, repeating a sequence of steps: first determine *current customers encounters*$_{m,n}$ and *potential customers fraction*$_{m,n}$ as intermediate steps to compute *new customers*$_{m,n}$. The values of *Potential customers*$_n$

and *Current customers$_n$* can be calculated using their values at time m and the number of *new customers* corresponding to the period m to n.

The quantity of *current customers encounters$_{0,1}$* is calculated by multiplying *Current customers$_0$* with *contact rate*: $5000 * 100 = 500\ 000$. The *potential customers fraction$_1$* is $995\ 000/1\ 000\ 000$ or 0.995. Therefore, *new customers$_{0,1}$* will be $500\ 000 * 0.995 * 0.1 = 4975$. From this follows that *Current customers$_{m=1}$* $= 5000 + 49\ 500$ and *Potential customers$_{m=1}$* $= 990\ 000 - 4975$.

Calculating one month is relatively easy. Each of the months is calculated in the same way; only the time indices increase each time by one. Repeating the calculations by hand is laborious and is prone to error, so using a spreadsheet is the typical tool for this task.

Figure 2.3 displays the spreadsheet using the columns to represent the variables *Potential customers, Current customers, current customers encounters, potential customers fraction,* and *new customers,* and the rows to store the values for each variable in the respective months. The numbers in the first row are the column indices and the numbers in the furthest column on the left are the row indices. The combination of a row and column identifies a

DIY 2.4:
Create a spreadsheet model to simulate the behaviour of *Current customers*

You may see the analogy between the rows 'month' in Tables 2.2 and 2.3 and the time index m. Based on this, create a spreadsheet similar to Table 2.2. Start with the same initial values for month 0 and write formulae to have the spreadsheet compute the values of the variables *Potential customers, Current customers, current customers encounters, potential customers fraction,* and *new customers* for months 1 to 12.

If you can, use the 'Formulas' menu in MS Excel© to assign names to the exogenous variables: *contact rate, conversion fraction,* and *population.* Moreover, adjust the way your spreadsheet software represents the columns and rows to have column numbers and row numbers. This will change the way the references to cells are displayed in your formulas and show how the current values of variables depends on previous values of these variables. If you use Excel, the 'Options' menu has a 'Formulas' sheet where you can adjust the representation of formula to the 'R1C1' style: R refers to 'row' and C to 'column'. Review your spreadsheet by comparing it to the values in Table 2.2. You can find the spreadsheet file 'C2 Data table example' on our companion website. Use the worksheet at the end of the chapter.

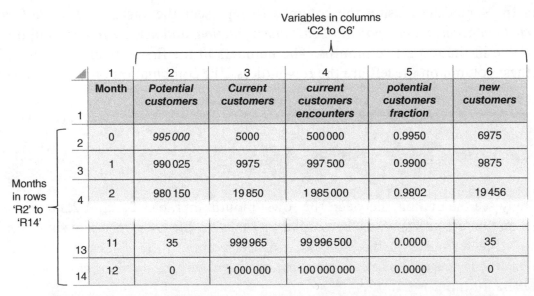

Figure 2.3 A spreadsheet for simulating the variables of the model

cell. To make clear references to columns and rows, the formulas use 'R' to refer to a row and 'C' to refer to a column. To be a bit more precise, the variables are recorded in the columns C2–C6, and the months are recorded in rows R2–R14. For example, the initial number of *Potential customers* is stored in cell R2C2.

The initial state, month 1, starts at time 0 and the numbers of *Potential customers* and *Current customers* are not calculated. These are shown in cells R1C2 (meaning 'row 1, column 2'; note that this is not the same as saying 'next row, 2 columns right' by writing R[1]C[2]) and R1C3. The *current customers encounters, potential customers fraction,* and *new customers* are calculated.

When the number of *current customers encounters* is calculated by formula, and we know that it depends on the number of *Current customers* in the same month, then the formula should have a reference to the cell in the same row one column to the left of where the formula is, i.e. RC[−1]. 'R' without a number means 'same row', and 'C' with a number x in square brackets means 'x columns away from here'; if x is negative, this means 'to the left', and if x is positive it is 'to the right'. Therefore, the formulas are:

- *current customers encounters* = 100 * RC[−1]
- *potential customers fraction* = RC[−3] / 1 000 000
- *new customers* = 0.01 * RC[−1] * RC[−2]

Figure 2.4 illustrates these relationships. The cells whose values are determined by formulas depend on values stored in other cells. Arrows show these dependencies, which represent causal relationships. The arrowheads indicate the direction of the information used. For instance, *current customers encounters* depends on *Current customers,* which is stored at RC[−1].

Once month 1 is completed, you can compute the values of *Potential customers* and *Current customers* for the beginning of the following month. They depend on the respective value just one month before ('one row up, same column' R[−1]C) and last month's *new customers* (*Potential customers* 'one row up, three columns to the right' and

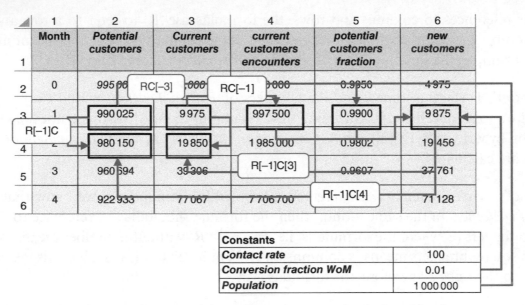

Figure 2.4 The references in spreadsheet formulae reveal relationships between variables

Current customers 'one row up, four columns to the right'). The formulas for *current customers encounters, potential customers fraction,* and *new customers* do not change; they can simply be copied to the row of month 2. From then on, you can copy the entire row until month 12.

To a certain extent, this spreadsheet with its formulas is a simulation model. However, you may agree that the tabular format does not reveal the causal structure of the situation, i.e. 'the model', and that it is difficult to interpret the formulas. In addition, the formulas are repeated for each time period and this repetition clutters the representation, when the underlying model becomes more complex and the number of variables increases. Analysis based on spreadsheet modelling becomes less efficient, and even impossible, when analysing highly dynamic and interdependent scenarios. For this reason, we will introduce new diagrams for you to consider.

2.2.4 Causal diagrams reveal the causal structure

The previous subsection introduced the concept of stocks and flows, and you might have noticed that *Potential customers* and *Current customers* are stocks, while *new customers* is a flow. There is a specific set of symbols used to map the causal structure of situations; these will prove highly useful for managing NewTel.

Let us do a simple thought experiment to see how a causal diagram can capture all structural features that are necessary to represent the dynamics unfolding over time (Figure 2.5). Imagine the market has a total of 12 individuals. At the end of month 1, *Potential customers$_1$* is 11 and *Current customers$_1$* is 1. We then stop time to count the individuals, thus making ou, flow of *new customers* grey (= inactive). During month 2, two individuals decide to purchase; therefore, we have two *new customers$_{1,2}$*. So at the end of month 2, these two individuals have left *Potential customers$_2$* (now nine individuals remain*)* and have moved to *Current customers$_2$* (now three).

Figure 2.5 illustrates the phases we go through when simulating one period of time. There are two stocks represented as rectangles and identified by the names *Potential customers* and *Current customers*. Between them, there is an arrow with a valve symbol and the variable name *new customers*. Think of this as a pipe through which the acquired customers (or anything else for that matter) flow, with the quantity (per month) controlled by a valve. This is the path which *Potential customers* take when they purchase a mobile phone and become NewTel's *Current customers*. This arrow-with-valve is the symbol for a 'flow rate'.

Figure 2.5 shows what happens between the end of month 1 and the end of month 2. In the upper third of the illustration, you see the final balances of the two stocks *Potential customers* and *Current customers* when month 1 ends: 11 and 1 respectively. These are the quantities in the stocks when the following month 2 begins. In the middle third, two individuals are moving ('flowing') from *Potential customers* to *Current customers*; this is the monthly flow of *new customers*. At the end of month 2, shown in the lower third, the information about the number of individuals

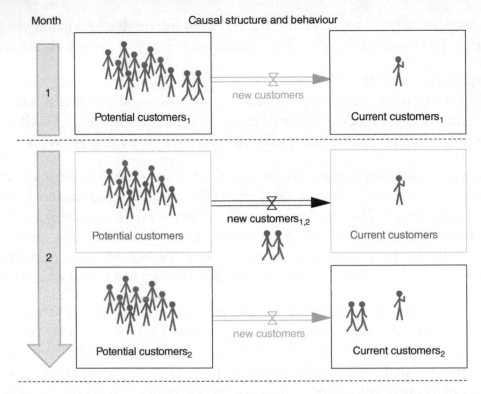

Figure 2.5 Symbolic representation of the two stocks *Potential customers* and *Current customers* and the flow of *new customers*

in each stock is updated. Causal diagrams based on stocks and flows are called 'stock-and-flow diagrams' (SFD). In slightly more general terms, this is how simulation operates:

- stock variables have an initial value at the beginning of the first month;
- during the month, the monthly flow values are calculated, and they depend on the current values of some stocks;

- at the end of each month, the stocks are updated depending on their value at the beginning of the month and the values of the flows during the month.

In Table 2.2, you could see the entire series of values of each variable; however, as Figure 2.4 shows, the causal structure that underlies the behaviour of the variables is difficult to understand in a tabular format. Diagramming and visualizing, as in Figure 2.5, improves your understanding and reveals insights about your management situation. The next step is to populate the SFD with equations specifying how the variables are calculated each month. This is equivalent to the formulas in the previous spreadsheet but is easier to comprehend.

Why are the two resources stocks *Potential customers* and *Current customers* considered? All businesses need customers. You might think that NewTel needs *Current customers* only. However, if your model fails to conceptualize *Potential customers* as a stock, how will you ever gain *new customers* and increase your stock of *Current customers*?

Toolbox 2.3:
Measuring resources

We can count how much there is in stocks at a given point in time. Some are easy to count, such as *Current customers*. They are tangible and visible. Others may be more difficult to count, even if they are tangible, for example *Potential customers*. There are also intangible resources that we can only estimate at best. But even *Staff motivation* or *Customer satisfaction* can, in principle, be measured. If *Staff motivation* is assumed to have an influence on productivity and an organization faces a productivity issue, then *Staff motivation* must be considered when looking for a solution. The empirical methods of organizational psychology provide approaches to measuring *Staff motivation*. As Galileo Galilei said: 'Measure what is measurable, and make measurable what is not so'.

The *Passengers aboard* an airplane are clearly visible and they can be counted. The *Citizens of the People's Republic of China* are also clearly visible, but for practical reasons they cannot be simply counted – their

Table 2.4 Measurement is sometimes direct, sometimes indirect

		Countable	
		Yes	No
Directly observable	Yes	Count	Estimate by polling or sampling
	No	Find conceptual model and infer from qualitative material	Estimate by expert judgment

number must be estimated based on polls. The *Satisfaction of restaurant guests* cannot be easily observed, but their level of satisfaction can be easily gauged. Marketing literature gives us a whole host of ways to infer satisfaction from qualitative data. The *Discontent of a country's population* on the verge of public unrest cannot be easily observed either, and it is practically impossible to circulate a questionnaire – so expert judgment may be the only practical way to make an approximate estimate (Table 2.4).

In this context, variables that can be directly observed and counted are often called 'hard variables', whereas the 'soft variables' are those that must be indirectly inferred because they are hard or impossible to observe.

> **Guideline 2 (G 2): Soft variables are difficult to quantify, but they matter**
> Soft variables are often crucial to solving challenges. If they are difficult to quantify, they should be approximated as accurately as the modeller's time and resources allow. Soft variables should not be excluded from the model, as doing so would assume a value of 0. And that might be the only value known to be wrong.

Remember that, especially in the case of soft variables, one may not be able to obtain precise data concerning their behaviour. However, if reference modes (see Toolbox 1.1) contain estimated turning points, extreme values, and value ranges, it is more likely that you will build a useful simulation model.

If you worked through DIY 2.4, then you have created a spreadsheet table like Table 2.2, and you have entered formulas into each of the rows representing one month. You will have noted that the formulas for all rows (time periods) after the initial one have the same reference structure. Consider the SFD in Figure 2.6: the diagram represents a causal structure that is valid for each month of the entire time horizon. Each variable is represented only once – not once per time period. If you could enrich each stock and each flow symbol in the SFD in Figure 2.6 with an equation equivalent to the formula in the respective spreadsheet row, then you would not need to replicate the diagram for each month, as in Figure 2.5.

A SFD can be improved by graphs showing how the model's variables behave over the duration of 12 months. In Figure 2.6, you see an S-shaped behaviour of *Current customers* and the inverted S-shape of *Potential customers*.

Figure 2.6 clearly displays both the causal structure of the situation for NewTel and the behaviour of this structure. The graphs direct your attention to the behaviour of the variables and not just to specific numbers when using tables (Figure 2.2). This leads to new questions about your management challenge. You are invited to answer one of these questions in the DIY2.5.

DIY 2.5:
Explain the behaviour of the variable *Potential customers*

In Figure 2.6, *Current customers* and *Potential customers* both display exponential behaviour first and then switch to goal-seeking behaviour. However, one of them has a positive slope whereas the other's slope is negative. Why is the shape of *Potential customers* the inverse of the 'S-shaped behaviour' shown by *Current customers*?

Consider an SFD of your situation together with the equations specifying the variables' behaviour as shown in Figure 2.7.

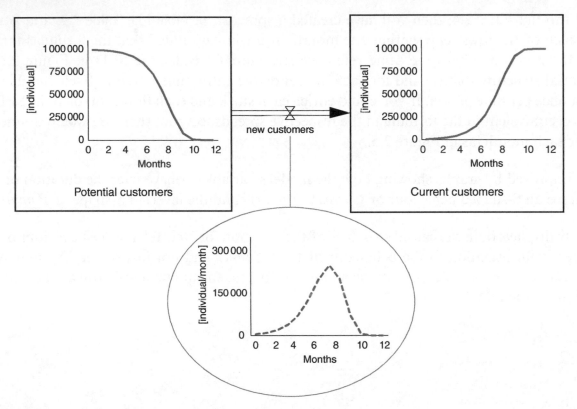

Figure 2.6 The causal structure underneath customer dynamics and its behaviour over time

Figure 2.7 shows a series of symbols with well-defined meanings, which we will discuss in turn. This subsection also provides more details about the stocks, the flows, and the causal links. Following that, Section 2.2.2 deals with the symbol ↻ with a letter 'R' or 'B', which represent 'feedback loops'.

Figure 2.7 also shows the equations describing the behaviour of the two stocks, *Potential customers* and *Current customers*, as well as the *new customers* flow, together with the symbols representing them in the stock-and-flow

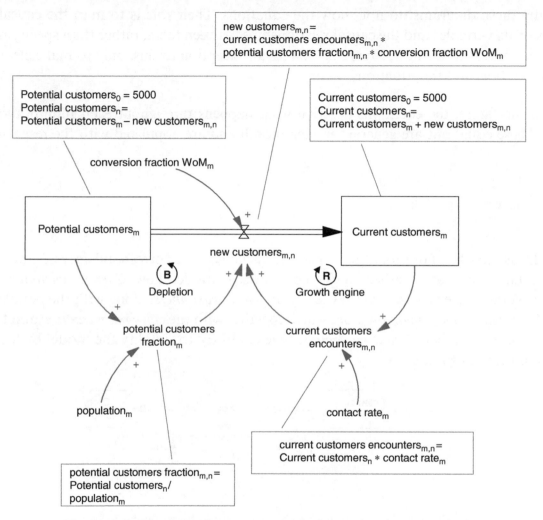

Figure 2.7 The causal structure with the respective equations

diagram. Normally these diagrams do not show the equations. Their role is to map the causal structure of the situation in terms of its variables and the causal relationships between them, rather than specifying the operational details, i.e. the equations. But, for now, Figure 2.7 makes an exception to this, only to make clear the equivalences between the SDF symbols and the equations.

As you can see in the figure, the equations describe what happens throughout each month and what is counted between months. These equations are general for each month and are populated with the respective values in each

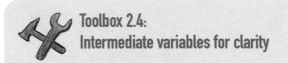

Toolbox 2.4:
Intermediate variables for clarity

A SFD usually has additional intermediate variables that correspond to relevant elements of the system but which are neither stocks nor flows. Consider how *Current customers* and *Potential customers* influence *new customers*. Clearly, *Potential customers*, along with the population combined into the *potential customers fraction*, which together with the *conversion fraction* and the *contact rate*, determine the number of *new customers*. One could try to simplify the model by formulating it the way it appears in Figure 2.8.

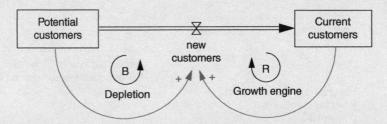

Figure 2.8 A diagram that does not show all the relevant factors

In this formulation, the flow of *new customers* would behave according to Equation (2.5), which is a formal way to state that 'the monthly *new customers* is the result of the following: the number of *Current customers* meet 100 other individuals each, out of whom (*Potential customers*/1 000 000)% are *Potential customers*, and 0.01 or 1% of the resulting number of individuals become *new customer* this month'. This is a long and complex sentence. Its meaning is represented in a formal and clear way by:

$$new\, customers[\text{individual}/\text{month}]=$$
$$Current\, customers[\text{individual}]*100*(Potential\, customers[\text{individual}]/1\,000\,000)*0.01 \qquad (2.5)$$

Where 100 represents *contact rate*, 0.01 stands for the *conversion fraction* and 1 000 000 corresponds to the *population*. The monthly number of *new customers* would be the same as in the previous formulation; we only substitute the placeholders for the exogenous variables by their values.

However, there is a drawback. When you look at this equation, you have to actively remember what these numbers stand for. And the diagram does not help you to remember that there are two relevant factors: *contact rate* and *conversion fraction*. When you compare this supposedly simplified version with the one shown in Figure 2.7, it becomes apparent that by explicitly representing the exogenous variables in the diagram, this diagram provides a more transparent representation of NewTel's situation. The same holds true for the intermediate variables such as *potential customers fraction*, which appears as (*Potential customers* / 1 000 000) in Equation (2.5): the diagram as well as the equation which explicitly contain *potential customers fraction* are easier to interpret and use. This is also true for other intermediate variables, e.g. *current customers encounters*. You could continue without them, but since they can play a relevant role in your strategic reasoning you should clearly illustrate them in diagrams and in equations.

> **Guideline 3 (G 3): Model parsimony**
> When developing and using causal diagrams, make sure that all relevant, and only relevant, variables and causal links are represented.
>
> You can follow this guideline by repeatedly asking yourself if the diagram is sufficiently explicit to understand the causal relationships that are relevant to understanding and describing each variable's behaviour. If the diagram can be simplified without losing clarity, do it. If the diagram is not explicit enough to explain a variable's behaviour, then add an intermediate variable. As you examine the situation, your understanding or mental model develops, and therefore you may decide to simplify a diagram later in the process. To guide you, remember what Einstein said: 'Everything should be as simple as possible, but not simpler'.

month. This is where the computer helps: it quickly carries out the computational steps without omissions or accidental mistakes. Since the time indices are mostly for mathematical consistency, and since you now understand their meaning, let us leave them out from here onwards to simplify our representations of the situation.

The causal links in Figures 2.7 and 2.8 have '+' signs at their arrowheads. These represent the link's 'polarities', which allow you to codify and to interpret how variables react to one another. For instance, *potential customers fraction* is the result of the number of *Potential customers* divided by the number of individuals in the total *population*. When there are <u>more</u> *Potential customers*, the *fraction* will be <u>higher</u>, and when there are <u>less</u> *Potential customers*, the *fraction* will be <u>lower</u>. You need to understand polarity to correctly map and analyse your situation.

You are now able to read the diagram in Figure 2.7 as a textual description: changes in *Potential customers* will lead to changes in the *potential customers fraction* in the same direction. The <u>higher</u> the *potential customers fraction* and the <u>more</u> *current customers encounters*, the <u>more</u> *new customers* there will be. Also, if the *potential customers fraction* and *current customers encounters* <u>decrease</u>, there will be <u>fewer</u> *new customers*.

Toolbox 2.5:
Causality and polarity

The single-line arrows are causal links: they represent cause and effect between pairs of variables. Let us define the variable where the effect occurs as e and the causing variable is c (Figure 2.9).

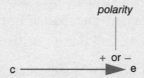

Figure 2.9 A causal link between two variables

The variable e changes according to changes occurring in c. The polarity represents the direction in which e reacts to changes in c. If we want to understand the polarity of the influence of c on e, then we must temporarily assume that all other variables linked to e are held constant. Of course, in the real world, several variables may affect e; however, if two variables $c1$ and $c2$ changed at the same time, how could we determine how much of the change in e is caused by $c1$? In science, the practice of holding all other variables constant is called 'ceteris paribus', i.e. 'all other things being equal'.

> **Guideline 4 (G 4): Ceteris paribus**
> Ceteris paribus (c.p.) is a way of analysing causal interconnections. Such analysis accounts for the changes that the change in one variable influences the effect variable. All the other variables which are also linked to the effect variables remain unchained in their value.

A positive polarity is when the change in c causes a change in e in the same direction. In other words, if c <u>increases</u>, then e will be <u>larger</u> than what it otherwise would have been. This can be surprising because it refers to 'what otherwise would have been'. Think of a case where a company's *sales* are <u>decreasing</u>. If it decides to <u>discount</u> the *price*, the effect may be that some <u>additional</u> *people buy* the product and the sales will <u>decrease less</u> than before, but still decrease. Hence, *sales* would be 'larger than what they otherwise would have been'. But the polarity also means: If *c* <u>decreases</u>, then *e* will be <u>smaller</u> than it otherwise would have been. Think of a savings account with a given *interest rate* (if it has a positive value: you may remember that this is sometimes not the case from the example in Toolbox 2.1): if the *interest rate* <u>sinks</u>, the *balance* on your savings account will still <u>increase</u>, but it will be 'smaller than it otherwise would have been'. When the change in the effect variable *e* is in the same direction as the change in the cause variable *c*, we call this a positive polarity which is represented by a '+'.

Then, there is also a negative polarity. If *c* <u>increases</u>, then *e* will be <u>lower</u> than what it otherwise would have been. And vice versa, if *c* <u>decreases</u>, *e* will be <u>larger</u> than it otherwise would have been. In other words, when the change in the effect variable *e* is in the opposite direction as the change in the cause variable *c*, we call this a negative polarity which is represented by a '−'.

The equation defined for a variable indicates how the variable is affected by other variables. There are two aspects. Firstly, any cause variable *c* linked to an effect variable *e* by a causal link must also be used on the right side of the equation describing *e*. Secondly, the mathematical operation carried out on the effect variable *e* must be consistent with the polarity of the causal link, i.e. + or −, from the cause variable *c*. Table 2.5 shows typical ways in which an arithmetic operator represents the polarity of a causal link.

For instance, imagine a company where management has defined a standard for *desired productivity*. In such a case, *actual productivity* must be compared to the standard and, therefore, management receives information about *measured productivity*. Figure 2.10 shows a causal diagram indicating that *measured productivity* depends on the amount of *work done* and the number of *hours worked*. Since we focus on the polarity, the figure does not show the *desired productivity* and how the

Table 2.5 Typical arithmetic operators representing positive and negative polarity

$$c \xrightarrow{+} e \qquad\qquad c \xrightarrow{-} e$$

Addition: $e = x + c$	Subtraction: $e = x - c$
Multiplication: $e = x * c$	Division: $e = x / c$
Exponential: $e = x^c$	Root: $e = x^{1/c}$
Power: $e = c^x$ (for $x > 1$)	Power: $e = c^x$ (for $x < 1$)

variables are used to control productivity. The right-hand side of Figure 2.10 displays two graphs. Each of them contains one of the two variables *work done* and *hours worked*, as well as *measured productivity*. Note that the ceteris paribus assumption is applied. Each of the behaviour-over-time-graphs (BOTG) shows two different cases: the dark blue line represents an <u>increase</u> in *work done* (or *hours worked*) and the effect on *measured productivity*. The light blue line represents a <u>decrease</u> in *work done* or *hours worked* and the reaction of *measured productivity*.

The relationship between *work done* and *measured productivity* has a positive polarity, while *hours worked* has a negative polarity on its link to *measured productivity*. *Measured productivity* is calculated using *work done* and *hours worked*. An <u>increase</u> in *work done* leads to <u>higher values</u> for *measured productivity*, ceteris paribus, and an <u>increase</u> in *hours worked* must <u>decrease</u> the *measured productivity*, ceteris paribus. As an equation, this is expressed as: *measured productivity = work done / hours worked*.

Of course, in real life situations several factors may have different effects simultaneously. For instance, *work done* and *hours worked* can vary at the same time. However, whatever the influence of *work done* may be, the polarity of the influence of *hours worked* on *measured productivity* will always be negative. Keep in mind the ceteris paribus assumption: if you changed *work done* and *hours worked* at once,

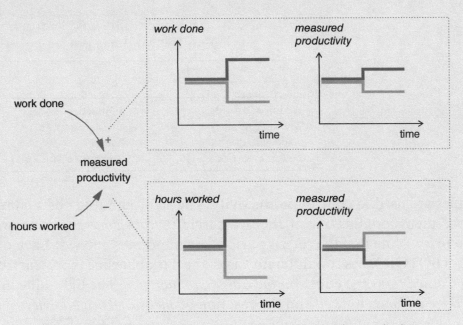

Figure 2.10 Examples of positive and negative polarity

how could you ever know which influence ought to be attributed to *hours worked* when you inspect *measured productivity*?

Caution is necessary when interpreting the polarity of causal links between flows and stocks. As a first example, when an *inflow* to a *stock* <u>decreases,</u> what happens to the stock?

<u>Reducing</u> the *inflow* will not lead the stock to <u>decrease</u> in absolute terms. What happens is that <u>less will be added</u> to the stock from that moment on, and therefore its slope will be <u>smaller</u> – but still positive. In Figure 2.11, the dotted line in the stock's **BOTG** shows what would have happened

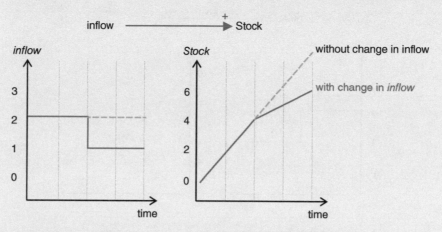

Figure 2.11 Positive polarity between an *inflow* and a *Stock*

otherwise: it is greater than the solid line showing what happens after reducing the *inflow*. When an *inflow* is reduced, the *stock* will be lower than what it would have otherwise been.

It can also be a little confusing at first when interpreting the negative polarity of *outflows* (Figure 2.12).

An *outflow* takes away units from the *stock*. A negative polarity does not imply that when the *outflow* sinks, the *stock* will rise. What happens is that fewer units are drained per period and, therefore, the *stock* declines less quickly than before. The solid line in the stock's graph is higher than the dotted line, showing that the actual behaviour is less negatively sloped than before. The *stock* still sinks, but slower than what would otherwise have been the case.

Please keep in mind that the polarity of a causal link refers to a comparative change, not an absolute change.

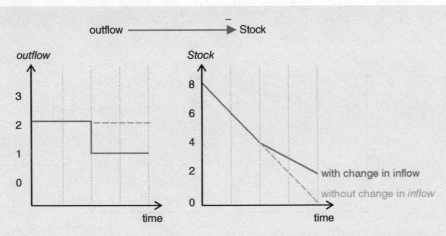

Figure 2.12 Negative polarity between an *outflow* and a *Stock*

Thanks to this coherence between the equations, the causal links, and their polarity signs, it is possible to understand the causal structure of a situation based on the diagram alone. There is no need to examine the equations. We consider this a relief, don't you?

Now you can map the causal structure of your business challenge with NewTel to see how the different variables interact. We also have a set of equations describing these relationships between the variables. Let us move on and simulate this.

2.3 Structure and dynamics of new product diffusion

2.3.1 Your first simulation model

Before you can simulate a model, you have to build it. From now on, you will develop a simulation model for your situation in Plutonia using simulation-modelling software. Such a model consists of variables, i.e. stocks, flows, intermediate variables, and causal links in the form of a SFD and several equations. The software allows you to map the structure, quantify the variables, and to simulate their behaviours. We use the diagram style and equation language of the software Vensim Personal Learning Edition (PLE). The software can be downloaded free-of-charge for personal uses from www.vensim.com. Our discussion in the text uses a series of models and you are invited to use these models too. Naturally, you will encounter the most effective learning experience when you use the text to reconstruct the models yourself. Alternatively, you can use the prepared models from the book's companion website. Figure 2.13 shows the SFD of the model 'C2 Word of Mouth'.

When you compare Figure 2.13 to the structure shown in Figures 2.7 and 2.8, you find that the variable *current customers encounters* has disappeared, but the variable *purchases WoM* has been added. Why such a change of intermediate variables? As you will recall from the discussion concerning intermediate variables, the main function of such variables, for instance *current customers encounters* and *purchases WoM*, is to show the understanding

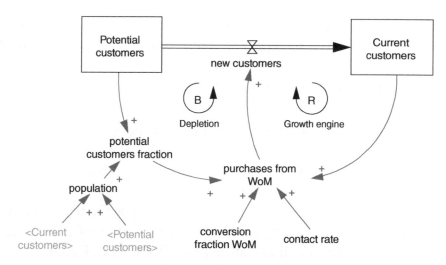

Figure 2.13 The core of the causal structure of the mobile phone case

system structure of the situation. During a first phase of the discussion, it was important to understand the causal structure behind the word-of-mouth diffusion, and it was functional to visualize *current customers encounters* in the diagram.

However, at present you are focused on how to acquire *new customers* for NewTel and to concentrate on the word-of-mouth dynamics to achieve this. The variable *purchases from WoM* reminds you that this is one essential part of winning *new customers*. But this structure is not the only reason for *new customers*. Later in the discussion, *advertising spending* will be added as a second reason for people to purchase your product, and it will be highly useful to see that there are two separate possibilities that motivate *Potential customers* to become your *Current customers*.

Equations (2.6) and (2.7) are equivalent to Equation (2.5): the multiplication of *Current customers* with *contact rate*, which was previously assigned to the variable monthly *current customers encounters*, is now a part of the variable *purchases WoM*.

$$purchases\ from\ WoM\ [\text{individual}\,/\,\text{month}] = Current\ customers\ [\text{individual}] * contact\ rate$$
$$[\text{individual}\,/\,\text{month}\,/\,\text{individual}] * potential\ customers\ fraction\ [\%] * conversion\ fraction\ WoM\ [\%] \quad (2.6)$$

$$new\ customers\ [\text{individual}\,/\,\text{month}] = purchases\ WoM\ [\text{individual}\,/\,\text{month}] \quad (2.7)$$

Since both sets of intermediate variables have the same effect on the *new customers* flow, the model shown in Figure 2.8 generates the same customer behaviour as the one shown in Figure 2.7. *Current customers, contact rate,* the *potential customers fraction,* and the *conversion fraction WoM* drive *purchases WoM,* which, in turn, constitutes the flow of *new customers.* This is at the same time more explicit than Equation (2.5) (a quick check: can you remember what 0.01 and 1 000 000 represent?) and does not occupy space in the diagram displaying intermediate variables that are not needed. The units of measure must match on both sides of an equation: this avoids comparing apples with oranges. This is obviously the case in Equation (2.7). But look at Equation (2.6). Each of the variables on the right-hand side of the equation has its own unit of measure. To assess if units are consistent at both sides of the equation, apply the arithmetic operations to the units. In the term 'individual × individual/month/ individual × % × %', the two percentages do not have an influence. The initial 'individual' cancels out with the denominator of 'individual/month/individual', so indeed the right-hand side of Equation (2.7) resolves to 'individual/month' and matches the left-hand side: individual = individual. This is what we call 'unit consistency' and we take great care to assure unit consistency amongst all equations of a model because unit inconsistencies reveal flaws in model conceptualization.

In addition, Figure 2.13 shows the initial values of the two stocks as separate variables, alongside the stock symbols. As you know, the stocks *Potential customers* and *Current customers* contain a given number of individuals at a certain point in time. In the briefing, you were told that as you take over responsibility for NewTel's Plutonia market development, you start with 5000 *Current customers*. This also means that you start with 995 000 *Potential customers*. You would not be able to start formulating your strategy without knowing the initial balances of the stocks. If you were not told the respective quantities, you would need to count the individuals to produce your initial inventory. In the same way, a simulation model needs to be 'told' the initial value for each stock variable.[1]

So, a stock variable, such as *Current customers*, has two components for its calculation: one for the simulated months and one for its initial value. The logic of the accumulation process appears in Equation (2.8). Two aspects of the equation might make you think: *Current customers* appears on both sides and TIMESTEP is mentioned. This is consistent as is discussed in the next paragraph.

$$\textit{Current customers}[\text{individual}]$$
$$= \textit{Current customers}[\text{individual}] + \textit{new customers}[\text{individual}/\text{month}] * \textit{TIMESTEP}[\text{month}] \tag{2.8}$$

---

[1] This can be done by directly specifying the initial quantity in the equations (which do not show up in the diagram); however, frequently it is useful to explore a model's behaviour with different initial conditions, and to do so you would need to go into the initial equations each time you want to change the initial conditions. It is much more practical to define a constant like *init Current customers* because this allows you to redefine the initial conditions without leaving the simulation and getting into the equations.

Pronounced in words, the equation states that '*Current customers* at a given point in time are what they were just before plus the *new customers* who arrived during the past period of time'. Recall for a moment that these variables have time indices and that Equation (2.8) requires the initial value of *Current customers*, that is, *Current customers*$_0$. The value for *customers*$_0$ will be read from the constant *init current customers*. You can imagine that at the onset of the simulation $m = 0$ and then *Current customers*$_n$ equals the stock of *Current customers*$_m$ plus the *new customers*$_{m,n}$.

What is TIMESTEP and why is it used in the stock equation? This becomes clear when you consider that there is an alternative way to formulate this relationship:

$$Current\ customers = \text{INTEG}\left(new\ customers, init\ current\ customers\right)^2$$

The simulation software carries out an 'integration'. This is a process of adding up portions of a given substance, which you may remember from your math courses. At NewTel, you want to manage *new customers*, which is the number of *Potential customers* who decide to become your *Current customers* over the period of one month. The basic time unit is one month. Until now, *new customers* have been treated as if a month was just one block of time and we implicitly took it for granted than we could accurately represent the flow by computing the equation once a month. However, it is evident that people make their purchasing decisions daily, not only once a month: the purchasing decisions of many individuals is a repeated process, rather than a one-time event.

For this reason, the simulation model must be run in 'time steps' much shorter than one month and, thus, imitate an actual purchasing process as explained in Toolbox 2.6 on methodology and tools.

---

[2] INTEG is a software internal function meaning 'integral' and its argument *new customers* represents the sequence of quantities that become integrated into *Current customers* over the 12 months; starting with the initial value.

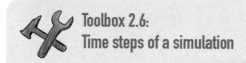

You receive reports and make decisions once a month – which is a typical for management decisions that are based on information that has been synthesized over time spans (rather than real-time data). However, the people in Plutonia make purchasing decisions daily. Also, the encounters between *Current customers* and *Potential customers* are distributed over a period of a month.

How does this all work? Let us assume the Plutonians meet and make decisions once a week and, hence, meet four times a month. At the end of the first week, a certain number of *contact rate* have taken place. Table 2.6 shows the respective values assuming 100 *contact rate* (and therefore 100 / 4 weeks = 25 *weekly encounters*) and a *conversion fraction* of 0.01 in each case; recall that this fraction refers to each encounter rather than a specific time interval and, therefore, it does not change if the length of the time spans is changed from month to week.

In the upper half of Table 2.6, you see the results as before if the results are calculated once per month. 5000 *Current customers* are WoM-promoters for the complete month, and they have 497 500 mixed encounters (with *Potential customers*). At the end of the month, the number of *Current customers* has increased to 9975.

In the lower half of the table, you see the results when the numbers are for each week, i.e. the time step is ¼ or 0.25 of the month. Each week, *Potential customers* become *new customers* and, therefore, are subtracted from the *Potential customers* and added to the *Current customers*. Since this happens already in week 1, in week 2 we have <u>more</u> *Current customers* who are WoM-promoters and <u>fewer</u> *Potential customers*. The total number of mixed encounters then adds up to 713 715, which is almost 50% more than in the first calculation. When the fourth week is over, there are 12 138 *Current customers* compared to 9975.

Table 2.6 Time step influences the accuracy of the results

Months	Potential customers	Current customers	new Customers
0	995 000	5000	4975
1	990 025	9975	
Total number of *new customers*			4975

Weeks	Potential customers	Current customers	new Customers
0	995 000	5000	1244
1	993 756	6244	1551
2	992 205	7795	1934
3	990 271	9729	2409
4	987 862	12 138	
Total number of *new customers*			7138

new customers based on:
monthly calculation	4975
weekly calculation	7138
relative difference	43%

When using a computer to calculate the results, the 'time step' of the actions in the model can be approximated with sufficient accuracy as compared to the real actions. In the current example, the time step is 0.25 month, which is expressed as a fraction of the basic time unit that is used. In the book's simulation models, the time step is even shorter: 0.0625. This means the set of formulas is evaluated 16 times per month, roughly every other day. Note that in some software packages this is called 'TIMESTEP', whereas in others it is called 'DT' or 'delta time'. Regardless of the software package you use, that or DT is a property of the execution of the entire model, not of its causal structure or even a specific variable. You can find a tutorial for setting the time step on this book's companion website.

Going back to Equation (2.8), you realize that TIMESTEP can be one or less. If it is one, then the flow will be calculated for the entire month in one single step. If it is 0.0625, the simulation software will carry out 16 calculations and the flow will be separated in 16 pieces. The result will be a higher accuracy of the quantities in the simulation. But anyway, the TIMESTEP (internal) variable has its own unit of measure, which is precisely the time unit of the model: month. Thus, multiplication of the flows with TIMESTEP leads to cancelling out the time unit and, therefore, the unit consistency is conserved in the equations that describe stocks.

You have now reached a thorough knowledge concerning the stocks, the flows and the intermediate variables. However, that is not the end of the story. In NewTel's situation, there is more to the model than stocks and flows. From Figure 2.1 onwards, you have seen feedback loops, for instance 'growth engines' and 'depletion'. Feedback loops are a fundamental part of dynamic systems and they need to be analysed.

2.3.2 Feedback loops

The signs ↺ with either an 'R' or 'B', which you have seen in the various SFDs, are iconic statements pointing your attention to the presence of 'feedback loops'. These loops are of fundamental importance for you to understand, as they determine how a system drives its own behaviour.

The word-of-mouth structure contains two feedback loops. One of them – named 'growth engine' – connects *new customers* to *Current customers* in a causal chain; denoted as 'R'. The other one is 'depletion' and it ties together

Toolbox 2.7:
Feedback loops

A feedback loop is a chain of variables and causal links that is logically closed. In short, when a change (<u>increase</u> or <u>decrease</u>) in a cause variable has an influence on the same variable which caused the initial change, then a feedback loop is present. In a way, the change is 'fed back' to where it came from.

There are many examples. Sometimes, the loops are present in nature. When your *body temperature* <u>falls</u> below normal levels, you start to shiver: your *muscle work* <u>increases</u> and that <u>increases</u> your *body temperature*. This is a balancing feedback loop, as it counteracts the initial change and, therefore, acts such as to conserve or re-establish a balance.

A *population of rabbits* that has a high *reproduction rate* produces <u>more</u> *births*, which <u>increases</u> the *population* of rabbits. <u>Even more</u> rabbits will be born in the future. As an additional example, if you deposit a given amount of money in a savings account and the *interest rate* is positive, such that the bank periodically deposits an *interest payment* on your account, assuming your *withdrawals* are <u>less</u> than the *interest payments*, then the *interest payments* <u>increase</u> your *balance*, which leads to <u>higher</u> *interest payments*. These are two examples of a reinforcing feedback loop. This type of loop is sometimes referred to as a 'vicious cycle' or a 'virtuous cycle', depending on your view of the world. In the case of the rabbit *population*, most people would call it a 'vicious cycle'. In the case of the savings account, customers will certainly call this a 'virtuous cycle', but the bank owners may have a different interpretation. The government of a heavily indebted country will probably perceive that the feedback loop of compound interests is a 'vicious cycle'. Frequently, the choice of the adjective 'virtuous' or 'vicious' depends on the perspective of an agent. For this reason, it is good practice to speak of 'reinforcing feedback loops' and not to use the value-laden terms 'virtuous' or 'vicious'.

Sometimes, a feedback loop is intended for management: when a company perceives a <u>loss</u> of *sales*, it may decide to <u>reduce</u> *price*s to <u>increase</u> *sales*. At other times, unintended feedback loops emerge: when a company <u>reduces</u> *price*, this <u>draws away</u> *customers* from a competitor. Then, the other company may decide to <u>reduce</u> *prices* too, trying to <u>win</u> back *customers*. If each company inflicts a <u>loss</u> of *customers* on its rival and then reacts to the loss with an attempt to <u>win</u> *customers*, this will inflict another <u>loss</u> on the rival company and *prices* will spiral down.

Feedback loops can be part of a policy, but they can also be part of how situations happen to be structured. One essential property of feedback loops is their self-determined functioning: once you have initial success in gaining *new customers*, this will set off a steady reinforcement of *new customers* that will continue on its own. And at the same time, it will deplete *Potential customers*, thereby steadily diminishing the force of the word-of-mouth effect. We say that its behaviour is endogenously generated. This means that a feedback loop determines its behaviour itself – you must consider this momentum in your management situation.

> **Principle 3 (P 3): Feedback loop**
> **A feedback loop is a circular chain of causal links. Loops have a closed logic which leads to endogenously driven (autonomous) behaviour. Loops have either a reinforcing (R) or a balancing (B) polarity.**

A loop's polarity can be deduced by applying a change to one of its variables and tracing the effects of the causal links back to the same variable. If the initial change is amplified, the loop is reinforcing ('R'); if the initial change is dampened or decreased, it is a balancing loop ('B'), which counteracts the initial change.

new customers with *Potential customers*; denoted as 'B'. *New customers* belongs to both feedback loops. Therefore, the loops interconnect in this variable.

These two feedback loops are essential for customer dynamics and you must understand them to find out how you can influence the system according to your objectives. In the following, the two different types of feedback loops are first analysed in isolation.

2.3.3 Reinforcing feedback and exponential growth

Consider the reinforcing feedback loop. Equations (2.6), (2.7) and (2.8) contain a certain number of variables that are interdependent. Table 2.7 shows the three equations as rows and separates each of them: the variable on the left-hand side of an equation appears in the column 'dependent' and the variables on the right-hand side of an equation in the column 'independent'.

You can easily see that each of the dependent variables also appear as an independent variable. Starting from the first row of Table 2.7, you can read that *purchases WoM* depends on *Current customers*, which depends on *new customers*, which, in turn, depends on *purchases WoM*. This operationally closed loop is shown as a causal loop diagram (CLD) in Figure 2.14.

DIY 2.6:
Building your first simulation model

Develop a simulation model to explore this reinforcing feedback loop. This model must represent *Current customers*, *new customers*, *purchases WoM*, the *potential customers fraction*, the *conversion fraction WoM*, and *contact rate*. The two latter variables keep the values we have used before (0.01 and 100 respectively). Also, your simulations should start with an initial balance of 5000 *Current customers*.

This model does not include the *Potential customers* stock. Therefore, the *potential customers fraction* cannot be computed. Instead, *potential customers fraction* will be a constant. Set it to 0.99. This value is almost identical to the one the *potential customers fraction* had initially when the model 'C2 Word of Mouth' was simulated earlier in this chapter. Keeping this value constant allows you to explore the behaviours generated by the 'growth engine' reinforcing loop without the effect of the balancing feedback loop.

Remember to set the time step to 0.0625. You can use the tutorial from the companion website to help you.

Table 2.7 Interdependencies amongst variables

Equation	Dependent	Independent
2.6	purchases WoM	Current customers
		contact rate
		potential customers fraction
		conversion fraction WoM
2.7	new customers	purchases WoM
2.8	Current customers	Current customers
		new customers

Figure 2.14 shows that *Current customers* <u>increase</u> *new customers*, which, in turn, <u>add to</u> *Current customers*. This is a 'reinforcing feedback loop' because each iteration reinforces the initial impulse. Note that these equations are equivalent to what is shown in the diagram in Figure 2.14.

If you have completed DIY 2.6, compare your model to the model 'C2 Loop reinforcing' (Figure 2.15). Make sure the equations and values are identical. Then, use your model in the 'SyntheSim' run-time mode of Vensim. A SyntheSim tutorial is on the companion website.

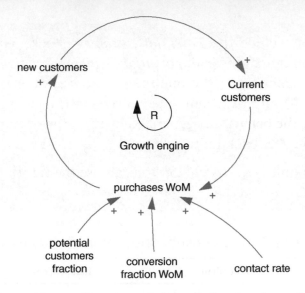

Figure 2.14 Causal loop diagram of the reinforcing loop 'growth engine'

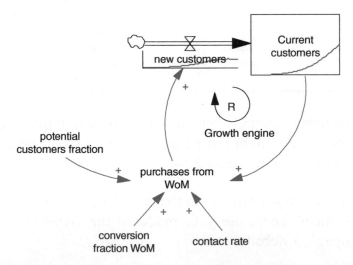

Figure 2.15 SFD of the reinforcing loop in the diffusion model and its behaviour over time (model 'C2 loop reinforcing')

The centrepiece of this model is a reinforcing feedback loop, labelled with 'R': any positive number of *new customers* will <u>add to</u> *Current customers*, which will then <u>increase</u> the number of *purchases from WoM* and, thus, further <u>increase</u> the number of *new customers*. If any of the variables *contact rate*, *conversion fraction WoM*, or *potential customers fraction* <u>increase</u>, the loop's strength, sometimes referred to as its gain, will increase. Of course, the opposite is also true: decreasing values of *contact rate*, *conversion fraction WoM*, or *potential customers fraction* decrease the loop's strength.

The SyntheSim mode shows the behaviour of each variable and it allows you to adjust the values of the exogenous variables during the simulation. *Current customers* begins with 5000 individuals; there are 100 *contact rate* and the *conversion fraction WoM* is 0.01. The *potential customers fraction* is constant at 0.99, with the approximate value of 995 000 *Potential customers*.

If a constant is changed by the sliders, the model immediately resimulates and the resulting behaviours are displayed. This makes it easy to explore the range of model behaviours under different parameter values. Now, let us analyse and understand what is happening in the model for our current set of parameter values.

Current customers and *purchases WoM* show exponential growth. This exponential shape is the consequence of the reinforcing feedback loop, which is why this type of feedback loop is called 'growth engine'. Table 2.8 shows how the dynamics unfold.

When the simulation is initialized with 5000 *Current customers*, month 1 yields 8066 *new customers* who are integrated into the stock of *Current customers*. In the following months, the same rule is applied, and *Current customers* more than double from month to month. Figure 2.16 shows how the growth of *Current customers* <u>accelerates</u> – this is exponential growth.

Current customers more than double each month because the number of *new customers* exceeds the number of *Current customers* – as does the number of *purchases WoM*. There are so many additional *purchases WoM* because

Table 2.8 The monthly <u>increase</u> of *Current customers*

Month	Current customers	new customers
0	5000	8066
1	13 066	21 078
2	34 144	55 082
3	89 226	143 941
4	233 167	376 148
5	609 315	982 952
6	1 592 267	

DIY 2.7:
Explain what drives exptonential growth

In Figure 2.16, *Current customers* displays exponential growth, which is one of the atomic behaviour modes. Why does *Current customers* show exponential behaviour? Explain how the causal structure of the model shown in Figure 2.15 generates this behaviour mode.

Hint: use the 'causes strip' tool in Vensim, which opens a window with the graphs of *Current customers* and the variable(s) it depends on. A tutorial on the causes strip tool is available on the web page.

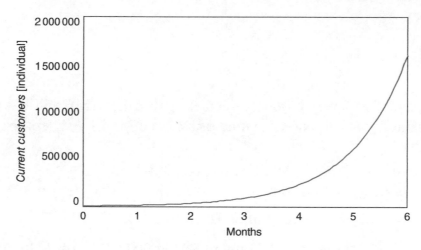

Figure 2.16 Exponential growth of *Current customers*

the number of promoters (*Current customers*) quickly increases, but the *potential customers fraction* never decreases. With the model structure as it is, no other behaviour can result.

However, there are many more *Current customers* than individuals in the total *population*. After six months, *Current customers* has grown beyond the million individuals in Plutonia, which is why only six months are shown. The fact that this model produces impossible numbers for *Current customers* clearly indicates that something is missing in our causal structure. Since you know that the logics of the two equations for *purchases WoM* and for *Current customers* are correct, the problem must be in one of the values the equations use.

If you have no indication which of these values could be erroneous, you can start exploring by reducing each of them, always one at the time. The simulation model you have built enables you to run several experiments.

Running the simulation several times with adjusted values for *potential customers fraction* (0.5 instead of 0.99), *contact rate* (50 instead of 100), and *conversion fraction WoM* (0.005 instead of 0.01) has provided you with

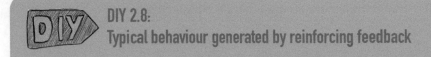

DIY 2.8:
Typical behaviour generated by reinforcing feedback

Run the model in SyntheSim mode (remembering that the TIME STEP is 0.0625) and modify the parameter values yourself one at a time using the appearing sliders for that purpose. Use the following values:

potential customers fraction=0.5(instead of 0.99);

contact rate=50(instead of 100);

conversion fraction=0.005(instead of 0.01).

Which aspects of the behaviour change and which aspects do not? Take a moment to look at the graphs showing *Current customers'* behaviour for each of these simulations. Note what they have in common and what distinguishes them from one another. Explain the similarities and differences in terms of the underlying causal structure. Use the worksheet at the end of the chapter.

behaviours that are all exponential but with quite different curvatures from the original one. Figure 2.17 shows the behaviours of six different simulations. Three of them are the ones just mentioned. However, the figure also contains the behaviour under default values as well as two simulations combining several changes of parameter values: one run combines *potential customers fraction*=0.5 and *contact rate*=50, and the other run uses *potential customers fraction*=0.5, *contact rate*=50 and *conversion fraction WoM*=0.005.

Figure 2.17 shows that the exponential behaviour of *Current customers* under different parameter values grows at very different speeds. When only one of the parameter values is reduced to half of its usual values, *Current customers* reach almost 100 000 after six months. There are three possible ways to reach this behaviour and the corresponding curves overlap one another. When two of the three parameters are set to half of their default value, *Current*

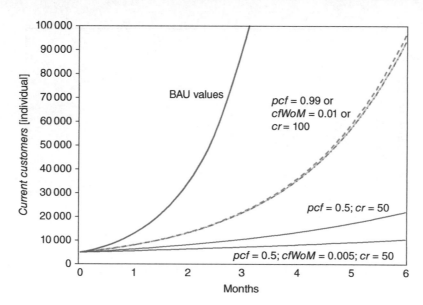

Figure 2.17 Different degrees of exponential growth of *Current customers* for different scenarios. (Legend: *pcf* is the potential customers fraction, *cr* is the *contact rate* and *cfWoM* is the *conversion fraction WoM*.)

customers only grows to around 20 000 individuals by the end of six months, and when all three parameters are reduced to half their default values, *Current customers* do not grow beyond 10 000.

Consider the time it takes *Current customers* to reach the 10 000 individuals mark: under the default values, this happens after roughly three weeks (remember that the time step is 0.0625, which means each month is subdivided into 16 steps; at time step 0.75 *Current customers* grows beyond 10 000 individuals). If only one of the parameters is reduced to half, then the mark is crossed at time step 1.4375 (half of the second month). If two parameters are halved, you have to wait until time step 2.8125 (practically three months), and if all three parameters are only half their default value, it happens at time step 5.625. You remember that all three parameters are used in the flow equation, which is a multiplication. Therefore, you can multiply them together and observe the relationship between

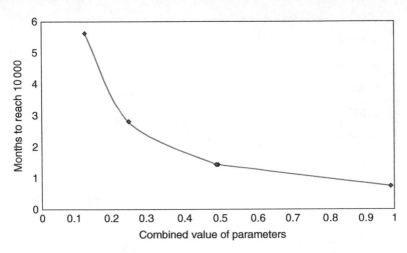

Figure 2.18 The relationship between the multiplied parameter values and the number of months needed to grow to 10 000 *Current customers*

their combined value and the number of months it takes before *Current customers* cross the mark of 10 000 individuals. This is shown in Figure 2.18.

In Figure 2.18, you see that when the combined value of the three parameters is <u>reduced</u>, the time required to reach the 10 000 *Current customers* mark <u>increases</u>. But it does not increase in a linear manner. If you <u>halve</u> the combined parameter value, the time necessary more <u>than doubles</u>. Since you always start with 5000 *Current customers,* it takes your <u>more</u> or <u>less</u> time to reach the 10 000 mark; it means that you are <u>growing less</u> or <u>more quickly</u>.

The time you take to go from one point to another point is your speed. If you look again at the curves in Figure 2.17, you will not only see that higher combined parameter values always come together with higher speeds of growth, but also that the higher speed is reached starting from the same point; in other words, there is a <u>higher acceleration</u> when the combined parameter values are <u>higher</u>. <u>Higher acceleration</u> goes together with a <u>greater curvature</u> of the graphs. And, indeed, the shape of *Current customers* curve remains exponential in each of these simulations; and when the combined parameter values are <u>greater</u>, it has a <u>higher</u> curvature. Therefore, it is only a question of time until *Current customers* grows beyond the *population*, thereby developing in a way which cannot happen in reality. Therefore, even if you know that <u>reducing</u> these values <u>reduces</u> the curvature of the graph, i.e. the <u>acceleration</u> of *Current customers* is <u>reduced</u>, the behaviour is still exponential: *Current customers* still <u>accelerates</u>. You have not yet solved the problem.

There is one inconsistency between the current behaviour of *Current customers* and what you may have noticed in the previous graphs (Figure 2.2) and in the SellPhone simulation, i.e. the current behaviour of your model with only a reinforcing feedback loop does not generate an S-shaped curve but rather an exponential curve. Exponential behaviour is one of the atomic behaviour modes discussed in Chapter 1. That means that the causal structure of a reinforcing feedback loop is the driver of one of the atomic behaviour modes; it is therefore essential. The reinforcing loop you are currently analysing can explain the first part of the behaviour shown in Figure 2.2. However, the current simulation model cannot completely recreate the S-shape pattern. This means that there is more to the causal structure of your situation than what is contained in our current model.

2.3.4 Balancing feedback and goal-seeking behaviour
Now, direct your attention to the balancing feedback loop.

DIY 2.9:
Build your second simulation model

Build a simulation model for the balancing loop 'depletion'. You need to represent *Potential customers* (initialized with 995,000 individuals), *potential customers fraction* (which now is calculated in the same way as indicated by Equation (2.2)), *purchases WoM* and *new customers*. Additionally, the two parameters *conversion fraction WoM* (=0.02) and *contact rate* (=100) must be in the model. Even though *conversion fraction WoM* has been equal to 1% up to now, this time we will use a value of 2% because it allows us to observe depletion more clearly. You may explore how switching back to 1% affects the behaviour of *Potential customers* under the effect of this balancing feedback loop. Later in the book, we will return to the original value of 1%. *Current customers* has to be held constant now, because the reinforcing 'growth engine' loop should not have any influence on the behaviour of the balancing loop. Set the value of *Current customers* to 200 000 individuals. The tutorial from the companion website guides you through these steps.

This corresponds to the model 'C2 Loop balancing', which you can download from the companion website. Compare and adjust your model to simulate the model with the default parameter values and initial value of *Potential customers*. Compare the behaviour of your *Potential customers* to the one generated by the reference model 'C2 Loop balancing'. Use the worksheet at the end of the chapter.

Figure 2.19 shows the model 'C2 Loop balancing' when simulated in SyntheSim mode.

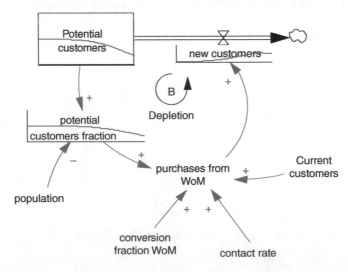

Figure 2.19 The balancing 'depletion' feedback loop of the diffusion model as SFD

This model separates the *Current customers* from the *new customers* flow; by doing this, you have the possibility to experiment with the feedback loop between *Potential customers*, *potential customers fraction*, and *purchases WoM* and *new customers*. The flow variable *new customers* <u>depletes</u> *Potential customers*, thereby <u>decreasing</u> the *percentage of Potential customers*, which then <u>diminishes</u> *new customers*, slowing down the <u>depletion</u> of *Potential customers*. Here, an initial <u>increase</u> in the cause variable leads to a subsequent <u>decrease</u> in the same variable after the causal chain is completed. This is a 'balancing feedback loop'; it compensates for an initial impulse and, thereby, tends to move to stability or equilibrium. Balancing feedback loops are denoted with a 'B'. The graph drawn into the *Potential customers* stock (also Figure 2.20) has a negative slope that approaches a stable equilibrium. So, too, do the other variables. This is goal-seeking behaviour.

The graph in Figure 2.20 reveals a negative slope of *Potential customers*. Initially, the negative slope is steep, but it steadily becomes flatter and eventually approaches zero. This is in stark contrast to the exponential growth seen in the case of the reinforcing feedback loop, and it is the second atomic behaviour mode encountered in Chapter 1.

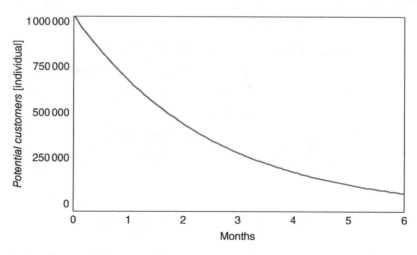

Figure 2.20 Behaviour of *Potential customers* when only the balancing loop is active

This means that the balancing feedback loop structure is of fundamental importance as well. Inspect the SFD with the causal structure to identify the reason for this change of the behaviour mode.

When looking at the SFD in Figure 2.19, it may appear surprising that it is a closed loop because no arrow is shown from *new customers* to *Potential customers*. Nevertheless, your understanding of the situation tells you that the *new customers* flow rate <u>reduces</u> the number of *Potential customers* because it moves individuals from the *Potential customers* stock to the *Current customers* stock. When *new customers* <u>increases</u>, *Potential customers* <u>decreases more rapidly</u>. Also, <u>decreasing</u> *new customers* <u>reduces</u> the number of *potential clients* <u>more slowly</u>. There is then a stable relationship between *new customers* and *Potential customers*. This relationship is not shown in the SFDs and, technically, it is an 'implicit causal link'. The cyclical nature of the chain of causation becomes more visible when you represent it as a causal loop diagram (CLD). In such diagrams, no difference is made between the different types of variables:

Each of the causal links in Figure 2.21 is a statement tying two variables together. An <u>increase</u> of the *potential customers fraction* <u>increases</u> in the number of *purchases from WoM*; this results in an <u>increase in</u> *new customers*,

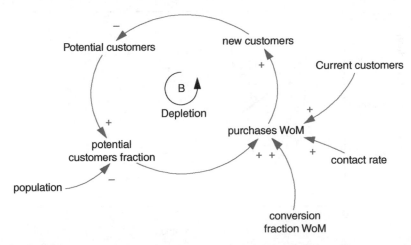

Figure 2.21 Causal loop diagram of the balancing 'depletion' loop

which, in turn, <u>accelerates the reduction</u> of *Potential customers*. The same polarity signs apply when the *percentage of Potential customers* <u>decreases</u>: in such a case the number of *purchases from WoM* also <u>decreases</u> and the resulting <u>reduction</u> of *new customers* will <u>slow down the loss</u> of *Potential customers*.

This means that a feedback loop has one causal structure but can drive the behaviour in different directions according to the nature of the initial impulse. Of course, the slope of *Potential customers* will always decrease – which expresses the reducing speed of depletion. However, when something falls short of achieving a target level and corrective action is taken to <u>increase</u> the *performance*, such as to <u>decrease</u> the *gap* between *target performance* and *observed performance*, the *observed performance* will <u>increase</u> and gradually come closer to the *target performance*. For instance, consider how the number of simultaneous calls supported by your hardware is kept at a desired level in the following example: you calculate the size of the *gap* between the *desired* and the *current number of simultaneous calls*; if the size of the *gap* <u>increases</u>, you <u>increase</u> *investments in server capacity*. This will <u>increase</u> the *current number of simultaneous calls* and <u>reduce</u> the *gap*. Over time, the *current number of simultaneous calls* will, therefore, increase towards the *desired number*. This causal structure is shown in Figure 2.22.

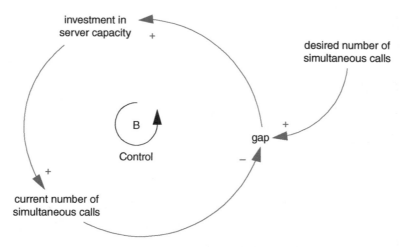

Figure 2.22 Causal loop diagram of a balancing loop 'control'

The underlying structure of causation is a balancing feedback loop and the behaviour it drives is literally goal seeking. This is the reason why we speak of goal-seeking 'behaviour' rather than 'decline'.

In addition, recognizing that one structure can drive increases as well as decreases makes it clear why it is so important to separate the causal structure from the behaviour it generates. You may not be able to change the fact that in a situation like NewTel's on Plutonia – there is a feedback loop – but you may be able to alter the direction of its behaviour.

When you deal with balancing loops, a causal loop diagram can make them easier to identify visually: there is no way people can become *new customers* without <u>reducing</u> the number of *Potential customers*. This means that the *potential customers fraction* must <u>sink</u>; therefore, <u>fewer</u> individuals would become *new customers* in the future. Figure 2.23 shows the characteristic behaviour of *Potential customers* and *new customers*.

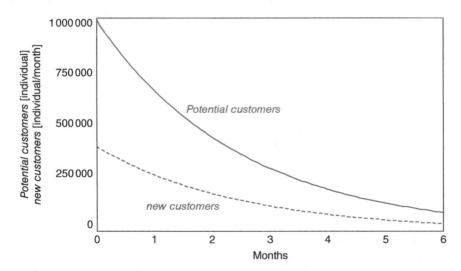

Figure 2.23 Goal-seeking behaviour of *Potential customers* and <u>decreasing</u> monthly number of *new customers*

The number of *Potential customers* decreases but at a diminishing rate. After month 5, it is practically zero. This shape is consistent with the behaviour of *new customers*: firstly, more individuals per month purchase mobile phones and, as time advances, the monthly number of *new customers* gets smaller and approaches zero (after five months). This means that each month a definite number of individuals move out of the *potential customer* state, but each month the number of *new customers* becomes smaller. Also, the shape of *new customers* is consistent with the behaviour of *Potential customers*: when you have less *Potential customers*, the *potential customers fraction* decreases, so *new customers* will decrease. You observe a stable relationship between the absolute level of *new customers* and the slope of *Potential customers*. A higher level of *new customers* means that the slope of *Potential customers* is more negative, whereas a lower level of *new customers* means a less negative slope of *Potential customers*.

Of course, the number of *Current customers* also has an influence. Simulating the model with a range of different numbers of *Current customers* allows you to see this influence. In particular, the higher the number of *Current customers* the quicker the loss of *Potential customers* is. At the same time, it becomes apparent that the number of *Current customers* cannot change the fact that the balancing feedback loop generates stabilizing behaviour. In other words, the loss of *Potential customers* slows down as it approaches zero. You may wonder why this is called goal-seeking behaviour, since there is no apparent goal or target compelling you to do whatever you can to deplete *Potential customers*. However, it is in the nature of a depletion process to gradually empty a stock. Think of what the consequence would be if Plutonia's entire *population* did not have children: those alive progressively grow old and die, and after a certain number of years the *population* would be exactly zero. You can think of this balancing feedback loop as having an implicit goal and gradually decreasing the *population* of the stock to that goal of zero.

There is a relationship between the number of *Current customers*, the speed at which *Potential customers* are lost, and how quickly this speed decreases. Figure 2.24 shows the behaviour of *Potential customers* for different numbers of *Current customers*, always starting with one million *Potential customers*. When you have more *Current customers*, greater numbers of *Potential customers* decide to purchase. For this reason, the slope of *Potential customers* is more negative. On the other hand, lower numbers of *Current customers* lead to a slower

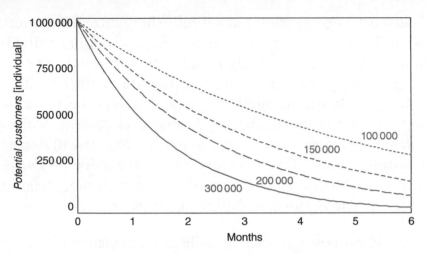

Figure 2.24 Different goal-seeking behaviours of *Potential customers* for varying values of the stock of *Current customers*

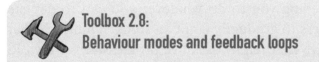

Toolbox 2.8:
Behaviour modes and feedback loops

In Chapter 1, the behaviour modes were introduced and it was shown that complex behaviour modes like S-shaped growth or oscillation can be decomposed into the atomic behaviour modes: exponential and goal seeking. These are fundamental and 'atomic' in the sense that they cannot be further decomposed; they are indeed the building blocks of complex dynamic behaviour. The previous two subsections have shown that beneath each of these atomic behaviour modes, there is a causal structure. Figure 2.25 illustrates what we have discovered so far:

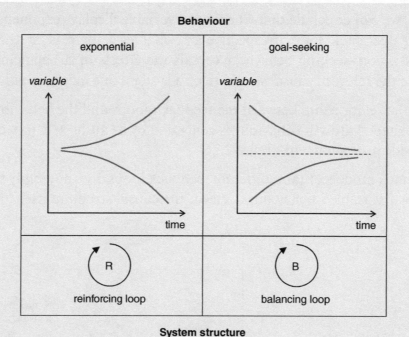

Figure 2.25 The causal structures driving the atomic behaviour modes

As we have seen, a reinforcing feedback loop can only generate exponential growth or exponential decrease behaviours. Also, a balancing feedback loop can only generate goal-seeking behaviour.

Principle 4 (P 4): Types of feedback loops and atomic behaviour modes
Reinforcing feedback loops drives exponential behaviour: they increase the speed of change.
Balancing feedback loops drive goal-seeking behaviour: they decrease the speed of change.

From this, we can conclude that whenever a variable displays exponential behaviour, it is driven by a reinforcing feedback loop irrespective of what else there is in the model and situation. And, analogously, goal-seeking behaviour reveals the effects of a balancing feedback loop. One cannot directly see the relevant causal structure of a system; one must expend analytical effort to discover it.

Based on the relationship between the feedback loops and the behaviour modes, it can be concluded that the S-shaped growth behaviour is generated by a causal structure composed of a reinforcing and balancing loop, as shown in Figure 2.26:

The fact that a model contains different feedback loops does not imply that they are equally important for driving a variable's behaviour. Indeed, the causal structure itself does not imply anything about

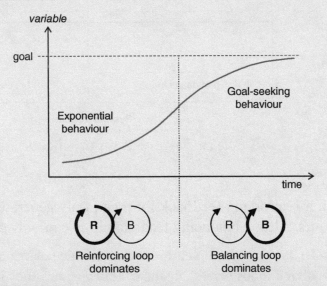

Figure 2.26 A combination of feedback loops drives S-shaped growth

the relative strength of the loops' influence. If the variables and causal links that are deemed to be relevant for a problem under study combine to form different feedback loops, for instance one reinforcing and one balancing loop, then these loops are present at all times in the causal structure.

We face such circumstances in the life of companies. For instance, when employees are part of a project that runs well, their *morale* and *productivity* will not display any worrisome signs. However, if things start falling behind schedule, their manager is likely to <u>increase</u> the *pressure* on the employees. This may lead to <u>increased</u> *efforts* for a while, but if the employees' *energy* is <u>burned faster</u> than <u>restored</u> over a longer period, their *performance* will <u>get worse</u> instead of better. The system structure does not change in such a case. What happens is that as particular variables reach a threshold, parts of the system which have been dormant become active.

Many sudden shifts of behaviour modes can be understood that way. Consider the following examples of such shifts.

The *satisfaction* of customers: while customers are satisfied, word-of-mouth may draw <u>additional</u> *customers* in. If *service capacity* is <u>not increased</u> sufficiently, early signs of *customers leaving* may be overseen. When the *loss of customers* (outflow) is <u>not compensated</u> *by new customers* (inflow), the problem becomes visible. But word-of-mouth already has turned negative, i.e. *Former customers* spreading bad opinions will <u>increase</u> the flow of *customers lost* and <u>decrease</u> the number of *new customers*, and <u>improving</u> *service capacity* turns out to take too much time to avoid a spiral of <u>decreasing</u> *Current customers*.

The scrutiny of regulatory bodies: think of the VolksWagen (VW) scandal with fraudulent particle emission from vehicles (Hotten, 2015; Gates *et al.*, 2017). While car *sales* developed as desired, <u>high</u> *expectations* about new engine emission technologies <u>built up</u> in the company. When the outlook on future *sales* became <u>dire</u> because of the <u>lacking</u> *capability* of building engines with low emissions, a shortcut to cover up this lack was welcomed and not much control was exercised to comply with legal regulations. When the shortcut was discovered, the resulting problem for the company was huge and, in the aftermath of the VW 'discovery', a series of models from other manufacturers has been found to be suspicious of similar manipulations. The <u>damage</u> to the *Reputation* is large and will <u>hamper</u> the company's *performance* for a substantial time.

The *financial stability* of a country: think of how the financial crisis placed indebted countries under critical pressure. Governments take *borrowed money*, for which *interest* has to be paid. Accordingly, they are supposed to dedicate these resources to productive purposes, which will not only pay the *interest* and the *debt* but will also help the country to become less needy in future. However, it is tempting to spend such resources on *politically rewarding uses*, keeping voters *satisfied* – and voters hardly feel the *debt burden* <u>increasing</u>. Do you know how long each citizen of your country would need to work to pay *the Accumulated debt* of your country? However, when the *interest due* <u>exceeds</u> the *yearly paying capacity*, *borrowed money* must be redirected from such popular uses to *interest payments*, and the problem becomes apparent. Those who have the possibility to move away, or transfer their money, will save themselves and leave the country. Since the *interest rates* can <u>increase</u> due to globally relevant events occurring outside such a country, there is a subjacent *vulnerability* <u>building up</u> but not considered – until the critical point is reached.

A *refugee* crisis unfolding as this book is being written. Think of how people live in many countries between Africa and Asia, particularly in the countries where the former colonial powers of Europe have exercised their influence in the past. It is not a secret that their *living conditions* are somewhere between <u>harsh</u> and <u>inhuman</u> – and, more than a few times, policies which have been popular have even worsened their situation. For example, Europe's common agricultural policy drove *overproduction*, which was partially dumped in developing countries at ruinous *prices*. This has helped to <u>keep high</u> *material living standards* in Europe, but insofar as it <u>hindered</u> *economic development* in the developing countries, it constantly <u>drove</u> individuals from such countries to *migrate* in search of *acceptable opportunities*. When the context of war in Arab countries <u>increased</u> the *number of people fleeing* their countries and it became visible that Europe might be accepting refugees, a word-of-mouth process was triggered in short time. If such a <u>quickly growing</u> number of *individuals* flee inhuman conditions, often accepting little less inhuman conditions while they do so, and returning them to their original countries is not an option, then only helping to <u>generate</u> *acceptable life conditions* in these countries will help. This, in turn, requires changing established policies and is slow to implement – while in the meantime, the *pressure of refugees* will be very hard to <u>reduce</u>.

The factors that drive sudden, unpredictable swings of behaviour of a variable, e.g. *orders coming in*, *fines* to be paid, *debt*, or *refugees*, have been here all the time, albeit they have not caused trouble.

When a firmly established policy ceases to produce the usual effects, it is time to ask ourselves what did we fail to consider.

Some orientation comes from knowing how typical system structures drive certain behaviour patterns or modes. If a variable displays exponential behaviour, the reinforcing loop is stronger than the balancing loop. And if the variable displays goal-seeking behaviour, then the balancing loop is stronger than the reinforcing one. If the behaviour of the variable switches from exponential to goal-seeking behaviour, this is the result of the balancing loop becoming stronger than the reinforcing one. The change of strength or dominance amongst feedback loops is called dominance shift and it is apparent in the case of S-shaped behaviour. The point of inflexion in the graph of the variable is reached in the moment when dominance shifts from the reinforcing to the balancing loop.

> **Principle 5 (P 5): Loop dominance**
> **Different loops are dominant under different conditions of certain variables.**
>
> **Guideline 5 (G 5): Shifts in behaviour reveal loop dominance shifts**
> **Shifts between atomic behaviour modes reveal dominance shifts amongst feedback loops.**

decline in *Potential customers*. The slope of *Potential customers* is always <u>negative</u> and always <u>decreases</u> over time. When the number of *Potential customers* <u>decreases</u>, the number of *Current customers* <u>increases</u>, as Plutonia's total *population* is constant at one million individuals. Note that the shape of the behaviour of *Current customers* is the one already seen as the second part of the S-shaped behaviour (Figure 2.2), starting at month 7. The second phase of the diffusion process is dominated by the balancing feedback loop.

2.3.5 When the two feedback loops are interconnected

The causal structure of both feedback loops combined (Figure 2.13) is, therefore, able to generate the typical behaviour shape of the diffusion process. The corresponding model is 'C2 Word of Mouth'. As the previous two subsections have shown, the reinforcing feedback loop 'growth engine' and the balancing feedback loop 'depletion' intersect in the flow *new customers*. The first half of the simulation displays exponential growth of *Current customers*. The relevant insight for NewTel is that the 'growth engine' feedback loop <u>drives</u> the number of *Current customers* <u>up</u> until the 'depletion' loop <u>reduces</u> the availability of *Potential customers* enough to limit this growth.

The number of *new customers* depends on four factors: *Current customers*, the *potential customers fraction*, *contact rate*, and the *conversion fraction WoM*. *Current customers* and the *potential customers fraction* are all endogenous, i.e. their values are determined by the respective equations. The *contact rate* and the *conversion fraction WoM* are external parameters and are constant. Their values can be changed to explore the range of behaviours the model can generate. In the Business as Usual (BAU) scenario, you assumed a *contact rate* of 100 and a *conversion fraction* of 0.01. Now, simulate the model with different values for *contact rate* and the *conversion fraction*. *Contact rate* changes between 50, 100, and 200; the *conversion fraction* will be 0.005, 0.01, and 0.02. Some of the combinations will be equivalent: for instance, if one of the parameters is reduced to half its original value and another parameter is doubled, then the calculation of both yields the same value. We exclude such combinations that would lead to identical combined values. Table 2.9 shows three different combinations for the *conversion fraction WoM* (rows) and three for *contact rate* (columns). The cells in the table enumerate the five possible combinations. Cells with an * indicate equivalent combinations.

For instance, combination 1 in Table 2.9 uses a *contact rate* of 50 and a *conversion fraction* of 0.005.

Table 2.9 Combinations of parameter values (* indicates equivalent combinations)

Scenarios		contact rate =		
		50	100	200
conversion fraction WoM	**0.005**	#1	#2	#3
	0.01	(*#2)	(*#3)	#4
	0.02	(*#3)	(*#4)	#5

DIY 2.10:
Evaluate the scenarios using the simulation model

Use your simulation model or 'C2 Word of Mouth' to conduct the five combinations as shown in Table 2.9.

There are two ways you can do this. If you 'run' the model in the SyntheSim mode, you can use the sliders rather than the parameters to adjust the parameter values. For instance, you can change *contact rate* from 50 to 100 without stopping the simulation.

An alternative way to carry out different 'runs' is to define a distinct 'data set' for each one. The data set of a simulation is like a spreadsheet table where the software stores each value of each variable for each time step of the simulation. The default name for a data set is 'Current'; it is displayed in the top tool bar. You can type data set names, such as 'Combination1' and 'Combination2', into the edit field, replacing 'Current'. If you then change the value of a parameter and simulate the model, this run of the model will not overwrite the values stored in 'Current' but will create a new data set with the simulation values. The different data sets can be handled in Vensim's control panel, which has a pane for data sets. All the data sets in the 'loaded' list will be displayed in tables and graphs. Vensim displays each data set in a different colour within the graphs.

Use the worksheet at the end of the chapter.

After simulating different parameter values, there are different ranges of behaviours to interpret (Figure 2.27).

The upper part of Figure 2.27 shows *Current customers*, the lower part displays the corresponding behaviour of *new customers*. Each curve is labelled according to the scenarios in Table 2.8. Note that for <u>lower</u> parameter values, the dynamics are <u>slower</u>. In combination 1, 12 months is not enough to reach the maximum number of *new customers*, where the behaviour *Current customers* changes from exponential to goal seeking. This does not mean that the system will not perform an S-shaped behaviour; it only means that the time horizon is not sufficient for the dynamics to be revealed completely. According to how the combined value of the parameters increases, the time to

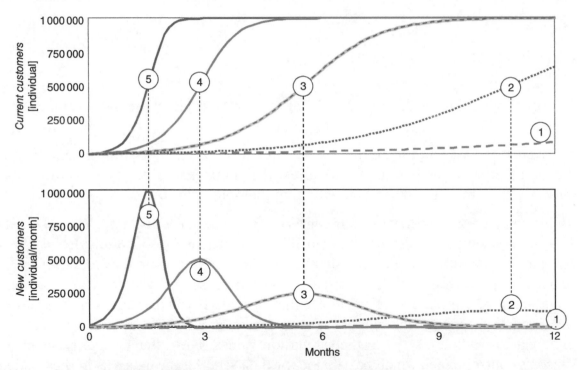

Figure 2.27 Typical variations of S-shaped growth

reach the peak becomes shorter, as you see in combinations 2 through 5. This also shows that some parts of the causal structure, even though they are in the SFD, may not have much influence on the system's behaviour during a specified time horizon. Of course, this does not mean that these structures are not there; we have isolated the two feedback loops and simulated their behaviour in the sections earlier in this chapter. In general, the absence of evidence of something is not equivalent to evidence of its absence. So be careful when defining the time horizon of a simulation model; it should be long enough for the slowest dynamics to become active.

Guideline 6 (G 6): The length of the time horizon
The time horizon of simulations must be long enough for the slowest relevant dynamics to unfold.

Considering the month in which the *new customers* of NewTel reaches its highest value, there is a pattern: when the combined parameter values of *contact rate* and *conversion fraction WoM* increase, the absolute number of *new customers* at its peak value increases, too. This faster growth of *new customers* means that *Potential customers* depletes more quickly and, therefore, the maximum is reached earlier (and increasing numbers of *new customers* are followed by decreasing numbers of *new customers*. Returning to *Current customers*, the turning point from exponential to goal-seeking behaviour is reached at the same time as *new customers* reach their highest value in each scenario. The number of *Current customers* when this turning point is reached is always 500 000 – half of the *population*. It is always an S-shaped curve, and the slope of the S is steeper for higher parameter values.

It is no coincidence that the peak in *new customers* occurs when *Current customers* shifts from exponential to goal-seeking behaviour. There is a fundamental relationship between *new customers* and *Current customers*, and it has to do with the cumulative nature of the stock of *Current customers*.

Figure 2.28 illustrates the behaviour of the stock of *Current customers*. Let us simplify and shorten the time horizon to only seven months. This will be enough months to understand the underlying idea. Assume that you have seven wooden blocks of a height that corresponds to the number of new customers in a given month, and that these numbers are 1, 2, 4, 8, 4, 2 and 1, respectively. Since the time horizon is seven months, the individuals represented by these blocks will be customers for different numbers of months: those who are *new customers* in the first month

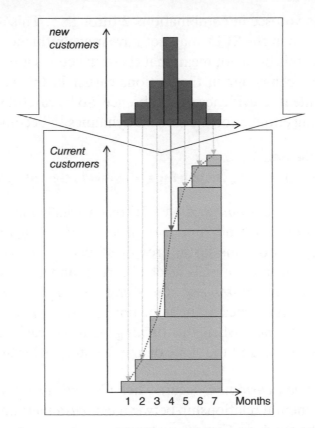

Figure 2.28 The highest value of *new customers* is the turning point for the behaviour in *Current customers*

will be there for seven months, those who arrive in the second month will be there only for six months, and so on. Assume further that the blocks' width represents the length of their stay. The situation is summarized in Table 2.10.

Now you start building a tower that will represent the *Current customers* stock. Figure 2.28 starts with a display of the seven *new customers* blocks aligned left to right according to the months. The blocks are turned so that their width is hidden. Then, for example, block 1 does not take the entire width and hides block 7.

Table 2.10 Blocks added earlier stay longer, and blocks added later are stacked on top of older blocks.

Individuals	Arrive at month (height)	Stay for (width)
1	1	7
2	2	6
4	3	5
8	4	4
4	5	3
2	6	2
1	7	1

In each of the seven months, you take the respective month's wooden block and move it down into the stock of *Current customers*. From month two on, any block added to the stock will be put on top of the most recently deposited block. The blocks in the stock are turned so that their width is now visible. This clearly shows that each month's *new customers* are counted on top of the *Current customers* who were already in the stock. A dotted line is drawn through the top of each *new customers* block in the *Current customers* stock, so you can see the shape of the slope: it is indeed S-shaped.

Over the complete time horizon, a positive number of *new customers* is added to the *Current customers* each month. Therefore, its slope is always positive. If the number of *new customers* grows from month to month, the slope of *Current customers* increases. When the number of *new customers* declines from month to month, the slope of *Current customers* decreases, but remains positive. A phase of increasing positive slope followed by another phase of decreasing positive slope looks like an S. The point of inflection must occur, when the flow of *new customers* reaches its highest value. This is an important management insight:

Management Insight 1 (MI 1): *new customers* **changes** *Current customers*
The number of individuals who are *new customers* **corresponds to the slope or the change of** *Current customers***.**

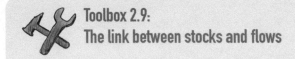

The previous explanation with the wooden blocks was an illustration of a general principle that applies to all dynamic systems in which resources flow into and out of stocks:

Principle 6 (P 6): Flow rates are the change of stocks over time
The level of a net flow corresponds to the slope or the change of the stock.

A stock represents the quantity of a given resource. If there is a different quantity in a stock at two different points in time, then something happened between these two points in time. As a matter of fact, there may be various dynamics adding to or draining from this stock; each of them provokes the stock to change over time. A mathematician would say that the stock is a function of the flow, the amount of change of the stock per period is the derivative of the stock with respect to time.

All flows move the same substance, which is tracked in the stock over a given period of time. They can be summed up into a *net flow*, which then represents the total amount of change of the stock over the period of time. This means that if the net flow over one period of time is, say, 10, the level of the stock at the end of the period will be 10 units higher than at the beginning of this period. In other words, during this particular period of time the slope of the stock is 10.

Therefore, the causal links between flows and stocks must be interpreted with great care.

Figure 2.29 shows a generic causal link, which can be read out as "*net flow* adds to *Stock*". This is always true, but keep in mind that *net flow* can be positive, zero or negative. When the net flow is equal to zero the stock will not change. When the net flow is not zero, the stock's slope will be equal to the flow's absolute value and have the same sign as the flow. A negative net flow means a negative slope; a positive net flow means a positive slope. Consequently, the shape of behaviour of the stock

net flow ————————→ Stock

Figure 2.29 How to interpret the causal link between a flow and a stock

is different to the shape of behaviour of the net flow. Figure 2.30 shows typical examples.

This figure illustrates three cases in which the stock's initial value is assumed to be 0. If a *flow* which is otherwise equal to 0 <u>rises</u> to 1 for one period of time and then <u>drops</u> back to 0, the *Stock* grows to 1 and then remains stable. If the *flow* <u>changes</u> from 0 to 1 and remains at the value, the *Stock* will <u>grow</u> linearly. And if the *flow* starts <u>growing</u> from 0 to 1, then 2 and so on, the *Stock* <u>grows</u> exponentially.

Empirical studies have shown that most individuals intuitively misunderstand <u>changes</u> in the *flow* and the resulting <u>changes</u> in the *Stock* (Sterman, 2010; Sterman and Sweeney, 2007). Be careful not to fall into the trap of flawed behavioural reasoning (Moxnes, 1998).

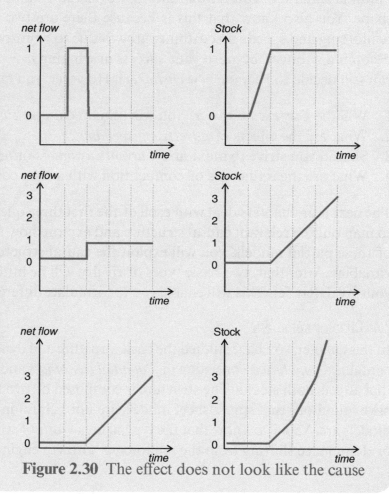

Figure 2.30 The effect does not look like the cause

At present, you have elaborated the core of your management situation: introducing NewTel's mobile phones in Plutonia's market. You have found that over the 12 months, *Current customers* will accumulate displaying an S-shape. You also know that this is because there are two feedback loops in the causal structure. The first one is reinforcing and speeds up customer growth due to word-of-mouth dynamics. At the same time, a balancing loop is becoming stronger, because your success at winning *new customers* exhausts the stock of *Potential customers* who can still decide to become *new customers*. However, you may ask yourself:

1. Will the *Current customers* you win remain *Current customers* forever or will they leave after a given time?
2. What are the effects of *advertising spending*?
3. Should you strive to maximize *Current customers* or *new customers* instead?
4. What are the influences of competition with a rival company?

The next four chapters deal with each of the first three questions in turn. We help you to develop simulation models to map out the relevant causal structure and explore how to answer each question. Once you have understood each of these partial models, you will exploit the causal structure to find out what the ideal values are for our decision variables. After that, two basic types of rivalry will be introduced and we will extend the model to also incorporate your rival, RivTel. This will enable you to formulate different competitive scenarios and design a policy for NewTel.

2.4 Chapter summary

In this chapter, you have studied the basic structure and dynamics of word-of-mouth. You now know that its structure contains a *population* consisting of *Potential customers* and *Current customers*, connected by a flow of *new customers* that affects both stocks. The structure is composed of two feedback loops, one reinforcing, the other balancing. You have found out that spreadsheet models are not helpful in representing such a causal structure, but stock-and-flow models are. You also know that the typical behaviour of word-of-mouth is S-shaped and that this is the consequence of dominance shifting from the reinforcing 'Growth engine' loop to the balancing 'Depletion' loop.

2.5 Questions and challenges

Questions

1. Why are *Current customers* an important resource for NewTel?
2. How does word-of-mouth result in *new customers*?
3. Why does word-of-mouth generate an S-shaped behaviour?
4. Why does one month's growth of *Current customers*, i.e. *new customers*, limit the possibilities of future growth?
5. What is a causal link?
6. What is the characteristic feature of a stock?
7. What does INTEG indicate?
8. What is the characteristic feature of a flow variable?
9. What is the characteristic feature of an intermediate variable?
10. What is the fundamental relationship between a net flow and the stock it affects?
11. What is market saturation and when does it occur?
12. What polarities are there? Explain them using examples.
13. What is a feedback loop? What are its relevant attributes?
14. What is the characteristic behaviour of each type of feedback loop?
15. Are all feedback loops equally important at all times? Explain why or why not?
16. Can observed behaviour be used to detect shifts in the dominance of feedback loops? How?
17. What is the time step of a simulation?
18. How can you measure variables?
19. What is the relationship between the number of *new customers* and the behaviour of *Current customers*?
20. What should you do with a variable you believe to be relevant but whose quantification is problematic? Why?

21. What is model parsimony?
22. Which pair of criteria must be satisfied to state that a causal diagram contains an appropriate set of variables?
23. When analysing how one causal link influences a variable, what should you do with all other causal links pointing at this variable? Why?
24. Which criterion must be satisfied by the selected time horizon of a simulation?
25. What are similarities and differences between simulation models and spreadsheet models?
26. What is the relationship between the system structure of a model and the behaviour modes introduced in Chapter 1?

Challenges

Imagine the case of a country entering a profound financial crisis. One million people have a bank account and 5000 have already heard the alarming news and are now *panicked customers*: They rush to the bank to withdraw their money if the bank still has reserves to pay out. The remaining individuals are still *unaware customers*. However, everybody out in the streets can see the panicking customers lining up in front of the bank offices. Assume that each hour, 1000 people walk by the bank offices and see what is happening. A certain share of them is still unaware of the crisis, but for each panicking customer they see in a queue for a cashier, the likelihood that they become *panicked customers* themselves is 0.1%.

How much time does it take before half of the 1 000 000 individuals are *panicked customers*? How many customers are *panicked customers* when 10 hours have passed?

In which ways is this case different from your business challenge of NewTel? In which ways is it similar?

References

Bloomberg. 2016. Bloomberg Markets: GBPUSD spot exchange rate. http://www.bloomberg.com/quote/GBPUSD:CUR (last accessed 7 November 2017).

CDC, 2009, 2008–2009 Influenza season summary. http://www.cdc.gov/flu/weekly/weeklyarchives2008-2009/08-09summary.htm (last accessed 7 November 2017).

Cox, J. and Copeland, R. 2015. Greek bank deposits fall to lowest level in more than 10 years. *The Wall Street Journal*, 29 May 2015. http://www.wsj.com/articles/greek-bank-deposits-fall-to-lowest-level-in-more-than-10-years-1432906601 (last accessed 7 November 2017).

Ewing, J., 2016. German bond yield goes negative on 'Brexit' fears and Central Bank policies. *The New York Times*, 14 June 2016. http://www.nytimes.com/2016/06/15/business/dealbook/germany-bonds-negative-ecb.html?_r=0 (last accessed 7 November 2017).

Gates, G., Ewing, J., Russell, K., and Watkins, D. 2017. How Volkswagen's 'defeat devices' worked. *The New York Times*, 16 March 2017. http://www.nytimes.com/interactive/2015/business/international/vw-diesel-emissions-scandal-explained.html?_r=0 (last accessed 12 November 2017).

HDCYT. 2007. Charly bit my finger again [online video]. www.youtube.com/watch?v=_OBlgSz8sSM (last accessed 7 November 2017).

Hotten, R. 2015. Volkswagen: The scandal explained. BBC News. http://www.bbc.com/news/business-34324772 (last accessed 7 November 2017).

Influenzanet. 2009. Netherlands (2008–2009) – Overview. https://www.influenzanet.eu/results/?page=results&group=overview&country=dk&casedef=ilit&lang=en&type=disease_base__ili&season=2008 (last accessed 7 November 2017).

Moore, E. 2016. Germany claims eurozone first with negative yield bond sale. *Financial Times*, 13 July 2016. http://www.ft.com/cms/s/0/25ae95da-48db-11e6-8d68-72e9211e86ab.html#axzz4EIg7iicM (last accessed 7 November 2017).

Moxnes, E. 1998. Not only the tragedy of the commons: misperceptions of bioeconomics. *Management Science*, **44**(9): 1234–1248.

PSY. 2012. Gangnam Style [online video]. www.youtube.com/watch?v=9bZkp7q19f0 (last accessed 7 November 2017).

Randow, J. and Kennedy, S. 2016. Negative interest rates. Bloomberg Quick Take. http://www.bloomberg.com/quicktake/negative-interest-rates (last accessed 7 November 2017).

Rogers, E.M. 2013. *The Diffusion of Innovations*, 5th edn. Free Press, New York, NY.

Sterman, J.D. 2010. Does formal system dynamics training improve people's understanding of accumulation? *System Dynamics Review*, **26**(4): 316–334.

Sterman, J.D. and Sweeney, L.B. 2007. Understanding public complacency about climate change: adults' mental models of climate change violate conservation of matter. *Climatic Change*, **80**(3–4): 213–238.

Weick, K.E. 1989. Theory construction as disciplined imagination. *Academy of Management Review*, **14**(4): 516–531.

Worksheet DIY 2.3:
Market saturation

Graph the behaviour of *new customers* and *Current customers* created by the simulation:

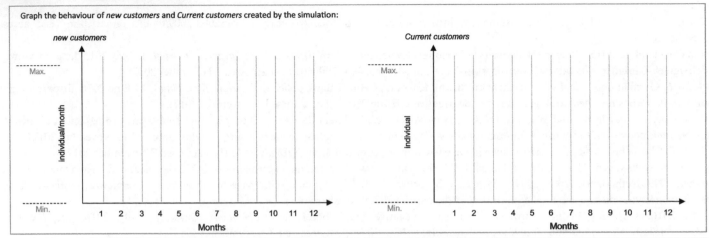

Graph the behaviour of the variables appearing in the Wikipedia page on "Market saturation"

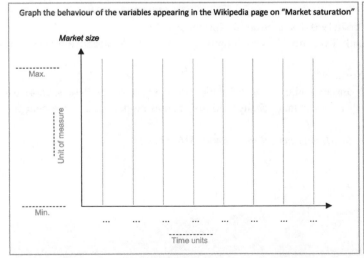

Describe similarities and differences. If there are differences, explain why.

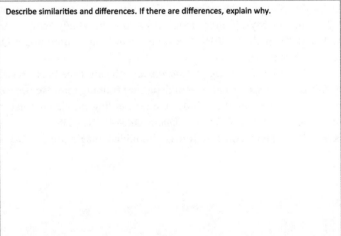

Worksheet DIY 2.4:

Create a spreadsheet model to simulate the behaviour of Current customers

Parameters	Population	1000000
	contact rate	100
	conversion fraction	0.01

Month	Potential customers	Current customers	Current customers encounters	Potential customers fraction	New customers
0	995,000	5,000	500,000	0.9950	4,975
1	990,025	9,975	997,500	0.9900	9,875
2	980,150	19,850	1,985,000	0.9802	19,456
3	960,694	39,306	3,930,600	0.9607	37,761
4	922,933	77,067	7,706,700	0.9229	71,128
5	851,805	148,195	14,819,500	0.8518	126,233
6	725,572	274,428	27,442,800	0.7256	199,117
7	526,455	473,545	47,354,500	0.5265	249,300
8	277,155	722,845	72,284,500	0.2772	200,340
9	76,815	923,185	92,318,500	0.0768	70,914
10	5,901	994,099	99,409,900	0.0059	5,866
11	35	999,965	99,996,500	0.0000	35
12	0	1,000,000	100,000,000	0.0000	0

Worksheet DIY 2.8:
Typical behaviour generated by reinforcing feedback

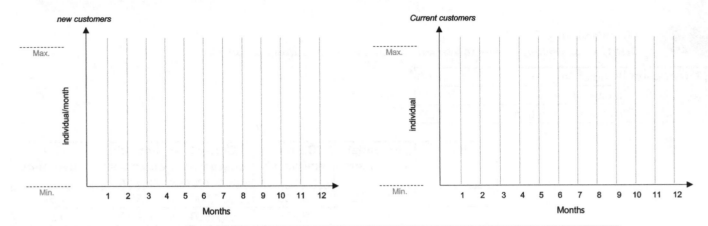

new customers

Max.

individual/month

Min.

1 2 3 4 5 6 7 8 9 10 11 12

Months

Current customers

Max.

individual

Min.

1 2 3 4 5 6 7 8 9 10 11 12

Months

Legend: (Use different colours to represent the behaviour of *new customers* and *Current customers* for each of the simulations.)

potential customers fraction = 0.5 (instead of 0.99):
contact rate = 50 (instead of 100):
conversion fraction = 0.005 (instead of 0.01):

Examine the graphs and describe similarities and differences. If there are differences, explain why.

Worksheet DIY 2.9:
Build your second simulation model

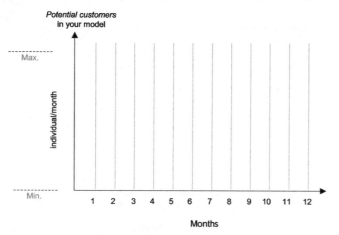

Potential customers in your model

Max.

Min.

individual/month

1 2 3 4 5 6 7 8 9 10 11 12

Months

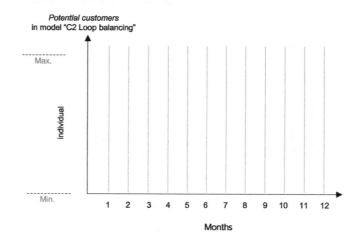

Potential customers in model "C2 Loop balancing"

Max.

Min.

individual

1 2 3 4 5 6 7 8 9 10 11 12

Months

Examine the graphs and describe similarities and differences. If there are differences, explain why.

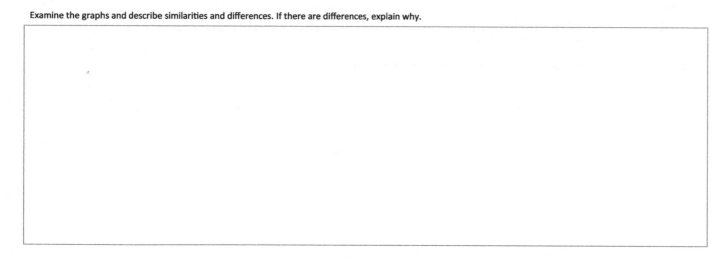

Worksheet DIY 2.10:
Evaluate the scenarios using the simulation model

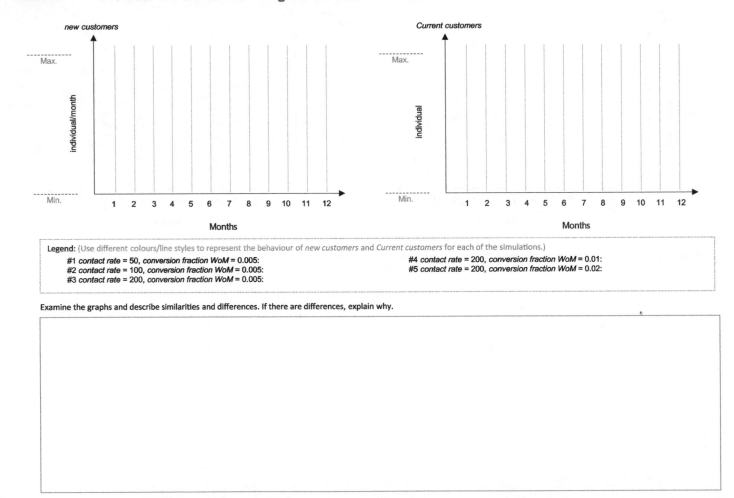

new customers

individual/month

Max.

Min.

1 2 3 4 5 6 7 8 9 10 11 12

Months

Current customers

individual

Max.

Min.

1 2 3 4 5 6 7 8 9 10 11 12

Months

Legend: (Use different colours/line styles to represent the behaviour of *new customers* and *Current customers* for each of the simulations.)

#1 *contact rate* = 50, *conversion fraction WoM* = 0.005:
#2 *contact rate* = 100, *conversion fraction WoM* = 0.005:
#3 *contact rate* = 200, *conversion fraction WoM* = 0.005:

#4 *contact rate* = 200, *conversion fraction WoM* = 0.01:
#5 *contact rate* = 200, *conversion fraction WoM* = 0.02:

Examine the graphs and describe similarities and differences. If there are differences, explain why.

EFFECTS OF A LIMITED PRODUCT *LIFE CYCLE DURATION*

3.1 Introduction

In this chapter, you learn about the consequences of a limited *life cycle duration* of a product or service for the accumulation of *Current customers*. In particular:

- those *Current customers* who reach the end of the *life cycle duration* are lost as *Current customers*;
- since they are not *Current customers* any longer, they may decide to purchase your product again;
- <u>reducing</u> or <u>increasing</u> the *life cycle duration* has distinct effects on the behaviour of the variables *Current customers* and *new customers*.

On the methodological level, you learn how to represent the *life cycle duration* and its effects in an evolving simulation model, and how to take advantage of this simulation model to improve your understanding of the dynamic consequences of changing the *life cycle duration*.

Growth Dynamics in New Markets: Improving Decision Making through Simulation Model-based Management,
First Edition. Martin F.G. Schaffernicht and Stefan N. Groesser.
© 2018 John Wiley & Sons Ltd. Published 2018 by John Wiley & Sons Ltd.
Companion website: www.wiley.com/go/Schaffernicht/growth-dynamics

3.2 The concept of *life cycle duration* and its effects on customer dynamics

The simulation model developed and analysed in Chapter 2 describes how individuals move from *Potential customers* to *Current customers*. It also assumes that *Current customers* cannot dispose of your product and service; in other words, your mobile phones have an unlimited *life cycle duration* and the service contract is also unlimited. This is not realistic. In Chapter 2, this assumption was reasonable in order to concentrate on the core of word-of-mouth dynamics. Now, since you have mastered this basic structure, let us relax this assumption and remember the briefing of your situation as responsible manager of NewTel in Plutonia: your product/service bundle has a limited *life cycle duration*. When your customers purchase mobile phones and sign up for subscription contracts, the product-service bundles are valid for nine months. Of course, there are at least two reasons why someone can stop using a mobile phone: the phone can reach the end of its technical life cycle, i.e. designed obsolescence, or the owner may prefer to replace the phone by a different one for personal reasons – is known as psychological obsolescence. Taking these details into account would complicate the task at hand and cloud the understanding of the relevant causal mechanisms. For the time being, assume that the mobile phone and the subscription are treated as one bundle. Chapter 8 relaxes this assumption.

The default *life cycle duration* is nine months. The status of a *current customer* changes nine months after the purchase when the service contract is not valid anymore and the phone is obsolete; from that moment on, this individual becomes a *potential customer* again. As we saw in Chapter 2, a given number of *Potential customers* purchase the bundle each month and thus become part of the stock of *Current customers*. You wonder which *Current customers* leave each month – surely this depends on the *life cycle duration*. The *Current customers* who leave will become clear after the following analyses. Firstly, you need to understand how the aging process that leads to *customers leaving* works depending on the *life cycle duration*. Secondly, you have to find out what the leaving of *Current customers* means for *Potential customers*. Thirdly, the previous findings must be integrated with the word-of-mouth dynamics studied in Chapter 2.

Let us consider how the stock of *Current customers* would fill up, if it were zero at the beginning. To keep everything as simple as possible, suppose that *life cycle duration* is now only two months. Figure 3.1 illustrates what happens.

Figure 3.1 considers four months and the number of *new customers* is held constant at two individuals each month. During the first month, there are no *Current customers* yet. In month 2, the *new customers* from month 1 become

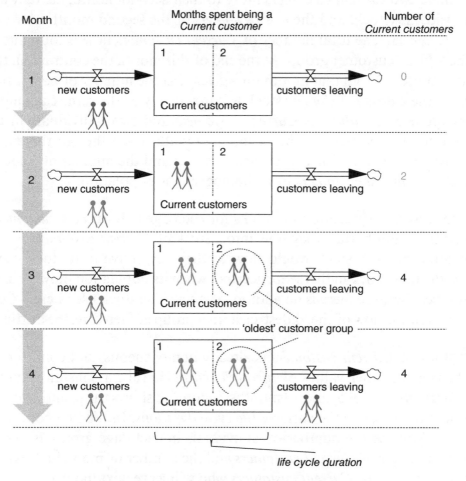

Figure 3.1 Stock of *Current customers* with a homogenous population

Current customers, and they spend their first month in this state. Figure 3.1 indicates this by dividing the *Current customers* stock into two areas, one for each month of the *life cycle duration*. The total number of *Current customers* is now two. In month 3, these two *Current customers* move to their second month; i.e. they have moved to the right and to the second area inside the stock, and the *new customers* of the second month have moved in the first space in the stock of *Current customers*. The total number of *Current customers* now is four, and the two individuals in the second month are the 'oldest' customer group. At the end of this month the contract, in this example, will expire and their phone becomes obsolete. From that month on – given that the number of *new customers* and the *life cycle duration* remain the same – the *Current customers* stock will practically be the same each month: two individuals in the first month of their *life cycle duration* as *Current customers* and two individuals in their second month as *Current customers*, who leave the company in the upcoming month. Even though there are different individuals during each month, the total number of *Current customers* is four and the number of 'oldest' *Current customers* is two. We say that the stock of *Current customers* has a homogeneous population.

You can think of this stock as an aggregation of stocks for each age cohort: *new customers* flow into a stock of *Current customers* in their first month, then they flow into a stock of *Current customers* in their second month and so on. The entire population of each stock would flow to their respective next stock each month. The 'oldest' customer group would be the final stock in this sequence and, when its population moves on, this oldest group leaves the stock of *Current customers* because there is no additional stock. The stock used here – *Current customers* – is the sum of all these age groups. The outflow of the 'oldest' customer group is, therefore, the outflow of *Current customers*.

Now, assume that your stock of *Current customers* is already homogeneous, and consider how *Current customers* and 'oldest' *customers* behave for other values of *life cycle duration*. Take a constant number of 10 monthly *new customers* and *life cycle durations* of 2, 3, 5, and 10 months. Figure 3.2 shows the resulting compositions of the stock *Current customers* for different values of the variable *life cycle durations*. In the first column, the different *life cycle durations* are shown. Then, you see the number of individuals in each 'age group' inside the *Current customers* stock, followed by the total number of *Current customers* and the number of individuals who find themselves in the 'oldest' *customers* group. These are the *Current customers* who will leave next month.

life cycle duration [month]	Current customers per 'age group' inside the stock [individual]										Total	Oldest	Equation for customers leaving [individual/month]
2	10	10									20	10	Current customers / life cycle duration
3	10	10	10								30	10	Current customers / life cycle duration
5	10	10	10	10	10						50	10	Current customers / life cycle duration
10	10	10	10	10	10	10	10	10	10	10	100	10	Current customers / life cycle duration
	1	2	3	4	5	6	7	8	9	10			

Months

Figure 3.2 Age composition of *Current customers*

The first row shows the case shown in Figure 3.1, where *life cycle duration* is two months. If 10 individuals buy a mobile phone each month and thereby become *Current customers*, there must be 10 individuals who bought the phone last month and 10 different individuals who purchased the phone the month before the last month. The total number of *Current customers* is 20 individuals. The 10 individuals who have bought two months ago are now in the last month of their *life cycle duration* – the 'oldest' customer group – and they will discontinue your service and cease to be *Current customers* next month.

The second row shows the case of a three-month *life cycle duration*. Compared to the case of a *life cycle duration* of two months, individuals now remain *Current customers* for an additional month. Therefore, there are three different age groups of 10 individuals each. The total number of *Current customers* is now 30 individuals, and again 10 of them are in the 'oldest' group – the individuals who leave the following month. In the case of a *life cycle duration* of five months, you have a total of 50 *Current customers*, and again 10 of them belong to the 'oldest' group. This is always the case because the total population consists of as many age groups as there are months in the *life cycle duration*, given your assumption of a homogeneous population. Each month 10 individuals become *new customers*, i.e. there is a monthly inflow of 10 individuals. You also know that the individuals in the 'oldest' group will leave the stock, thus, there will be an outflow. In each scenario with a different value of *life cycle duration*, there is both an inflow of 10 *new customers* per month as well as an outflow of 10 individuals per month named *customers leaving*. You can compute this number of individuals by dividing *Current customers* by *life cycle duration*.

When the *life cycle duration* increases from two to three months – and assuming the causal mechanisms are the same – then you will have 30 *Current customers* (10 per age group, i.e. per month). Similarly, 10 *Current customers* would leave each month. In that case, one third of *Current customers* leave each month. The rule to approximate the number of *customers leaving*, i.e. *Current customers* divided by the *life cycle duration*, still works. With a *life cycle duration* of five months, 10 out of 50 *Current customers* will leave per month.

DIY 3.1:
Customer dynamics

From the preceding paragraphs, you know how the loss of *Current customers* can be calculated. Determine which proportion of the *Current customers* leave the stock each month for *life cycle durations* of 9 and 10 months. How does this proportion <u>change</u> when you <u>increase</u> the *life cycle duration*? Use the worksheet at the end of the chapter.

There is a pattern: the flow of individuals leaving the stock of *Current customers* equals the number of *Current customers* divided by the *life cycle duration*. This is an important systems insight.

Systems Insight 1 (SI 1): Calculating the loss of an aging resource
When a stock accumulates individual units over several discrete time steps and the stock content is homogenous, then the number of individual units leaving per time step can be calculated as the number of individual units in the stock divided by average time spent in stock. This time can be based on a contract or on estimates of customers' average behaviour.

For you with NewTel, this means that you can determine the monthly number of individuals leaving the *Current customers* stock by:

$$customers\ leaving[\text{individual}/\text{month}]=Current\ customers[\text{individual}]/life\ cycle\ duration[\text{month}] \qquad (3.1)$$

NewTel's customers have a contract with a given number of nine months, so you might have expected that the number of *customers leaving* in a given month corresponds exactly to the number of *new customers* nine months before. However, some individuals always opt out of using their current mobile phone before the *life cycle duration* is over, for example because they want to start using a newer model. Therefore, it is reasonable to assume that there is no exact relationship between *new customers* and *customers leaving*.

DIY 3.2:
Customer dynamics under different customer intakes

How many *Current customers* would leave if the inflow of *new customers* is 500 and 1000, respectively?

In addition, figure out how many *Current customers* would leave if the *life cycle duration* approached an infinite value. Use the worksheet at the end of the chapter.

The simulation model developed in Chapter 2 has no *life cycle duration*. Note that if *life cycle duration* is infinite this is equivalent to the mobile phones not growing old and the subscription never ending. In this case, the number of *customers leaving* each month would correspond to *Current customers* / ∞, which is, by definition, zero. Just as for *life cycle duration*, a flow of *customers leaving* which is always zero is equivalent to not having such a flow variable in your model – and in such a case this variable would be eliminated from the model. However, if your model does not contain a variable, you cannot change it to see what the effects are; you cannot adjust the model to changing conditions in the real world, either. To re-emphasize: you cannot manage a factor of the real situation that you did not include as a variable in your model of that situation. Recall **Guideline 3**: 'When developing and using causal diagrams, make sure that all relevant, and only the relevant, variables and causal links are represented'.

There is one additional reason why variables are preferred to absolute values like '0.1' or '100' in models: each time you formulate an equation containing an absolute value, this equation becomes useless as soon as the real system contains a different value. Think of *life cycle duration*: it would not be practical to have to use three different models to assess what happens when *life cycle duration* is 6, 9 or 12 months, respectively. It is much more efficient to use the variable *life cycle duration* and adjust the value of *life cycle duration* as needed and, therefore, be able to assess many different *life cycle duration* scenarios using the same model.

> **Guideline 7 (G 7): Conceptual clarity and flexibility by naming variables**
> Strive to include all factors as named variables instead of using absolute values directly in an equation. A general formulation can be used in many specific settings, whereas a specific formulation can only be used in one setting.

Equation (3.1) generates the flow of *customers leaving*, i.e. the customers NewTel loses each month. According to this equation, *customers leaving* depends on *life cycle duration* and on *Current customers*. At the same time, *customers leaving* influences *Current customers*. This causal structure is best represented by the feedback loop 'B' shown in Figure 3.3 (see also the model 'C3 Life cycle duration outflow 1'):

Figure 3.3 shows the entire causal structure; the stock of *Current customers* and the new outflow *customers leaving*, which depends on *Current customers* and *life cycle duration*. The dependence of *customers leaving* on *Current customers* is straightforward: the <u>more</u> individuals are in the stock, the <u>more</u> *Current customers* can leave each month and vice versa. This is indicated by the positive polarity of the causal link between these two variables (see Toolbox 2.4). What about the influence of the *life cycle duration* on *customers leaving*? Here we have the <u>longer</u> the

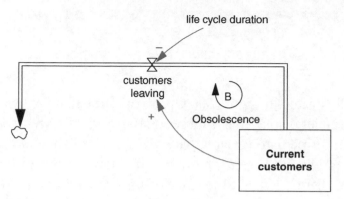

Figure 3.3 If the *life cycle duration* of the product is limited, the stock of *Current customers* is reduced over time

life cycle duration, the <u>fewer</u> *Current customers* leave and vice versa, as suggested by the negative polarity of that causal link.

Even though the stock-and-flow diagrams (SFD) does not show a causal link going from *customers leaving* to *Current customers*, clearly the *customers leaving* outflow reduces the number of *Current customers* remaining in the stock. This causal link is, again, an 'implicit' one and it is not shown on the diagrams because this effect is already contained in the flow; recall that any stock's equation states that the stock changes according to the associated flow variables. Because of the implicit character of that causal link, you may find it surprising that the diagram indicates a balancing feedback loop 'B' – just as in the case of the 'depletion' loop in Chapter 2. But consider that if *Current customers* <u>increases</u> from, say, 100 000 to 200 000, then, of course, there will be <u>more</u> *customers leaving*. And, of course, an <u>increased</u> *customers leaving* outflow means that *Current customers* is <u>reduced faster</u>. Clearly, there is interdependence between these two variables. Since there would be <u>less</u> *Current customers* left, in the following month there would be <u>less</u> *customers leaving*, and you can see that (ceteris paribus) both *Current customers* and *customers leaving* would stabilize: This is the balancing feedback loop known as 'obsolescence'.

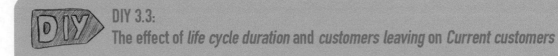

Build the model illustrated in Figure 3.3. Open your modelling software and create a new model file. Then enter the variables displayed in Figure 3.3: the stock of *Current customers*, the *customers leaving* outflow, and the intermediate variable *life cycle duration*. Then, add the two causal links from the stock to the flow and from *life cycle duration* to the flow; if your software package allows you to add polarity signs, add them. Now, set the value of *life cycle duration* to nine months, remembering that '9' is the value and 'month' the unit of measure. Next, set the initial value of *Current customers* to one million (unit: individual). Your modelling software automatically generates the stock equation: by connecting the flows to the stocks, you have already provided the necessary information.

Eventually, you need to input the equation for the flow of *customers leaving*. You only type the right-hand side of the equation because your software knows which variable you are working on. In the dialog window for writing equations, your software shows you the variables to be used in the equation in a list: these are the variables that are connected by causal links you have drawn before. To compose an equation, you can click on the variables in that list and the software writes the corresponding words into the editing field. You only must take care of the arithmetic operators used to carry out the computation. On the companion website, you can find a video tutorial to guide you through the development of this model. If you do not want to compare your model to a reference model, you can also download the model 'C3 Life cycle duration outflow 1' from the website.

Make sure that the simulation is over 12 periods of time (months) and that the 'time step' or 'DT' is set to 0.0625.

There is a worksheet for this DIY on the companion website. Use it to draw the graphs of *Current customers* and *customers leaving* that you expect to see when the model is simulated for different *life cycle durations*: 6, 9, or 12 months. Then, simulate the model for each of these *life cycle durations*. You may have to stop the simulation and change the value of *life cycle duration* for each of these simulations.

Compare your sketched graphs to the ones generated by the simulation: Did the slopes on your graphs have the same sign (negative or positive) as the simulated runs? Is the change of the slopes in your sketched graphs the same as in the simulated runs? Are the differences in slope between the graphs for different *life cycle durations* in your expected graphs roughly the same as in the simulated ones?

Corroborate the validity of the following assertions based on the causal model structure of Figure 3.3:

- When the *life cycle duration* increases, *customers leaving* decreases.
- When the *life cycle duration* decreases, *customers leaving* increases.
- When *customers leaving* has a positive value during month 1, *Current customers* in month 2 is less than in month 1.
- When *Current customers* is less in month 2 than in month 1, *customers leaving* during month 2 is lower than during month 1.

Use the worksheet at the end of the chapter.

Figure 3.4 shows the results for *Current customers* when the model 'C3 Life cycle duration outflow 1' is simulated for three different *life cycle durations* (i.e. 6, 9, and 12 months).

Figure 3.4 shows *Current customers* in the upper part and *customers leaving* below. For each scenario for *life cycle duration*, *Current customers* starts with 1 000 000 individuals. According to Equation (3.1), the number of *customers leaving* for the six-month scenario must be twice the number of *customers leaving* for the 12-month scenario. Indeed, *customers leaving* during month 1 starts with about 82 000 individuals when the *life cycle duration* is 12 months and

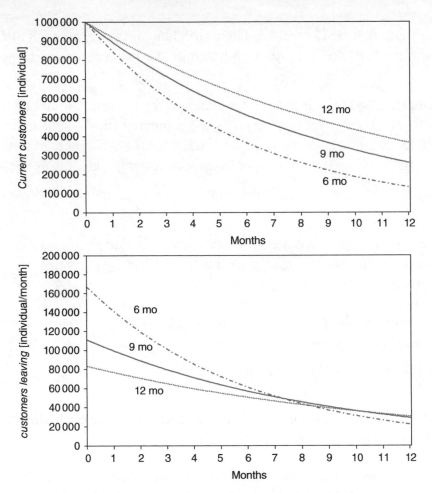

Figure 3.4 Impact of different *life cycle durations* on *Current customers* and *customers leaving* over 12 months (abbreviated as 'mo')

approximately 164 000 people when the *life cycle duration* is six months. From this, it follows that the slope of *Current customers* (upper part of the figure) is twice as steep for a *life cycle duration* of 12 months. The scenario using nine months is inbetween the two other scenarios.

When *Current customers* diminishes, which you can see happening from month to month, then the flow of *customers leaving* becomes smaller. Accordingly, the *customers leaving* flow decreases quicker in the six-month scenario than in the 12-month scenario. Also, when the flow of *customers leaving* is smaller, the flow drains less *Current customers*: the slope of the curves is still negative but the absolute value of the reduction becomes smaller. Hence, for shorter *life cycle durations*, the reduction of *Current customers* is larger. *Life cycle duration* changes have an inverse impact on *customers leaving*. In addition, this outflow has an indirect positive impact on *Current customers*: a decrease in *life cycle duration* leads to fewer *Current customers*, while an increase in *life cycle duration* leads to more *Current customers*.

It is important to realize that currently the outflow *customers leaving* leads to a cloud symbol which indicates the model boundary (Toolbox 1.1), i.e. the individuals going through this outflow exit the model and are not considered any longer. This violates the assumption of a constant *population*, as the *population* is reduced. For the purposes of studying what happens between *Current customers* and *customers leaving*, this simplification is reasonable. However, as *customers leaving* become *Potential customers*, this change should now also be accounted for. The assumption of the constant *population* includes the implicit assumption that nobody will withdraw from the *population* susceptible to purchase and use a mobile phone. This is equivalent to stating that *Current customers* never disappear from the *population*. The model in Figure 3.3 lacks the variable *Potential customers* and so it can be added to the model (Figure 3.5; 'C3 Life cycle duration outflow 2').

The cloud in Figure 3.3 has now been replaced by the stock of *Potential customers*. In other words, *customers leaving* are not leaving the model boundary. This means that during simulation the total number of individuals in the model is constant, and each individual lost from the *Current customers* stock is added to the *Potential customers*

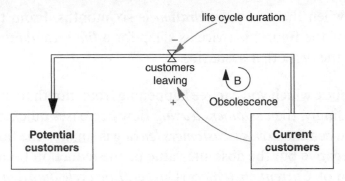

Figure 3.5 *Customers leaving* enter the stock of *Potential customers*

stock. Therefore, the <u>more</u> *customers* that are *leaving* from the stock of *Current customers*, the <u>more</u> *Potential customers* there are:

$$Potential\ customers[\text{individual}] = Potential\ customers[\text{individual}] +$$
$$(customers\ leaving[\text{individual} / \text{month}] - new\ customers[\text{individual} / \text{month}]) * \textbf{TIMESTEP}[\text{month}] \quad (3.2)$$

 DIY 3.4:
The effect of *life cycle duration* and *customers leaving* on *Potential customers*

How does the *Potential customers* stock develop when the model is simulated with the default *life cycle duration* of nine months? How does it develop when the *life cycle duration* is changed to six or twelve months?

Use the worksheet from the companion website and draw graphs of your expected behaviour of *Potential customers* for the *life cycle duration* scenarios 6, 9, and 12 months.

To corroborate your expectations, you need a proof, such as the results of the simulation model. However, you do not need to start from scratch; rather adapt your model from your previous DIY tasks.

If you have carried out DIY 3.3, then create a copy of the simulation model you have built and add the stock of *Potential customers* to it (otherwise you can make the changes to a copy of 'C3 Life cycle duration outflow 1' which you can download from the companion website, or you can download the model 'C3 Life cycle duration outflow 2'). After adding the stock, you need to establish the causal relationships between the new variable and those that are already in the model: the *customers leaving* flow is still draining individuals from the stock of *Current customers*. Next, you must connect the *customers leaving* flow to the *Potential customers* stock. Remember that you can watch the video tutorial on our companion website.

Once the flow is connected to the stock, you have to set the initial value of *Potential customers*, which shall be zero. Recall that the *Current customers* stock is initialized with 1 000 000 individuals to investigate the effects of *customers leaving*. The time parameters and the model settings remain unchanged. As alternative to creating your own model, you can download 'C3 Life cycle duration outflow 2'. Simulate the model and compare your expected to the simulated one. What is the polarity of the effect of *life cycle duration* on *Potential customers*? Use the worksheet at the end of the chapter.

Similar to the *new customers* flow in Chapter 2, since *customers leaving* is an inflow to *Potential customers* and an outflow from *Current customers*, one should expect the respective stocks *Current customers* and *Potential customers* to have slopes with opposite signs, but with the same absolute value. *Current customers* should have a negative slope while *Potential customers* should have positive one. After running the model with a *life cycle duration* of nine months, Figure 3.6 shows the behaviour of the two stocks *Potential customers* (light blue) and *Current customers* (dark blue).

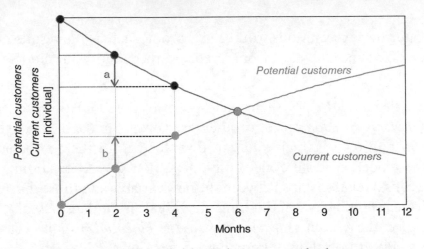

Figure 3.6 Total number of individuals is conserved when customers return
from *Current customers* to *Potential customers*

The number of *Current customers* <u>decreases</u> over the simulated time, while *Potential customers* <u>increases</u>. Make no mistake, this does not mean that one is causing the other. It just means that both stocks change. You know that the cause of the change in the stocks is the flow of *customers leaving*.

The simulated slopes of the graphs should confirm your expectations. In Figure 3.6, *a* represents the net change in number of *Current customers* from months 2 to 4, and *b* represents the net change of *Potential customers* over the same period of time. By measuring, you can verify that $a=-b$, and this is necessarily the case: the net change of *Current customers* is *new customers* minus *customers leaving*, and the net change of *Potential customers* is *customers leaving* minus *new customers*. Near month 6, the two lines cross when you have 500 000 *Current customers* and 500 000 *Potential customers*.

You should also observe that the speed of change, i.e. the slope of the graphs, slows down over time. The reason for this is in Equation (3.1). The size of the flow *customers leaving* depends on *Current customers*; since this number gets <u>smaller</u> from month to month, the flow gets <u>smaller</u> as well, <u>draining less</u> individuals from the *Current customers* stock; at the same time it <u>adds less</u> individuals to the *Potential customers* stock. This is the typical behaviour of a balancing feedback loop.

Now, after discussing the two models in Figure 3.3 and 3.5, concentrate again on the basic model you developed in Chapter 2. The model represented the transformation of *Potential customers* to *Current customers* by the word-of-mouth dynamics ('C2 Word of Mouth'). Now, add *life cycle duration* and the flow of *customers leaving* to that model. Figure 3.7 shows the result ('C3 Life cycle duration').

Recall that the *Current customers* displayed an S-shaped behaviour that was driven by the reinforcing loop 'growth engine' during the exponential phase and then by the balancing loop 'depletion' during the goal-seeking phase. Now, there is a new balancing loop 'obsolescence' formed by the chain of *Current customers* and *customers leaving*.

There is also a new reinforcing feedback loop 'replenishment' between *customers leaving*, *Potential customers*, *new customers*, and *Current customers*. It is printed in grey for a specific reason. Let us first consider how it operates. For example, <u>increasing</u> *new customers* <u>increases</u> *Current customers*, which <u>increases</u> the flow of *customers leaving* and, thus, <u>increases</u> the stock of *Potential customers*. Recall that an inflow always adds to a stock and an outflow always drains from a stock. This is **Principle 6** from Chapter 2. Accordingly, when *new customers* <u>increases</u>, this means that more individuals are added per month and, as a consequence, *Current customers* will <u>grow faster than before</u>. However, even though there is a circular relationship here, and certainly the *customers leaving* flow replenishes *Potential customers*, it cannot be said that this loop drives a reinforcing dynamic: this would mean that an initial number of *new customers* leads to an exponential growth of both *Current customers* and *Potential customers*, i.e. it would generate individuals out of nothing. Recall that we work with a constant *population*. In the model, the two balancing loops dominate and guarantee that *population* will not increase. For each of the stocks we have to take into account that if it <u>increases</u>, the respective outflow will also <u>increase</u> and this will <u>reduce</u> the level of the stock. Additionally, at the level of the stocks and flows, the model cannot <u>add</u> one individual to one of the stocks without <u>subtracting</u> it from the respective other stock.

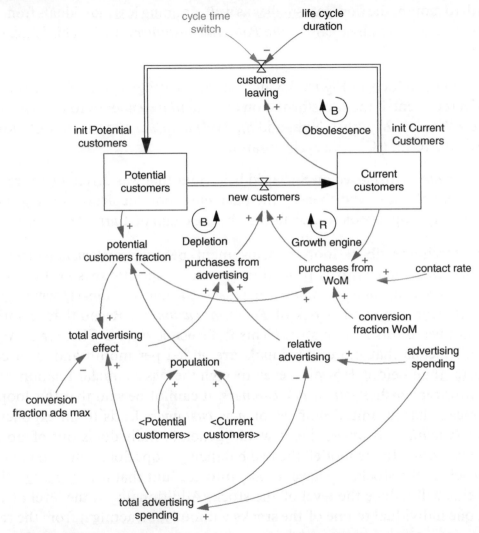

Figure 3.7 Diffusion of a product with a limited *life cycle duration*

Following **Guideline 3** (Chapter 2) and recognizing that this is not a relevant feedback loop, it is not marked with the loop symbol and does not receive a name in the figures that follow.

Hence, the new model has three relevant feedback loops that will synchronously influence the flows. This increases the model's complexity. Now it becomes almost impossible for most people to mentally simulate this system. The essential characteristics of the word-of-mouth dynamics from Chapter 2 were:

a. S-shaped <u>growth</u> of *Current customers*;
b. at the end of the year all individuals in the *population* are *Current customers*;
c. therefore *new customers* <u>decreases</u> to zero;
d. a shift from exponential to goal-seeking behaviour in month 6.

This is what happens when *life cycle duration* is unlimited, which is conceptually the same as having no *life cycle duration*. But now *life cycle duration* is limited. How will the essentials (a)–(d) be affected by this change of the causal structure?

DIY 3.5:
Adding the limited *life cycle duration* to the word-of-mouth dynamics

Create a copy of your current model from Chapter 2 and add the *life cycle duration*, the *customers leaving* flow, and the necessary causal links to the new model. Be sure to set *life cycle duration* to nine months.

Use the worksheet from the companion website to sketch your expected graph of *Current customers*, *new customers*, and *customers leaving*. Your graph should show what you expect will change concerning the four essentials mentioned above.

Then, simulate the model and compare your expected and the simulated behaviour of *Current customers*, *new customers*, and *customers leaving*. If there are differences between your graph and the simulated ones, ask yourself which aspect of the changed causal structure you did not consider properly.

Finally, compare the behaviour of *Current customers*, and *new customers* to the behaviours generated by the model in Chapter 2; the inflexion point (when exponential behaviour shifts to goal-seeking behaviour on the S-shaped curve) in the behaviour of *Current customers*; the moment when *new customers* reach their peak and the approximate number of *new customers* at the peak; the final number of *Current customers* as well as of new *customers*. If there are differences between the graphs in Chapter 2's and the simulated ones with respect to some of these characteristics, explain how the change in the causal structure leads to these changes of behaviour. Use the worksheet at the end of the chapter.

Figure 3.8 shows the behaviour of the two flows and the stock of *Current customers*:

In Figure 3.8, *Current customers* seems to behave as in Chapter 2. As always, the inflection point for changing from exponential to goal-seeking behaviour coincides with the peak of *new customers* in month 6. At that time, the slope of *Current customers* is equal to the difference between *new customers* and *customers leaving*, and this difference is at its maximum at that time. The shape of behaviour for *customers leaving* mirrors the behaviour of the stock *Current customers* since its values are the result of dividing the number of *Current customers* by the constant *life cycle duration*.

However, an additional look at the graphs reveals that now the final number of *Current customers* in month 12 is lower than one million individuals; 885 300 to be precise. A further difference is that now *new customers* do not diminish to zero but remains at a steady value of around 114 700 individuals per month. This is the case as some *Current customers* reach the end of their product bundle's *life cycle duration* and *customers leaving* return to the stock of *Potential customers*, and then some of them purchase a new mobile phone and, thereby, become again

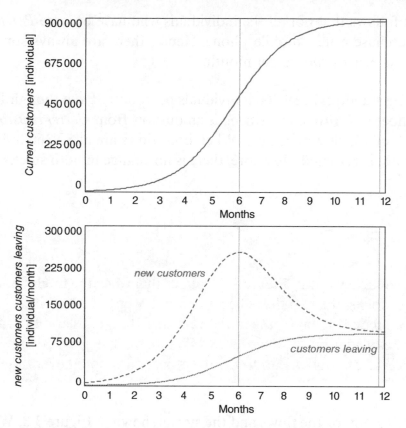

Figure 3.8 Behaviours with a *life cycle duration* of nine months

your *Current customers*. Without the *customers leaving* flow, *Potential customers* would be entirely depleted; but, with this flow, there will be a replenishment of *Potential customers* as long as there are *Current customers*. In other words, with a constant *total population*, there will always be some individuals moving to the *Potential customers* stock. However, the word-of-mouth effect is not powerful enough to make all the *Potential customers* become *new customers* in one month. It follows that not all the individuals who have become *Potential customers* in any given month will immediately purchase a new mobile phone. Hence, there are always some *Potential customers* and, consequently, there are always *new customers* per month.

The flow of *customers leaving* stabilizes at 89 360 individuals per month. Even though Figure 3.8 shows both flows with positive values, remember that *customers leaving* is an outflow from *Current customers* and *customers leaving* is subtracted from the stock of *Current customers*. When both flows are at 89 360 individuals per month, the net flow, i.e. inflow minus outflow, is zero and, therefore, there is no change in both stocks.

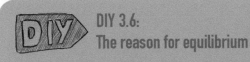

DIY 3.6:
The reason for equilibrium

In the simulated behaviour in Figure 3.8, you see that when the model starts with the default initial values for the stocks, the two flows become equal over time, leading to a net flow of zero. Is this always the case independent of the initial values of the stocks and the value of *life cycle duration*? Give a verbal explanation of how the two flow rates change the two related stocks and how the changing levels of the stocks lead to the flows becoming equal over time.

You have observed the stabilization of the flows and the stocks shown in Figure 3.8. What are the reasons that the initial <u>growth</u> and later <u>decline</u> of *new customers* finally moves into a steady state, that is, each month *new customers* has the same value? In Chapter 2, the S-shaped growth leading into the complete depletion of *Potential customers* and no more *new customers* was explained by the combined effects of the 'growth engine' and 'depletion' feedback lops. **Principle 3** (Chapter 2) stated that feedback loops 'have a closed logic which leads to endogenously driven (autonomous) behaviour'. This was certainly confirmed for the two loops studied in Chapter 2: you can accelerate the dynamics by <u>increasing</u> the *monthly encounters* or the *conversion fraction*, and you can slow it down by <u>decreasing</u>

these parameters, but you cannot change the S-shape, which is the consequence of the reinforcing loop dominating when there are many *Potential customers* and the balancing loop dominating once *Potential customers* are less than half the *population*. In the simulation of the latest model, the S-shape still exists. The difference is that the stock of *Potential customers* is not completely depleted and a steady flow of *new customers* exists. This must be a consequence of the combined effect of all three feedback loops in the model. Figure 3.9 shows the causal structure of the three feedback loops as a causal loop diagram (CLD) you need to analyse.

Because of polarity (Toolbox 2.5) and the relationship between flows and stocks (**Principle 6** from Chapter 2), analysing a CLD requires attention when interpreting causal links.

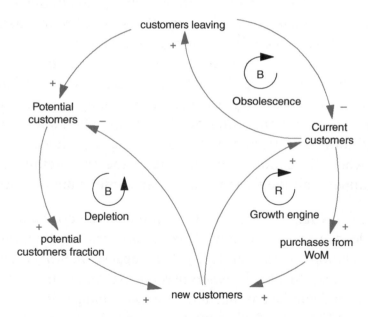

Figure 3.9 CLD of the three feedback loops

The flow *customers leaving* is a constant proportion of the stock of *Current customers*. *New customers* is a changing proportion of the stock *Potential customers*, because it depends on *Current customers* and *Potential customers*, and both stocks change over time.

1. Starting with only 5000 individuals out of one million as *Current customers*, *new customers* is larger than *customers leaving*.
2. When *new customers* is larger than *customers leaving*, there are two consequences:
    a. *Current customers* <u>increases</u>, which causes *customers leaving* to <u>increase</u> as well;
    b. *Potential customers* <u>decreases</u>, which will first <u>reduce the growth</u> of *new customers* and later force *new customers* to <u>decrease</u>.
3. If initially *new customers* is greater than *customers leaving* (step 1), and *customers leaving* <u>increases</u> (Step 2a) and *new customers* <u>decreases</u> (Step 2b), then the values of the flows must become increasingly close to one another and, sooner or later, converge. If *customers leaving* <u>increases</u>, then *Current customers* <u>diminishes</u> and *Potential customers* <u>replenishes</u>. If *new customers* <u>decreases</u>, *Current customers* <u>grows less</u> and *Potential customers* is <u>depleted less</u>. This is the circular logic of a feedback loop between stocks and flows in action.
4. When *new customers* equals *customers leaving*, the net rate of change of the two stocks is zero, and no stock changes thereafter. From that moment on, both flows keep their values and remain equal. This is because the reinforcing 'replenishment' loop is restricted by the balancing 'obsolescence' and 'depletion' loops, which push towards a condition where the exponential pressure of the reinforcing loop is counteracted by the balancing loops. When this happens, all the variables are in an equilibrium or a steady state (Toolbox 1.1).

The model 'C2 Word of Mouth' in Chapter 2 assumed an unlimited *life cycle duration*. Now, *life cycle duration* is reduced to nine months. This leads to a steady flow of *new customers*, together with a lower number of *Current customers* at the end of the simulation (i.e. in month 12). This suggests that *life cycle duration* has an influence on how the number of *Current customers* and *new customers* develop over time when the transient phase of exponential growth is over and the market is in dynamic equilibrium. How will changes in the *life cycle duration* influence *new customers* and *Current customers*? Figure 3.10 displays *Current customers* and the two associated flows for three different values of *life cycle duration*: 6 (dark blue), 9 (blue), and 12 (light blue) months.

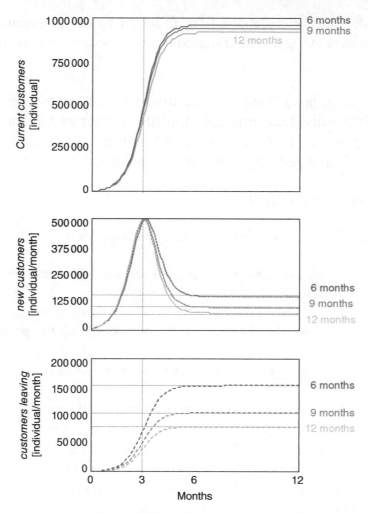

Figure 3.10 The effect of different *life cycle durations* on *Current customers*, *new customers*, and *customers lost*

Figure 3.10 shows the stock of *Current customers* first, followed by the associated flows. In each of the three scenarios, the peak in *new customers* indicates the transition from exponential growth to goal-seeking behaviour of the stock of *Current customers*.

When the *life cycle duration* is <u>reduced</u> from nine months to six months, the long-term value of *Current customers* is <u>reduced</u> to 912 000 individuals and the monthly number of *new customers* <u>increases</u> to 152 000. On the other hand, <u>increasing</u> the *life cycle duration* to 12 months <u>increases</u> the long-term value of *Current customers* to 954 000 individuals and <u>reduces</u> monthly *new customers* to 79 500.

This leads to an important management insight:

Management Insight 2 (MI 2): The life cycle duration has opposing effects

The *life cycle duration* influences which fraction of the *population* will be *Current customers* in the mature market and the size of the *new customers* flow:

a. the <u>shorter</u> the *life cycle duration*, the <u>the smaller</u> the percentage of the *population* that will be *Current customers* in the long run;
b. the <u>shorter</u> the *life cycle duration*, the <u>higher</u> the monthly number of *new customers* you can expect in the long run.

Until now, you could influence the behaviour of *Current customers* and *new customers* by changing the *life cycle duration* of the mobile phones and associated services. You also have seen in Chapter 2 that changes in the number of *monthly encounters* and changes in the *conversion fraction* can increase or decrease the speed of the diffusion. For the time being, assume that both *monthly encounters* and the *conversion fraction* are constant. One additional assumption is that NewTel has 5000 *Current customers* at the beginning; you have already seen that as soon as the value of 500 000 *Current customers* is passed, the growth loop is dominated by the balancing feedback loop.

Even though you have changed the *life cycle duration* in several ways, the moment when *new customers* peaks and the initial phase of exponential growth changes to goal-seeking behaviour remain unchanged. In other words, the transition from the initial growth phase into maturity does not change. This transition always occurs when the *potential customers fraction* sinks below 50%. This is a threshold value. To conclude, the *life cycle duration* cannot affect the point in time when the shift between growth phase and maturity occurs. In other words, the *life cycle duration* is not a condition that determines when the transition occurs. This leads us to two management insights:

Management Insight 3 (MI 3): *Life cycle duration* **does not influence loop dominance**
In a market with a stable *population*, *life cycle duration* does not influence the moment when the market evolves from its initial growth phase into maturity.

Management Insight 4 (MI 4): The *potential customers fraction* influences loop dominance
In a market with a stable *population*, the *potential customers fraction* influences the moment when the market evolves from its initial growth phase into maturity: the quicker the *potential customers fraction* decreases (since less *new customers* are replaced by *customers leaving*), the sooner the market enters maturity.

There are reasons why many companies make substantial efforts to shorten the *life cycle duration* of their products. **Management Insight 2** has a connection with the business model that specifies how a company creates or influences revenue streams. And indeed: *Potential customers* become *new customers* by making a purchase; your model represents this by *purchases from WoM*. <u>More</u> *new customers* then means <u>more</u> *revenues*, and a <u>shorter</u> *life cycle duration* causes *new customers* to be <u>larger</u> in the longer run. This is an important aspect for deciding the *life cycle duration*. Even more so if you consider that *Current customers* frequently have to pay some kind of fees or rates for making use of the product and service they have purchased; in such cases, *revenues* from these fees <u>diminish</u> when there are <u>less</u> *Current customers*. *Life cycle duration* influences *new customers* and *Current customers* in opposing directions.

The streams of revenues associated to *new customers* and *Current customers* are the subject of Chapter 5. However, you can already analyse and evaluate the impact of *life cycle duration* on *new customers* and *Current customers* – but this requires being able to assess the accumulated impact rather than the impact for a month. We will take you through this step by step in the next section.

3.3 Tracking *Accumulated purchases* and *Accumulated customer-months*

3.3.1 Structure

Since NewTel depends on *revenues* from *new customers'* phone purchases and on *revenues* from *Current customers'* service contracts, the following two statements are valid:

- the <u>more</u> *new customers*, the <u>higher</u> the *revenues*;
- the <u>more</u> *Current customers*, the <u>higher</u> the *revenues*.

With a constant customer *population* in the market and a *life cycle duration* that is practically unlimited, each individual in the target market can purchase only once. If every individual can *purchase* only once, it is not possible to achieve more *new customers* than there are individuals in the *population*. However, since now your model for NewTel has a limited *life cycle duration*, the situation is different. As this chapter has shown, if the *life cycle duration* is limited, there is a certain number of *customers leaving* every month, thereby <u>diminishing</u> *Current customers* and <u>replenishing</u> the stock of *Potential customers*. After the initial months, this leads to a number of *new customers* per month which is larger than zero. This means that some individuals purchase more than once and, consequentially, there can be more purchases than individuals in the *population*.

The sooner a *Potential customer* turns into a *new customer*, the better this is for NewTel because they will be a paying NewTel *current customer* during more months of this year: *Current customers* generate revenues for each month of the *life cycle duration* they are in NewTel's *Current customers* stock.

You will be responsible for the cumulative situation at the end of the year; you want to know:

a. How many times has the *purchasing price* been payed?
b. How many times the *subscription rate* has been payed?

The first question can be answered by counting the number of individuals who have passed through the *new customers* flow when the year is over. Quantifying this will allow you to know the *Accumulated purchases*. Assuming that *Accumulated purchases* is set to zero at the start of the year, Equation 3.3 describes the calculation:

$$Accumulated\ purchases[\text{purchase}] = Accumulated\ purchases[\text{purchase}] +$$
$$purchases\ added[\text{purchase} / \text{month}]*\textbf{TIMESTEP}[\text{month}] \tag{3.3}$$

The answer to the second question is summing up the number of times each *current customer* pays the *subscription rate*. This sum will be the *Accumulated customer-months* and since you use the number of *Current customers*, the unit of measure is 'individual'. The name 'customer-months' refers to the total number of months of service that NewTel has delivered. In the base scenario, each *current customer* will be served during nine months. If we had 10 *Current customers*, that would make a total of $10 \times 9 = 90$ months. This variable also expresses the total number of times *Current customers* have paid the *subscription rate* to NewTel. In project management, for example, people are used to planning with person-months; customer-months are similar to this:

$$Accumulated\ customer - months[\text{individual}] = Accumulated\ customer - months$$
$$[\text{individual}] + customer - months\ added\ [\text{individual/month}]*\textbf{TIMESTEP}[\text{month}] \tag{3.4}$$

You can interpret the total number of *new customers* as *Accumulated purchases* and the monthly headcount of *Current customers* as *Accumulated customer-months* because we have made the simplifying assumption that one

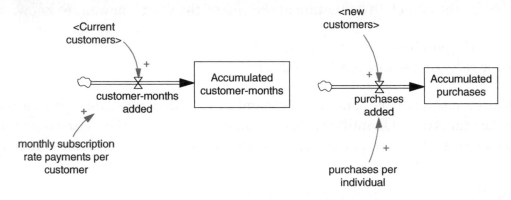

Figure 3.11 Structure for *Accumulated customer-months* and *Accumulated purchases*

customer equals one mobile phone and one contract. This is convenient as long as the assumption is held up; in Chapter 8, you will discover how the model would need to be modified if you drop this assumption.

The SFD in Figure 3.11 shows this new part of the model:

The consistency of units is conserved by introducing the variables *subscription rate payments per customer* and *purchases per individual*. Equations (3.5) and (3.6) show the calculations:

$$customer-months\ added[\text{subscription rate payment} / \text{month}] = Current\ customers[\text{individual}] *$$
$$monthly\ subscription\ rate\ payments\ per\ customer[\text{subscription rate payment} / \text{individual} / \text{month}] \tag{3.5}$$

$$purchases\ added[\text{purchase} / \text{month}] = new\ customers[\text{individual} / \text{month}] * purchases\ per\ individual$$
$$[\text{purchase} / \text{individual}] \tag{3.6}$$

At the moment your current model lacks the variables *Accumulated purchases* and *Accumulated customer-months*. Make a copy of your current model and incorporate the necessary variables and links. You can compare yours to the model 'C3 Life cycle duration' from the companion website.

To reiterate, each variable has a unit of measure. The flow of *new customers* is defined as 'individuals per month'. Recall that *purchases from WoM* are what causes individuals to become *new customers* and per that assumption one individual buys one mobile phone and has one contract. One new customer [individuals/month] is equivalent to one additional purchase and the unit of *purchases added* [purchase/month] results from multiplying a new constant *purchases per individual* [purchase/individual], whose value is one. The *Accumulated purchases* stock measures purchases.

Now, consider which unit to define for the stock *Accumulated customer-months*. Each *current customer* pays the *subscription rate* each month. The stock represents how many times NewTel receives a *subscription rate* payment for the simulated year. If you define that *Accumulated customer-months* represents the accumulated value of monthly subscription rate payments over time, it is reasonable to set the stock's unit to [subscription rate payments]. Then, the flow will be [subscription rate payments/month].

This is important: it is a way to assure that the model contains only elements which are meaningful to your business situation.

Now simulate the model for three different *life cycle durations*: 9, 6, and 12 months respectively. Use the table formats to record the resulting *Accumulated purchases* and *Accumulated customer-months*. How different are the results for 12 and 6 months as compared to the standard nine months? Use the worksheet at the end of the chapter.

3.3.2 Behaviour

The simulation model (initialized with *Potential customers* = 995 000; *Current customers* = 5000) allows us to evaluate what changes of *life cycle duration* (in our case from 9 months to 6 months and 12 months) would yield in terms of *Accumulated purchases* at the end of the 12 months (Table 3.1).

Increasing the *life cycle duration* from 9 to 12 months reduces *Accumulated purchases* by roughly 95 000 over the year, while decreasing the *life cycle duration* to six months increases *Accumulated purchases* by 143 000. The increase in *new customers* is – at least partly – compensated for by decreasing *Current customers* because of the flow of *customers leaving*. Each *new customer* will be a *current customer* for the time beginning with the purchase until either the end of the simulation or the end of the *life cycle duration* of the product bundle.

After you have extended the model, investigate what the effects of changing the *life cycle duration* from 9 to 12 and 6 months respectively are for the *customer-months* at the end of the year (Table 3.2).

When the *life cycle duration* is changed from 9 to 12 months, 297 000 *Accumulated customer-months* are gained. Reducing the *life cycle duration* to six months reduces *Accumulated customer-months* by 589 000. In comparison to the effect of changing the *life cycle duration* on *Accumulated purchases*, the effect of *customer-months* works in the opposite direction. Since *purchasing price* and the *subscription rate* have been not considered yet (you will deal with them in Chapter 5) you cannot decide if changing the *life cycle duration* would increase your revenue streams.

Table 3.1 *Accumulated purchases* won or lost by changing the *life cycle duration*

Life cycle duration	Accumulated purchases	Difference with respect to 9 months life cycle duration
9 (standard)	1 477 000	0
12	1 382 000	−95 000
6	1 620 000	143 000

Table 3.2 *Accumulated customer-months* won or lost by changing the *life cycle duration*

Life cycle duration	Accumulated customer-months	Difference with respect to 9 months *life cycle duration*
9	5 374 000	0
12	5 671 000	297 000
6	4 785 000	−589 000

However, you now know that changing the *life cycle duration* has two simultaneous effects with opposite directions. You can use your simulation model to quantify and compare these effects.

Management Insight 5 (MI 5): *Life cycle duration* **has opposing effects on the different types of revenues Changing the** *life cycle duration* **does not affect the rate at which NewTel wins** *new customers***, and it cannot change the fact that exponential growth is followed by goal-seeking growth from the moment when the** *potential customers fraction* **sinks below 50%. However,** *life cycle duration* **can be used to increase either the** *Accumulated customer-months* **or** *Accumulated purchases* **at the expense of the respective other variable.**

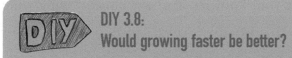

DIY 3.8:
Would growing faster be better?

Suppose that you can <u>increase</u> the speed at which NewTel wins *new customers*. Could this lead to an increase in *customer-months* or *Accumulated purchases* without a loss of the other variable?

Use Worksheet 3.8 from the companion website to develop your hypothesis concerning the impact on *Accumulated purchases* and on *Accumulated customer-months*. Keep the worksheet for Chapter 4, where you will corroborate your hypothesis with a simulation. Use the worksheet at the end of the chapter.

Increasing the speed of customer dynamics might be relevant for you. The question is: if *life cycle duration* cannot be used for this purpose, what variable could you possibly use? Chapter 4 discusses if and to what extent *advertising spending* can be used for this purpose.

3.4 Chapter summary

You now know that the limited *life cycle duration* of mobile phones alters the basic S-shaped growth of NewTel's *Current customers*: you have slightly <u>fewer</u> *Current customers* but, in exchange, you maintain a steady flow of *new customers*. The <u>shorter</u> the *life cycle duration*, the <u>stronger</u> the effect. Looking at the final outcome at the end of the year, you can therefore influence whether you want to have <u>more</u> *Accumulated customer-months* or <u>more</u> *Accumulated purchases* – bearing in mind the trade-off between these two variables. In addition, you are by now used to performing activities such as:

- recognizing variables and causal links in the description of the situation;
- formulating equations to represent the way behaviours of variables are driven;
- experimenting with the simulation model to explore its range of behaviours;
- interpreting behaviour-over-time graphs to analyse simulated behaviours;
- analysing the causal structure to understand behaviour patterns, using your knowledge of systems principles like when *new customers* and *customers leaving* cancel each other out.

Thanks to all this, you should now understand the conditions under which the customer *population* enters a 'steady state equilibrium'.

By adding *life cycle duration* and *customers leaving* to the model, you have expanded the model boundary to include two variables which we have identified as relevant. However, we have yet to consider the impact of advertising. The next step is to expand model boundary even further to consider this.

3.5 Questions and challenges

Questions

1. What is the impact of limiting the *life cycle duration* on *Current customers*?
2. What is the impact of limiting the *life cycle duration* on *Potential customers*?
3. What is the impact of <u>decreasing</u> the *life cycle duration* on *Current customers* and *new* customers once the market matures?
4. Assuming a constant *population*, which variable has a decisive influence on the moment the market evolves from its initial growth phase into its maturity phase?
5. Why does *life cycle duration* not have an impact on the moment when the market evolves from its initial growth phase into maturity when the *population* is constant?
6. Can changes to the *life cycle duration* have an influence market development from initial growth into maturity? Why/why not?
7. What is the age composition of a stock, for instance, *Current customers*?
8. How can the outflow of a stock be calculated?
9. How should external variables like the *life cycle duration* be included in a simulation model?

Challenges

1. One of the assumptions in the previous discussions has been that all of the *customers leaving* will return to the *Potential customers* stock. The previous assumption was that there would be no additional individuals arriving at Plutonia. Taken together, these two assumptions assure that the total *population* is constant. This is, of course, an unrealistic assumption. The following two challenges motivate you to explore the consequences of changing these assumptions.

   Assume that each month, 50 000 additional individuals will be added to the overall *population*. At the beginning, they do not own a mobile phone. Develop a simulation model that incorporates this new assumption. How would the behaviour of the two customer stocks and two flows be affected by this new situation? Compare it to our model in Chapter 3. Explain how the change to the structure generates these differences.

Assume that only half of the *customers leaving* flow back into the *potential customer* stock, the other half *drop out*, i.e. leave the market. Modify your model from Chapter 3 to express that a certain percentage of the *customers leaving* leaves the market and the remaining of *customers leaving* move to the stock of *Potential customers*. How would the behaviour of the two customer stocks and two flows be affected by this situation? Compare it to our model from Chapter 3. Explain how the change to the structure generates these differences.

Finally, combining these challenges, suppose now that a given fraction of *customers leaving* leaves the market (challenge 3-2). In addition, there is a possibility that new people join the market (challenge 3-1). Assume the initial number of additional customers is zero, but you are free to decide how many individuals enter the market through this inflow each month. Your goal is to compensate for the loss of those *customers leaving* who did not go back to *Potential customers* but left the market. Can you modify the model in such a way that there is not total loss of individuals in the *population*?

2. When a stock represents a certain quantity of a resource, such as clients, and when you can assume a relatively homogenous age composition for the individuals in, e.g. the stock of *Current customers*, then you can apply the logic used in the previous case of the *life cycle duration* to replicate the *loss of customers*. Now think of the two flows *new customers* and *customers lost* as they move individuals from the stock *Current customers* to *Potential customers* and vice versa. At the same time the flows are influenced by the two stocks. How do you expect the age composition of *Potential customers* to be after six months of simulation? Tip: you can imagine the stock as a sequence of compartments, similar to Figures 3.1 and 3.2.

Worksheet DIY 3.1:
Customer dynamics

Assume that you have 1,000,000 *Current customers* and that there is an homogenious age distribution.

life cycle duration	Current customers										customers leaving	Proportion of customers leaving to *Current customers*
	per "age group" inside the stock									Total	*leaving*	
9												
10												

1   2   3   4   5   6   7   8   9   10
Months

Develop a causal diagram showing the polarity of the relationship between

Graph your results:

life cycle duration   and $\dfrac{customers\ leaving}{Current\ customers}$

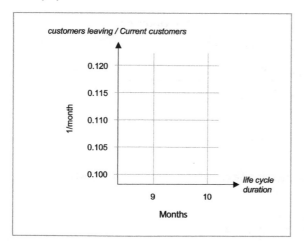

The assumption of a homogenous age distribution means that the *Current customers* has the same number of individuals for each age group. Also, there are as many age groups as months of *life cycle duration*. It follows that the total number of *Current customers* is *life cycle duration* multiplied by the monthly inflow of *new customers*. In this DIY, *new customers* is either 500 or 1,000 individuals.

Calculate the number of individuals in the stock of *Current customers* for each *life cycle duration* and each number of *new customers*:

Current customers		new customers	
		500	1,000
life cycle duration	6		
	9		
	18		

Then calculate the number of *customers leaving* for each *life cycle duration* and each number of *new customers*:

customers leaving		new customers	
		500	1,000
life cycle duration	6		
	9		
	18		

If the total population in Plutonia is 1,000,000, all of them are your *Current customers,* and *life cycle duration* was infinite (∞), what would be the number of *customers leaving*?

$$\text{customers leaving} = \frac{\text{Current customers}}{\infty} = \text{.......................................}$$

Worksheet DIY 3.3:
The effect of *life cycle duration* and *customers leaving* on *Current customers*

Draw the behaviours you expect as dotted lines and the simulated behaviours as solid lines (or use two different colours for expected and simulated behaviours):

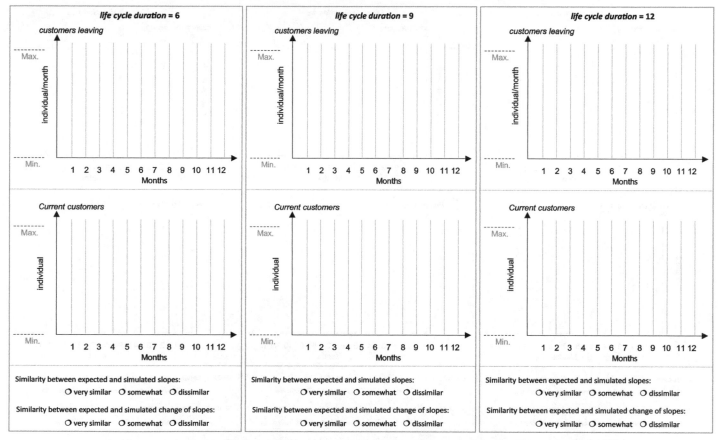

Are the differences in slope between the graphs for different *life cycle durations* in your expected graphs roughly the same as in the simulated ones?

O very similar   O somewhat   O dissimilar

Worksheet DIY 3.4:
The effect of *life cycle duration* and *customers leaving* on *Potential customers*

Draw the behaviours you expect as dotted lines and the simulated behaviours as solid lines (or use two different colours for expected and simulated behaviours):

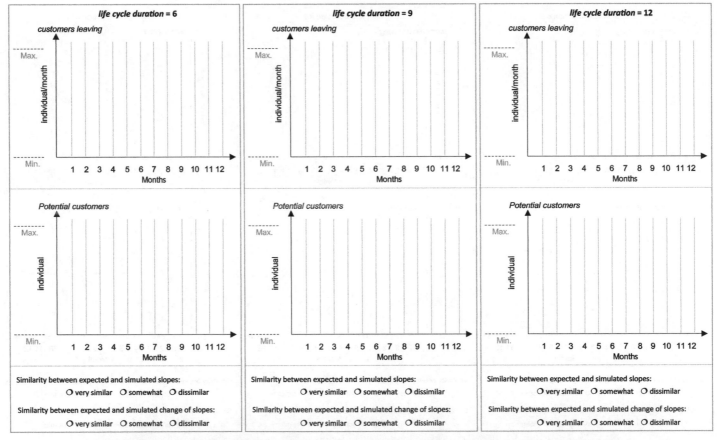

Are the differences in slope between the graphs for different *life cycle durations* in your expected graphs roughly the same as in the simulated ones?

O very similar   O somewhat   O dissimilar

Draw the behaviours you expect as dotted lines and the simulated behaviours as solid lines (or use two different colours for expected and simulated behaviours):

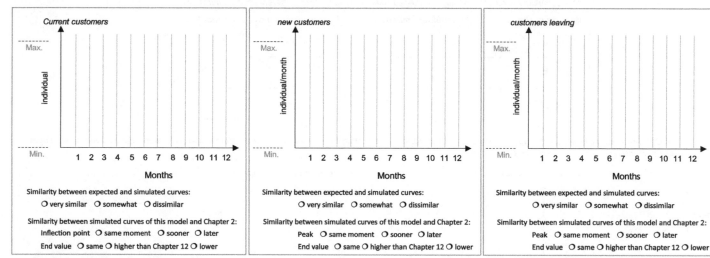

Similarity between expected and simulated curves:
○ very similar ○ somewhat ○ dissimilar

Similarity between simulated curves of this model and Chapter 2:
Inflection point ○ same moment ○ sooner ○ later
End value ○ same ○ higher than Chapter 12 ○ lower

Similarity between expected and simulated curves:
○ very similar ○ somewhat ○ dissimilar

Similarity between simulated curves of this model and Chapter 2:
Peak ○ same moment ○ sooner ○ later
End value ○ same ○ higher than Chapter 12 ○ lower

Similarity between expected and simulated curves:
○ very similar ○ somewhat ○ dissimilar

Similarity between simulated curves of this model and Chapter 2:
Peak ○ same moment ○ sooner ○ later
End value ○ same ○ higher than Chapter 12 ○ lower

If there are differences between Chapter 2's graphs and the simulated ones with respect to some of these characteristics, explain how the change in the causal structure leads to these changes of behaviour.

Worksheet DIY 3.7:
Modelling and exploring *Accumulated customer-months* and *Accumulated purchases*

Determine the end values of *Accumulated purchases* and *Accumulated customer-months* for three different *life cycle durations*:

life cycle duration	Accumulated purchases	Accumulated customer-months
6		
9		
12		

For each result from the tables, draw a dot in the two graphs representing the relationship between *life cycle duration* and *Accumulated purchases* and *Accumulated customer-months*, respectively. Then connect the dots.

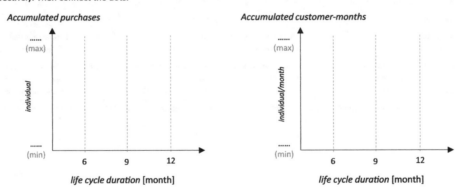

What are the consequences of <u>increasing</u> or <u>reducing</u> the *life cycle duration* for *Accumulated customer-months* and *Accumulated purchases* (end values)?

Worksheet DIY 3.8:
Would growing faster be better?

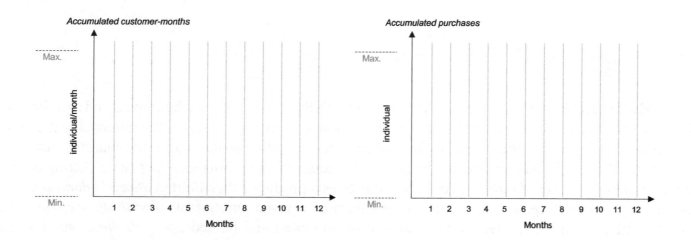

Accumulated customer-months

Accumulated purchases

Draw the default behaviour of both *Accumulated customer-months* and *Accumulated purchases* and the behaviour you would expect if NewTel could win *new customers* more quickly. Now explain how the differences (in behaviour and/or in end values) could occur:

THE EFFECT OF *ADVERTISING SPENDING*

4.1 Introduction

This chapter introduces the effects of advertising on your customers. Section 4.2 defines the context and assumptions under which advertising is considered. Then, you will discover how advertising influences the purchasing decisions of *Potential customers* and what the consequences for NewTel's *Accumulated purchases* and *Accumulated customer-months* are. In Section 4.3, our initial scenario assumes a fixed amount of *advertising spending* on marketing mobile phones with an unlimited *life cycle duration*. Section 4.4 addresses a product with a limited *life cycle duration*. This section considers, in a second scenario, the cumulative effects of a given amount of *advertising spending* in a particular month and compares the effects on products with unlimited and limited *life cycle durations*. From a methodological point of view, you will learn how to use switches and test inputs in a simulation model to quickly experiment with different scenarios and compare the resulting behaviours.

4.2 Turning the attention of *Potential customers* to a product

In Chapter 2, you gained a general understanding of how mobile telephony can spread in Plutonia. As it turned out, by means of word-of-mouth dynamics you could acquire all *Potential customers* in Plutonia, i.e. they became *Current customers* of NewTel in approximately six months. One question resulting from the simplified conceptualization of the diffusion process in Chapter 2 was about the *life cycle duration* of your product-service

Growth Dynamics in New Markets: Improving Decision Making through Simulation Model-based Management,
First Edition. Martin F.G. Schaffernicht and Stefan N. Groesser.
© 2018 John Wiley & Sons Ltd. Published 2018 by John Wiley & Sons Ltd.
Companion website: www.wiley.com/go/Schaffernicht/growth-dynamics

bundle. In Chapter 3, you saw that even though a limited *life cycle duration* has an influence on your stock of *Current customers* as well as on your *new customers*, it does not change the fact that after approximately six months equilibrium in the stocks of *Current customers* is reached. How then can promoting your product-service bundle by *advertising spending* influence this equilibrium situation?

Advertising is a corporate response to the need to inform *Potential customers* about a company's products and services. '*Advertere*' is Latin and means 'to turn attention to' something. Indeed, people need to know that certain products or services exist before they purchase them and, thereby, become *Current customers*. Advertising serves to inform and motivate *Potential customers* to become *Current customers* (Rogers, 2013). In your situation, advertising promotes mobile telephone services in Plutonia with the objective of <u>increasing</u> *new customers*. Many ways of advertising exist. For instance, print media, radio, TV commercials, webpages, product placement at (large-scale) public events, on TV shows, in movies or social media (Dent, 2011). In the face of numerous options, marketing research is needed to establish which is most effective.

For the time being, assume that all ways of advertising are equally effective and efficient. Moreover, limit advertising to the typical TV commercials, advertisements in newspapers, and online advertising, influencing the flow of *new customers*. Let us exclude social events and other influences on the *contact rate*, the *word-of-mouth conversion fraction*, or the sensitivity to price changes. With these assumptions, it becomes possible to focus on the essential question: How many *new customers* will advertising attract to your company?

4.3 The effect of fixed *advertising spending*

4.3.1 Structure

You should recall the fundamental structure of word-of-mouth diffusion from Chapter 2 (Figure 2.9): *Current customers* attract *Potential customers* and, each month, some of the latter decide to become *new customers*, thereby *increasing* the *Current customers* and <u>reducing</u> the *fraction of potential customers*. *Life cycle duration* was not an issue in Chapter 2. Now, you start to explore the effects of *advertising spending* in the context of this simplified causal structure. In the forthcoming sections, you will first integrate the concept of *advertising spending* in the word-of-mouth model from Chapter 2 ('C2 Word of Mouth') and then expand your analysis considering also the case of a limited *life cycle duration*. Following these two steps allows you to begin as simply as possible and add complexity later. Figure 4.1 shows the model 'C4 Advertisement monthly'. It builds on Chapter 2 and adds a series of new variables.

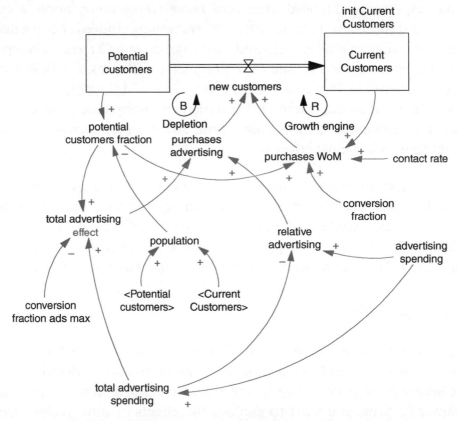

Figure 4.1 *Advertising spending* influences *new customers*

Advertising introduces the following causal mechanism: each month NewTel devotes a certain amount of financial resources to *advertising spending*; the maximum you are permitted to invest is $1 million. Even though you have not added your rival RivTel to the model yet, it is clear that RivTel also can spend money on advertising. The *Potential customers* perceive all advertising, irrespective of which company makes it, and as far as mobile telephone products and services are new to customers in Plutonia, any such advertisement will gain their attention. This means that NewTel's *advertising spending* will also promote RivTel, and RivTel's *advertising spending* will promote NewTel's service. In other words, when thinking about Plutonia as one market, using mobile telephones is promoted by the sum of both companies' *advertising spending*. Both NewTel and RivTel will be able to benefit from this *total advertising effect*. The *total advertising effect* depends on *total advertising spending*, which will be the sum of NewTel's and RivTel's *advertising spending* (as soon as RivTel is introduced to the model). The percentage of the *total advertising effect* that can be appropriated by NewTel is directly related to NewTel's relative *advertising spending* as a fraction of *total advertising spending*: the <u>larger</u> the share of *total advertising spending* coming from NewTel, the <u>more</u> of the *total advertising effect* goes to NewTel. This is represented by the variable *relative advertising NewTel*. It represents the fact that, even if NewTel's *advertising efforts* also helps RivTel, the main effect of the corresponding spending benefits NewTel. Note that this is done to allow introducing RivTel into the model in Chapter 7; if NewTel were the only mobile phone company in Plutonia, necessarily all *advertising spending* would be NewTel's and, therefore, it would be useless to calculate *total advertising spending*: NewTel's *relative advertising spending* would always be 100%. However: you already know that RivTel must be represented in the model, as soon as all important causal structures dealing with one single company have been articulated. It is wise to design your model in this flexible manner. Equations (4.1)–(4.3) represent this structure:

$$\textit{advertising spending}\left[\$/\,\text{month}\right]=0 \tag{4.1}$$

In Equation 4.1, the default value is zero, but you can adjust it within the range 0 to 1 000 000.

$$\textit{total advertising spending}\left[\$/\,\text{month}\right]=\textit{advertising spending}\left[\$/\,\text{month}\right] \tag{4.2}$$

$$relative\ advertising[\text{dimensionless}] = advertising\ spending[\$/\text{month}]\ /\ total\ advertising\ spending[\$/\text{month}] \quad (4.3)$$

The *conversion fraction advertising max* represents the relationship between the amount of *advertising spending* and the number of *Potential customers* persuaded by this to purchase and, thereby, become *new customers*. Think of this as a kind of exchange rate between two currencies; if you travel from one country to another one – which uses a different currency – you must convert some money from the original currency to the foreign currency. The exchange rate tells you how many units of the foreign currency you can buy with one unit of your own currency. The *conversion fraction advertising max* has the same function: it expresses how much effect one dollar of *advertising spending* has in terms of *new customers*:

$$conversion\ fraction\ advertising\ max[\text{individual}/\$] = 0.01 \quad (4.4)$$

This means that in the best possible case, you need to allocate \$100 to *advertising spending* to persuade one additional *potential customer* to purchase. We assume this fraction to be independent of the amount spent and to be constant for the sake of keeping the model as concise as possible. Chapter 8 discusses possible extensions. With the current value *advertising spending* is sometimes profitable and sometimes not: you must decide which amount you want to invest for each of the 12 months.

The *total advertisement effect* depends on the monthly amount of *total advertising spending* and the *conversion fraction advertising max* [\$/individual]. For instance, if NewTel spends \$100 000 in month 1, in principle 1000 additional individuals would become *new customers*. There is one further aspect to consider: advertising can only persuade *Potential customers*: *current customer* have already bought their mobile phone and cannot become *new customers* by definition. The assumption is that nobody uses two mobile phones at the same time. Therefore, the *total advertisement effect* also depends on the *potential customers fraction* in the total *population*:

$$total\ advertisement\ effect[\text{individual}/\text{month}] = total\ advertising\ spending[\$/\text{month}]\ /$$
$$conversion\ fraction\ advertising\ max[\text{individual}/\$]\ /\ potential\ customers\ fraction[\text{dimensionless}] \quad (4.5)$$

As stated before, *relative advertisement* corresponds to NewTel's share of *new customers* who decide to buy because of advertising. Taken together, this share of the total effect represents the number of purchases that NewTel will generate as a consequence of its own *advertising spending*:

$$purchases\ from\ advertising[\text{individual / month}] =$$
$$total\ advertising\ effect[\text{individual / month}] * relative\ advertising[\text{dimensionless}]$$

(4.6)

After introducing and explaining the new variables, it should now have become clear why in Chapter 2 *purchases from WoM* was separated from *new customers*: There are two separate reasons for customers to purchase.

4.3.2 Behaviour

The structure put forward in the previous subsection showed how *advertising spending* influences the flow of *new customers*. This structure helps you to improve your understanding of how the behaviour of *new customers* will change in response to different amounts of *advertising spending*.

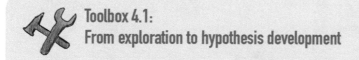

Toolbox 4.1:
From exploration to hypothesis development

In Chapters 2 and 3, the simulation models were mainly used to explore the behaviours implied by the word-of-mouth diffusion dynamics and by limiting the *life cycle duration*. If you are not familiar with a problem's causal structure and its behavioural implications, exploring, i.e. simulating to see what may happen, is a fruitful way to use a simulation model: exploration helps to structure and develop an initial mental model of the dynamic system under study.

Once you have created and refined your mental model of the relevant dynamic system you try to understand, it will begin to suggest the expected behavioural outcomes of important variables (Sterman, 2000).

Thus, you can use the understanding of the causal structure of the relevant system to develop a 'hypothesis' concerning what ought to happen to certain variables over time. In general terms, dictionaries define hypothesis as 'a tentative assumption made to draw out and test its logical or empirical consequences'. In science, a hypothesis is an 'idea or explanation that you then test through study and experimentation' (www.vocabulary.com/dictionary/hypothesis). We adhere to the latter definition: a hypothesis is a tentative estimation of expected behaviour derived from the causal structure of a model. A hypothesis has in general three elements:

1. a causal structure;
2. an assumed change in a variable;
3. a change in the behaviour or values of one or several variables which is caused by the assumed change in 2.

The ensuing simulations are then equivalent to tests carried out in a laboratory. Developing and testing hypotheses is an iterative process (Figure 4.2).

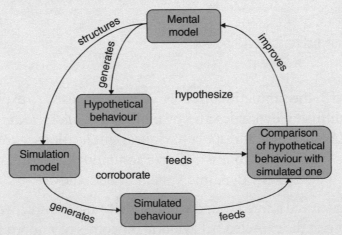

Figure 4.2 The iterative hypothesis development process

As Figure 4.2 shows, the simulation model is structured according to the current mental model. The mental model allows to formulate hypotheses with the objective to corroborate them. The simulation generates the simulated behaviour which is compared to hypothetical, expected behaviour resulting from the mental model.

The mental effort of predicting what would happen prepares the mind to process the simulated behaviours (Mayer, 2006). If the simulation confirms the expected behaviour, the reasoning leading to the prediction will be reinforced in the mind. If the simulation leads to a 'surprise', that is the expectation was wrong, then one asks about what was not understood and consequently improves the mental model (Mass, 1991).

This iterative process helps you to learn and understand problems and opportunities (Homer, 1996). It is also the reason why you must do this mental work yourself – it cannot be delegated. This is also the reason why you should work through the DIY sections, which motivate you to develop and test your own hypotheses.

As in the previous chapters, please work through the following 'Do-It-Yourself' tasks before continuing.

DIY 4.1:
The expected effect of *advertising spending* with an unlimited *life cycle duration*

Use what you have recently learned to interpret the causal structure in Figure 4.1 and develop hypotheses about how your *advertising spending* will influence the behaviour of *new customers* and *Current customers* over time.

Focus on what you expect to change as compared to the behaviours studied before. In Chapter 2, the word-of-mouth dynamics generated S-shaped growth in the number of *Current customers* until the pool of *Potential customers* was exhausted. If needed, use the model 'C2 Word of Mouth' to refresh your memory.

Do the graphs of *new customers* and of *Current customers* show different behaviours? What aspect of their behaviour changes? How is this difference caused by *advertising spending*? You can use the worksheet from the companion website to develop your hypotheses concerning expected changes of behaviour.

Thereafter, corroborate your hypotheses. Develop your own simulation model to find out how the variables' behaviour changes when *advertising spending* <u>increases</u>. Hint: you can start from the model you developed in Chapter 2 or download the model 'C2 Word of Mouth' from the companion website. Save the model with a new file name, insert the additional variables, and then populate the variables with the *advertising spending* equations. Your result should then be equivalent to the model 'C4 Advertisement monthly'.

Which of your hypotheses were confirmed by the simulations? When did the simulation results 'surprise' you, i.e. when were your hypotheses not confirmed? Use the worksheet at the end of the chapter.

The model structure in Figure 4.1 can be used to develop several hypotheses concerning the *total advertising effect* on the behaviour of *Current customers*, *Potential customers*, and *new customers*.

If *advertising spending* <u>increases</u> *new customers*, the stock of *Current customers* will <u>grow more</u> (with a larger slope) than otherwise would have been the case (H 4.1).

If *advertising spending* <u>increases</u> *new customers*, the stock of *Potential customers* will <u>decrease quicker</u> (with a more negative slope), which will lead to a <u>decrease</u> in the *potential customers fraction* (H 4.2).

If *advertising spending* increases *new customers*, the ensuing decrease in *potential customers fraction* reduces the *total advertising effect* from this time on. Therefore, the increase in *new customers* in one month induced by *advertising spending* will decrease *new customers* in the months thereafter (H 4.3).

To test these three hypotheses, simulate three scenarios for *advertising spending*: no spending, $500 000 per month, and $1 million per month for the variable *advertising spending*.

Figure 4.3 displays the first seven months of the behaviour of the stock of *Current customers* in the upper chart and the flow of *new customers* in the lower chart (dark blue = *advertising spending* = $0; blue = $500 000; light blue = $1 million). The information needed to corroborate the hypotheses is generated during these months, so it is not necessary to look at the remaining months of the year. Examining the flow of *new customers* first, the dotted black horizontal line shows that the magnitude of the peak is not affected: *new customers* always peaks at 250 000 individuals per month. However, as the dotted vertical lines indicate, the peak shifts from the original moment, i.e. after half of month 5 is over, to earlier moments: three weeks earlier if *advertising spending* equals $500 000 and five weeks earlier if it is $1 million. The dotted vertical lines also allow us to corroborate that the moment when the maximum of *new customers* is reached is also the moment when *Current customers* reaches the inflection point.

Shifting a curve with a positive slope to the left means that for each month, *Current customers* has a larger slope and is greater for higher amounts of *advertising spending*; this supports hypothesis H 4.1.

Since the magnitude of the flow corresponds to the slope of the increase or decrease in the stock, it follows that the moment of the shift of behaviour mode, i.e. the inflexion point, of the number of *Current customers* from exponential to goal-seeking occurs earlier when more money is allocated to *advertising spending*. As you have learned in the previous chapters, the inflexion point always occurs when the *potential customers fraction* reaches 0.5, i.e. 500 000 individuals out of a *population* of one million are *Potential customers*. When this number is reached, the *potential customers fraction* has become so small that the balancing 'depletion' feedback loop becomes stronger than the reinforcing 'growth engine' loop, and from then on, the monthly number of *new customers* diminishes. A look at

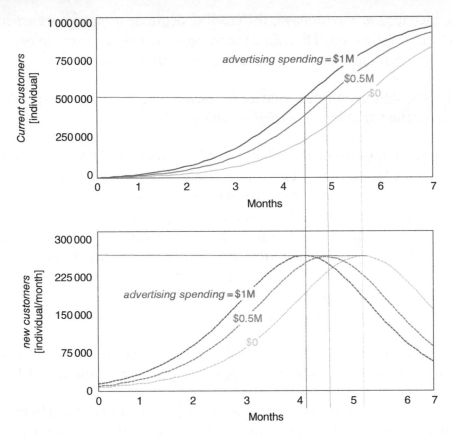

Figure 4.3 Effects of different amounts of *advertising spending* on *Current customers* and *new customers*

the graph of *Current customers* reveals that this always happens when there are 500 000 *Current customers*. This cannot be changed by allocating different amounts of *advertising spending*. Indeed, as the CLD in Figure 4.4 shows, *advertising spending* – through its effect on *purchases from advertising* – gives additional strength to the balancing 'depletion' loop.

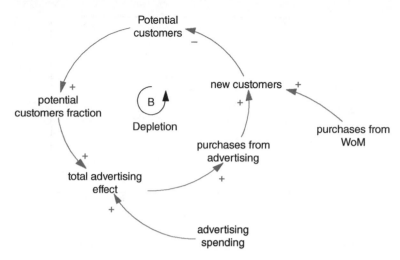

Figure 4.4 *Advertising spending* strengthens the balancing 'depletion' loop

The argument given above is confirmed by the data from simulating the three *advertising spending* scenarios; holding all other parameters constant, according to **Guideline 4** (Chapter 2). Figure 4.5 shows the behaviour of the *potential customers fraction* when *advertising spending* is $0 (light blue), $500 000 (blue) or $1 million (dark blue). Clearly, <u>higher</u> *advertising spending* leads to a <u>quicker decrease</u> in the *fraction of potential customers*, leading to a <u>quicker decrease</u> of *total advertisement effect, purchases from advertising, new customers*, and *Potential customers*: when the *potential customers fraction* <u>diminishes</u>, the *total advertisement effect* for a given amount of spending <u>decreases</u>. At the outset, almost the entire *population* is in the stock *Potential customers*, and the *potential customers fraction* has no recognizable influence on the word-of-mouth effect. When shifting from exponential growth behaviour to goal-seeking growth behaviour, this *fraction* has decreased to 50%, and therefore $100 spent on advertisement will only have half of the original effect on *purchases from advertising*. This supports hypotheses H 4.2.

The lower part of Figure 4.3 confirms that if *Current customers* is higher in one month, it will be lower in later months. This hypothesis requires at least two simulations to check if *Current customers* is higher for a given month

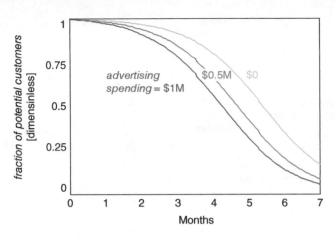

Figure 4.5 The effect of *advertising spending* on the *potential customers fraction*

in one of them. You have three simulations, for $0, $500 000 and $1 million *advertising spending* respectively. You have already corroborated that <u>increasing</u> *advertising spending* leads to a <u>quicker ascent</u> of *Current customers* until the peak is reached at an earlier month. After the peak, *new customers* for $1 million is below *new customers* for $500 000, which, in turn, is below *new customers* without *advertising spending*. Therefore, hypothesis H 4.3 can also be supported. You can also see that after the inflexion point, the slope of *Current customers* is lower for higher amounts of *advertising spending*, which is a consequence of **Principle 6** (Chapter 2).

To conclude, *advertising spending* cannot increase the total number of purchases stemming from *new customers* in the current version of the model. Recall that the effect of advertising is currently limited to the initial purchase, and that by excluding the effect of a limited *life cycle duration*, there will be no repurchases. What advertising achieves is that individuals decide to purchase a mobile phone earlier. This also means that those individuals who have purchased earlier than they would have without advertising will not purchase in the month anymore they would have originally purchased. Consequently, <u>increased</u> *new customers* attracted by advertising in one month are offset by diminishing purchases in later months. Chapter 3.2 introduced the variables *Accumulated customer-months* and *Accumulated purchases* to capture the effects of changes in *life cycle duration*. The variables capture also the effects of *advertising spending*:

Augmenting *advertising spending* leads to <u>higher</u> *Accumulated customer-months* but does <u>not increase</u> *Accumulated purchases*. As Table 4.1 shows, spending $500 000 per month throughout the year does not change *Accumulated purchases*, but there are almost 800 000 <u>more</u> *Accumulated customer-months*. The maximum *advertising spending* of $1 million will yield 1.12 million <u>more</u> *Accumulated customer-months* until the end of the year. You cannot decide yet if the corresponding *revenues* will be greater than this amount; Chapter 5 addresses this by discussing *purchasing price* and *subscription rate*. However, Table 4.1 shows that <u>doubling</u> the monthly *advertising spending* <u>does not double</u> the *Accumulated customer-months*. *Accumulated purchases* <u>cannot be increased</u> due to *advertising spending* as long as the *life cycle duration* is not limited.

The $500 000 spent on advertising persuades some *Potential customers* to purchase, i.e. *advertising spending* <u>diminishes</u> the *potential customers fraction* remaining in the *population*. This means that the inflexion point from exponential growth to goal-seeking behaviour is reached earlier during the year. This also means that the effects of any future *advertising spending* as well as the word-of-mouth dynamics will be weaker for the rest of the year. <u>Doubling</u> the *advertising spending* from $500 000 to $1 million <u>reduces</u> the *potential customers fraction* even quicker,

Table 4.1 The effect of *advertising spending* on *Accumulated purchases* and *Accumulated customer-months* over 12 months with an unlimited *life cycle duration*

Scenario for *advertising spending*	*Accumulated purchases* (millions)	Difference in *new customers*	*Accumulated customer-months* (millions)	Difference in Accumulated *customer-months* (millions)
0	0.994	0	6.569	0
500 000	0.994	0	7.277	0.708
1 000 000	0.994	0	7.689	1.120

and the effect of future advertising and of the word-of-mouth dynamics is weaker. You can summarize this in the following five systems insights:

Systems Insight 2 (SI 2): Advertising leads to earlier purchases
As long as there are *Potential customers*, *advertising spending* influences and motivates them towards purchasing earlier than they would have done otherwise.

Systems Insight 3 (SI 3): Early *Current customers* spend more time as agents of diffusion
Every additional *current customer* reinforces the word-of-mouth dynamics and, if the purchase occurs early, while the *potential customers fraction* is still high, additional *new customers* can be won by the word-of-mouth process.

Systems Insight 4 (SI 4): Advertising and word-of-mouth drive *Accumulated customer-months*
Advertising spending as well as word-of-mouth increases the overall number of *Accumulated customer-months*.

Systems Insight 5 (SI 5): Advertising needs *Potential customers* and depletes them
The depletion of *Potential customers* is accelerated by *advertising spending*; at the same time, the effect of *advertising spending* depends on having many *Potential customers*. Therefore, the impact of *advertising spending* on *Accumulated customer-months* decreases over time, as the *potential customer fraction* decreases.

Systems Insight 6 (SI 6): Every *Potential customer* purchases only once
With a constant (limited) customer *population* in a market and with an unlimited *life cycle duration*, advertising cannot increase the total number of *Accumulated purchases*.

Now, the initial effect of *advertising spending* is established. To analyse the additional effects of *advertising spending* on customer dynamics in Section 4.5, the concept of a limited *life cycle duration* (Chapter 3) is re-introduced in the analysis, since it is relevant to how the two stocks *Potential customers* and *Current customers* change over time.

4.4 The effect of constant *advertising spending* with a limited *life cycle duration*

4.4.1 Structure

The previous section did not consider a limited *life cycle duration* of the product-service bundle when analysing the effect of *advertising spending* on customer dynamics. Now, it is time to uncover if the effect of *advertising spending* is different given a limited *life cycle duration*. For this purpose, *life cycle duration* and *customers leaving* are re-introduced to the model. *Life cycle duration* is a constant with a default value of nine months. The monthly number of *customers leaving* is calculated as the *Current customers* divided by *life cycle duration*. Figure 4.6 shows the SFD of this model. The model can be downloaded from the companion website as 'C4 Advertisement monthly limited *life cycle duration*'.

A new aspect of this model is the *cycle time switch*. It is not a variable belonging to the causal logic of your Plutonia model but, from the standpoint of the simulation software, it is a variable because it is used in an equation. Its function is to switch the *customers leaving* flow on and off. This functionality is achieved by limiting the switch values to either '1' or '0'and modifying the flow equation from its original version in Equation 3.1 to Equation 4.7.

$$customers\ leaving\ [\text{individual} / \text{month}] =$$
$$Current\ customers[\text{individual}] / life\ cycle\ duration[\text{month}] * cycle\ time\ switch[\text{dimensionless}] \qquad (4.7)$$

This small change leaves the causal structure of the model untouched, but now you can use the model to compare its behaviour between the scenarios with an unlimited and a limited *life cycle duration*. Creating variables is one possibility to enable you to alter the execution of simulations.

4.4.2 Behaviour

Will the effect of *advertising spending* change if the *life cycle duration* of your mobile phones is limited? In Chapter 3, you found that, due to the limited *life cycle duration*, some *Current customers* leave each month and, therefore, *Current customers* is less than the *population*, *Potential customers* never reaches zero, and *new customers* does not

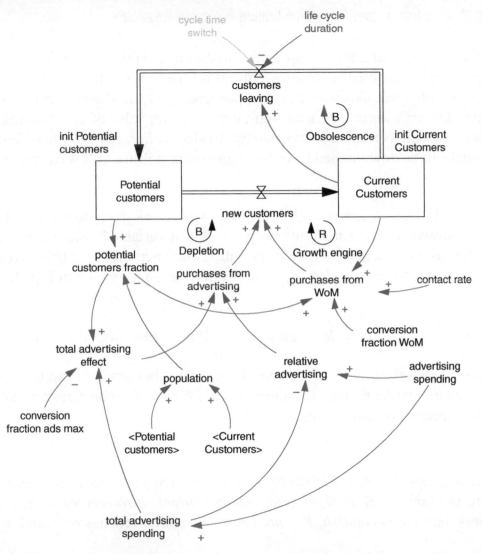

Figure 4.6 Causal structure for *advertising spending* with a limited *life cycle duration*

drop to zero. In other words: a <u>shorter</u> *life cycle duration* leads to a <u>reduced number</u> of *Current customers* at the end of the 12 months and to an <u>increase</u> in *new customers* each month, since individuals who used to own a mobile phone but became *Potential customers* after finishing their product's *life cycle duration* repurchase. These effects are <u>stronger</u> for <u>shorter</u> *life cycle durations*.

Advertising spending causes a <u>rise</u> in *purchases from advertising*, which leads to <u>earlier growth</u> in *new customers*. This causes an <u>increase</u> in *Accumulated customer-months*, but not in *Accumulated purchases*, if the *life cycle duration* is unlimited. However, as soon as *life cycle duration* is limited, the stock of *Potential customers* will be replenished by the flow of *customers leaving* and there will be individuals who purchase again. What are the effects of *advertising spending* on customer dynamics and on *Accumulated customer-months* and *Accumulated purchases*, when *life cycle duration* is limited?

DIY 4.2:
Does a change in *life cycle duration* change the effect of *advertising spending* on *customer-months*?

In Chapter 3, DIY 3.8 asked you if an increase in the speed at which NewTel wins *new customers* could lead to a gain of *customer-months* or *Accumulated purchases* without a loss of the respective other variable. Now that you know how *advertising spending* changes the customer dynamics when *life cycle duration* is unlimited, the question is how a limited *life cycle duration* changes these customer dynamics. Will the customer stocks and flows behave differently?

Elaborate hypotheses concerning the behaviour of *Accumulated purchases* and *Accumulated customer-months*. Use the SFD and reason for your hypotheses. Use the worksheet from the companion website to sketch the behaviours you expect.

Copy your model from the previous steps of this chapter (or copy the model 'C4 Advertisement monthly') and introduce the flow of *customers leaving* and the *life cycle duration* as in the final model of Chapter 3 ('C3 Life cycle duration'); remember to incorporate the *cycle time switch* as well.

A tutorial to develop the model is on the website. Or, alternatively, you may also use the model 'C4 Advertisement monthly limited life cycle duration' from the website.

Then, simulate the model with $0 monthly *advertising spending* and with $1 million monthly *advertising spending* for the following *life cycle duration* scenarios (12, 9, and 6 months). Observe how the behaviour-over-time-graph of *purchases from advertising* changes and then record the *Accumulated customer-months* and the *Accumulated purchases*. Use the worksheet at the end of the chapter.

According to what has already been found out, a number of hypotheses are proposed. Since a shorter *life cycle duration* increases the *customers leaving* flow, there will be more *Potential customers* to respond to *advertising spending*; consequently, the *potential customers fraction* will be higher than it would otherwise have been. Since this variable then has a higher value, a same amount of *advertising spending* will lead to more *purchases from advertising*, which increases the gain in *new customers* (because of additional *purchases from advertising*) and, thereby, slows the rate of decrease in *Current customers* (from *customers leaving*, which cannot be avoided and increases as *life cycle duration* gets shorter).

If the causal chain is as described as in the previous paragraph and *advertising spending* >0, then shortening the *life cycle duration* could have the following effects:

If *advertising spending* >0, then shortening the *life cycle duration* will increase *purchases from advertising*. Consequently, the number of *new customers* is increased (H 4.4).
If *advertising spending* >0, then shortening the *life cycle duration* will increase *Accumulated purchases* (holding the amount of *advertising spending* constant) due to increased *new customers* (H 4.5).

If *advertising spending* >0, then <u>shortening</u> the *life cycle duration* will <u>increase</u> the number of *Accumulated customer-months* (holding the amount of *advertising spending* constant) due to <u>increased</u> *new customers* (H 4.6).

Simulating the model with different values for *life cycle duration* allows for testing these hypotheses. By means of the graphs of *purchases from advertisement* in Figure 4.7, the hypothesis H 4.4 can be evaluated:

Figure 4.7 shows the behaviour of *purchases from advertisement* for four different *life cycle durations*. Even though the overall shape reveals an inverted S-shaped behaviour, clearly a <u>shorter</u> *life cycle duration* leads to a <u>higher</u> number of *purchases from advertising*. Hypothesis H 4.4 is therefore supported.

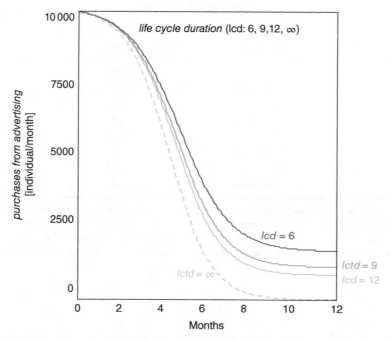

Figure 4.7 Graphs of *purchases from advertisement* for different *life cycle durations* (abbreviated here as *lcd*)

The validity of hypotheses H 4.5 and H 4.6 can be evaluated by looking at Table 4.2. The data in Table 4.2a show how many *Accumulated customer-months* and *Accumulated purchases* (in million units) are achieved according to *life cycle duration* and *advertising spending*. Note that setting the *cycle time switch* to zero is equivalent to setting an infinite *life cycle duration*. Table 4.2b shows how many units are won by increasing *advertising spending* from 0 to $1 million per month, according to different *life cycle durations*. Table 4.2c shows how many units are won when *life cycle duration* is changed from infinite to 12, 9, or 6 months, respectively.

Table 4.2 Simulation data for evaluating hypotheses H 4.4 to H 4.6

		4.2a: Simulation results		
cycle time switch	life cycle duration	advertising spending	Accumulated customer-months (million)	Accumulated purchases (million)
0	∞	0	6569	994
0	∞	1 000 000	7689	995
1	12	0	5671	1382
1	12	1 000 000	6855	1483
1	9	0	5374	1477
1	9	1 000 000	6581	1615
1	6	0	4785	1620
1	6	1 000 000	6038	1835

	4.2b: Won by *advertising spending* $1M/month			4.2c: Won by shortening *life cycle duration*	
life cycle duration	Accumulated customer-months (M)	Accumulated purchases (M)	life cycle duration	Accumulated customer-months (M)	Accumulated purchases (M)
∞	1120	1	12	64	100
12	1184	101	9	87	137
9	1207	138	6	133	214
6	1253	215			

Independent of *life cycle duration*, both *Accumulated customer-months* and *Accumulated purchases* are <u>higher</u> when *advertising spending* <u>rises</u> from 0 to $1 million per month. Comparison of the values for different *life cycle durations* reveals that <u>shorter</u> *life cycle durations* lead to <u>higher</u> *Accumulated customer-months* and to markedly <u>higher</u> results in *Accumulated purchases*. The gains in *Accumulated customer months* and in *Accumulated purchases* resulting from <u>reducing</u> *life cycle duration* from nine to six months are <u>larger</u> than the gains from <u>reducing</u> *life cycle duration* from 12 to 9 months. Hypotheses H 4.5 and H 4.6 are therefore confirmed.

Advertising does not change the effect of limiting or shortening the *life cycle duration*. The peak of *new customers*, and therefore the end of the exponential growth, is reached when the *potential customers fraction* has <u>sunk</u> to 50% because NewTel has 500 000 *Current customers*. None of this changes when *advertising spending* is <u>increased</u> from 0 to 1 million per month. The effect of *advertising spending* on *new customers* remains the same as in Chapter 3: it makes *Potential customers* decide to purchase one or several months earlier than they would have without the *advertising spending*. Consequently, the *new customers* peak is reached earlier because the threshold value of the *potential customers fraction* to switch from exponential growth to goal-seeking behaviour is reached quicker. This threshold value does not change as a function of *life cycle duration*. You now have gained another systems insight.

> **Systems Insight 7 (SI 7):** <u>Shortening</u> the *life cycle duration* leads to <u>loss</u> of *Current customers* and to repurchasing
> When the *life cycle duration* is limited, those *Potential customers* who purchase <u>earlier</u> also leave <u>earlier</u>. If they now reach the end of their bundle's *life cycle duration* before the end of the simulated year, this <u>loss</u> of *Current customers* <u>partly offsets</u> the <u>increase</u> of *Accumulated customer-months* yielded by *advertising spending*; however, in so far as some *Current customers* <u>leave earlier</u>, they will repurchase, thereby <u>increasing</u> the number of *Accumulated purchases;* this can <u>offset</u> the resulting <u>losses</u> in *Accumulated customer-months*.

4.5 The effect of advertising for one month

4.5.1 Structure

As one month's *advertising spending* changes the distribution of individuals between *Potential customers* and *Current customers*, it is important to quantify this effect. The moderating effect of varying *life cycle durations* on how *advertising spending* affects customer dynamics is now known. The assumption of an unlimited *life cycle duration*, as made in the initial sections of this chapter, is now relaxed: the following exploration of advertising is carried out assuming a *life cycle duration* of nine months.

To explore the impact of *advertising spending* on the *Accumulated customer-months* and *Accumulated purchases*, and the influence of timing when advertising is carried out, you need to be able to allocate your *advertising spending* to a specific month. Currently, in the model *advertising spending* is a constant, and the value you define will be applied for each of the 12 months. However, there is no reason to assume that the same amount of *advertising spending* will be spent in each month: you need to be able to set different values of *advertising spending* over the months.

For this, you must make a twofold change in the model: the amount of *advertising spending* needs to be adjustable to any particular month, which can be freely defined by you. Toolbox 4.2 shows how this can be done.

Toolbox 4.2:
Test inputs

Frequently one asks what would happen if a change occurs in a given variable at a specific time for a specific duration. This change may take quite different shapes. Including such changes in a variable is useful to see the behaviour or development of the system given this change. A simple change is a PULSE, which is just a temporary modification of the underlying value of a variable (Figure 4.8).

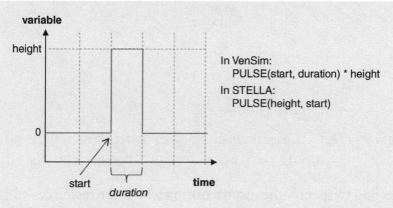

Figure 4.8 A PULSE function applies a change in a given variable at a specific time with a specific duration and magnitude

Most simulation modelling software packages have built-in functions for this. However, the details of the PULSE function vary between these software packages. In Vensim, the PULSE function needs two parameters: *start* and *duration*. *Start* refers to the simulation period in which the value returned is applied. *Duration* is the number of simulation periods during which the PULSE function will be active, i.e. it will return a non-zero value. The function itself returns the value '1' starting at period *start* and lasting *duration* periods. If a value greater than one is needed, the function must be multiplied with the desired *height*. In iThink/STELLA, the PULSE function implicitly assumes that the *duration* is always '1'. Therefore, only the *start* and *height* parameters are passed to the function. In PowerSim, the function is passed three parameters: *volume*, *start*, and *interval*. *Volume* is internally divided by the *timestep* set for the model (DT) to determine the height. *Start* specifies the first time the function will be triggered, and from then on it will be activated according to the *interval*. More details can be found in the respective software manuals.

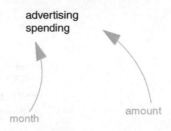

advertising
spending

month

amount

Figure 4.9 The PULSE function allows you to control the amount and the
month parameters for advertising spending

The second change enables you to specify the month during which the resources will be spent. Figure 4.9 shows how you have to change the model structure.

Now, the equation for computing *advertising spending* has to be adjusted as shown in Equation 4.8, using the function PULSE with its two arguments. Note that only the first argument, the month of *advertising spending*, can be adjusted. The second argument, the duration, is always equal to one.

$$advertising\ spending[\$/\mathrm{month}] = PULSE(\mathrm{month},1)*amount[\$/\mathrm{month}] \tag{4.8}$$

The default value for *advertising spending* is zero, and in the month that you specify the PULSE-function will return a value of one for one month, which is multiplied by the value you defined for *amount*. Since you will need to know the effect of exactly one month's *advertising spending*, the duration of the PULSE will be one.

For now, *month* and *amount* are exogenous variables and you will be able to define their values freely, i.e. as long as you keep the value of month between 1 and 12 and the value of amount inside the defined budget of $1 million.

Now, you can adapt your model from the previous section (Section 4.4) or use the model 'C4 One new customer' to explore the effect of the timing of *advertising spending* (all changes are implemented in model 'C4 One new customer').

DIY 4.3:
The effect of a single month's *advertising spending* on *Accumulated customer-months*
and *Accumulated purchases*

Your model from the previous section can easily be adjusted by adding the two new variables *month* and *amount*, linking them to *advertising spending*, and defining the equation according to Equation (4.6).

Firstly, what is the effect on *Accumulated purchases* and *Accumulated customer-months* when *advertising spending* is allocated to a later month instead of the first month? Formulate hypotheses using the worksheet from the companion website.

Next, plan some simulation experiments that help you test your hypotheses. The base case for evaluating the effects of month-wise *advertising spending* is *Accumulated customer-months* and *Accumulated purchases* without any *advertising spending* (see Table 4.2). Then you need to know the values for the same two variables in case you spend $500 000 or $1 million in month 1, 2, 3, or 4.

To summarize, simulate your model for the eight scenarios, spending either $500 000 or $1 million in month 1, 2, 3, or 4 and record the values of *Accumulated customer-months* and *Accumulated purchases* in the DIY worksheet from the companion website. Remember that *life cycle duration* is now nine months.

Then compare: how the final values for *Accumulated customer-months* and *Accumulated purchases* change in response to the amount and the month when advertisement is spent? Use your causal understanding of the situation to explain the differences. Use the worksheet at the end of the chapter.

4.5.2 Behaviour

The reason for examining the effect of spending on advertising in different months was that one month's *total advertising effect* will lead to *purchases from advertising* that <u>increase</u> the flow of *new customers* and, thereby, <u>reduce</u> the stock of *Potential customers*. This then <u>decreases</u> the *potential customers fraction* and, thereby, <u>diminishes</u> the *total advertising effect* in the future. All these effects have already been confirmed in the previous sections. You also know that the *potential customers fraction* will decrease due to the word-of-mouth dynamics, even if you do not spend money on advertising. In other words: in the presence of word-of-mouth dynamics, the *potential customers fraction* <u>decreases</u> over time. You know that the *total advertising effect* is such a variable: if the *potential customers fraction* <u>decreases</u>, the *total effect of advertising* will <u>decrease</u>, ceteris paribus.

Your hypothesis for this section might be:

> When a given amount of *advertising spending* is made <u>later</u> in the year the <u>diminishing</u> *total effect of advertising* <u>lowers</u> the <u>increase</u> of *purchases from advertising*, and therefore *new customers* <u>increase by a lower amount</u>, leading to a <u>smaller increase</u> in *Accumulated purchases* and *Accumulated customer-months* than when *advertising spending* is invested earlier in the year (H 4.7).

Simulating the model without any *advertising spending* yields 5.35 million *Accumulated customer-months* and 1.47 million *Accumulated purchases*.

Figure 4.10 shows the *Accumulated customer-months* and the *Accumulated purchases* (that are the result of spending $500 000 or $1 million in different months varying the month from 1 to 6. The light blue columns represent *advertising spending* of $500 000, while a spending of $1 million is shown in dark blue.

Figure 4.10 clearly shows spending $1 million always yields more *Accumulated customer-months* and *Accumulated purchases* than spending $500 000, and that both the absolute values and the difference achieved by spending more quickly diminish when the money is spent in later months. If *advertising spending* occurs in month 6, there is practically no difference between the two advertisement scenarios.

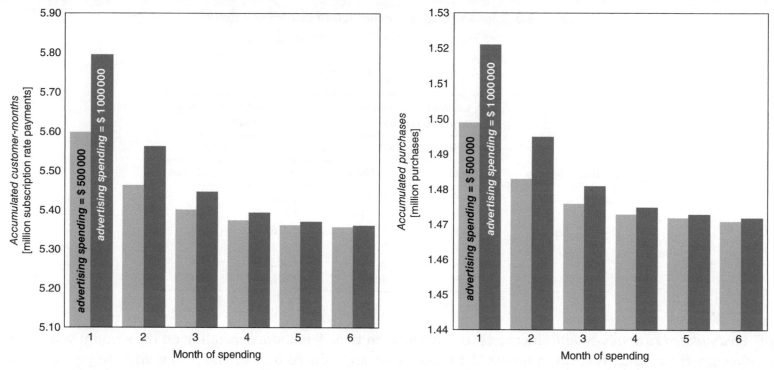

Figure 4.10 The total effect of one month of *advertising spending* on *Accumulated customer-months* and *Accumulated purchases*. The number at the bottom represents in which month the investment is made

This observation already supports hypothesis H 4.7 in principle. However, some additional information concerning how quickly the advertising effect <u>decreases,</u> when the *advertising spending* is deferred to <u>later</u> months, still has to be extracted from the simulation data. The numbers are reported in Table 4.3.

When there is no *advertising spending* at all, then you complete the year with 5.353 million *Accumulated customer-months* and with 1.471 million *Accumulated purchases*. If *advertising spending* occurs in month 1, the total number

Table 4.3 Final values of *Accumulated customer-months*
and *Accumulated purchases* resulting from *advertising spending*
in different months. The outcomes without *advertising spending*
are shown as 'base line'

		Accumulated customer-months (million)		Accumulated purchases (million)	
		Baseline = 5.353		Baseline = 1.471	
advertising spending		500 000	1 000 000	500 000	1 000 000
Month	1	5.598	5.795	1.499	1.521
	2	5.464	5.563	1.483	1.495
	3	5.401	5.447	1.476	1.481
	4	5.374	5.394	1.473	1.475
	5	5.362	5.371	1.472	1.473
	6	5.357	5.361	1.471	1.472

of *Accumulated customer-months* increases to 5.59 and even to 5.79 million, depending on the amount you decide to allocate. If the same is spent in month 2, the outcomes are reduced to 5.46 and 5.56 million respectively and then quickly converge to approximately 5.36, regardless of the amount spent. Looking now at *Accumulated purchases*, if *advertising spending* occurs in month 1, then you can achieve 1.49 or even 1.52 million purchases. If you wait until month 2, the numbers descend to 1.48 and 1.49; after month 4, the two spending scenarios yield practically the same outcomes.

How many additional *Accumulated customer-months* and *Accumulated purchases* can you expect to gain from allocating $500 000 or $1 million to *advertising spending* in one month or another? To answer this question, you subtract the outcomes with no *advertising spending* to those achieved by spending the respective amounts in one of the months, as shown in Table 4.4.

Table 4.4 Gains in *Accumulated customer-months* and *Accumulated purchases* with respect to no *advertising spending* resulting from different amounts of *advertising spending* in different months

advertising spending		Accumulated customer-months won (million)		Accumulated purchases won (million)	
		500 000	1 000 000	500 000	1 000 000
Month	1	0.245	0.442	0.028	0.050
	2	0.111	0.210	0.012	0.024
	3	0.048	0.094	0.005	0.010
	4	0.021	0.041	0.002	0.004
	5	0.009	0.018	0.001	0.002
	6	0.004	0.008	0.000	0.001

Table 4.4 compares the two spending scenarios ($500 000 and $1 million), indicating the difference between the *Accumulated customer-months* and *Accumulated purchases* obtained and the results without *advertising spending* (as displayed in Table 4.3). Looking at *Accumulated customer-months*, there are two relevant observations you can make: firstly, each time you spend a given amount one month later, you lose about half of the gain, regardless of the amount you are spending. For instance, from month 1 to 2 the *Accumulated customer-months* won decrease from 0.24 million (for spending $500 000) and 0.44 million (for spending $1 million) to 0.11 and 0.21 million, respectively. And when you compare the differences between spending $500 000 and $1 million for the same month, it turns out that spending twice as much money does not translate into twice as much *Accumulated customer-months* won. 0.44 is not quite two times 0.24.

The same proportions between months and between amounts spent occur again when you examine the numbers for *Accumulated purchases*: 0.028 is a little more than two times 0.12 (spending $500 000 in month 1 or 2), and 0.050 is a little less than two times 0.028 (spending $500 000 or $1 million in month 1).

Even though financial resources have not been introduced yet, you can already intuitively anticipate that the resources spent on advertising would not always be reimbursed by additional profits. If you assume for a moment that neither the *sales price* nor the *subscription rate* will be changed from their BAU values, you can do a quick multiplication. *Sales price* minus *purchasing price* (paid to the supplier Samuria Technologies for each mobile phone) is $50 − 40, so each purchase by a *new customer* gives you $10 profit. Similarly, *subscription rate* minus *Service costs* is $20 − 10 and you will have $10 profits for each *customer month*. Compare the profits expected when spending $1 million in month 1 or in month 6. In month 1, you will have 442 000 <u>additional</u> *customer months* and 50 000 <u>additional</u> *purchases*. You multiply each by 10 and compute your <u>additional</u> *profits* as $4 920 000, which is much more than the $1 million of *advertising spending*. However, for month 6, there are only 8000 *customer months added* and 1000 additional *purchases*. This will yield only $90 000 in <u>additional</u> *profits*, not enough to compensate for the *advertising spending*. Other possible indirect effects of *advertising spending* on *profits* and interdependencies with other relevant variables aside, spending money on advertising which is not profitable is not a good idea for your first year in Plutonia.

Of course, you should take this finding with caution, as you have not determined the best possible *sales price* and *subscription rate* yet. You must assume that you will change the *sales price* and the *subscription rate* from their default values to different values. However, when such changes happen, you should expect that they have an influence the decisions taken by *Potential customers* and *Current customers*. But if customer dynamics change, you cannot assume that the values of *Accumulated customer-months* and *Accumulated purchases* will be the ones that have been calculated by the current model – which does not include the causal structure representing the way how customers take such changes into account.

It becomes necessary to find out how changes in *sales price* and *subscription rate* – end even in other variables – influence customer dynamics and how the combined effect of all the influences plays out in *Accumulated profits*. Chapter 5 will introduce financial resources and enable you to fully explore these aspects. Two management insights follow from the current analysis:

Management Insight 6 (MI 6): Advertising needs *Potential customers* to be effective
Advertising is effective only in the initial months, when the number of *Current customers* has not yet reached a stable value.

Management Insight 7 (MI 7): Advertising is effective only for a short time
One single month of *advertising spending* by NewTel influences the distribution of individuals between the *Potential customers* and the *Current customers* stocks. This change influences the effectiveness of future *advertising spending*. This is important because it suggests that *advertising spending* should be analysed and decided upon for periods of months and not for an entire year.

4.6 How many *Current customers* are won by winning one *new customer*?

4.6.1 Structure

Why does the month in which advertising is used make such a big difference? To answer this question, recall that each new *current customer* will act as a diffusion agent for the remaining months of the year. As seen in Chapter 2, the effectiveness of these forces depends, among other things, on the *fraction of potential customers*. The question is: how many additional *new customers* can be won through word-of-mouth dynamics from one additional customer who is won by *advertising spending*? Since any additional *new customers* will alter the flow of *customers leaving* – as will any change in *life cycle duration* – and any changes in that flow will alter the number of *Potential customers* who are sensitive to the word-of-mouth dynamics, how do changes in *life cycle duration* impact this effect?

Answer this question by using your simulation. However, the model must give you the opportunity to make an experiment with just one additional *new customer*. Only a slight modification of the previous model from Section 4.5 is needed, as shown in Figure 4.11 and Equation 4.9.

The flow of *new customers* still contributes to *purchases from advertising* and *purchases from WoM* (as in Figure 4.6) but, in addition, it depends on two new exogenous variables. *Additional customer switch*, which will be '0' or '1' – if you want to run the model in the normal model, then the value should be '0'; with one

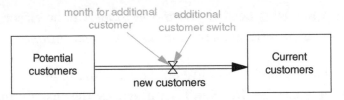

Figure 4.11 Adding the possibility to experiment with one additional *new customer*

additional *new customer*; the value should be '1'. *Month for additional customer* indicates the month in which the additional *new customer* will be added to the flow. Equation 4.9 shows the modified flow equation:

$$new\ customers[\text{individual / month}] =$$
$$purchases\ from\ WoM[\text{individual / month}] + purchases\ from\ advertising[\text{individual / month}] + \qquad (4.9)$$
$$pulse(month\ for\ additional\ customer, 1)[\text{individual / month}] * additional\ customer\ switch[\text{dimensionless}]$$

4.6.2 Behaviour

Each *current customer* reinforces the word-of-mouth diffusion – but how much, and how does the strength of the effect depend on the month in which a new customer is won and on the *life cycle duration*? Since you only have 12 months in total, the month in which a *new customer* appears determines how many months they will be in the *Current customers* stock before the year is over. In addition, if *life cycle duration* is limited, the time spent in the stock of *Current customers* may be even shorter.

According to the causal structure represented in the model, an additional *Current customer* will help to persuade other *Potential customers* to *purchase from WoM* and become *new customers*. Since this happens every single month, the earlier this additional *new customer* is won, the stronger his or her impact on winning more additional *new customers* and its consequence for *Accumulated purchases* and *Accumulated customer-months*. Due to the

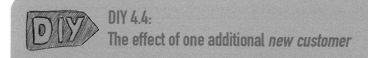

DIY 4.4:
The effect of one additional *new customer*

Given what you have already found out about the customer dynamics, propose your hypothesis concerning how many additional *Accumulated customer-months* and *Accumulated purchases* result from winning one additional *new customer* either in month 1, 2, 3, 4, 5, or 6.

You can use your own model and implement the necessary modifications, or download the model 'C4 Advertisement one new customer', to examine the effect of winning one additional *current customer* in a specific month.

How many additional *new customers* will this one customer attract during the remaining months of the year? Explore the scenarios for each of the first six months and *life cycle durations* of 6, 9, and 12 months respectively. Perform 18 simulations in total.

replenishment effect from a limited *life cycle duration* (as discussed previously), a <u>shorter</u> *life cycle duration* will increase the number of *Potential customers* susceptible to be persuaded by word-of-mouth and, therefore, will <u>strengthen</u> the effect one additional *Current customer* has. Therefore, the hypotheses are:

The <u>earlier</u> one <u>additional</u> *new customer* is won, the <u>more</u> additional *new customers* will there be, leading to <u>additional</u> *Accumulated purchases* and <u>additional</u> *Accumulated customer-months* (H 4.8).
A <u>shorter</u> *life cycle duration* <u>increases</u> the number of <u>additional</u> *Accumulated purchases* and *Accumulated customer-months* for a given amount of *advertising spending* (H 4.9).

Table 4.5 Total effects of winning one additional *new customer*

| | life cycle duration | | | | | |
| | 6 | | 9 | | 12 | |
Month	*Accumulated customer-months*	*Accumulated purchases*	*Accumulated customer-months*	*Accumulated purchases*	*Accumulated customer-months*	*Accumulated purchases*
None	4 765 818	1 612 283	5 352 708	1 470 616	5 648 239	1 375 066
1	4 765 879	1 612 293	5 352 762	1 470 622	5 648 296	1 375 071
2	4 765 845	1 612 288	5 352 732	1 470 619	5 648 262	1 375 068
3	4 765 832	1 612 286	5 352 716	1 470 617	5 648 250	1 375 067
4	4 765 824	1 612 284	5 352 712	1 470 617	5 648 244	1 375 067
5	4 765 821	1 612 284	5 352 709	1 470 616	5 648 241	1 375 066
6	4 765 820	1 612 284	5 352 708	1 470 616	5 648 241	1 375 066

Table 4.5 shows the total number of *Accumulated customer-months* and the *Accumulated customer-months* resulting from the one additional purchase made by one additional *new customer*. Simulations have been carried out for three different *life cycle durations* (6, 9, and 12 months) and for the months 1 through 6.

Your first thought upon looking at these figures may be that not much is won here: the overall size of the *Accumulated customer-months* stock is 4.7 million, and you can only see differences in the last two digits. Besides this, it is confirmed again that shorter *life cycle durations* come with less *Accumulated customer-months* and more *Accumulated purchases*. But do not rush to conclude that the effect of an additional *new customer* is negligible. After computing the differences between the respective results for the different months with the 'no additional new customer' scenario, you detect just how different the effect sizes are (Table 4.6).

Table 4.6 shows the consequences of winning one additional *new customer* in different months according to three different scenarios for *life cycle duration*: 6 months, 9 months (this is the BAU scenario), and 12 months. If you

Table 4.6 *Accumulated purchases* and *Accumulated customer-months* gained from winning one additional *new customer*

| | life cycle duration | | | | | |
| | **6** | | **9** | | **12** | |
Month	**Accumulated customer-months won**	**Accumulated purchases won**	**Accumulated customer-months won**	**Accumulated purchases won**	**Accumulated customer-months won**	**Accumulated purchases won**
1	61	10	54	6	57	5
2	27	5	24	3	23	2
3	14	3	8	1	11	1
4	6	1	4	1	5	1
5	3	1	1	0	2	0
6	2	1	0	0	2	0

could win one additional *new customer* by *advertising spending* in month 1, there would be between 5 and 10 additional *Accumulated purchases* recorded at the end of the year (depending on the assumed *life cycle duration*). Since one of these purchases corresponds to the *new customer* attracted by advertising, the other ones only purchased because of this individual acting as a diffusion agent. The additional *Accumulated customer-months* vary less between the *life cycle duration* scenarios. If *life cycle duration* is 12 months, you win a total of 57; recall that with the *life cycle duration* being as long as the simulation's time horizon, there is not much repurchasing. If *life cycle duration* is six months, many more *Current customers* leave, become *Potential customers* again, and then some of them repurchase earlier, while others repurchase later. The fact that only a fraction of the individuals who return to the stock of *Potential customers* and then repurchase immediately explains why you acquire more *Accumulated customer-months* with a *life cycle duration* of 12 months than with nine months. At 12 months, hardly any *Current customers* leave; at nine months, quite a few will leave but only part of them repurchase in the brief remaining simulation time. At six months, the remaining months are enough to have a significant fraction repurchase.

You conclude that hypothesis H 4.8 is supported: 'buying' additional *new customers* by advertising earlier yields more additional *new customers* due to word-of-mouth dynamics. And as stated in H 4.9, this effect is stronger when *life cycle duration* is shorter.

Advertising as well as the word-of-mouth dynamics address *Potential customers*. Consequently, if efforts are to be made to accelerate the dynamics because winning *Current customers* earlier in the year leads to increased *revenues*, then *advertising spending* should occur as early as possible.

Word-of-mouth is cheap – it is, in principle, free. Advertising is not. The question becomes: how to compare the value of additional *customer-months* to *advertising spending*? This leads you to recognize that you need to incorporate more financial variables, i.e. *prices*, *revenues*, and *costs*, into the discussion and the model.

4.7 Chapter summary

Advertising spending is useful for making *Potential customers* become *new customers* earlier than they would have been when word-of-mouth diffusion is the only existing mechanism for persuading them to buy your product. Therefore, advertising is only effective when there are sufficient *Potential customers*. Since its effect is an accelerated depletion of *Potential customers*, the effectiveness of *advertising spending* and of word-of-mouth promotion will decrease faster than without *advertising spending*.

Advertising is now integrated in your set of management decisions to achieve the highest possible *Accumulated purchases* and *Accumulated customer-months*. However, without taking account of *sales price* and *subscription rate*, you cannot tell how exactly the flows and the accumulation of financial resources are affected by advertising. This will be looked at in the next chapter.

4.8 Questions and challenges

Questions

1. Does *advertising spending* make people purchase <u>more</u> or purchase <u>earlier</u>? Explain.
2. Explain how *advertising spending* can <u>increase</u> the effect of word-of-mouth.
3. How does *advertising spending* affect *Accumulated customer-months*?
4. Is the impact of *advertising spending* on *Accumulated customer-months* constant or does it change over time? Explain.
5. Why can *advertisement spending* only affect *Accumulated purchases* when the *life cycle duration* is limited?
6. Why is *advertising spending* effective and worthwhile only in the initial months?
7. Why does *advertising spending* in one month <u>decrease</u> the effectiveness of *advertising spending* in a later month?
8. How can *advertising spending* with limited *life cycle duration* <u>increase</u> *Accumulated purchases*?
9. How does the formulation and evaluation of hypotheses help to understand the behavioural implications of the causal structure of your management situation?
10. What does the simulated model behaviour tell you?
11. What is the process of iterative hypothesis development?

Challenges

In Chapter 3, DIY 3.2 and DIY 3.3 dealt with two ways the susceptible *population* may change: drawing in additional *Potential customers* and losing *Current customers*. Assume that, in addition to the limited *life cycle duration*, there was a steady inflow of 100 000 additional Potential customers per month. How would that affect the impact of *advertising spending* on *Accumulated customer-months* and *Accumulated purchases*? You can find the solution on the book's companion website.

References

Dent, J. 2011. *Distribution Channels: Understanding and Managing Channels to Market*, 2nd edn. Kogan Page, London.

Homer, J.B. 1996. Why We Iterate: Scientific Modeling in Theory and Practice. *System Dynamics Review*, **12**(1): 1–19.

Mass, N.J. 1991. Diagnosing surprise model behavior: a tool for evolving behavioral and policy insights. *System Dynamics Review*, **7**(1): 68–86.

Mayer, R.E. 2006. Cognitive theory of multimedia learning. In Meyer R.E. (ed), *The Cambridge Handbook of Multimedia Learning*. Cambridge University Press, Cambridge, pp. 1–31.

Rogers, E.M. 2013. *The Diffusion of Innovations*, 5th edn. Free Press, New York, NY.

Sterman, J.D. 2000. Learning In and About Complex Systems. *Reflections*, **1**(3): 24–51.4.9

Worksheet DIY 4.1:
The expected effect of *advertising spending* with an unlimited *life cycle duration*

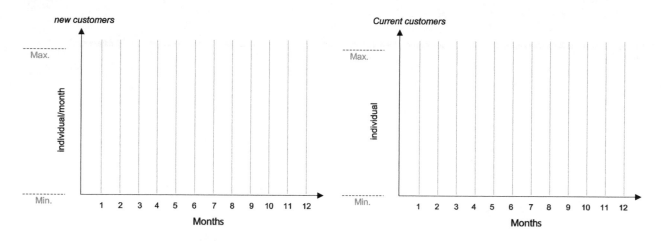

Your hypotheses:

Your assessment of your hypotheses after simulation:

Worksheet DIY 4.2:
Does a change in *life cycle duration* change the effect of *advertising spending* on *customer-months*?

How does <u>increasing</u> or <u>decreasing</u> *advertising spending* lead to different consequences for *Accumulated customer-months* and *Accumulated purchases, contingent* on different values of *life cycle duration*?

Your hypotheses:

(Continue on next page.)

Worksheet DIY 4.2:

Does a change in *life cycle duration* change the effect of *advertising spending* on *customer-months*? (continued)

Draw the expected (dotted line) and the simulated behaviour (solid line) for *advertisement spendings* of $0 and $1 million in these graphs, then continue on next page.

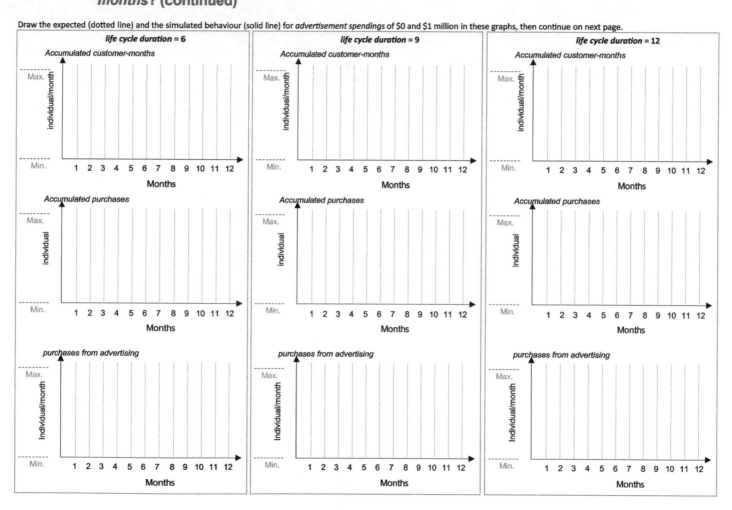

Worksheet DIY 4.2:
Does a change in *life cycle duration* change the effect of *advertising spending* on *customer-months*? (continued)

Compare your expected behaviours to the simulated ones in terms of slope, mode (exponential, goal-seeking), peaks and inflection points. If there are significant differences, explain them by means of the causal structure:

Worksheet DIY 4.3:
The effect of a single month *advertising spending* on *Accumulated customer-months* and *Accumulated purchases*

Record the end values of both variables for each of the simulations:

Accumulated customer-months		advertising spending		
		0	$ 500,000	$ 1,000,000
Month of advertising spending	1			
	2			
	3			
	4			

Accumulated purchases		advertising spending		
		0	$ 500,000	$ 1,000,000
Month of advertising spending	1			
	2			
	3			
	4			

Graph the values from the tables:

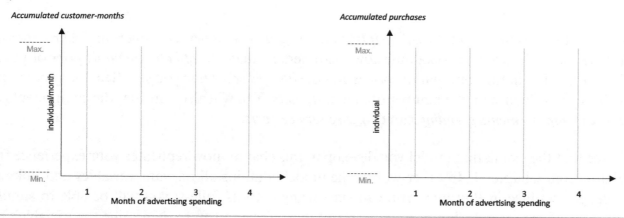

Accumulated customer-months

Accumulated purchases

By which sequence of causal relationships does the month of *advertising spending* affect *Accumulated customer-months* and *Accumulated purchases*?

FINANCIAL RESOURCES

5.1 Introduction

This chapter deals with NewTel's *revenues*, *costs*, and *profits*: the accumulation of *financial resources* in general. It poses the questions: What drives *revenues* and *costs*? How do *revenues* and *cost* relate to the variables from the previous chapters?

You will explore how the *sales price* and the *subscription rate*, together with *new customers* and *Current customers*, influence NewTel's *revenues*. You will also examine how customers evaluate the *effective monthly price* of purchasing and using mobile phones. It will turn out that the *prices* and the *life cycle duration* you set affect the *effective monthly price* and, hence, have an influence on the number of *new customers*. You will also consider the components of *total costs* and how *process improvements spending* can <u>decrease</u> *service costs*.

Overall, you will see that the simulation model you develop in this chapter now replicates your experience from the SellPhone simulator from Chapter 1. In other words, the model contains all relevant variables and links to fully describe the challenge you face in Plutonia. You can start using it to its fullest; you will be able to simulate the multiple simultaneous effects of changing one decision variable, allowing you to determine the variable's optimal value.

Growth Dynamics in New Markets: Improving Decision Making through Simulation Model-based Management,
First Edition. Martin F.G. Schaffernicht and Stefan N. Groesser.
© 2018 John Wiley & Sons Ltd. Published 2018 by John Wiley & Sons Ltd.
Companion website: www.wiley.com/go/Schaffernicht/growth-dynamics

5.2 The structure of *revenues*

5.2.1 The direct influence of *prices* on *revenues*

NewTel's telephone service is appreciated by part of Plutonia's *population* and, therefore, they are willing to pay for your service. You have two revenue streams: *new customers* pay the *sales price* upon purchasing the mobile phone and *Current customers* pay a *subscription rate* for its use. There are multiple other examples of payment before consumption or use: eating at a fast food restaurant, watching a movie, getting fuel for your car, buying at the supermarket, purchasing a watch, or buying a car. Payment during use occurs in cases such as renting a flat, TV and internet subscriptions, or insurance policies. In some cases, both forms appear together. For instance, when you buy a new car, the warranty requires you visit a certified garage regularly. In your mobile telephony market in Plutonia, customers pay the *sales price* for the phone at the beginning of the contract and then a fixed monthly *subscription rate* for the service. Keep in mind that there is no prepaid telephone service available.

NewTel's *total revenues* are the sum of revenues stemming from the *sales price* paid by each month's *new customers* and from the *subscription rates* received from each *Current customer* each month. You decide the *sales price* and the *subscription rate* for each month, and, of course, you will do that with the structure of both revenue streams in mind. If it turns out that customers react quickly to price changes, you might consider weekly decisions. However, in the context of this book, you would have to make 52 decisions in the SellPhone simulator, which tests your patience and endurance. All the content and principles discussed up to here are also valid when decisions are taken once a month.

From **Guideline 3** (Chapter 2), you know that when a resource or a factor is recognized as relevant, it must be included in the model. Since this section addresses *revenues*, you need to add the following variables to the existing model: *sales price, subscription rate, monthly profit, revenues, Accumulated profits*, and intermediate variables that help to clearly visualize the logic. Figure 5.1 represents NewTel's *revenues* and the variables they depend on. It is an important first step towards a new incarnation of your model you developed in previous chapters. Associated costs are discussed in the next section. The model file name is 'C5 Financial resources'.

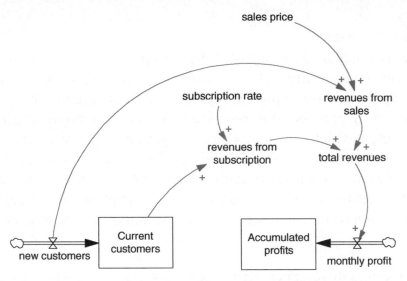

Figure 5.1 The *total revenues*, their sources, and their influence on *Accumulated profits*

The monthly *total revenues* add up the *revenues from sales* and the *revenues from subscription*. *Revenues from sales* depend on the number of monthly *new customers* and the *sales price*. Your *revenues from subscription* depend on *Current customers* and the *subscription rate*. *Total revenues* add to NewTel's *monthly profit* flow, which adds to the *Accumulated profits*. The *monthly profit* is also influenced by *costs* and is discussed in Section 5.3. Equation (5.1) describes this in other, precise, words:

$$total\ revenues[\$ / \text{month}] = new\ customers[\text{individual} / \text{month}] * sales\ price[\$ / \text{individual}] +$$
$$Current\ customers[\text{individual}] * subscription\ rate[\$ / \text{individual}] \qquad (5.1)$$

However, if all revenue calculations were performed in one equation, the diagram would be less explicit and it would not be able to differentiate between *revenues from sales* or *revenues from subscription*, i.e. without referring each time to '*new customers × sales price*' or '*Current customers × subscription rate*'. As suggested in **Guideline 2**

(Chapter 2), it is good modelling practice to explicate all relevant system structures. Following this advice, Equations (5.2), (5.3), and (5.4) are written:

$$total\ revenues[\$/month] = revenues\ from\ sales[\$/month] + revenues\ from\ subscription[\$/month] \tag{5.2}$$

$$revenues\ from\ sales[\$/month] = new\ customers[individual/month] * sales\ price[\$/individual] \tag{5.3}$$

$$revenues\ from\ subscription[\$/month] = Current\ customers[individual] * subscription\ rate[\$/individual] \tag{5.4}$$

Initially, the *sales price* is $50 per phone and the *subscription rate* is $20 per phone per month. Of course, when one of these variables increases, *revenues* will increase, and any decrease in one of these *prices* or, for that matter, in *new customers* or *Current customers* would reduce *revenues*. Since your objective of achieving the highest possible *Accumulated profits* depends on *total revenues*, Equations (5.2)–(5.4) suggest that it would be beneficial to have the highest possible numbers of *new customers* and *Current customers* at the highest possible *sales price* and *subscription rate*.

But you cannot directly determine the monthly number of *new customers* or the number of *Current customers*. All you can do is have some influence on their decisions by using those of your decision variables that are perceived by the Plutonians. As became clear in Chapter 3, changes in *life cycle duration* have two different effects. Increasing *life cycle duration* increases *new customers* and decreases *Current customers*; and decreasing *life cycle duration* has the opposite effect. *Current customers* and *new customers* change in opposite directions. Therefore, you need to carefully assess how the resulting changes in *Current customers* and *new customers* would play out.

In addition, everything that affects the costs people face when buying and using mobile phones will influence *Potential customers'* purchasing decisions. If phones become more expensive due to an increase in *sales price*, fewer *Potential customers* will be converted by word-of-mouth or advertising. Increasing the *sales price* risks diminishing *new customers* and *revenues from sales* may increase less than expected because it depends on the multiplication of these two variables (Equation (5.3). Similarly, <u>increasing</u> the *subscription rate* results in <u>fewer</u> *new customers*. <u>Fewer new customers</u> also mean <u>fewer</u> *Current customers*. And since all customers – you assume that there are no relevant differences between individual customers with respect to their decision behaviour – consider the *subscription rate*, too, <u>increasing</u> the *subscription rate* is likely to have the same effect as <u>increasing</u> the *sales price*. What combination of *sales price* and *subscription rate* will yield the highest *revenues*?

The answer to this question depends on the effect of your *prices* on *Potential customers'* purchasing decisions. Understanding these effects is essential to being able to purposefully influence your *revenues*; therefore, you need to understand them before continuing. Of course, *profits* are also influenced by *costs*, and your assessment of the combined effects of changes in the decision variables needs to also account for *costs*. Section 5.3 looks at this in detail.

5.2.2 The indirect influence of *price* and *life cycle duration* on *Potential customers'* purchasing decisions

As mentioned previously, to assess the effect of price changes on *revenues* and *profits*, you first have to understand how different price levels influence *Potential customers'* decisions to become *new customers*. After all, *revenue from sales* is *sales price* multiplied by the number of *new customers*. And as you already know, the relationship ought to be inverse: when the *sales price* is perceived to <u>increase</u>, the number of individuals who decide to purchase in a month will <u>decrease</u>.

NewTel's marketing research suggests that the individuals base their decisions on the *effective monthly price* (or *EMP*), i.e. the monthly *subscription rate* plus a fraction of the *purchasing price*. This fraction is calculated as the *purchase price* divided by the *life cycle duration*:

$$\textit{effective monthly price}[\$/\text{individual}] = \textit{sales price}[\$/\text{individual}]/\textit{life cycle duration}[\text{month}]+ \\ \textit{subscription rate}[\$/\text{individual}] \tag{5.5}$$

Figure 5.2 shows the causal structure implied by Equation (5.5).

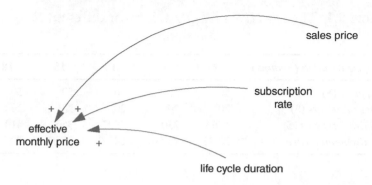

Figure 5.2 Causal structure of the *effective monthly price* (EMP)

This way to look at how expensive a mobile phone is allows the comparison of the commercial conditions offered by different companies, even if they include different *life cycle durations*. For instance, if NewTel and RivTel have identical *sales prices* and *subscription rates*, but NewTel's *life cycle duration* is 12 months whereas RivTel's is nine months, then NewTel's *effective monthly price* will be less than RivTel's, even if the total sum of amounts paid by customers is still the same.

Given the current assumptions, the *effective monthly price* is $50 divided by 9 plus $20 (Equation (5.5)), which yields $25.56. At this *effective monthly price*, all the individuals who feel tempted by the *word-of-mouth* diffusion or of *advertising*, will do so: they feel a want to own the product and they are not put off by the *price* it takes. This means that a <u>lower</u> *effective monthly price* would not <u>increase</u> *new customers*. However, a higher *effective monthly price* would <u>decrease</u> *new customers*.

How does the *life cycle duration* influence the *effective monthly price*? Table 5.1 shows how different *life cycle durations* lead to different *effective monthly prices* – while holding *sales price* and *subscription rate* constant.

The *effective total cost* <u>diminishes</u> by $60, from $230 to $170, when *life cycle duration* is <u>reduced</u> from nine to six months. And vice versa, <u>increasing</u> the *life cycle duration* by three months <u>increases</u> the *effective total cost* by $60.

Table 5.1 The *effective monthly prices* for different *life cycle durations*

life cycle duration (months)	6	9	12	15	18
sales price ($)	50	50	50	50	50
subscription rate ($)	20	20	20	20	20
effective total cost ($)	170	230	290	350	410
effective monthly price ($)	28.33	25.56	24.17	23.33	22.78

Customers are rational enough to compute the *effective monthly price* and perceive that <u>reducing</u> the *life cycle duration* <u>increases</u> the *effective monthly price* because the *sales price* is spread over <u>fewer</u> months. Figure 5.3 shows this relationship.

In Figure 5.3, the horizontal axis represents the range of possible values for the *life cycle duration* and the vertical axis represents the *effective monthly price*. By associating the *effective monthly prices* of the five different *life cycle durations* from Table 5.1, the figure visualizes the inverse relationship. In terms of the language used in this book, there is a causal link with a negative polarity between *life cycle duration* and *effective monthly price*.

The question is then just how the *effective monthly price* is considered in the Plutonians' purchasing decisions. Assume that people react to the absolute level of the *effective monthly price*; this means that if someone finds, say, $30 per month 'too expensive', but $26 per month 'affordable', and NewTel's *effective monthly prices* <u>increases</u> from $26 to $30, then this individual will not buy a mobile phone; the reason will not be the fact that it has become more expensive (the change) but the absolute level of the *effective monthly price*.

Further assume that small differences of *effective monthly prices* make only little difference for people. It will only matter to a small portion of the *Potential customers* if the *effective monthly price* is $26 or $26.2, for example. This is a sensible assumption: mobile telephony is new in Plutonia and using such a device affords status to its owner,

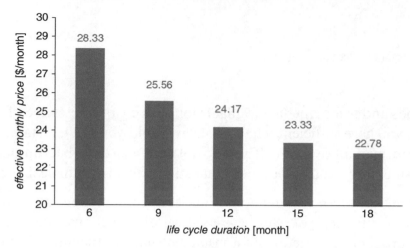

Figure 5.3 <u>Increasing</u> the *life cycle duration* <u>lowers</u> the *effective monthly price*

and, for this reason, the *effective monthly price* must <u>become</u> quite expensive before it turns off a substantial portion of interested individuals.

Sometimes, how customers react to what they have to pay is conceived of as 'elasticity': the elasticity expresses the percentage of behaviour change in response to a percentage of change in costs. For instance, an elasticity of one would mean: if the *effective monthly price* <u>increases</u> by 10%, then *new customers* <u>decreases</u> by 10%. Elasticity can be less than one when people's reaction is relatively small, or larger than one if people react strongly. However, according to this logic, the strength of the reaction would not depend on the absolute level of the *effective monthly price*: a 5% change starting from $26 would lead to the same relative change in *new customers* as if it started from $34.

But you are assuming that the reaction of Plutonians is more complex. Therefore, you will use a device that can represent the nonlinear relationship between *effective monthly price* and *new customers*.

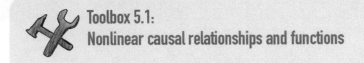

Toolbox 5.1:
Nonlinear causal relationships and functions

Different methods and techniques are available for working out the shape of the relationship between two variables. If you have sufficient reliable data available, you can use statistical methods to estimate this shape in the form of an equation. If you do not have such data, but time and money are sufficiently available, you can gather the data you need and still perform a statistical estimation.

The resulting equation will be a 'function'. Functions convert input into output. If you are familiar with a spreadsheet software, you will have used certain functions. And, yes, mathematics is a field where functions are rigorously defined: for instance, 'sum' is a function which takes two or more input values and returns one output value. In your model, you can also think of *purchases from WoM* as a function of *Current customers*, *potential customers fraction*, *contact rate*, and *conversion fraction WoM*.

However, there are situations when extensive data sampling is not feasible or when the efforts required would outweigh the benefits. In such cases, use the best judgement of experts in the field to approximate the shape of a nonlinear relationship (Ford and Sterman, 1997). The resulting functions are sometimes referred to as 'table functions', 'graphical functions', or 'lookup functions'. These names stress a kind of representation of the searched function; however, both graphical and table formats are typically used together. Independently of the name, they usually represent nonlinear relationships, and frequently these representations are based on expert estimates (Sterman, 2000). Figure 5.4 gives an example.

Figure 5.4 illustrates the essential steps when using expert estimations. Step 1 is to define the range of feasible input values: what is the smallest possible value the input variable can take? What is the greatest possible value? If this range is defined too narrowly, the experts' best judgement will only cover part of the values the input variable might assume in reality and in a simulation. If the range is set too wide, then the experts will tell you.

Step 2 is to ask each expert to indicate the output values that are typically observed for different input values. Experts are often able to draw a curve such as the grey curves in Figure 5.4. Most often,

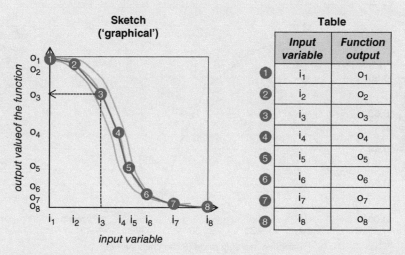

Figure 5.4 Capturing the shape of nonlinear relationships

different experts draw slightly different curves. However, an average can be determined and a representative curve (black in Figure 5.4) can be drawn. This curve is the best available estimate of the relationship.

Step 3 is to set a series of points on the nonlinear shape such that the lines between the points replicates the nonlinear shape of the relationship. These points can then be transferred to the modelling software. You can find a tutorial for nonlinear relationships on the companion website.

Step 4 is when the modelling software uses the data to compute the variables' values during simulations. Your estimated curve is stored in a table. For each cycle of the simulation, the input variable's current value is searched for in the input variable's column of this table. If the table contains exactly this value, then the output value is read from the output column in the same row of the table. If the input value is in between two of the stored data points, then the software interpolates the corresponding output value. Therefore, it is important to define enough data points to achieve a close enough fit between the interpolated lines and the originally estimated nonlinear shape.

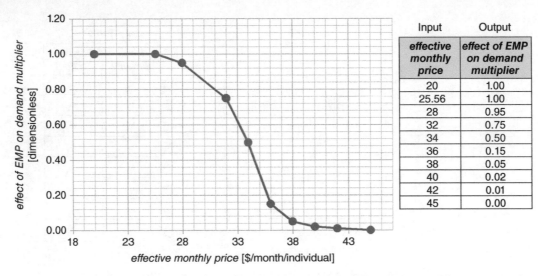

Input	Output
effective monthly price	effect of EMP on demand multiplier
20	1.00
25.56	1.00
28	0.95
32	0.75
34	0.50
36	0.15
38	0.05
40	0.02
42	0.01
45	0.00

Figure 5.5 The nonlinear relationship between *effective monthly price* and the *effect of EMP on demand multiplier*

Figure 5.5 displays the different values of the *effect of EMP on demand* which correspond to the values of *effective monthly price*.

As mentioned above, at an *effective monthly price* lower than $26, no *Potential customer* will refrain from purchasing. At a level of $30 per month, 10% of the *Potential customers* who are keen to have a mobile phone because of the word-of-mouth or the advertising will not purchase this month. When *effective monthly price* is $32 per month, more than 25% of the possible *new customers* will not purchase in that month. Only 50% of the potential *new customers* will become *Current customers* if the *effective monthly price* rises as high as $34 per month, and this percentage falls 25% at $38 per month. This inverted S-shape means that smaller increases of the *effective monthly price* provoke little reaction, but the decrease in customer accrual accelerates as *effective monthly price* continues to rise.

Figure 5.6 displays the causal structure of how the *effective monthly price* modifies the *purchases from WoM* and *purchases from advertising*.

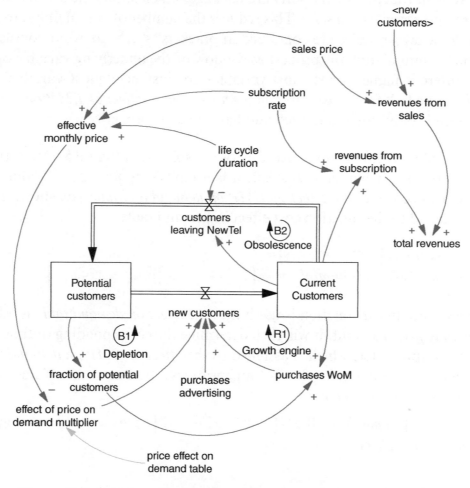

Figure 5.6 A <u>higher</u> *effective monthly price* <u>reduces</u> *new customers*

Figure 5.6 contains some details that require explanation. Firstly, in the upper right corner of the diagram, there is <*new customers*>; this is a so-called 'shadow variable' – it is just a visual copy of the already existing variable *new customers*. This is a convenient function of the software package, which allows the avoidance of a causal link from the *new customers* flow rate to *revenue from sales*. This reduces the number of causal links crossing over the diagram making it hard to read. Shadow variables are contained in brackets '<…>' to avoid confusion. If you click on a shadow variable with the 'equation' tool, the properties window of the underlying variable opens. Other modelling software packages use different names for shadow variables, for instance 'ghost variable', but their function is always the same. Secondly, the link from *cost effect on demand table* to *effect of EMP on demand multiplier* is grey to indicate that information is only stored and used and has no real causal effect.

The cost effect on demand table stores the nonlinear function displayed in Figure 5.5. It is, therefore, not a normal variable in the sense as defined in Chapter 1. Instead, it is a repository for the *x*-*y*-values of the function and, thereby, enables the model to compute the *effect of EMP on demand multiplier*, as shown in Equation (5.6). The *effective monthly price* is passed to the function cost effect in demand table:

$$effect\ of\ EMP\ on\ demand\ multiplier\,[\text{dimensionless}] = \\ cost\ effect\ on\ demand\ table\,(effective\ monthly\ price\,[\$/\text{individual}])\,[\text{dimensionless}] \tag{5.6}$$

Equation (5.6) shows how a nonlinear function is used: the *cost effect on demand table* is a 'function' that is given the value of *effective monthly price* as input. It will then determine the corresponding output value according to the table and then return this output value, which is assigned to the *effect of EMP on demand multiplier*. The unit of measure of *effect of EMP on demand multiplier* is 'dimensionless' because it is a fraction that will be used to calculate the monthly values of *new customers*:

$$new\ customers\,[\text{individual/month}] = (purchases\ WoM\,[\text{individual/month}] + purchases\ advertising\,[\text{individual/month}])* \\ effect\ of\ price\ on\ demand\ multiplier\,[\text{dimensionless}] \tag{5.7}$$

Equation 5.7 indicates that if the *effective monthly price* increases due to a higher *sales price* or *subscription rate* or a shorter *life cycle duration*, then *new customers* will be lower than it otherwise would have been. For example, if *purchases WoM* and *purchases advertising* add up to 1000 individuals, and the *effective monthly price* is $25.56, then the *effect of price on demand multiplier* is equal to one and there will be 1000 *new customers*. However, if the *effective monthly price* is $34, then the *effect of price on demand multiplier* is equal to 0.5, and therefore there will be only 5000 *new customers*.

5.2.3 How the *effective monthly price* affects *new customers* and *total revenues*

Which combination of *purchase price, subscription rate*, and *life cycle duration*, i.e. which *effective monthly price*, leads to the highest possible *revenue*? You know that a higher *effective monthly price* increases the *revenues from sales*, but at the same time it decreases the *effect of EMP on demand multiplier* and, thereby, decreases *new customers*; it also reduces the number of *Current customers*, which also affects *total revenues* via *sales from subscriptions*. Moreover, changes in *life cycle duration* not only affect the *effective monthly price* but also change the dynamics between *new customers* and *Current customers*.

If a rise of, say, 10% in *effective monthly price* triggers a decrease of 10% in the *effect of EMP on demand multiplier*, you might believe the *revenues* would not change. However, the relationship between *effective monthly price* and the *cost effect on demand* is nonlinear (Figure 5.5). If your *revenues from sales* are defined as *new customers* multiplied by *sales price*, and a given *sales price* increase leads to a smaller decrease in *new customers*, you would consider this a good decision because *revenues from sales* would increase. But if you assess the effects of changes in *effective monthly price* erroneously, *revenues from sales* might actually decrease. To avoid wrong decisions when changing variables which affect *effective monthly price*, you need to understand how they impact the *revenues from sales*.

It is not possible to directly set the *effective monthly price* and look for its effect on revenue; instead, you have to search for the best combination in a space with three dimensions, defined by the *sales price, subscription rate*, and *life cycle duration*. This space has many combinations: there are 13 possible *life cycle durations*, 71 possible *sales prices*, and 21 different values for the *subscription rate*, resulting in about 8500 combinations (Table 5.2).

Table 5.2 Search space for the optimal *effective monthly price*

Variable	Value range		Number of combinations
	Minimum	**Maximum**	
sales price ($)	40	70	31
subscription rate ($)	10	30	21
life cycle duration (months)	6	18	13
Combinations			8463

In principle, *sales price* can vary between $0 and $70, and the *subscription rate* between $0 and $30. However, *sales prices* below $40 and *subscription rates* below $10 are not very promising because of the *purchasing cost* of $40 and *service costs* of $10 per phone per month – charging <u>lower</u> prices would be 'dumping'; while it is not illegal and can be used as a competitive means against rivals, it inevitably means financial loss, and you can be sure that such low prices will not be the ones that maximize your *Accumulated profits*. *Life cycle duration* can vary between 6 and 18 months. The fact that these three decision variables combine in the *effective monthly price* allows the analysis to be simplified:

If any <u>increase</u> in *effective monthly price* offsets at least part of the direct revenue effect of an <u>increase</u> in *sales price* or *subscription rate*, this effect will be transmitted by *effective monthly price*, which does not have many different values. The maximum value of *effective monthly price* is $42, i.e. maximum *subscription rate* plus *sales price* divided by minimum *life cycle duration*. An *effective monthly price* <u>less</u> than $25.56 would <u>not</u> yield <u>more</u> *new customers*: due to income levels and distribution in Plutonia, at that *effective monthly price* nobody would find it too expensive. Therefore, it is not worth while trying if combinations resulting in a lower *effective monthly price* would lead to <u>higher</u> *Accumulated profits*.

This means that <u>reducing</u> the *sales price* or the *subscription rate* below their default values <u>will not increase</u> NewTel's *new customers*. Therefore, the resulting number of reasonable combinations is 3003. *Life cycle duration* has not only an effect on *effective monthly price* but also changes *customers leaving* and, thereby, the proportions between *new customers* and *Current customers*: a <u>shorter</u> *life cycle duration* leads to <u>less</u> *Current customers* and <u>more</u> *new customers* and a <u>longer</u> *life cycle duration* has the opposite consequence. If you expect that a <u>longer</u> *life cycle duration* will <u>reduce</u> the *effective monthly price* below the value $25.56 – where it will <u>not increase</u> the number of *new customers* – and at the same time <u>increase</u> the number of *Current customers* who pay the *subscription rate* for an increased number of months, this is reason enough to evaluate different values of *life cycle duration*.

You can exploit this causal structure to perform a preliminary exploration of a value range of *effective monthly price* that are likely to <u>increase</u> your *Accumulated profits*. To do so, you compute a list of *effective monthly price* values for each combination of *sales price, subscription rate*, and *life cycle duration*. You can download this example from the companion website which can be found in the spreadsheet file 'Section 5_2_3 combinations for EMP'. Once the rows are ordered by ascending values of *effective monthly price*, delete the rows where *effective monthly price* <25.56 (because the *effect of EMP on demand multiplier* cannot grow beyond the value of 1, which it has for this *effective monthly price*) and then use the lookup table (Toolbox 5.1) from Figure 5.5 to find the corresponding values of *cost effect on demand*. Multiplying of *effective monthly price* and the *cost effect of demand multiplier* yields a number which represents one month's *revenues from sales*. You know that in the business as usual scenario (BAU), this is $25.56. If *effective monthly price* multiplied by the *cost effect of demand multiplier* < $25.56, it means that you would <u>lose</u> *revenues from sales*. If *effective monthly price* multiplied by the *cost effect of demand multiplier* > $25.56, you would <u>gain</u> *revenues from sales*. However, this calculation is carried out without considering the consumer dynamics triggered by changing *new customers* and what it implies for *total revenues* when combined with the respective *sales price* and *subscription rate*.

Figure 5.7 displays the results of the corresponding calculations for all indicated combinations of *effective monthly price* and *effect of EMP on demand multiplier*. On the horizontal axis, you see a range of values for the *effective monthly price*. The vertical axis shows the values of *effective monthly price* multiplied by the *price effect of demand multiplier*. This indicates for each value of the *effective monthly price* if the combined effect of <u>increasing</u> the *effective monthly price* and thereby <u>decreasing</u> the *effect of EMP on demand multiplier* would be <u>larger than</u> the initial *effective monthly price*.

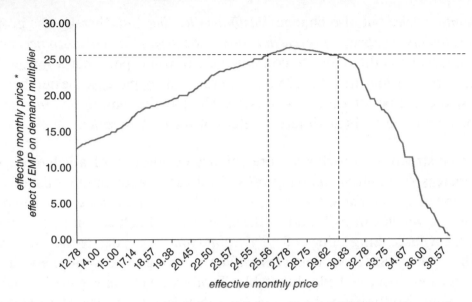

Figure 5.7 The *effective monthly price* and the *effect of EMP on demand multiplier*

The horizontal axis in Figure 5.7 represents the *effective monthly price* and the vertical axis displays values resulting from multiplying the *effective monthly price* with the *effect of EMP on demand multiplier*. The leftmost vertical dotted line in Figure 5.7 indicates the BAU value for the *effective monthly price*, which corresponds to the BAU scenario for *sales price*, *subscription rate*, and *life cycle duration*. The height of the curve for this *effective monthly price* (where the vertical dotted line crosses the horizontal dotted line) is identical to the *effective monthly price*. If the *effective monthly price* <u>decreases</u>, the curve is <u>below</u> the horizontal dotted line: your *revenues* would be <u>less</u> than in the BAU case (because the *effective monthly price* is <u>lower</u>, but the *effect of EMP on demand multiplier* <u>cannot rise</u> over 1, so the result of the multiplication is less than for the BAU value). Right of the second vertical dotted line, the *effective monthly price* is <u>greater than $30.8</u>. The resulting *effect of EMP on demand multiplier* is so <u>low</u> that again the multiplied value is below the horizontal dotted line: you would <u>lose</u> *revenues*. If you continue <u>increasing</u>

the *effective monthly price*, the *effect of EMP on demand multiplier* <u>decreases steeply</u>. The graph is not perfectly continuous because the underlying data, i.e. the combinations of *sales price*, *subscription rate*, and *life cycle duration*, vary in larger steps. This does not affect the relevant insights to be gained: all the combinations leading to a <u>smaller</u> *effective monthly price* <u>reduce</u> the value of *effective monthly price* multiplied by *price effect on demand* meaning that *revenues* <u>diminish</u>. Figure 5.7 also shows that some values of *effective monthly price* >25.56 would indeed <u>increase</u> *revenues from sales*; however, the maximum is attained somewhere between 27 and 28, and around *effective monthly price* = 30, the value is back to 25.56.

This means that if the *effective monthly price* which *Potential customers* perceive <u>rises</u> beyond $30, you will have <u>less</u> *new customers* than you would have had otherwise. From Chapters 3 and 4 you know that each *new customer* results in *Accumulated customer-months* and attracts additional *new customers* due to the word-of-mouth dynamics. Therefore, deciding to do something that will reduce *new customers* will mean <u>less</u> *Accumulated purchases* and *Accumulated customer-months* at the end of the year. Keep this in mind when you decide on the *sales price*, the *subscription rate*, and the *life cycle duration* in Chapter 6.

From now on, the causal structure accounts for the two different *prices* and their different effects: one directly on *revenue* and the other on *new customers*. At the same time, *life cycle duration* also has two different effects, one on the flow *leaving customers*, and therefore the balance between *Current customers* and *new customers*, and the other on *new customers*. Purchases also affect the proportions between *Current customers* and *new customers*. Even though the model is currently made up of no more than 30 variables, the multiple effects resulting from any change in the decision variables *sales price*, *subscription rate*, and *life cycle duration* already makes it impossible to find out which values would yield the highest possible *Accumulated profit* for NewTel without simulating the model. In the following, we summarize some systems insights and management insights.

Systems Insight 8 (SI 8): Influences on *total revenue*
An <u>increase</u> in any of the variables *new customers*, *sales price*, *Current customers*, or *subscription rate* will <u>increase</u> the *total revenue*.

Systems Insight 9 (SI 9): Influences on *effective monthly price*

An <u>increase</u> in any of the variables *sales price, subscription rate,* or *life cycle duration* will <u>increase</u> the *effective monthly price*, which, for values over $30, will lead to a <u>decrease</u> of *new customers*.

Management Insight 8 (MI 8): Avoid low values for *effective monthly price*

A value of *effective monthly price* <u>lower than</u> $25 <u>reduces</u> *total revenues* because the <u>decrease</u> in *sales price* and/or *subscription rate* is <u>not</u> offset by an <u>increase</u> in *Accumulated purchases* or *Accumulated customer-months*. Do not go lower than $25.

Management Insight 9 (MI 9): Avoid high values for *effective monthly price*

A value of *effective monthly price* <u>higher</u> than $30 *reduces total revenues* because the <u>increase</u> in *sales price* and/or *subscription rate* is <u>more than</u> outweighed by a <u>decrease</u> in *Accumulated purchases* or *Accumulated customer-months*. The optimal combination of *sales price, subscription rate,* and *life cycle duration* is one where the corresponding *effective monthly price* is in the range between $25 and $30.

Management Insight 10 (MI 10): *Accumulated profits* **as key performance indicator (KPI)**

The diverse influences of your decision variables on customer dynamics are all summarized in *Accumulated profits*. You can therefore monitor *Accumulated profits* to know if adjustments to the decision variables' values have the desired effect.

5.3 The structure of costs

5.3.1 The components of *total costs*

NewTel invests financial resources. To sell mobile phones to *new customers*, you buy them at a unit *product cost* of $40. To serve one *Current customer* during a month, you need employees and equipment costing $10 per phone. In addition, if you decide to use *advertising spending* to speed up the acquisition of *new customers* you must spend financial resources. Remember the simplifying assumptions from Chapter 2: in real life, the unit cost of phones will not be constant but depend on the amount purchased. Furthermore, the cost of buying these phones from your

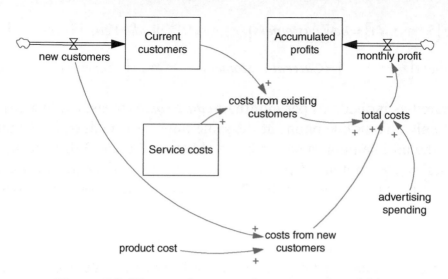

Figure 5.8 The *total costs* and connected variables

suppliers will not necessarily occur in the same month as they are sold to your *new customers*. Also, the average monthly unit cost per *Current customer* depends on NewTel's overall company size. However, all these attributes of real situations would only add unnecessary complexity to our discussion and distract your attention from the underlying dynamics and principles. Later, in Chapter 8, these assumptions will be revisited. Incorporating *costs* in the discussion means inserting some additional variables into the causal structure (Figure 5.8).

Firstly, the monthly *total costs* <u>reduces</u> your *monthly profit* and, therefore, <u>increases</u> *Accumulated profits*: the *monthly profit* flow is a net flow and could, in principle, even be negative. Equations (5.8)–(5.10) describe the behaviour of the cost related variables:

$$total\ costs[\$/\text{month}] = costs\ from\ new\ customers[\$/\text{month}] + costs\ from\ existing\ customers$$
$$[\$/\text{month}] + advertising\ spending[\$/\text{month}] \tag{5.8}$$

$$costs\ from\ new\ customers [\$/\text{month}] = new\ customers [\$/\text{month}] * product\ cost [\$/\text{month}] \tag{5.9}$$

$$costs\ from\ existing\ customers [\$/\text{month}] = Current\ customers [\$/\text{month}] * Service\ costs [\$/\text{month}] \tag{5.10}$$

New customers are measured as individuals per month, *product cost* is measured in $ per individual because one individual buys one and only one mobile phone at the same time. As explained in the introduction (Chapter 1), NewTel has to purchase the mobile phones before being able to sell them. When both variables are multiplied, mathematically 'individual' cancels out and $ per month remains, since *Current customers* are in individual units and *service costs* are $ per individual per month. The three components of *total costs* have the same unit of measure.

5.3.2 Reducing *Service costs* by improving processes

NewTel cannot reduce the unit *product cost* it pays to the producer of mobile phones. But it can invest in process improvements to diminish its *service costs*, i.e. the option is open to you to invest in activities that help NewTel keep its customers satisfied while using less actual resource. Consultants analyse and redesign your business processes, employees can be trained, and software tools can be developed or improved.

Since you have to manage NewTel for one year in Plutonia, you estimate that the *minimal service cost* cannot be below $9 per *Current customer* per month. At the beginning, there is a margin of $1 in reducing *Service costs*. It may appear to be a small number, but it means a yearly cost reduction of 10%, and if it was possible to achieve it at once, NewTel would add $1 for each customer-month to its *Accumulated profits*.

It is sensible to start process improvement with the 'low hanging fruit': if your efforts focus first on the improvements that are the easiest to achieve, then you will initially make relatively important improvements. But as you advance, it will get progressively more difficult to make additional improvements. The fact that a given amount of effort yields ever smaller progresses is often referred to as diminishing marginal returns. You can introduce it in the model in the form of an indicator of how close the current *Service costs* are to the *minimal service costs*. This indicator – the *process improvability ratio* – is current *Service costs* minus the *minimal service costs*. This describes the effect of a balancing feedback loop, where the *minimal service cost* operates as an implicit goal; if you make a progress and <u>reduce</u> *Service costs*, then the *process improvability ratio* will <u>decrease</u> and, therefore, a constant <u>amount of</u> *process improvement spending* will yield <u>decreasing</u> *reductions of service costs*. This is a balancing feedback loop with the name 'cost reduction'. *Service costs* are the only costs you can reduce in this case. The *product cost* is assumed to be constant and the *advertising spending* follows the policy you use but you cannot reduce the *cost per customer converted*. Equation (5.11) contains the 'cost reduction' loop:

$$\textit{process improvability ratio}[\text{dimensionless}] = \left(\textit{Service costs}[\$/\text{month}] - \textit{minimal service costs}[\$/\text{month}]\right)/ \\ \textit{minimal service costs}[\$/\text{month}] \tag{5.11}$$

During your first month, when *Service costs* are \$10/individual/month, the *process improvability ratio* will be a little higher than 10%. If you successfully reduce *Service costs* to, say, \$9.5, the *process improvability ratio* will decrease to around 5%. This is the 'cost reduction' feedback loop, which is a part of the situation you cannot change. The consequence of this is that a given amount of monthly *process improvement spending* will not always yield the same amount of *reduction of service costs*; rather, the amount of reduction will be modulated by the *process improvability ratio*. Figure 5.9 shows the overall logic of *reduction of service cost* by *process improvement spending*.

Figure 5.9 shows the three components of *total costs*: *costs from new customers, cost from existing customers*, and *advertising spending*. Now, there is *process improvement spending* as fourth component. It follows that using financial resources to reduce *Service costs* is a double-edged sword: it reduces *Service costs* by a given amount but at the same time it is a cost factor itself.

It is therefore important that you recognize the nonlinear nature of the relationship between *process improvement spending* and the *process improvement effect on costs*. Figure 5.10 shows how different amounts of monthly *process improvement spending* translate into *process improvement effect on costs*. The range of input values reaches is from

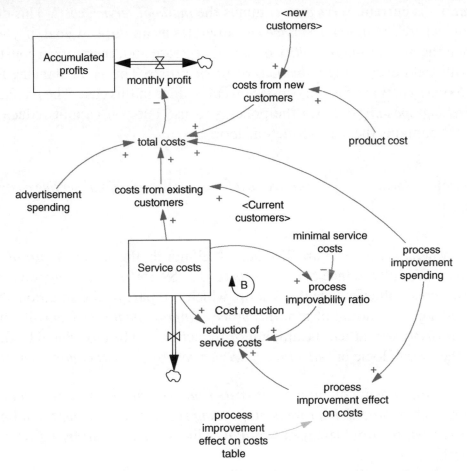

Figure 5.9 Causal structure of how *process improvement spending* <u>reduces</u> *Service costs*

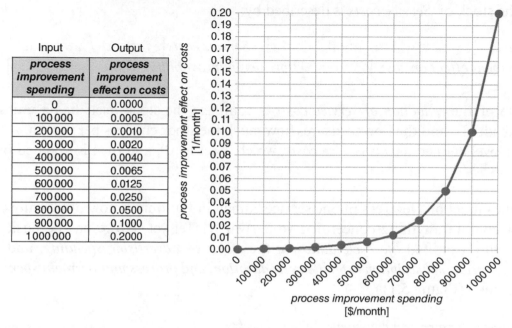

Input	Output
process improvement spending	process improvement effect on costs
0	0.0000
100 000	0.0005
200 000	0.0010
300 000	0.0020
400 000	0.0040
500 000	0.0065
600 000	0.0125
700 000	0.0250
800 000	0.0500
900 000	0.1000
1 000 000	0.2000

Figure 5.10 The nonlinear relationship between *process improvement spending* and *process improvement effect on costs*

zero to one million. The reason for the maximum value of a million per month is that internal policy (see Chapter 1) in NewTel limits *process improvement spending* in countries such as Plutonia.

In the model, this relationship is stored as a lookup function in *process improvement effect on costs table*, and it is read by the equation of *process improvement effect on costs*:

$$process\ improvement\ effect\ on\ costs\left[1/\text{month}\right] = process\ improvement\ effect\ on\ costs\ table$$
$$\left(process\ improvement\ spending\ NewTel\left[\$/\text{month}\right]\right)\left[1/\text{month}\right]$$

(5.12)

The outflow from the stock of *Service costs* is described by:

$$
\begin{aligned}
reduction\ of\ service\ costs\ [\$/\text{month}/\text{individual}/\text{month}] &= Service\ costs\,[\$/\text{month}/\text{individual}/\text{month}]\ * \\
process\ improvement\ effect\ on\ costs\,[1/\text{month}]\ * &\ process\ improvability\ ratio\,[\text{dimensionless}]
\end{aligned}
\tag{5.13}
$$

The unit of measure of the *reduction of service costs* is complex; the stock itself has a unit composed of three parts – $/month/individual – and the flow measures how much the stock changes per month. And, finally, the stock starts with an initial level defined as *init service costs*, which is set to 10, and then is updated by the flow rate over time.

The structure of your model of NewTel's phone service launch in Plutonia is now practically complete. Certainly, the model does not contain anything concerning your rival RivTel yet. However, the basic logic of the WoM diffusion dynamics with a limited *life cycle duration*, the effect of *advertising spending*, and the effects of your decision variables *sales price*, *subscription rate*, *life cycle duration*, and *process improvement spending* on *revenues* and *costs* are already included (Figure 5.11).

5.4 Behaviour: customer dynamics and the accumulation of profits

The model in its current version ('C5 Financial resources') combines the word-of-mouth dynamics, the limited *life cycle duration*, the possible advertising with the monthly cash flow (*revenues* and *costs*), and the accumulation of *profits* over the year. The new elements in the model have not changed the structure of the previous models. The introduction of the *effective monthly price* and the *effect of EMP on demand multiplier* should not affect the customer's dynamics as long as you keep the default values of your decision variables.

In Chapter 1, you have used the SellPhone simulator in a BAU scenario, where *sales price* = $50, *subscription rate* = $20, and *life cycle duration* = 9 months. Further, there was neither *advertising spending* nor *process improvement spending*. If the current simulation model is to be used to find the combination of decision variables which leads to

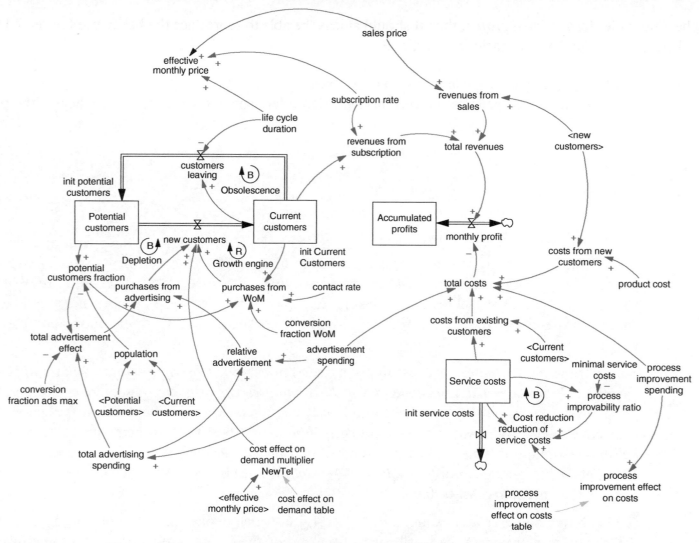

Figure 5.11 Causal structure of NewTel's challenge without competitor

the highest possible *Accumulated profits*, then it should at least be able to reproduce the behaviours observed when you worked through the BAU scenario in SellPhone.

Guideline 8 (G 8): Replicate past behaviour to gain confidence
Before using a model to design policies for your organization's development, make sure it replicates the past behaviours.

DIY 5.1:
Contrasting the model behaviour with the SellPhone BAU scenario

In this chapter, we have looked at the logic of a series of new variables and the operational details in the equations and figures. Now, you are ready to integrate these new elements. Make a copy of your model from Chapter 4 and add the new stocks, flows, intermediate variables, and causal links, so that the resulting model resembles the one displayed in Figure 5.11. If you are not sure how to specify the details of the nonlinear functions, please use the tutorial from the book's companion website.

Simulate the model under BAU assumptions: *sales price* = 50, *subscription rate* = 20 and *life cycle duration* = 9. No *advertising spending*, no process *improvement spending*. Also, make sure that the parameters *conversion fraction WoM* and *monthly encounters* are correctly set at 0.01 and 100, respectively. The initial value of *Current customers* should be 10 000 to be comparable with the SellPhone simulator, where the total number of *Current customers* (NewTel plus RivTel) was 10 000 at the beginning. Accordingly, *Potential customers* must be initialized with 990 000 individuals. Finally, the time step must be 0.0625.

Go back to Chapter 1 and examine Figures 1.4–1.6, which depict the behaviour observed in the SellPhone simulator. Use the work sheet at the end of the Chapter to record when the inflexion point is reached and how many *Current customers* there are at the end of the year. Also record the *Accumulated profits* achieved by the end of the year. Copy the graphs of *Current customers* and *monthly profits*. Then, record the same information from the simulation of your current model and compare both sets of information.

In Chapter 1, the BAU scenario generated data but the model underpinning the simulation was not visible. By consequence, it is not possible to directly compare your model to the SellPhone model. Some structural differences are obvious: your current model contains neither RivTel's variables nor the variables and links needed to represent the interactions between both companies. But in the BAU scenario, both companies' decision variables had identical values, and therefore the Plutonians could not make a difference between NewTel and RivTel. Accordingly, your current model with only NewTel should generate behaviours equal to the sum of NewTel plus RivTel in the SellPhone BAU. The behaviour modes generated by your current model should be exponential when the original data is exponential, and particular moments such as inflexion points and maxima should occur at the same time.

Compare your sketched graphs of *Current customers* and *monthly profits* with the one your current model generates for both variables and answer these two questions:

Are the modes of behaviour similar (for instance: either exponential or goal-seeking)?
Are the final values of *Current customers* and *Accumulated profits* similar?

Hint: keep in mind that in Chapter 1 both NewTel and RivTel were considered, whereas the current model does not account for your rival. Use the worksheet at the end of the chapter.

Indeed, simulating the current model under the BAU assumptions generates behaviours and outcomes that are similar to the SellPhone BAU. Consider the behaviours shown in Figure 5.12.

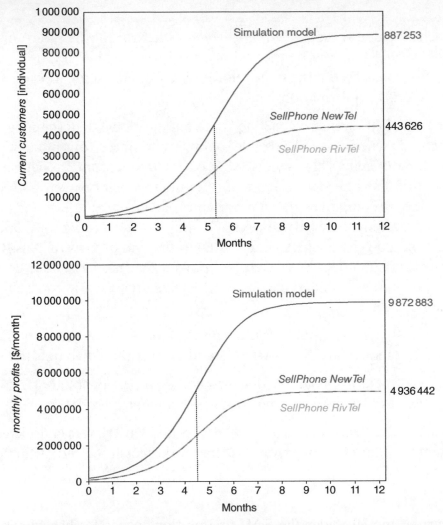

Figure 5.12 Comparison of *Current customers* and *monthly profits* between the SellPhone BAU scenario from Chapter 1 (with NewTel and RivTel) and the current simulation model

In the SellPhone simulator, NewTel had to share customers with RivTel; therefore, the graph displays the variables for both companies. In both the SellPhone BAU and your current simulation, the behaviour of *Current customers* and of *monthly profit* is clearly S-shaped. The inflection point when the number of *Current customers* stops growing exponentially and starts showing goal-seeking behaviour is marked in each graph as a dotted line. It cannot be determined with precision in the graphs, but this is possible by looking up the flows of *new customers* and *monthly profits*. When *new customers* reaches its maximum – that is, it switches from growth to decrease – then the *Current customers'* graph switches from exponential to goal-seeking growth. Subtracting the current value of *new customers* from its value at the previous time step allows you to know whether *new customers* is growing or decreasing. So if it switches from a positive difference to a negative one, you have found the two time steps delimiting the brief lapse of time during which the inflection point has been reached. Performing this process allows you to find out that for *Current customers* the point of inflection is reached between time steps 6.1875 and 6.25, that is between days 6 and 8 of the seventh month (remember that the time step is set to 0.0256 or 1/16; if a month has an average number of 30.5 days, this means that every time step corresponds to approximately two days of the month). The equivalent search in the data of *monthly profits* detects the switch from growth to decrease between time steps 5.3125 and 5.375, which corresponds to the time between days 10 and 12 of the sixth month.

The simulation model does not include RivTel, and for this reason all *new customers* become NewTel's *Current customers*. Therefore, it is not surprising that in your own simulation *Current customers* is as high as NewTel's and RivTel's from the SellPhone BAU combined. For the same reason all *monthly profits* in the simulation accrue to NewTel. Table 5.3 shows the comparison of the final outcomes in *Current customers* and *Accumulated profits*.

Table 5.3 Comparison of your simulated data with the SellPhone data
for the BAU scenario

Compared elements	SellPhone	Your current simulation model
Current customers at the end of the year (million)	0.89	0.89
Accumulated profits at the end of the year (million)	75.5	76.4

The *Current customers* and *Accumulated profits* for SellPhone reported in Table 5.3 are the sums of the data for NewTel and RivTel. Only in this circumstance can you compare the SellPhone results to the data generated by your simulation model, in which NewTel gains all the *new customers* and all the *monthly profits*. The simulation comes close to reproducing the exact number of *Current customers* at the end of the year. The difference is a consequence of the initial difference between the total number of *Current customers* in the simulation and the SellPhone data: SellPhone starts with 10 000 and your simulation with 5000. Consequently, word-of-mouth diffusion is quicker in SellPhone. *Accumulated profits* are roughly 9% lower in the simulated model. This difference is larger than the one in *Current customers*, but this again is a consequence of starting points of the simulation – SellPhone's extra 5000 *Current customers* generate more *Accumulated customer-months*. How many of these 5000 individuals will repurchase during the year once their products' *life cycle duration* is over? If you multiply these numbers with the $10 of profit coming in for each customer-month and for each purchase, you can probably see that there must be a difference in *Accumulated profits*.

To conclude this chapter, let us take a closer look at the way in which monthly *revenues* and *costs* combine into *monthly profit*. The *revenues from sales* and *revenues from subscriptions* are shown in Figure 5.13 together with the *total costs* and the resulting *monthly profit*.

In Figure 5.13, *total costs* (dotted light blue line) take negative values, which is what they are with respect to *monthly profits*. But if you look at the monthly values of *total costs* contained in the intermediate variable in the simulation, they appear as positive numbers. You know that to compute the *monthly profit*, you have to calculate *total revenue* minus *total costs*.

Figure 5.13 shows the *revenue from sales* (dotted dark blue line) and the *revenue from subscription* (light blue line). The thick black line representing *monthly profit* has positive values, indicating that the sum of the two *revenue* streams is greater than the *total costs* in every month. You see that *revenue from sales* rises exponentially until the end of month 5, then soon peaks and decreases until reaching a plateau towards the end of the year. This is a consequence of the balancing 'depletion' loop (Figure 5.11), in which the diminishing *potential customers fraction* slows down the word-of-mouth dynamics. As you should remember, using a limited *life cycle duration* leads to *revenue from sales* not diminishing completely to zero but remaining at a low level. It is logical that the shape of *revenue from sales* mimics

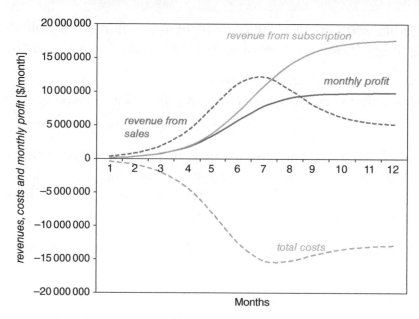

Figure 5.13 Behaviour of *revenues, costs* and *profits*

the shape of *new customers*. Of course, as long as NewTel keeps selling <u>more</u> mobile phones each month, the *total costs* will also become exponentially <u>more important</u>. Remember that you purchase the phones for a fixed cost of $40 each. For the same reason, *total costs* also become <u>lower</u>, when the number of monthly *new customers* <u>sinks</u>.

Current customers follows an S-shaped path, which drives the shape of *revenue from subscription*. When *revenue from sales* peaks, this is due to the fact that *new customers* peaks, and then *Current customers* switches from exponential to goal-seeking growth, which explains the change of behaviour from exponential to goal-seeking occurs in *revenue from subscription*. A part of the slope of *revenue from subscription* is offset by the negative *revenue from sales* slope; but both revenue streams have values <u>larger than</u> zero, so the *total revenue* may <u>rise</u> <u>slower</u> than prior to the peak in *revenue from sales*, but nevertheless it keeps <u>rising</u>. At the same time, *total costs* have <u>diminished</u> and, in total, the *monthly profit* <u>slope approaches</u> zero, so that the amount of *monthly profit* stabilizes. This is why the slope of *Accumulated profits* also <u>stabilizes</u>. Based on these observations we can derive one further systems insight:

> **Systems Insight 10 (SI 10): Bounded** *reduction of service costs*
> *Service costs* **can be decreased within a certain range by allocating financial resources to** *process improvement spending.*

5.5 Chapter summary

In this chapter you have completed an important part of your journey to systematically exploring what you can achieve with NewTel in Plutonia and how you best use your decision variables to achieve this. You have captured the basic word-of-mouth dynamics (Chapter 2), the limited *life cycle duration* (Chapter 3), *advertising spending* (Chapter 4), and now financial resources in your systems model.

We have guided you through this process of incremental modelling not by chance, but because we are following two important guidelines:

> **Guideline 9 (G 9): Start with only the most important causal structure**
> **When approaching a complex problem, start modelling with what you or member of the modelling team, including decision makers, believe to be the most fundamental piece of causal structure. Then, incrementally add new pieces of causal structure as you discover the need.**

> **Guideline 10 (G 10): Simulate after each model modification**
> **After changing the causal structure of a model, simulate it often to ensure that the model behaves correctly.**

By working in this step-by-step approach, you avoided creating large new pieces of causal structure that are difficult to analyse and keep under control. And, in only four steps, you have developed a simulation model that will allow you to answer the following core questions systematically and with rigour:

- How much *Accumulated profits* can you achieve for NewTel in Plutonia?
- What should the values of the decision variables be to maximize *Accumulated profits*?

This is what you will start working on in Chapter 6.

5.6 Questions and challenges

Questions

1. How exactly does an <u>increase</u> in any of the variables *new customers, sales price, Current customers*, or *subscription rate* <u>increase</u> the *total revenue*?
2. How exactly does an <u>increase</u> in any of the variables *sales price, subscription rate*, or *life cycle duration* <u>increase</u> the *effective monthly price*?
3. Why will an *effective monthly price* <u>larger than</u> $30 lead to a <u>decrease</u> of *new customers*?
4. Why would your *profits* be <u>reduced</u> if the value of *effective monthly price* <u>decreases</u> below $25?
5. Why would *total revenues* be <u>reduced</u> if the value of *effective monthly price* <u>increases</u> over $30?
6. Why is monitoring *Accumulated profits* sufficient to know if adjustments to the decision variables' values have the desired effect?
7. Why does a given amount of *process improvement spending* not always lead to the same <u>reduction</u> of *Service costs*?
8. Why is it important to make sure that a model replicates the behaviours observed in the past before using it to design policies for your organization's development?
9. What are the advantages of starting to model a complex problem with the most fundamental piece of causal structure and incrementally adding new pieces of causal structure as you discover that they are needed?
10. What problems can be caused if you do not simulate your model after having changed its causal structure?

Challenges

In this chapter, we have assumed the *product cost* to be constant at $40 for each mobile phone you buy from your supplier Samuria. However, imagine that you could negotiate an agreement to obtain price discounts according to how many mobile phones you buy from your provider each month. Assume the data shown in Figure 5.14.

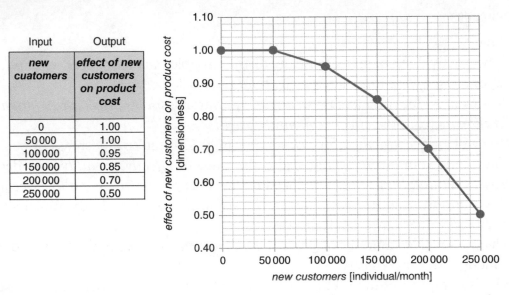

Input	Output
new cuatomers	**effect of new customers on product cost**
0	1.00
50 000	1.00
100 000	0.95
150 000	0.85
200 000	0.70
250 000	0.50

Figure 5.14 The nonlinear shape of the effect that *new customers* has on *product cost*

What modifications do you need to make to your model to take this new situation into account? How would your *total costs* and the *monthly profits* change in this case? (Hint: you can implement a switch 'provider discount switch' in a similar way to the 'cycle time switch' used in Chapter 4. If the switch has value = 0, the model takes the *normal product price* of $40, and if the switch is = 1, the model takes the table function into account.)

References

1   Ford, D.N. and Sterman, J.D. 1997. Expert knowledge elicitation to improve formal and mental models. *System Dynamics Review*, **14**(3): 309–340.
2   Sterman, J.D. 2000. *Business Dynamics: Systems Thinking and Modeling for a Complex World*. McGraw-Hill, Boston, MA.

Worksheet DIY 5.1:
Contrasting the model behaviour with the SellPhone BAU scenario

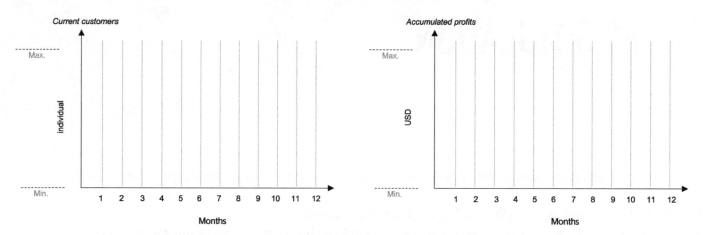

Use different colours to represent the behaviour of *Current customers* and *Accumulated profits* for each simulation.

Then observe the graphs and describe similarities and differences in terms of behaviour modes and inflection points, as well as end values. If there are differences, explain why.

ANALYSING THE MARKET SITUATION WITH THE SIMULATION

6.1 Introduction

In this chapter, you learn to exploit the simulation model to answer two important questions:

1. What level of *Accumulated profits* for NewTel is a good result?
2. What values of the decision variables allow you to achieve that level of *Accumulated profits*?

To answer these questions, you will extensively experiment with the simulation model. You will learn to systematically explore the simulation and to define the values of the decision variables. You will address each variable in isolation first, before combining them in more complex parameter configurations. You will also learn how to minimize the number of simulation experiments needed to find the optimal value for a decision variable.

Growth Dynamics in New Markets: Improving Decision Making through Simulation Model-based Management,
First Edition. Martin F.G. Schaffernicht and Stefan N. Groesser.
© 2018 John Wiley & Sons Ltd. Published 2018 by John Wiley & Sons Ltd.
Companion website: www.wiley.com/go/Schaffernicht/growth-dynamics

6.2 Planning the search for the highest possible *Accumulated profits*

After analysing different aspects of NewTel's situation in Plutonia in Chapters 2 to 4, Chapter 5 added financial resources; and simulating the model showed that it replicates the relevant features of the behaviour observed in the SellPhone simulator, with which you had your first experience in Chapter 1. In both simulations, you must use same default values of the decision variables to obtain approximately the same result. We concluded that the model is useful for helping us plan for financial success in your first year in Plutonia. With this model you now can test possible policies, before implementing them in reality – and being responsible for the results.

Currently you know that NewTel can make around $70 million *Accumulated profits* in the first year of operation in Plutonia. But it is unclear if this is even a good outcome, or if you could even do better. In fact: what is the highest possible value of *Accumulated profits*? And to what values should you set your decision variables to achieve this level of *Accumulated profits*? Perhaps the final *Accumulated profits* of roughly $70 million resulting from the default values is not the best possible outcome and, therefore, the values are not the 'most' optimal combination. You will now use the simulation model to find the highest possible *Accumulated profits*.

Each decision variable influences several other variables, i.e. you cannot change any decision variables without triggering several effects at the same time. Thus, it is important that you plan your policies using a map which helps you visualize and consider these multiple effects and interdependencies. The stock and flow diagram (SFD) in Figure 5.11 gives a detailed overview of all variables and their causal relationships. A SFD is highly informative, because it shows all relevant details as well as the different types of variables. However, there are times when you do not want to see all the details because you need to concentrate on the feedback loops in a situation and their interaction. This is best achieved with a causal loop diagram (CLD) (Lane, 2008).

Right now you need to focus on the different ways the decision variables affect *monthly profits* and *Accumulated profits*. It is not essential to differentiate between stocks and flows. Therefore, a CLD helps to ease understanding. The CLD in Figure 6.1 is derived from the simulation model in Figure 5.11:

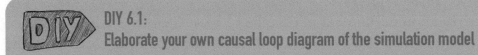

The structure driving the diffusion process remains at the core of the model considering the limited *life cycle duration*. Comparing Figure 6.1 to Figure 3.9, which shows only four feedback loops consisting of two stocks and two flows as well as the *potential customers fraction* and *purchases from WoM*, there are several differences. The CLD in Figure 6.1 does not show certain intermediate variables. From Toolbox 2.4, you recall that intermediate variables are useful to make details of the causal structure explicit, but they can be aggregated into the flows if a detailed representation is not needed. In Figure 6.1, they have been aggregated into the causal structure because we want to emphasize the feedback loops (**Guideline 3**, Chapter 2), and therefore the links belonging to feedback loops are printed thicker than the other links. For instance, *effective monthly price* is now directly linked to *new customers* with negative polarity; this conserves the polarity of the pathway from *effective monthly price* to *new customers* through the intermediate variables that belong to the simulation model. This is similar to looking at a road map of the entire country instead of a city map: many details are hidden. The simulation model 'C6 Monopoly', which contains the causal structure examined in Chapter 5 and some user interface objects to help in the search process, is like a city map that helps you to find precise directions. The CLD is the country map and gives you an overview.

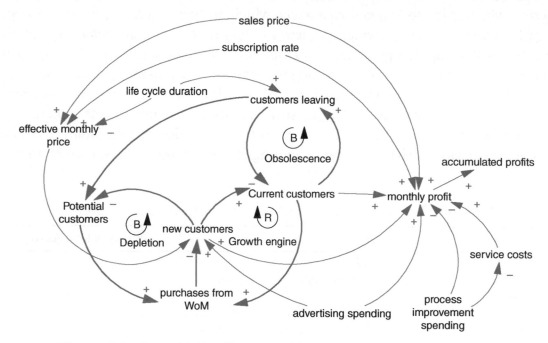

Figure 6.1 Causal loop diagram of the current simulation model

The CLD allows us to look at the causal pathways from the decision variables to *Accumulated profits* including the feedback loops, which give the system considerable autonomy in determining its behaviour. You may remember that during the initial phase, you can increase or decrease the speed of the exponential growth of *Current customers* but you cannot avoid it being exponential, because there is the reinforcing 'growth engine' loop. Likewise, you cannot avoid a point of inflexion being reached and growth switching to a goal-seeking mode because of the balancing 'depletion loop'.

When *sales price* and the *subscription rate* are <u>increased</u>, there are two effects: <u>increased</u> *profits* and <u>increased</u> *effective monthly price*, which leads to <u>less</u> *new customers*, which, in turn, <u>decreases</u> *profits*. A <u>decrease</u> in *life cycle duration* will <u>diminish</u> *customers leaving*, which <u>reduces the loss</u> of *Current customers*, which leads to <u>increased</u> *profits*. The other effect is that <u>increasing</u> *effective monthly price* ultimately leads to <u>decreasing</u> *profits*. <u>Increased</u> *advertising spending* will <u>increase</u> *new custom*ers, leading to <u>higher</u> *profits*, and <u>increased</u> *costs*, which <u>reduces</u> *profits*. <u>Increasing</u> *process improvement spending* will <u>increase</u> *total costs* immediately (after all, you are spending money) and later <u>diminish</u> *Service costs*, which then will <u>decrease</u> *total costs*: it is an investment, generating a cost now from which you should benefit later. Tracing these different paths from your decision variables to *monthly profits* allows you to establish that each decision variable has two opposing effects on *profits*, as shown in Table 6.1.

Table 6.1 Multiple influences of the decision variables on profits

Decision variable	Path	Polarity of influence on *profits*
sales price	Direct	+
	effective monthly price → new customers	−
subscription rate	Direct	+
	effective monthly price → new customers	−
life cycle duration	*effective monthly price → new customers*	−
	customers leaving → Current customers	+
advertising spending	Direct	−
	new customers	+
process improvement spending	Direct	−
	Service costs	+

Table 6.2 Value ranges of the decision variables

Variable	Value range			Number of integer values in range
	Initial	Minimum	Maximum	
sales price ($)	50	50	70	21
subscription rate ($)	20	20	30	11
life cycle duration (months)	9	6	18	14
advertising spending ($)	0	0	1 000 000	11
process improvement spending ($)	0	0	1 000 000	11

Since each of your decision variables has two influences on *profits*, moving from the default values will make you gain and lose something at the same time. Are there particular values of your decision variables for which the difference between what you gain minus what you lose is largest? You will need to search the range of possible values for each of your decision variables to identify the best combination. Table 6.2 recapitulates the ranges for each decision variable.

Note that the minimum values of *sales price* and *subscription rate* are not zero anymore. You found out in Chapter 5 that reducing these prices below their default level cannot increase *new customers*, but unavoidably diminishes *revenue* and *profits*.

You need to know the effect of each of these variables on *profits*. If you changed two or more of the decision variables at the same time, you would not be able to attribute the individual influence to either of them. It follows that you need to explore the effects of changes to the values of each decision variable, ceteris paribus, i.e. while holding the other decision variables constant.

But before executing this search, note that the first four decision variables in Table 6.1 transmit one of their effects through *new customers*. This means that the effect of each of these variables on *profits* is possibly influenced by the values of the other variables. Consequently, you cannot find the ideal value for each of these decision variables by varying its value and maintaining the other variables constant at any value of your choosing, for instance, the default value. You remember that the polarities of the causal links represent what would happen under the 'ceteris paribus' assumption (**Guideline 4** in Toolbox 2.5), i.e. that all other variables remain unchanged.

One way to be sure that you have explored the effect of each decision variable, holding the other decision variables' values constant, would be to test all possible combinations. A quick calculation leads a discouragingly high number of such combinations: if there are 21 different *sales prices* (assuming you use only integer numbers), 11 *subscription rates*, and 14 *life cycle durations* there are 3234 combinations of *sales price, subscription rate*, and *life cycle duration*. Suppose you tried with *advertising spending* and *process improvement spending* in steps of $100 000, so that you have 11 possible values for each, under the restriction that the sum of both amounts must not become greater than $1 million, there are $11 \times 11 = 121$ combinations minus those combinations that exceed $1 million. Next, we detail how to find the number of acceptable combinations. If you set one of the variables at $0 (the lowest possibility), then the other one can go through the whole range of 11 values, yielding 11 combinations. When one variable is set at $100 000, then the other one can only be set to 10 of its values, leading to 10 combinations. If you continue to increase the first variable's value to the next higher value, the number of possible combinations decreases by 1, successively to 9, 8, 7, 6, 5, 4, 3, 2, and eventually 1. There are 66 allowed combinations. Multiplication with the 3234 combinations of *sales price, subscription rate*, and *life cycle duration* results in 213 444 possible combinations of the decision variables awaiting your best efforts to evaluate their corresponding *profit*. Ready? Let us begin…

But wait! There is an alternative available to you: you can determine the highest *profit* achievable by varying each of the decision variables one by one. This would, in the worst case, take 21 trials for the *sales price*, 11 for the *subscription rate*, 14 for the *life cycle duration*, and 11 for each the *advertising spending* and the *process improvement spending*, making a total of 68 combinations (the sum of individual variations in the range of each variable's values). Once you know the best value for each decision variable, given that the respective other decision variables are constant, you can combine these values, assess the corresponding *profit* and eventually make small adjustments to further increase the final profit.

In the light of these considerations, we have outlined a plan of action for you: start with partial searches, while varying one variable. You start with a search for the optimal *subscription rate* – where 'optimal' means 'the value which yields the highest *Accumulated profits*' – leaving the other decision variables at their default values. Then search for the optimal *sales price* and afterwards the optimal *life cycle duration*. Since you cannot be sure that, for instance, the optimal *subscription rate* of the partial search is still optimal when the *life cycle duration* is changed from its default value to the result of the partial search, you should test for possible improvements in *Accumulated profits* with minor variations of the decision variables. After that, you can search for the best *advertising spending* for the different months of the year, assuming already the new values of *sales price*, *subscription rate*, and *life cycle duration*. In the separate final step, find the effect of *process improvement spending*. Then combine *advertising spending* and *process improvement spending* to find the optimal combination given a restriction on the maximum combined spending (*advertising spending* plus *process improvement spending*) of $1 million. Finally, combine the variables and search for the optimal combination. For all the necessary simulations, please use the model 'C6 Monopoly'. The logic used here is an application of a more general guideline:

Guideline 11 (G 11): Finding the optimal combination of values for sets of decision variables
When you need to find the optimal combination of values for more than one decision variable, you first search the best value for each of the variables in a partial analysis and then combine them.

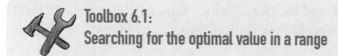

Toolbox 6.1:
Searching for the optimal value in a range

When the value of an objective variable is influenced by a parameter, we frequently need to know which parameter value leads to the optimal value of the objective variable.

Rather than starting at one end of the parameter value range and looking at each possible value, we use a half-interval search method (Figure 6.2).

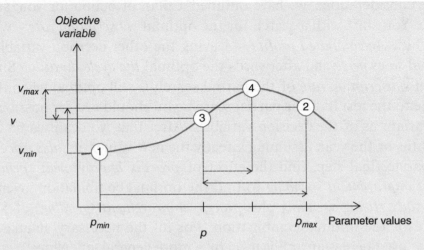

Figure 6.2 Half-interval search for the best parameter value

The horizontal axis shows the parameter value; the vertical axis indicates the values of the objective variable that is to be optimized. The range of parameter values is limited by a minimum and a maximum; start at the minimum at point 1 in Figure 6.2. For each parameter value p, there is a corresponding value $v(p)$ of the objective variable defined by an equation. One of the values of the objective variable, v_{max}, will be higher than all others, and the corresponding parameter value p_{max} is what is to be discovered.

However, *ex ante* nobody knows where the optimum is: nobody can directly see the summit. The optimum must be found in a stepwise way. Imagine that you are hiking and want to climb a summit: Make a step in a given direction and then observe whether that was a step upwards or not. If it was a step upward, continue in the same direction; if it was a step downward, make a step backwards and continue your search in a different direction.

The analogy has a weak point: firstly, the mountaineer has to search into many possible directions because the space has three dimensions, while you in the example have only two dimensions to consider. Therefore, only choose between going right (increasing p) or left (decreasing p). What follows translates the mountaineer analogy into a procedure.

Since the lowest and the highest possible parameter values p_{max} and p_{min} are known, it is clear that the searched parameter value p_{opt} is in-between these limits.

The question is: How many parameter values p must be evaluated by using the equation to find the best value p_{opt}? Here is the procedure to employ:

- the current value of p;
- the direction you are heading to (that is: will it increase p or decrease it?);
- the step size: by how much will you vary p in the next search step?

The general logic is: if after changing p according to the step size, $v(p)$ has increased, keep searching in the same direction; if $v(p)$ has decreased, switch to the opposite direction. After making a step, the current step size is halved – this assures that you evaluate for different values of p, instead of jumping back and forth between ever the same two values. At the start of the procedure, first set an initial value for p and determine a *step size* and a *direction*:

- set p to p_{min} and evaluate $v(p)$;
- set *step size* to $p_{max} - p_{min}$;
- set the *direction* to 1.

For the second step, the procedure must apply a special rule:

- set p to $p +$ direction $\times$ step size;
- evaluate $v(p)$;

- invert the current direction of search setting direction to direction $\times (-1)$;
- set step size to step size / 2.

In step 2, you have reached the upper limit of the parameter value range: note that if the initial value of p is p_{min} and you add $(p_{max} - p_{min})$, then $p = p_{min} + (p_{max} - p_{min})$, which is p_{max}. You cannot increase p beyond p_{max}, therefore invert the direction irrespectively of whether $v(p)$ has <u>increased</u> or <u>decreased</u>. At this current stage of your search, you know which of the two limits of the parameter value range yields a higher value $v(p)$ of the objective variable, but not if there is a value even higher than the current $v(p)$ within the range. Continue from step 3 on:

- set p to $p + $ direction $\times$ step size;
- evaluate $v(p)$;
- if $v(p)$ has decreased, then set direction to direction $\times (-1)$;
- set step size to step size / 2.

You can carry out as many steps you need until the <u>increases</u> in $v(p)$ become so small that you are satisfied with the value.

How does the procedure work in the example shown in Figure 6.2? From step 1 to step 2, $v(p)$ *increases*. From step 2 to 3 (now in the middle between p_{min} and p_{max}), v(p) decreases. This means that you went too far (p is too low) and, therefore, you have to turn around, inverting the direction. Divide the step size by 2 once again and move to point (4). Now, the $v(p)$ <u>increases</u>. In this example, you are lucky and your fourth point, p is practically at the maximum value of the objective variable; therefore, you have found p_{opt}. However, if you wanted to come even closer to the highest possible value, you could repeat these steps.

This method leads to good results in a small number of steps given that there is only one maximum value of the objective variable in the possible range of parameter values. However, it is a relatively simple method and, therefore, it can encounter two types of problems. Firstly, if the highest value of the objective variable corresponds to one of the extreme values of the parameter, i.e. v_{max} is $v(p_{min})$ or $v(p_{max})$, then the method causes p to converge to a suboptimal value, because the step size becomes ever smaller, and the method cannot go back to a previous value of p. As a precaution, it is possible to compare the values of $v(p)$ reached after three steps or more to detect this trap: in such a case, the procedure can be stopped and the highest value of $v(p)$ reached so far is kept as v_{max} and the corresponding p is considered as p_{opt}.

The second type of problem happens when there are two peaks – local maxima – for $v(p)$, separated by a valley. In such a case, the search method described here can converge on either of these peaks, and it might be the lower one. There are more sophisticated search methods that from time to time make random steps of a large step size to avoid this kind of early convergence. While searching manually, i.e. without the help of computer programs, it is, in principle, possible to make such random steps, but there would be a practical limit to the number of steps we want to carry out. For instance, in the example above, when we appear to have found p_{opt} at step 4, we could make a last evaluation in the middle between steps 1 and 2, just to be sure that we did not converge on a local maximum of v.

You will use this search logic to identify the optimal combination of your decision variables. However, the logic is useful in general, and you should keep it as a guideline:

Guideline 12 (G 12): The logic of optimization
When searching for the value of a parameter that optimizes the value of an impacted variable, start at one boundary of the value range and then iteratively approach the searched value, decreasing the step width with each iteration.

6.3 Searching for optimal values for the decision variables

6.3.1 Searching for the best *subscription rate* given a constant *sales price* and *life cycle duration*

Your first search concentrates on finding out what *subscription rate* in the range of \$20–30 per month leads to the highest *Accumulated profits*; given that *sales price* is fixed at \$20 and *life cycle duration* is constant at nine months. To keep the number of search steps low, let us evaluate only integer values for the *subscription rate*.

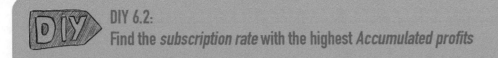

With the help of the simulation model 'C6 Monopoly', you can determine the level of *Accumulated profits* at the end of the year for different *subscription rates*. Decide on the set of different *subscription rates* you want to use. The minimum is $20 and the assumed maximum is $30 (remember your briefing in Chapter 1).

Take the worksheet provided on the companion website and using the half-interval search logic, decide what the first two values for the *subscription rate* are and record them on the worksheet. Then, execute the simulations and write down the final balance of *Accumulated profits* next to the respective *subscription rate*. Next, decide in which direction to further change the *subscription rate* and what the step size should be; write down the new *subscription rate*, simulate and, again, write down the new value of *Accumulated profits*. Continue this process until you believe that the resulting *Accumulated profits* cannot be improved further. Use the worksheet at the end of the chapter.

When searching for the best *subscription rate*, it is interesting to observe some other variables and not just *Accumulated profits*. The *effective monthly price*, which influences *new customers*, is certainly relevant to our understanding of *Accumulated profits*. In addition, the month in which the flow of *new customers* peaks tells you the moment in which the balancing 'depletion' loop starts to dominate the reinforcing 'growth engine' loop. It is also interesting to know from which month on the flow of *new customers* stabilizes, because from that month on your *Current customers* will also be stable. The total number of times NewTel receives the payment of a *subscription rate* is reported in *Accumulated customer-months*, and the total number of mobile phones sold is calculated in the variable *Accumulated purchases*. Table 6.3 shows the values of these variables for different *subscription rates*. The variables and months are presented in rows. The steps carried out in the search are numbered from 1 to 6 and appear as column titles. The last row shows the respective *Accumulated profits*.

Table 6.3 Results for different *subscription rates* when *sales price* = $50 and *life cycle duration* = 9 months

Step	1	2	3	4	5	6
subscription rate ($)	20	30	25	23	22	24
effective monthly price ($)	25.56	35.56	30.56	28.56	27.56	29.56
Month when new customers peak	6	After 12	8	7	7	8
Month when new customers stabilize	10	After 12	12	10	10	11
new customers	5288	2077	28 922	11 478	7982	18 470
Current customers	880 871	19 594	831 457	866 060	873 892	851 924
Accumulated customer-months	5 352 708	128 182	4 026 905	4 826 600	5 085 739	4 445 184
Accumulated purchases	1 470 616	28 836	1 273 890	1 397 348	1 433 974	1 340 833
Accumulated profits ($)	68 233 240	2 852 009	73 142 464	76 719 256	75 368 592	75 640 880

The lowest interesting value of the *subscription rate* is equal to its default value of $20 because, for lower values, the *effective monthly price* will <u>sink</u> below $25.56; the *effect of EMP on demand* would <u>not grow</u> beyond 100% (remember the discussion of this effect at Figure 5.7 in Chapter 5), so you would <u>not</u> have <u>more</u> *new customers*, so you would <u>reduce</u> your *revenues from sales*. Therefore, step 1 is executed with the default *subscription rate*. This reproduces the outcomes of the business as usual scenario (BAU), which you simulated at the end of Chapter 5. For the next step, you add $10, which brings you from $20 to $30, which is the upper limit of the value range. <u>Increasing</u> the *subscription rate* to $30 also <u>increases</u> the *effective monthly price*, in that case to more than $35. The simulated horizon of 12 months of the year is not sufficient time to see *new customers* peak or even stabilize. As compared to the BAU scenario, all the variables you are monitoring in this run finish the simulated year with significantly <u>reduced</u> values. You would have only around 20 000 *Current customers* and roughly 2000 *new customers* per month, meaning less than 30 000 *Accumulated purchases* and only 130 000 *Accumulated customer-months*. The *Accumulated profits* are lower than $3 million.

According to the logic of the half-interval search method, you have two reasons to change the direction of the search: the results have worsened and you have reached the limit of the range of values. Therefore, the next step is to decrease the *subscription rate* and it will be half of the step size, this is, five dollars <u>less</u>. The results of this evaluation are reported in the column with step 3. After <u>decreasing</u> the *subscription rate* from $30 to $25, the *effective monthly price* <u>sinks</u> to roughly $30 and *new customers* now reach their peak value after eight months and arrive at a stable value in month 12. All the other reported variables dramatically <u>increase</u>. Comparing the result from step 2 with step 3 shows that the objective values are higher: *Accumulated profits* of almost 73 million are almost 10% higher than *Accumulated profits* in the BAU scenario.

Since the move from step 2 to step 3 has increased your outcome, you keep searching in the same direction and just halve the step size. If you applied the 'halved step size' rule strictly, it would now become 2.5. But this clashes with your plan to search in steps of integer values for *subscription rate*. Therefore, when seeking the optimal *subscription rate,* you do not strictly divide the step size by 2, but round it to $2, from $25 to $23. If you had decided to reduce the *subscription rate* by $4, the sequence of steps would have been slightly different: you would have evaluated for *subscription rates* $22, $24, and $23 that is steps 5, then 6 and finally 4. The final result and the total number of steps would have been the same. *New customers* now peaks and stabilizes one month earlier. As the data in the column of step 4 show, your results have once again improved: almost five million *Accumulated customer-months*, practically 1.4 million *Accumulated purchases* and almost $77 million *Accumulated profits*.

Following the logic of your search, you must now evaluate the results that would follow from a *subscription rate* of $22. You can see in the column of step 5 that, in this case, *Accumulated profits* would be <u>reduced</u>. This shows you that you do not need to keep searching in the same direction: you know that by changing the *subscription rate* from $23 downwards, you cannot improve your *Accumulated profits*. This does not necessarily prove, however, that between $23 and $25, there might be even higher *Accumulated profits* to be achieved. To find out if this is the case, step 6 evaluates for the case of a *subscription rate* of $24, but this reduces *Accumulated profits*.

When you visualize the combinations of *subscription rate* and *Accumulated profits*, it becomes clear that you have indeed found the *subscription rate* which maximizes *Accumulated profits* given fixed values for *sales price* and *life*

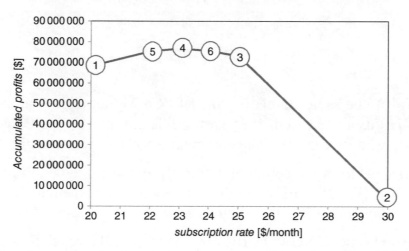

Figure 6.3 Searching the optimal *subscription rate* when sales *price* = 50 and *life cycle duration* = 9

cycle duration. Figure 6.3 is analogous to Figure 6.2: it shows the parameter – *subscription rate* – on the horizontal axis and the objective variable – *Accumulated profits* – on the vertical axis. The search steps are shown with their respective numbers:

Figure 6.3 clearly shows how your search has converged from the limits of the parameter value range towards the optimal value of the *subscription rate*. This is your first partial finding: the highest level of *Accumulated* profits to be achieved by any *subscription rate* in the allowed range of values is $76 719 256 and the corresponding *subscription rate* is $23.

6.3.2 Searching the optimal *sales price* given a constant subscription *rate* and *life cycle duration*
Table 6.4 presents a search in four steps in which different *sales prices* lead to different *Accumulated profits* and one identifies the best *sales price*.

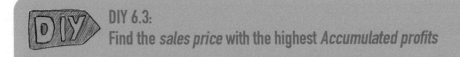

DIY 6.3:
Find the *sales price* with the highest *Accumulated profits*

With the help of the same simulation model ('C6 Monopoly'), you can also find the level of *Accumulated profits* at the end of the year for different *sales prices*. Decide on the set of different *sales prices* you want to evaluate. The minimum is $50 and your assumed maximum is $70.

Take the worksheet from the companion website and using the half-interval search logic, decide what the first two values for the *sales price* will be and record them in the worksheet. Remember to set the *subscription rate* to $20 in the simulation model.

Then, execute the simulations and write down the final balance of *Accumulated profits* next to the respective *sales price*. Next, decide in which direction to further change the *sales price* and what the step size should be; write down the new *sales price*, simulate and, again, write down the new value of *Accumulated profits*. Continue this process until you believe that the resulting *Accumulated profits* cannot be improved further. Use the worksheet at the end of the chapter.

Table 6.4 Results for different *sales prices* when *subscription rate* = $20 and *life cycle duration* = 9 months

Step	1	2	3	4
sales price ($)	50	70	60	65
effective monthly price ($)	25.56	27.78	26.67	27.22
Month when *new customers* peak	6	7	7	7
Month when *new customers* stabilize	10	10	10	10
new customers	5288	8352	6651	7456
Current customers	880 871	873 015	877 185	875 165
Accumulated customer-months	5 352 708	5 054 718	5 207 190	5 131 774
Accumulated purchases	1 470 616	1 429 651	1 450 761	1 440 363
Accumulated profits ($)	68 233 240	**93 436 672**	81 087 120	87 326 824

You vary only the *sales price*; all other decision variables remain at their default levels. The table starts at *step* 1, where the *sales price* is at its default level $50. Again, the other variables' values are provided by the simulation, which has been run once per step. For step 1, the *effective monthly price* is equal to the one calculated above. As before, the row 'Month when *new customers* peak' refers to the month when *purchases* reach the highest value and when *Current customers* switches from exponential growth to asymptotic growth. The row 'Month when *new customers* stabilize' represents the month when the stock of *Current customers* has stabilized. The stable values of *Current customers* and *new customers* are around 880 000 and 5000 respectively. After 12 months, NewTel has 5.3 million *Accumulated customer-months* and 1.5 million *Accumulated purchases*. You can multiply the *Accumulated customer-months* by (subscription rate − Service cost) to determine the amount of *Accumulated profits* due to *revenues from subscription*. Analogously, multiplying the *Accumulated purchases* by (*sales price* − *product cost*) yields the amount of *Accumulated profits* due to *revenues from sales*. The sum of both amounts is equal to the simulated amount of *Accumulated profit*, i.e. $68 million, and this number is the basis for comparisons.

For step 2 you set the step to $20 and <u>increase</u> the *sales price* to $70, its maximum value. This <u>increases</u> the *EMC* 27.78, which is little more than two additional dollars. Due to the small size of this difference, *peak* of *new customers* is reached only one month later and *Current customers* still achieves stability in month 10. After that, there are around 8300 *new customers* each month and you have 873 000 *Current customers*. In comparison with the outcome of step one, you <u>lose</u> only 300 000 *customer-months* and 40 000 *Accumulated purchases*, and the *Accumulated profits* rise as high as $93 million: approximately 25 million <u>more</u>.

Since <u>increasing</u> the *sales price* led to an <u>increase</u> in *Accumulated profits*, you might be interested in exploring even higher *sales prices*. However, you have already reached the upper limit of the range of allowed values, and therefore you cannot proceed in the same direction. After having looked at the extreme values of *sales price*, you cannot tell yet if there would not be any higher *Accumulated profits* to be achieved by a *sales price* somewhere in between these extreme values. For this reason, you turn around, reduce the step size to $10, and examine the outcomes of simulating the model for a *sales price* of $60 (shown in the column of step 3). It turns out that the *effective monthly price* now falls back to just in the middle between steps 1 and 2, as do the final values of the *Accumulated purchases* and *Accumulated customer-months*. *Accumulated profits* terminate around $81 million, which also lies halfway between the *Accumulated profits* reached in the two previous steps.

You conclude that you would not find any better results in terms of *Accumulated profits* for *sales prices* below $60. On the other hand, you cannot be sure that between $60 and $70 you will not find a *sales price* leading to even higher *Accumulated profits*. To find out, you switch directions, reduce the step size to $5 and simulate the model for a *sales price* of $65. The outcomes appear in the column of step 4. A look at the values reported in that column supports the conclusion that the *Accumulated profits* reaches its highest value when the *sales price* is $70.

And, indeed, Figure 6.4 shows that the four steps you executed lie on a straight line; tracing the line through the different combinations of *sales price* and *Accumulated profits* gives you confidence that there is not a hidden local maximum somewhere in between these values.

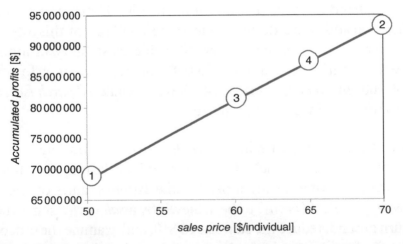

Figure 6.4 Searching the optimal *sales price* when *subscription rate* = 20 and *life cycle duration* = 9

You conclude that – at least when the *life cycle duration* and the *subscription rate* are at their BAU value – the sales price should be $70.

6.3.3 Searching the optimal *life cycle duration* given a constant *sales price* and *subscription rate*

DIY 6.4:
Find the *life cycle duration* with the highest *Accumulated profits*

With the help of the same simulation model ('C6 Monopoly'), you can also find the level of *Accumulated profits* at the end of the year for different *life cycle durations*. Decide on the set of different *life cycle durations* you want to evaluate. We will take a minimum of six months and maximum of 18.

Once again, take the worksheet from the companion website and using the half-interval search logic as explained above, decide what the first two values for the *life cycle duration* will be and record them in the worksheet. Remember to set the *sales price* to $50 in the simulation model.

Then, execute the simulations and write down the final balance of *Accumulated profits* next to the respective *life cycle duration*. Next, decide in which direction to further change the *life cycle duration* and what the step size should be; write down the new *life cycle duration*, simulate and, again, write down the new value of *Accumulated profits*. Continue this process until you believe that the result cannot be improved further. Use the worksheet at the end of the chapter.

In your third search, the question is which value of *life cycle duration* will lead to the highest *Accumulated profits* given the initial *sales price* and *subscription rate*? The search is reported in Table 6.5.

Table 6.5 Results for different *life cycle durations* when *sales price* = $50 and *subscription rate* = $20

Step	1	2	3	4	5	6
life cycle duration (months)	9	6	18	15	17	16
effective monthly price ($)	25.56	28.33	22.78	23.33	22.94	23.13
Month when *new customers* peak	6	7	n.a.	7	8	8
Month when *new customers* stabilize	10	10	n.a.	10	12	11
new customers	5288	15 517	3340	3666	3433	3540
Current customers	880 871	803 820	937 682	926 383	934 361	930 623
Accumulated customer-months	5 352 708	4 287 920	5 944 942	5 826 132	5 909 982	5 870 666
Accumulated purchases	1 470 616	1 513 474	1 262 956	1 309 791	1 277 007	1 292 540
Accumulated profits ($)	68 233 240	58 013 940	**72 079 000**	71 359 232	71 869 896	71 632 056

As before, step 1 replicates the BAU scenario and you already know the outcomes. However, compared to the previous two partial searches, the initial *life cycle duration* of nine months is not very close to either of the limits of the range of possible values. Therefore, your plan will be to first <u>decrease</u> *life cycle duration* three months. From the former chapters you remember that a <u>reduction</u> in the *life cycle duration* brings <u>more</u> *new customers* and <u>less</u> *Current customers* due to the obsolescence of the mobile phones. You might suspect that <u>shortening</u> the *life cycle duration* will <u>increase</u> *Accumulated profits* because of the <u>increased</u> *new customers*. However, the *effective monthly price* <u>rises</u> to over $28, and you already know that this <u>diminishes</u> the word-of-mouth effect on *Potential customers*. And indeed, the <u>additional</u> *new customers*, 15 000 instead of 5000, are not able to set off the <u>loss</u> of *Current customers*: in the end, there are roughly one million less *Accumulated customer-months*. Accordingly, *Accumulated profits* <u>decrease</u> to $58 million in step 2.

Will it <u>increase</u> if you <u>increase</u> the *life cycle duration*? In step 3 you set *life cycle duration* to the other extreme value: 18 months. This time, the *effective monthly price* <u>sinks</u> to less than $23, but you know that below $25.56 <u>no increase</u> of *new customers* can be triggered by <u>reducing</u> the *effective monthly price*. The customer dynamics are slow in this case and *new customers* do not reach a peak during the 12 months. Due to the <u>lower size</u> of the *customers leaving* flow, the final values of *new customers* are <u>lower</u> and you have <u>more</u> *Current customers*. In terms of *Accumulated customer-months*, you now almost reach six million (as compared to the BAU results, this is roughly 10% <u>more</u>) and 1.2 million *Accumulated purchases* (200 000 <u>less</u>). You have <u>won</u> many additional *customer-months* than you have <u>lost</u> *Accumulated purchases*. Since the *subscription rate* is a little less than half the *sales price*, the relationship between these two prices reduces the effect of this difference. Still, the total effect is that *Accumulated profits* go <u>up</u> to $72 million, which is $4 million <u>more</u> than in the BAU case and $14 million <u>more</u> than for a *life cycle duration* of six months.

At present, you now ask yourself if there might be an intermediate *life cycle duration* that reaches even higher *Accumulated profits*, somewhere between the previously evaluated *life cycle durations*. Therefore, you successively try with 15, then 17, and, finally, 16 months, but the results (columns for steps 4 to 6 in the table) show that no other *life cycle duration* leads to higher *Accumulated profits* than 18 months – given the *sales price* of $50 and the *subscription rate* of $20. Figure 6.5 shows the pathway of the search across the different values of *life cycle duration*:

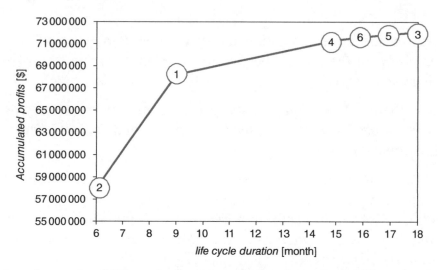

Figure 6.5 Searching the optimal *life cycle duration* when *sales price* = $50 and *subscription rate* = $20

You conclude that as long as the *sales price* is $50 and the monthly *subscription rate* is $20, 18 months is the most desirable *life cycle duration* if our aim is to achieve the highest possible *Accumulated profits*.

6.3.4 Searching for the optimal combination of *sales price*, *subscription rate*, and *life cycle duration*

Up to now, you have carried out partial searches and have determined the optimal value for each of the decision variables *sales price*, *subscription rate*, and *life cycle duration*, varying one decision variable at a time and holding all the other decision variables constant. Having analysed the consequences of changing one variable at a time, now the question is whether the optimal values from the partial searches are still optimal when you change the values of each of these variables to the value found in the partial searches.

DIY 6.5:
Find the combination of *sales price*, *subscription rate* and *life cycle duration* with the highest *Accumulated profits*

With the help of the same simulation model ('C6 Monopoly'), you can also find the level of *Accumulated profits* at the end of the year for different combinations of *sales price*, *subscription rate*, and *life cycle duration*.

Assuming that there will be no *advertising spending* and no *process improvement spending*, which combination of values for *sales price*, *subscription rate*, and *life cycle duration* will yield the highest value of *Accumulated profits*, and what values will they be?

You can use the worksheet provided on the companion website. Define the initial level for *sales price*, *subscription rate*, and *life cycle duration* according to what you have found in the three previous sections. Record the resulting *Accumulated profits*. Then explore the outcomes for nearby values of *sales price*, *subscription rate*, and *life cycle duration* to see if it is possible to further increase *Accumulated profits*.

Remember to set the variables to the values found in the previous subsections. Then, execute the simulations and write down the final balance of *Accumulated profits* next to the respective combination of *sales price, subscription rate*, and *life cycle duration*. Next, decide in which direction to further explore possible combinations in the neighbourhood of the current values of the decision variables. Continue this process until you believe that the result cannot be improved further. Use the worksheet at the end of the chapter.

Thanks to your partial searches, you now know what the most desirable value is for each of the decision variables *sales price, subscription rate*, and *life cycle duration* when the other variables are held at their default level. Table 6.6 recapitulates the respective *Accumulated profits* achieved by these partial searches:

This does not guarantee, though, that the combination of *sales price* = $70, *subscription rate* = $23 and *life cycle duration* = 18 months, will lead to the highest possible *Accumulated profits*. However, it is a good idea to evaluate just how high *Accumulated profits* is in that case, with special attention to if it is higher than the best *Accumulated*

Table 6.6 *Accumulated profits* achieved in partial searches by varying one decision variable at a time

Variables	Partial searches (variables changed by search in bold, other variables in grey)		
	subscription rate	sales price	life cycle duration
subscription rate ($)	**23**	20	20
sales price ($)	50	**70**	50
life cycle duration (months)	9	9	**18**
Outcome of searches: *Accumulated profits* ($)	**76 719 256**	**93 436 672**	**72 079 000**

profits you could achieve by changing only one of the decision variables at a time. If, as you hope, this combination yields the highest *Accumulated profits* so far, the next question becomes how you can find out if it can be further increased in a small number of evaluations. Remembering the shapes of the relationships between each of these decision variables and *Accumulated profits* (shown in Figures 6.3 to 6.5), you notice that for the *sales price* and the *life cycle duration*, the highest reachable *Accumulated profits* were at the upper limit of the respective decision variable, and that decreasing the *sales price* or the *life cycle duration* would make the values you observe descend the slope of *Accumulated profits* in each case. You will not find higher profits for lower values of these two decision variables. However, the *subscription rate* has its optimal value somewhere in between the highest and the lowest value you can decide for it. Maybe, the optimal *subscription rate* is not any longer at $23 after having changed the *sales price* and *the life cycle duration* from their default values to their optimal values?

Your plan for this search process is to start with the default values, then evaluate the combination *sales price* = $70, *subscription rate* = $23 and *life cycle duration* = 18 months. Provided that the resulting *Accumulated profits* are <u>higher</u> than in the BAU case (step 1), you will then assess if any <u>increase</u> or <u>decrease</u> of the *subscription rate* further <u>improves</u> *Accumulated profits* and identify the optimal *subscription rate* given the *sales price* = $70 and *life cycle duration* = 18 months. Finally, you will test whether a <u>decrease</u> of the *sales price* or *life cycle duration* further <u>increases</u> *Accumulated profits* or not.

This means you know more than in the beginning, but not enough. Therefore, you now must search for the best combination. Of course, in this search you can change several of these variables at a time. If you start with a *sales price* of $50, but would prefer it to be $70, start with *subscription rate* of $20, but would prefer it to be $23, would the combination of *sales price* = $70, *subscription rate* = $23 and *life cycle duration* = 18 months still be better? And would 18 months then still be the most desirable *life cycle duration*? Table 6.7 shows the results of the step from the BAU scenario to the combination of the values found in the partial searches:

As in the partial searches, step 1 replicates the BAU scenario. Step 2 corresponds to the combination of the values found in the partial searches: *sales price* $70, monthly *subscription rate* $23, and *life cycle duration* 18 months. The

Table 6.7 Results for combining the values from the partial searches of *sales price*, *subscription rate*, and *life cycle duration*

Step	1	2
sales price ($)	50	70
subscription rate ($)	20	23
life cycle duration (months)	9	18
effective monthly price ($)	25.56	26.89
new customers	5288	4437
Current customers	880 871	935 329
Accumulated customer-months	5 352 708	5 783 395
Accumulated purchases	1 470 616	1 251 628
Accumulated profits ($)	68 233 240	112 733 000

effective monthly price rise to $26.9, we have less *Current customers* and a few less purchases, and the *Accumulated profits* rise to $112 733 000, which is much higher than those achieved in the partial searches. A quick look at the nonlinear function of how purchases relate to the *effective monthly price* (Chapter 5, Figure 5.7) reminds you that such a rise in the *effective monthly price* will cause the *price effect on demand multiplier* to sink and eventually reduce *purchases* to almost half of what they might be. You wonder: maybe your product has become so costly to *Potential customers* that the diminished *purchases* harm your own *Accumulated profits*? Indeed, NewTel has almost $200 000 *Accumulated purchases* less as compared to the BAU scenario, but 400 000 more *Accumulated customer-months*.

You decide to test if variations in the three decision variables could increase *Accumulated profits* even further. Since the new value of *Accumulated profits* is so much higher than in the BAU scenario, you believe that if there are better combinations they must be in the neighbourhood of the values assumed in step 2, that is: the three decision variables should be varied slightly to check for further increases in *Accumulated profits*.

It is still important to test partial variations first. So, you evaluate if *Accumulated profits* <u>rise</u> if you <u>decrease</u> the *life cycle duration* from 18 to 17 months (<u>increasing</u> it is not a possible choice), but *Accumulated profits* <u>decrease</u> to $112 228 568. When you restore *life cycle duration* to 18 months and <u>reduce</u> the *sales price* from $70 to $69, the *Accumulated profits* are $111 585 680, which is even <u>less</u>. You turn the *sales price* back to $70 and now you have only the *subscription rate* left to vary. But you can <u>decrease</u> it as well as <u>increase</u> it, so you first try with a <u>decrease</u> to $22, but *Accumulated profits* <u>sink</u> to $108 675 904. You try again with an <u>increase</u> to $24. Now *Accumulated profits* <u>increase</u> to $116 460 024.

You now know that – assuming a *life cycle duration* of 18 months and a *sales price* of $70 – a *subscription rate* of $23 is too low to reach the highest possible *Accumulated profits*. The best possible value for the *subscription rate* must be somewhere between $24 and $30. You follow the search method used above and vary the values in this range, which is $6 now. Table 6.8 shows the steps you take before settling at a subscription rate:

You have now searched across the value range of *subscription rate* and found that when *life cycle duration* is 18 months and *sales price* is $70, a *subscription rate* of $25 yields even higher *Accumulated profits* than the $23 found in the partial searches. You still cannot be sure that this is the highest possible value of *Accumulated profits*, which can be reached by combining *subscription rate*, *sales price*, and *life cycle duration*: could it be, say, that for a *subscription rate* of $25, slightly <u>reducing</u> the *sales price* or <u>reducing</u> *life cycle duration* or both decision variables <u>increases</u> *Accumulated profits* even further? If you simulate the model with *sales price* = $69 or *life cycle duration* = 17 months, you will find out that this is not the case.

Table 6.8 Results for different *subscription rates* when *sales price* = $70 and *life cycle duration* = $18

Step	1	2	3	4
subscription rate ($)	30	27	25	26
Accumulated profits ($)	49 755 628	112 375 112	116 766 664	115 371 480

DIY 6.6:
Find the *advertising spending* with the highest *Accumulated profits*

Knowing the optimal values for the *sales price*, the *subscription rate*, and the *life cycle duration* when there is no *advertising spending*, you can use the same simulation model and the same search logic to find out the values of your monthly *advertising spending* that leads to the highest *Accumulated profits*, assuming that there will be no *process improvement spending*.

The procedure is no different to the previous searches. Using the worksheet from the companion website, define the initial level for *sales price*, *subscription rate*, and *life cycle duration*, according to what you have found in the three previous sections.

Try an amount of $1 million for each month from 1 to 6 separately before using combinations. For each possibility, run the simulation and write down the final balance of *Accumulated profits* next to the respective *advertising spending* pattern. Continue this process until you believe that the result cannot be improved any further. Use the worksheet at the end of the chapter.

Now you know that when *advertising spending* is $0 and *process improvement spending* is $0, the highest possible *Accumulated profits* are $116 766 664, and this result can be achieved by setting the *sales price* to $70, the *subscription rate* to $25, and the *life cycle duration* to 18 months – these values, by the way, result in an *effective monthly price* of $28.90.

The last decision variable that can influence *total revenues* is *advertising spending*. In the BAU scenario, its value is zero, but it can be any amount up to $1 million per month. The results from Chapter 4 are that after the first three months, the effect of $1 million of monthly *advertising spending* on *Accumulated purchases* and *Accumulated customer-months* quickly becomes very small. With a *life cycle duration* of 18 months without *advertising spending*, you finish the year with \$1 470 616 *Accumulated purchases* and 5 352 708 *Accumulated customer-months*.

Preliminary analysis based on the simulations of the BAU scenario allows you to determine how much additional *Accumulated profit* could be achieved by allocating \$1 million to *advertising spending* in either of the first three months. Depending on how *advertising spending* is allocated in either of the three months, *Accumulated purchases* and *Accumulated customer-months* will vary. As long as there is no *advertising spending*, you can calculate the value of *Accumulated profits* at the end of the year as *Accumulated purchases* × (*sales price* − *product price*) + *Accumulated customer-months* × (*subscription rate* − *Service cost*). If the only thing you change between two runs of the simulation model is to allocate a certain amount of money to *advertising spending*, then you can calculate the impact on *Accumulated profits* based on the difference between *Accumulated purchases* and *Accumulated customer-months* caused by *advertising spending*. To do so, you can carry out the following two steps. For step 1, let us call the simulation without *advertising spending* 'BAU' and the one 'with *advertising spending*' (WAS) and use both abbreviations as subindices for *Accumulated purchases* and *Accumulated customer-months*.

Step 1: Expected additional gross Accumulated profits from sales and subscriptions = (*Accumulated purchases*$_{WAS}$ − *Accumulated purchases*$_{BAU}$) × (*sales price* − *product price*) + (*Accumulated customer-months*$_{WAS}$ − *Accumulated customer-months*$_{BAU}$) × (*subscription rate* − *Service cost*)

Note that (sales price − product price) is the sales margin and (subscription rate − Service cost) is the subscription margin.

Step 2: Expected additional net Accumulated profits = Expected additional gross Accumulated profits from sales and subscriptions − sum of amounts allocated to *advertising spending*

Note that since the two values calculated here are not variables in the model, they are not printed in italics. However, the steps are easy to carry out and can be used to store and compare the results from runs with different amounts of *advertising spending*. The results of this analysis for five different allocations of *advertising spending* are shown in Table 6.9:

Table 6.9 Additional *Accumulated profits* expected from different allocations to *advertising spending* under BAU assumptions

advertising spending = $1 million per month			Additional *Accumulated purchases*	Additional *Accumulated customer-months*	Expected additional gross *Accumulated profits* from *sales* and *subsctiptions* ($)	Sum of amounts allocated to *advertising spending* ($)	Expected additional net *Accumulated profits* ($)
1	2	3					
Yes	No	No	96 037	845 432	9 414 690	1 000 000	8 414 690
No	Yes	No	50 537	442 778	4 933 150	1 000 000	3 933 150
No	No	Yes	24 128	210 552	2 346 800	1 000 000	1 346 800
Yes	Yes	No	120 323	1 061 230	11 815 530	2 000 000	9 815 530
Yes	Yes	Yes	129 150	1 139 744	12 688 940	3 000 000	9 688 940

According to Table 6.9, it does make a difference on *Accumulated profits* if you allocate $1 million to *advertising spending* in month 1, 2, or, 3. While the additional *total revenues* to be expected from spending $1 million in month 1 clearly outweigh the additional costs of *advertising spending* in month 3, when the total effect is very low. If *advertising spending* is allocated in several months, the effect achieved on *new customers* in the first month <u>depletes</u> *Potential customers* and, thus, <u>decreases</u> the effect of *advertising spending* in the following month. Therefore, the difference in expected additional *Accumulated profits* between spending $1 million in months 1 and 2 and spending $1 million in all three months is negative: the <u>depletion</u> of *Potential customers* resulting from *advertising spending* in months 1 and 2 is so large that the additional effects of the third month of *advertising spending* on *Accumulated purchases* and *Accumulated customer-months* cannot recover the $1 million *advertising spending*. Even if you reduce the third month's *advertising spending* to $100 000, the net effect on expected *Accumulated profits* is negative.

This is a useful intermediate result, for you can conclude that, under BAU assumptions, you would only need to corroborate the net effect of *advertising spending* during the first three months under the assumption of the new values for the three decision variables already explored. So you simulate the model assuming that *sales price* = $70, *subscription rate* = $25, and *life cycle duration* = 18 months. Under BAU assumptions, *advertising spending* turned uneconomic after the first two months, so you should concentrate on the first three months now. But simulating with different values for *sales price*, *subscription rate*, and *life cycle duration* might cause a change in the way *advertising spending* affects *Accumulated profits* over the months of the year. Since you cannot be sure before you try, we will go through the first four months together this time.

You allocate $1 million to *advertising spending* in the first four months of the year, firstly month by month and then in combinations. Table 6.10 shows the results.

Table 6.10 presents the outcomes of seven different *advertising spending* scenarios, showing firstly the effects of spending $1 million in only one single month. As you might have expected from the previous simulations, the additional *Accumulated profits* achieved by spending $1 million in the first month are sizable and delaying the spending to later months quickly <u>diminishes</u> these additional *Accumulated profits*. The additional *Accumulated purchases* and *Accumulated customer-months* <u>decrease</u> to approximately half their size each time you wait one more month. When comparing these results to those from the BAU simulation (Table 6.9) you should notice that now the number of additional *Accumulated purchases* is significantly <u>lower</u> but there are slightly <u>more</u> *Accumulated customer-*

Table 6.10 Additional *Accumulated profits* from different *advertising spending* when *sales price* = $70, *subscription rate* = $25, and *life cycle duration* = 18 months

advertising spending = $1 million per month				Additional Accumulated purchases	Additional Accumulated customer-months	Additional Accumulated profits ($)
1	**2**	**3**	**4**			
Yes	No	No	No	52 508	879 623	13 769 600
No	Yes	No	No	28 407	469 389	6 893 032
No	No	Yes	No	14 043	229 452	2 863 088
No	No	No	Yes	6565	106 162	789 392
Yes	Yes	No	No	66 293	1 117 310	16 748 440
Yes	Yes	Yes	No	71 455	1 206 638	17 243 176
Yes	Yes	Yes	Yes	73 585	1 243 407	16 858 688

months. According to the analysis of the effects of *life cycle duration* on the customer dynamics (Chapter 3), it was to be expected that increasing *life cycle duration* from 9 to 18 months would result in fewer *new customers* and slightly more *Current customers*. When you consider that the margin between *sales price* and *purchasing price* ($40) has increased from $10 to $30, and that the new *subscription rate* has increased the margin over *Service costs* from $10 to $15, it becomes clear that the loss of *Accumulated purchases* has been more than compensated by the increased margin and the increased number of *Accumulated customer-months*. Combining the changes in customer dynamics and in the margins, it turns out that now spending $1 million on advertising will pay off – at least when spending the money as a one-off investment.

The three lower rows in Table 6.10 show the outcomes of spending $1 million on advertising in several months: the first two, the first three, or the first four months. As now the *advertising spending* of month 1 already increases the depletion of *Potential customers* – exactly the same way it was discussed for the previous simulations – the effect of later months' *advertising spending* diminishes. Under these circumstances, the highest possible increase in *Accumulated profits* as well as *Accumulated purchases* and *Accumulated customer-months* are reached when you allocate $1 million to *advertising spending* in months 1 to 3. This results in $17 million additional *Accumulated profits*, i.e. from $116 766 664 to $134 009 840.

As you know, both *advertising spending* and *effective monthly price* (expressed in your model as *price effect on demand multiplier*) have an influence on *Potential customers* purchasing decisions. In turn, the *effective monthly price* is influence by the *life cycle duration*, the *sales price,* and the *subscription rate*. In Chapter 4, you learned that a certain increase in *sales price* or in the *subscription rate* can sometimes increase *total revenues*, this is the case when the *price* increase is larger than the reduction in *new customers* induced by the effect of *effective monthly price* on the *price effect on demand multiplier*. However, if the reduction of *new customers* is stronger than the effect of the *sales price* or *subscription rate* increase, then *total revenues* will decrease. In your current situation, the *sales price* can only be decreased to affect *Accumulated profits* because the current value of $70 is the highest allowed value. The *subscription rate* can be decreased and increased to evaluate the impact of such a change on *Accumulated profits*.

Could it be then that a <u>lower</u> *sales price* or a <u>lower</u> or <u>higher</u> *subscription rate* <u>increases</u> *Accumulated profits* even more? Simulating with *sales price* at $69 and *subscription rate* at $24 and then $26 reveals that <u>reducing</u> the *sales price* and <u>reducing</u> the *subscription rate* <u>reduces</u> *Accumulated profits*, but <u>increasing</u> the *subscription rate* to $26 <u>increases</u> *Accumulated profits* to $134 922 240. You would finish the year with 6 552 111 *Accumulated customer-months* and 1,290,941 *Accumulated purchases*. $134 922 240 is the highest value for *Accumulated profits* so far.

6.3.6 Searching for the optimal pattern of monthly *process improvement spending*

All the previous searches dealt with decision variables that have an impact on *total revenues*. This is immediately clear for the *sales price* and the *subscription rate*; but *life cycle duration* and *advertising spending* have an influence on customer dynamics and, therefore, indirectly influence *total revenues*, too. But *profits* also depend on *total costs*. You have already examined the effects of *advertising spending*, which is one component of *total costs*, you have not yet searched for the best values of monthly *process improvement spending*.

 DIY 6.7:
Find the *process improvement spending* leading to the highest *Accumulated profits*

Using your model with the optimal values for *sales price*, *subscription rate*, *life cycle duration*, and zero *advertising spending*, you can now employ the same search logic to find out the values of monthly *process improvement spending* that leads to the highest *Accumulated profits*.

Use the worksheet from the companion website and leave the values of *sales price*, *subscription rate*, and *life cycle duration* unchanged from the previous DIY.

Try an amount of $1 million for each month from 1 to 6 separately before using combinations. For each possibility, execute the simulation and write down the final balance of *Accumulated profits* for each combination of *process improvement spending*. Continue this process until you believe that the result cannot be improved further. Use the worksheet at the end of the chapter.

At the beginning of the year, the *Service cost* is $10 per month for each *Current customer*, so the difference to the minimal *Service costs* is at its highest possible value. Recall the discussion of process improvement in Chapter 5.3.2 (Figure 5.9). When the *Service costs* are <u>high</u>, the *process improvability ratio* is <u>high</u> and a given amount spent will have a larger effect compared to a situation the level of *Service costs* has been already reduced. This <u>reduction</u> of *Service costs* will <u>decrease</u> the *process improvability*: this is the effect of the balancing 'cost reduction' loop. Therefore, the shape of *Service costs* for a constant *process improvement spending* must show a <u>diminishing slope</u>, as shown in Figure 6.6.

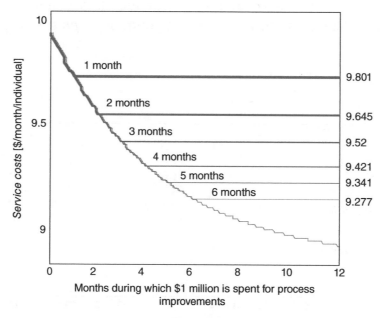

Figure 6.6 *Service costs* <u>decrease</u> achieved by dedicating $1 million to *process improvement spending* during 1, 2, 3, 4, 5 or 6 months

If you spend $1 million starting with a *Service costs* level of $10, as is the case in month 1, *Service costs* are reduced more than if you spend the same amount and *Service costs* are already at $9.8 due to the previous round of *process improvement spending*. So if you spend $1 million in each of the months 1 to 6, *service costs* progressively descend to $9.3. Spending the same amount has less effect when the *Service costs* are already relatively low. At the same time, the number of *Current customers* swiftly underline(increases) (Figure 6.7).

So if you can reduce *Service costs* by $0.5 and you have 500 000 *Current customers*, this would make for a monthly cost underline(reduction) of $250 000. Therefore, you reflect: if you achieved a total of 6 552 111 *Accumulated customer-months* with the default *Service costs* level, the accumulated *costs from Current customers* would be $65 521 110. If you could reduce the *Service costs* from $10 to $9.85, this would reduce the accumulated *costs from Current customers* by 6 552 111 × $0.15 = $982 812. The question is then which amount of *process improvement spending* would be needed to achieve this effect?

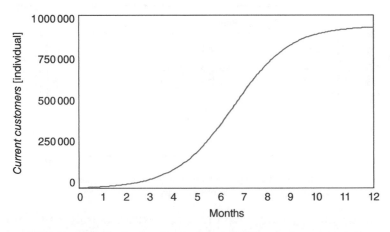

Figure 6.7 S-shaped growth of *Current customers*

To better understand how *process improvement spending* in different months plays out in cost reductions, simulate the model with several configurations for allocating $1 million to *process improvement spending*. As you are not allowed to spend more than $1 million per month on advertising and process improvement taken together, base the simulations on a *sales price* of $70, a *subscription rate* of $25 and a *life cycle duration* of 18 months without *advertising spending*.

Per the results shown in Table 6.11, you can save a little more than $1 million *costs from current customers* if you allocate $1 million to *process improvement spending* during one of the first five months. The net savings in *Service costs* are $61 776 if you spend the amount on process improvements in the first month and descend to $17 908 if you do it in month 5. Spending $1 million once always means that the unit *Service costs* <u>sink</u> from $10 to $9.8, but if you achieve process improvement one month later, you have already lost the opportunity to do it the previous month. In month 6, it is too late: the total cost savings are smaller than the amount spent to achieve them.

Table 6.11 Cost savings due to *process improvement spending* of $1 million in different months

Months of spending						Sum of *costs from*	Saving from *process*	
1	2	3	4	5	6	current customers ($)	improvement spending ($)	Net cost saving ($)
Yes	No	No	No	No	No	52 392 936	1 061 776	**61 776**
No	Yes	No	No	No	No	52 395 288	1 059 424	59 424
No	No	Yes	No	No	No	52 400 572	1 054 140	54 140
No	No	No	Yes	No	No	52 412 220	1 042 492	42 492
No	No	No	No	Yes	No	52 436 804	1 017 908	17 908
No	No	No	No	No	Yes	52 484 660	970 052	−29 948
Yes	Yes	No	No	No	No	51 557 844	1 896 868	−103 132
Yes	Yes	Yes	No	No	No	50 898 124	2 556 588	−443 412
No	No	No	Yes	Yes	No	51 609 868	1 844 844	−155 156

If you spend $1 million in each of the initial two months, you will not recover the second million entirely. Remember that by committing $1 million in month 1 for *process improvement spending*, the *process improvability ratio* already has <u>decreased</u>, and therefore the second million does not achieve as big an effect on process improvement and the ensuing reduction in *Service costs* do not offset this second million.

From this analysis, you discover that *process improvement spending* makes sense to improve *Accumulated profits*, if it is made during the first five months and it is ideally made in month 1.

6.3.7 Combining *advertising spending* and *process improvement spending*

DIY 6.8:
Find the overall combination with the highest *Accumulated profits*

Now you know the values that *sales price, subscription rate,* and *life cycle duration* should have to maximize *Accumulated profits.* You also know that an *advertising spending* of $1 million during months 1 to 3 <u>increases</u> *Accumulated profits.* But you have also found out that a *process improvement spending* of $1 million <u>increases</u> *Accumulated profits,* albeit less than *advertising spending.* You remember the limit of $1 million monthly for the combined spending on advertisings and process improvement.

How can you combine *advertising spending* and *process improvement spending* such as to achieve the highest *Accumulated profits*? Will minor modifications in *sales price, subscription rate,* or *life cycle duration* increase *Accumulated profits* even further?

Use the same model and the worksheet from the companion website to set up and carry out some explorative simulations and to see if you can find the overall best combination of values for the decision variables. Use the worksheet at the end of the chapter.

The simulations exploring the best allocations of *advertising spending* (Table 6.6) showed that by spending $1 million in each of the first three months, you can increase A*ccumulated profits* by $17 243 176. The experiments to find the best way to go about *process improvement spending* (Table 6.11) revealed a decreasing net effect: if you spend $1 million in month 1, you can expect a cost reduction of $61 000 and if you spend the same amount in month 5, it will be only $17 000.

Advertising spending is profitable during the first four months; *process improvement spending* is profitable during the first five months. Even though *advertising spending* is more profitable than *process improvement spending,* you would like to benefit from both effects: increasing *total revenues* through *advertising spending* and reducing *total costs* thanks to *process improvement spending*. However, you must stay within the budget of $1 million per month for both *advertising spending* and *process improvement spending* combined. Therefore, you must decide in which sequence to allocate the funds.

The gains in *total revenues* from *advertising spending* are greater than the *total cost* reductions from *process improvement spending*. It is important to recognize that even though the sum of *advertising spending* and *process improvement spending* must not be greater than $1 million (and so these two ways of spending interact because they compete for the same financial resources), there is no causal interaction between these two variables. *Advertising spending* does not affect *Service costs* and *process improvement spending* does not affect customer dynamics and the resulting *revenues*. For this reason, any mixes of *advertising spending* and *process improvement spending* in a given month lead to lower *Accumulated profits*. For instance, in month 3, *advertising spending* increases *revenues* by more than *process improvement spending* can reduce *Service costs*. Therefore, if you decided to reallocate $100 000 from *advertising spending* to *process improvement spending*, your *monthly profit* would decrease. Accordingly, the available financial resources will be either allocated to *advertising spending* or to *process improvement spending*.

Table 6.12 presents the different combinations of $1 million *advertising spending* and *process improvement spending* in months 1 through 5, ordered by the additional *Accumulated profits* they yield:

Table 6.12 The most profitable way to allocate $1 million between *advertising spending* (A) and *process improvement spending* (PI)

Month 1	2	3	4	5	Additional Accumulated profits ($)
A	A	A			17 243 176
A	A	A	A		16 858 688
A	A				16 748 440
A					13 769 600
	A				6 893 032
		A			2 863 088
			A		789 392
PI					61 776
	PI				59 424
		PI			54 140
			PI		42 492
				PI	17 908

For the first three months, clearly allocating $1 million monthly to *advertising spending* is the most effective way to use your budget. Under the assumption of having spent $1 million on advertising during months 1 through 3, continuing to do so would cause a loss (additional *Accumulated profits* would decrease from $17.2 million to 16.8 million). But *process improvement spending* in month 4 and 5 increases the additional *Accumulated profits* by some thousand dollars.

Therefore, your decision is to allocate $1 million to *advertising spending* during the first three months, then $1 million to *process improvement spending*. Afterwards, no *advertising spending* and no *process improvement spending* for the remaining months. Will this allow you to increase *Accumulated profits* over the $134 922 240 that was the best result so far?

Simulating the model with *sales price* = $70, *subscription rate* = $26, *life cycle duration* = 18 months, *advertising spending* = $1 million for months 1, 2 and 3 and *process improvement spending* = $1 million in month 4, you achieve the following outcomes:

- *Accumulated profit*: $135 117 552
- *Accumulated customer-months*: 6 241 871
- *Accumulated purchases*: 1 268 871

Indeed, the current combination of values for the decision variables allows you to achieve even higher *Accumulated profits*.

6.4 Decisions, behaviours, and outcomes in the best case monopoly

You have now reached a point where a comprehensive summary of the factors and relationships of your situation and their implications for your decisions can be made. Table 6.1 showed that, except for process *improvement spending*, each of your decision variables has more than one influence, and therefore each change you decide to make in the value of these decision variables will cause several simultaneous effects. Decisions leading to increases in the *effective monthly price* for customers increase the *total revenues*, ceteris paribus, but decrease *new customers* because the *price effect on demand multiplier* is reduced. Changes in *life cycle duration* change the flow of *customers leaving* and with it the entire customer dynamics. *Advertising spending* first increases *new customers* but at the same time increases the depletion of *Potential customers* and, therefore, reduces the future flow of *new customers*. To finish, you must choose between *advertising spending* and *process improvement spending*. Your exploration of the space of possible values for the decision variables took several steps.

1. You have explored the three decision variables influencing the *effective monthly price* one at a time and found that:
   - The best *sales price* when the *subscription rate* is $20 and the *life cycle duration* is nine months is $70, and it leads to *Accumulated profits* of $76 719 256.
   - The best *subscription rate* when the *sales price* is $50 and *life cycle duration* is nine months is $23; this allows you to reach *Accumulated profits* of $93 436 672.

- The best *life cycle duration* when the *sales price* is $50 and the *subscription rate* is $20 is 18 months; *Accumulated profits* amount to $72 079 000.
2. After the isolated explorations, you evaluated the effects of setting these three variables at the values found in step 1:
   - When you combined the three values *sales price* = $70, *subscription rate* = $22, and *life cycle duration* = 18 months, *Accumulated profits* were $112 733 000.
   - You found that by increasing the *subscription rate* to $25, you can increase *Accumulated profits* to $116 766 664.
3. You then turned to *advertising spending* using the values from step 2:
   - The best allocation *advertising spending* then turned out to be: spend $1 million in each of the first three months and then nothing. *Accumulated profits* increased $17 243 176 to reach $134 009 840.
   - Exploring minor variations of the *subscription rate* allowed you to find out that if the *subscription rate* is increased from $25 to $26, *Accumulated profits* increase to $134 922 240.
4. Eventually, an allocation of $1 million to *process improvement spending* in month 4 (in the previous month, you use the allowed budget for *advertising spending*) further increases *Accumulated profits* to $135 117 552.

Over the entire search, you have been able to include ever more decision variables. Table 6.13 gives a summary of the process. It shows the different decision variables in columns. Each row corresponds to one of the 'steps' above; whenever in a step, decision variables were kept at their respective default values from the BAU scenario, they are printed in grey:

As you can see in Table 6.13, *Accumulated profits* were immediately higher than the BAU outcomes when you started searching varying only one decision variable at a time. In moving on to combining the partial findings, *Accumulated profits* increased hugely and kept improving until you had defined specific values for each of the decision variables and each month of the year. This is the best result you can achieve assuming you have the monopoly in Plutonia; we will call this the best case monopoly (BCM) scenario.

The final value of *Accumulated profits* is what you will be held responsible for at the end of the year. However, beyond knowing the final outcomes for *Accumulated profit*, you also need to understand what has happened over

Table 6.13 Summary of the search for the best values of the decision variables

| Combinations | Decision variables (variables changed by search in bold, other variables in grey) | | | | | |
	sales price ($)	subscription rate ($)	life cycle duration (months)	advertising spending ($)	process improvement spending ($)	Accumulated profits ($)
BAU	50	20	9	0	0	68 233 240
sales price	**70**	20	9	0	0	93 436 672
subscription rate	50	**23**	9	0	0	76 719 256
life cycle duration	50	20	**18**	0	0	72 079 000
subscription rate, sales price	**70**	**23**	**18**	0	0	112 733 000
and life cycle duration	**70**	**25**	**18**	0	0	116 766 664
advertising spending	**70**	**25**	**18**	**1 million** in months 1–3	0	134 009 840.
	70	**26**	**18**	**1 million** in months 1–3	0	134 922 240.
All decision variables	**70**	**26**	**18**	**1 million** in months 1–3	**1 million** in month 4	135 117 552

the months of the year and why. The graphs of the variables representing customers and financial resources allow us to answer this twofold question (Figure 6.8).

Figure 6.8 shows the stocks *Potential customers* and *Current customers* in the upper part and the customer flows in the lower one. *Current customers* follows an S-shape and grows exponentially until month 6, when the behaviour switches to goal-seeking. It stabilizes around 931 000 individuals, leaving the remaining individuals as *Potential customers*. *New customers* includes a number of individuals who purchase because of the *advertising spending* of the first three months; it grows exponentially until peaking in month 6 and descending to 55 000 individuals, while *customers leaving* grows by following an S-shape up to about 51 000 individuals.

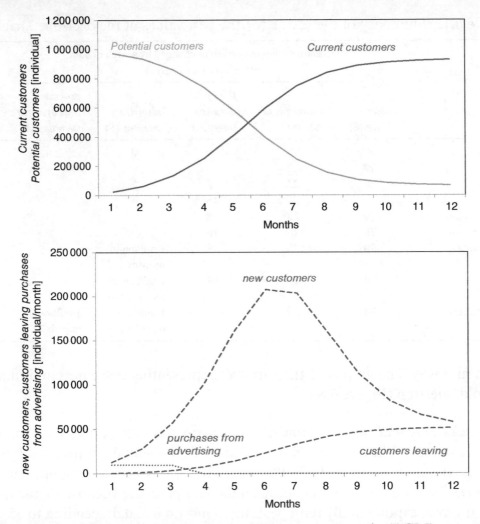

Figure 6.8 Customer dynamics in the best case monopoly (BCM) scenario

Figure 6.9 shows the financial flows resulting from these customer dynamics. In the upper part, you see how *revenues from sales* and *revenues from subscription* add up to *total revenues. Revenue from sales* follows the shape of *new customers* (multiplied by the *sales price*) and, therefore, grows exponentially until it peaks in month 6 and declines to a stable value of $3.8 million. Until the peak, they are more important than *revenue from subscriptions*, which follow the S-shape of *Current customers* (multiplied by the *subscription rate*) and grow up to around $24 million. The shape of *total revenue* combines the bell-shape of *revenue from sales* and the S-shape of *revenue from subscriptions*.

Thus, there will be a phase when *total revenue* will decrease slightly. You know that beforehand, and you also know that this is part of achieving the highest possible *Accumulated profits*. If you wanted to reduce the relative importance of *new customers* and the *revenue from sales*, this would only be possible together with a reduction of *total revenues*. Remember: it is not part of your task at NewTel to avoid *total revenues* <u>sinking</u> at any point in time: You are responsible for the final value of *Accumulated profits*.

The middle part of Figure 6.9 shows how the different cost combine into *total costs. Advertising spending* during months 1 to 3 appears as fine dotted line, and *process improvement spending* in month 4 is shown as line with longer dots. In relative terms, these two components of *total costs* are not of huge importance. *Costs from new customers* represent the *new customers* bell-shaped curve multiplied by the *purchasing price* NewTel pays for each mobile phone it buys; only to sell it on to the *new customers. Costs from Current customers* roughly replicate the S-shaped *Current customers* behaviour, though its slope is slightly diminished due to the *process improvement spending* in month 4. The shape of *total costs,* similar to *total revenues*, grows exponentially until the peak in *new customers* is reached in month 6. Afterwards, *total costs* <u>diminishes</u> more than *total revenues*, which is why it pays off to spend $1 million on process improvements.

The lower part of Figure 6.9 shows the initial losses, followed by an S-shaped growth in *monthly profit* until levelling out around $17 million.

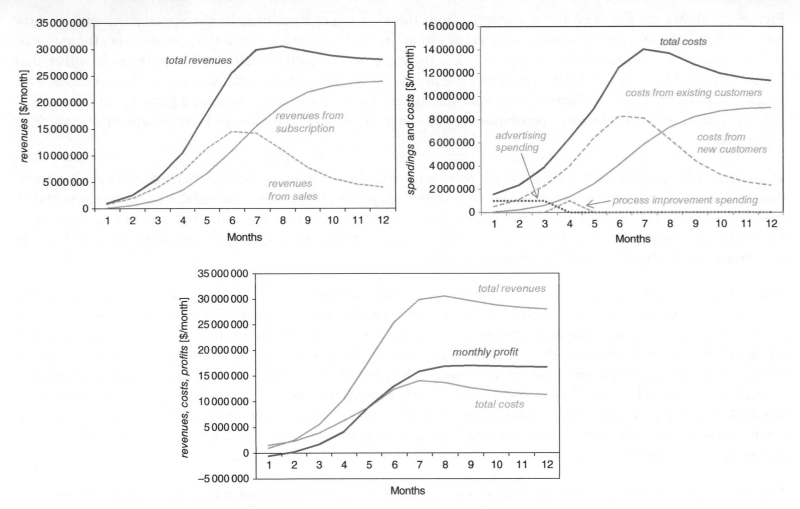

Figure 6.9 Financial flows in the best case monopoly (BCM) scenario

6.5 Setting your objectives

The benefit of evaluating the different possible value combinations for the decision variables is that now you know what a 'good' result for *Accumulated profits* is: around $135 million. Note that this was not obvious when you played through the BAU and 'competing for customers' (CFC) scenarios with SellPhone in Chapter 1. When the CFC scenario lead to hardly any profits at all, making $67 million in the BAU scenario may have looked quite good. But now you know that much more could be achieved in the BCM scenario and you also know how you can achieve this result. You have found the optimal values for all decision variables; these are summarized in Table 6.14.

Is it not remarkable that you needed to search for the values of the decision variables which resulted in the highest possible *Accumulated profits* to find out what the maximum *Accumulated profit* will be? The benefit of developing and using a simulation model for your operations at NewTel is, therefore, twofold: you find out what is possible to achieve and how to achieve it at the same time.

> **Systems Insight 11 (SI 11): Business performance depends on all decision variables**
> The performance of a business, as measured by outcome variables such as *Accumulated profits*, is the consequence of the combined effects resulting from the values of all decision variables and their interdependencies. To define an objective level that it is possible to reach requires a systematic evaluation of the feasible combinations of all decision variables.

Table 6.14 The best case monopoly (BCM) values of the decision variables

Decision variable	Initial value	Optimal value
sales price ($)	50	70
subscription rate ($)	20	26
life cycle duration (months)	9	18
advertising spending ($)	0	1 000 000 in months 1 and 2, then 0
process improvement spending ($)	0	1 000 000 in month 3

This is an important step towards launching your operations. Let us briefly recapitulate what you have done so far and what it allowed you to achieve. Throughout Chapters 2 to 6, you have developed a simulation model in several iterations, starting with a representation of the most fundamental aspects of your business situation and adding causal structure until the content of the model and its behaviour proved to be satisfying.

This is a typical way to go about modelling (Homer, 1996) and at the end of the process your model is a theory of your current situation (Schwaninger and Groesser, 2008; Weick, 1989): it is logically and empirically coherent, but at the same time remains open to be revised in the face of newly discovered aspects (Mass, 1991). Until now you have discovered a set of feedback loops that are, in general, difficult to understand (Moxnes, 1998). You also comprehend the ways in which your target population accumulates either in the stock of *Current customers* or *Potential customers* according to how you set the *life cycle duration*. Correctly understanding stock accumulation is oftentimes counterintuitive (Sterman and Sweeney, 2007) but your efforts in developing your simulation models have helped you to correctly understand these aspects of your business challenge. Summing up, you have realized quite some progress and we invite you to compare your experience with the descriptions offered by Sterman (2000, 2001, 2010).

The fact that you can use the simulation model you developed so far to define your objectives and the way to achieve those objectives is an example of model-based management (Schwaninger, 2010). Model-based management means that you design business policies derived from your mental model of the business situation and test it using the simulation models whose development allowed you to sharpen your mental model.

However, everything analysed so far has been done without taking RivTel into account. It was correct not to account for your direct rival: firstly, you had to develop a clear understanding of the situation. But it is obvious that RivTel will carry out the same analysis as you did and come to the same insights and similar conclusions: it knows there are $135 million *Accumulated profits* to be made in Plutonia and it will do whatever it can to capture a substantial part of this amount. And it also knows the BCM scenario and the optimum values of the decision variables. Finally, it also knows that you know the same things and that you are there to capture a substantial part of the possible profits, too.

Therefore, it does not seem reasonable to simply jump from the current values of the decision variables to the optimum values and hope that everything will work out just nicely. There are new questions arising in the context of the rivalry between NewTel and RivTel:

- What effects would differences in *effective monthly price* between the two companies have in terms of capturing customers and in terms of revenues?
- What effects would advertising have if one company spends more for it than the other?
- Should you compete for *Potential customers* or for *RivTel's Current customers*, or for both?

In answering these questions, you must consider that RivTel also tries to answer the same question. It is true that your current model has helped a lot already, but to answer these new questions some additional work is required. Chapter 7 discusses how to take advantage of the work you have already done and to expand the model such as to find answers to these questions.

6.6 Chapter summary

In this chapter, you have planned and carried out a sequence of simulation experiments that considered possible values for each decision variable. You learned to set the values to be evaluated in steps of variation from large to smaller so as to achieve the optimal value of your objective variable as efficiently as possible. You also learned that each variable's contribution to *Accumulated profits* is first studied in an isolated manner, before you combine them.

This has allowed you to find out that the highest possible value of *Accumulated profits* is $135 million and you know the optimal values for each decision variable in the BCM scenario.

The many simulations carried out with the model have allowed you to develop familiarity with the use of simulation and with the causal structure of your model.

6.7 Questions and challenges

Questions

1. How can a quantified simulation model help set an objective level for *Accumulated profits* which is attainable and suitably high?
2. How do you proceed if you search for the optimal combination of two decision variables?
3. What is the procedure of the half-interval search method? Describe its procedure.
4. What is the relationship between decision variables and performance?

Challenges

One of the assumptions up to here is that the *conversion fraction WoM* is 0.01. How would the highest possible *Accumulated profits* and the optimal values of the decision variables change if *the conversion fraction WoM* is increased to 0.02?

References

Homer, J.B. 1996. Why we iterate: scientific modeling in theory and practice. *System Dynamics Review*, **12**(1), 1–19.

Lane, D.C. 2008. The emergence and use of diagramming in system dynamics: a critical account. *Systems Research and Behavioral Science*, **25**(1), 3–23.

Mass, N.J. 1991. Diagnosing surprise model behavior: a tool for evolving behavioral and policy insights. *System Dynamics Review*, **7**(1), 68–86.

Moxnes, E. 1998. Not only the tragedy of the commons: misperceptions of bioeconomics. *Management Science*, **44**(9), 1234–1248.

Schwaninger, M. 2010. Model-based management (MBM): a vital prerequisite for organizational viability. *Kybernetes*, **39**(9/10), 1419–1428.

Schwaninger, M. and Grösser, S. 2008. System dynamics as model-based theory building. *Systems Research and Behavioral Science*, **25**(4): 447–465. doi:10.1002/sres.914.

Sterman, J.D. 2000. Learning in and about complex systems. *Reflections*, **1**(3), 24–51.

Sterman, J.D. 2001. System dynamics modeling: tools for learning in a complex world. *California Management Review*, **43**(4), 8–24.

Sterman, J.D. 2010. Does formal system dynamics training improve people's understanding of accumulation? *System Dynamics Review*, **26**(4), 316–334.

Sterman, J.D. and Sweeney, L.B. 2007. Understanding public complacency about climate change: adults' mental models of climate change violate conservation of matter. *Climatic Change*, **80**(3–4), 213–238.

Weick, K.E. 1989. Theory construction as disciplined imagination. *Academy of Management Review*, **14**(4), 516–531.

Worksheet DIY 6.2:
Find the *subscription rate* with the highest *Accumulated profits*

Using the half-interval search logic, explore the values of *Accumulated profits* you can achieve setting the *subscription rate* at different values inside the permitted range (20 to 30), approximating the *subscription rate* which leads to the highest *Accumulated profits*.

Use the table to carry out the steps of the search. Upon finding the highest *Accumulated profits*, report the data points to the graph and connect the dots.

Step	subscription rate	Accumulated profits
1		
2		
3		
4		
5		
6		
7		

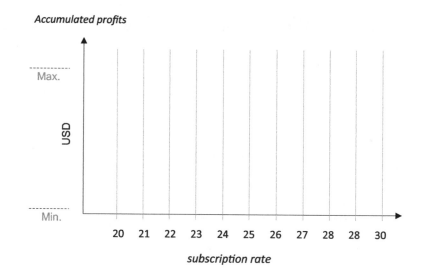

Highest possible *Accumulated profits*: ....

Optimal *subscription rate*: ....

Worksheet DIY 6.3:
Find the *sales price* with the highest *Accumulated profits*

Using the half-interval search logic, explore the values of *Accumulated profits* you can achieve setting the *sales price* at different values inside the permitted range (50 to 70), approximating the *sales price* which leads to the highest *Accumulated profits*.

Use the table to carry out the steps of the search. Upon finding the highest *Accumulated profits*, report the data points to the graph and connect the dots.

Step	sales price	Accumulated profits
1		
2		
3		
4		
5		
6		
7		

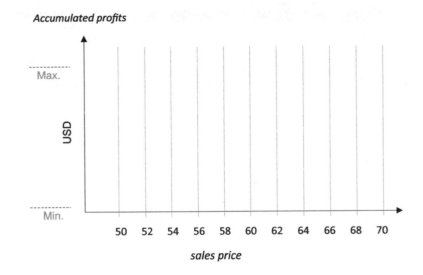

Highest possible *Accumulated profits*: ....

Optimal *sales price*: ....

Worksheet DIY 6.4:
Find the *life cycle duration* with the highest *Accumulated profits*

Using the half-interval search logic, explore the values of *Accumulated profits* you can achieve setting the *life cycle duration* at different values inside the permitted range (5 to 18), approximating the *life cycle duration* which leads to the highest *Accumulated profits*.

Use the table to carry out the steps of the search. Upon finding the highest *Accumulated profits*, report the data points to the graph and connect the dots.

Step	life cycle duration	Accumulated profits
1		
2		
3		
4		
5		
6		
7		

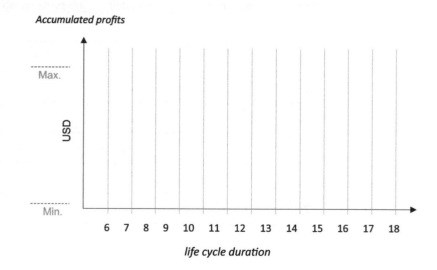

Highest possible *Accumulated profits*: ……………………….

Optimal *life cycle duration*: ………………………..

Worksheet DIY 6.5:
Find the combination of *sales price*, *subscription rate* and *life cycle duration* with the highest *Accumulated profits*

Set the initial values of *subscription rate*, *sales price* and *life cycle duration* to the values you have found in the DIYs 6.2, 6.3 and 6.4. Then explore if variations to the values of the three variables (if the bounds of the value range of each variable allow it, and one variable at a time) are able to further increase the *Accumulated profits*.

Use the table to record each trial's outcomes (since you cannot draw a 4D graph, the table is the only practical way to represent the results):

Step	*subscription rate*	*sales price*	*life cycle duration*	*Accumulated profits*
1				
2				
3				
4				
5				
6				
7				

Highest possible *Accumulated profits*: ....

Optimal

　　　subscription rate: ....

　　　sales price: ....

　　　life cycle duration: ....

Worksheet DIY 6.6:
Find the *advertising spending* leading to the highest *Accumulated profits*

Set the initial values of *subscription rate, sales price* and *life cycle duration* to the values you have found in DIY 6.5. Then find out in which months committing USD 1 million to *advertising spending* further increases your *Accumulated profits*.

Step	advertising spending in month						Accumulated profits
	1	2	3	4	5	6	
1	1,000,000						
2		1,000,000					
3			1,000,000				
4				1,000,000			
5					1,000,000		
6						1,000,000	
7							
8							
9							
10							
11							
12							

Highest possible *Accumulated profits*: ………………………….

advertising spending starts in month …….. and the last month when to spend USD 1 million is …….

Worksheet DIY 6.7:
Find the *process improvement spending* leading to the highest *Accumulated profits*

Set the initial values of *subscription rate*, *sales price* and *life cycle duration* to the values you have found in DIY 6.5. Then find out in which months committing USD 1 million to *process improvement spending* further increases your *Accumulated profits*.

Step	process improvement spending in month						Accumulated profits
	1	2	3	4	5	6	
1	1,000,000						
2		1,000,000					
3			1,000,000				
4				1,000,000			
5					1,000,000		
6						1,000,000	
7							
8							
9							
10							
11							
12							

Highest possible *Accumulated profits*: ....

process improvement spending starts in month .... and the last month when to spend USD 1 million is ....

Worksheet DIY 6.8:
Find the overall combination with the highest *Accumulated profits*

Set the initial values of *subscription rate, sales price* and *life cycle duration* to the values you have found in DIY 6.5. Then find out how to distribute USD 1 million in each of the first five months such as to maximize your *Accumulated profits*.

Step	Allocation of a total of USD 1 million to	Month					Accumulated profits
		1	2	3	4	5	
1	advertising spending						
	process improvement spending						
2	advertising spending						
	process improvement spending						
3	advertising spending						
	process improvement spending						
4	advertising spending						
	process improvement spending						
5	advertising spending						
	process improvement spending						
6	advertising spending						
	process improvement spending						

Highest possible *Accumulated profits*: ....

The optimal combination of *advertising spending* and *process improvement spending* is Step # ....

MARKET DYNAMICS WITH A COMPETITOR

7.1 Introduction

In this chapter, you are going to incorporate your competitor RivTel into the simulation model. What you have found out in the previous chapters will continue to be useful and, if it is possible to set the values of the decision variables to the values you found in Chapter 6, *Accumulated profits* will still be maximized. Now, however, the *population* and the *profits* will have to be split between you and RivTel.

- The *Potential customers* have a choice between NewTel and RivTel.
- Each company's *Current customers* have the choice of switching to the respective other company.

This twofold choice has a consequence for the ways in which rival companies compete and we distinguish between two types of rivalry (Warren, 2008): rivalry type I refers to competing for *Potential customers*, while competition for each other's *Current customers* is called rivalry type II.

We are going to adjust the model so that the simulation experiments help you to design a strategy to implement the optimal values of your decision variables and achieve the highest possible *Accumulated profits* at the end of the year. RivTel's manager is not unknown to you: it is Mary Roamer, the person who preceded you at NewTel. It is plausible that you have a good grasp of how RivTel will go about competition – and RivTel's management can be

Growth Dynamics in New Markets: Improving Decision Making through Simulation Model-based Management,
First Edition. Martin F.G. Schaffernicht and Stefan N. Groesser.
© 2018 John Wiley & Sons Ltd. Published 2018 by John Wiley & Sons Ltd.
Companion website: www.wiley.com/go/Schaffernicht/growth-dynamics

assumed to have as well a grasp on your approach to competition. As you might expect, there is a difference between competing for *Potential customers* and competing for your rival's *Current customers*. So firstly we will analyse competition for *Potential customers* and then we will examine competition for *Current customers*. This process includes figuring out how RivTel will react to your decisions, which will be taken into account when making decisions for NewTel. The model will, therefore, also have to be adjusted to reflect how each company reacts to the other company's decisions. Once these changes have been made, the simulation model will be ready for you to define policies, compare the resulting *Accumulated profits*, and decide which policy is most useful for your purpose.

7.2 Competing for *Potential customers*: rivalry type I
7.2.1 Structure
Initially, almost the entire *population* is available as a *Potential customer*: NewTel and RivTel each have 5000 *Current customers;* leaving 990 000 *Potential customers* to be persuaded to become *Current customers*. In such an immature market situation, it is simply not necessary to chase the rival company's customers. Rather, you will first strive to attract *Potential customers* and you know that RivTel will do the same. In terms of the stocks and flows structure, this requires you to expand the latest version of the model ('C6 Monopoly') as shown in the Figure 7.1.

The elements of the model representing with NewTel's *Current customers* is duplicated for RivTel. Thus, the model has two stocks of *Current customers*, one for NewTel and one for RivTel. Moreover, there is a flow of *new customers*

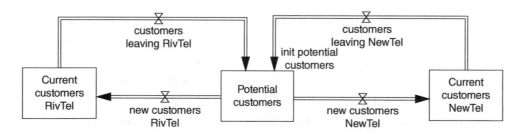

Figure 7.1 Rivalry type I means companies compete for *Potential customers*

to each company's *Current customers* stock and a flow of *customers leaving* from these two stocks back to the *Potential customers* stock. Each flow of *new customers* is driven by the respective company's word-of-mouth dynamics, its *advertising spending*, and its *effective monthly price*. While each *customers leaving* flow is regulated by the company's product *life cycle duration*.

You can decide the value of your decision variables each month and RivTel's manager can do the same. For example, both you and your competitor can freely set your own company's *sales price* and *subscription rate*.

This gives prices and the *life cycle duration* an additional role: if one of the companies sets its decision variables in such a way that <u>increases</u> its *effective monthly price* above the rival's *effective monthly price*, then its flow of *new customers* <u>becomes smaller</u> than that of its rival. Therefore, the *effective monthly price* now becomes a means to compete for *Potential customers* (the effects on demand discussed in Chapter 5 notwithstanding).

Since the *population* is homogenous in its purchasing decisions, the number of *monthly encounters*, the *conversion fraction WoM*, and the *conversion fraction advertising max* have the same values for everyone, regardless of which company they are customers of. All the other variables concerning the effects of word-of-mouth, *effective monthly price*, and *life cycle duration* are included in the model once for NewTel and RivTel too. The resulting model is almost twice as large as the latest model 'C6 Monopoly' but in terms of causal structures the new elements only duplicate the same logic for your competitor RivTel.

All the time that NewTel was the only company offering mobile phone services, the *effective monthly price* and *advertising spending* only influenced the flow of *new customers*. But with the introduction of RivTel, there are now two such flows: *new customers NewTel* and *new customers RivTel*. Thanks to the existence of two different companies offering the same kind of service, *Potential customers* can choose between NewTel and RivTel. To choose they must compare both companies. Let us consider the effects of *advertising spending* and *effective monthly price*. To do so, word-of-mouth dynamics will not be considered. This allows us to focus on advertising (Figure 7.2).

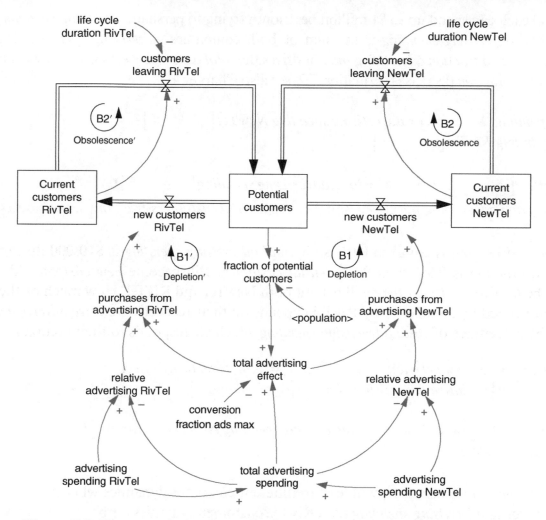

Figure 7.2 The causal structure of *advertising spending* with rivalry type 1

NewTel and RivTel each can spend up to $1 million per month trying to persuade *Potential customers* to become their *new customers*. *Total advertising spending* is the sum of both companies' *advertising spending* (Equation 7.1), and according to the *conversion fraction advertising max*, it drives the *total advertising effect*, which will also <u>decrease</u> when the *potential customers fraction* <u>decreases</u> (Equation 7.2, see also Chapter 4).

$$total\ advertising\ spending\,[\$/month] = advertising\ spending\ NewTel\,[\$/month] +$$
$$advertising\ spending\ RivTel\,[\$/month] \tag{7.1}$$

$$total\ advertising\ effect\,[individual/month] = total\ advertising\ spending\,[\$/month]\,*$$
$$conversion\ fraction\ advertising\ max\,[individual/\$]\,*\ potential\ customers\ fraction\,[dimensionless] \tag{7.2}$$

Conversion fraction advertising is equal to 0.01, so if *total advertising spending* is $10 000 during one month and *potential customers fraction* is 0.99, then 99 *Potential customers* will become *new customers* during that month (Equation 7.3). The *total advertising effect* will benefit both NewTel and RivTel. How much of the *total advertising effect* can be appropriated by NewTel or by RivTel depends on their respective *relative advertising* (Equation 7.4). In other words: the percentage of *total advertising spending* which corresponds to their company.

$$purchases\ from\ advertising\ NewTel\,[individual/month] = total\ advertising\ effect$$
$$[individual/month]\,*\ relative\ advertising\ NewTel\,[dimensionless] \tag{7.3}$$

$$relative\ advertising\ NewTel\,[dimensionless] = advertising\ spending\ NewTel\,[\$/month]\,/$$
$$total\ advertising\ spending\,[\$/month] \tag{7.4}$$

Since changes in the *new customers* flow will lead to different customer dynamics whenever you allocate more or less financial resources to *advertising spending* than RivTel, customer dynamics for both companies will also change. If you spend, for instance, twice as much on advertising as RivTel, you will be able to capture a larger share of

Potential customers. Of course, your opponent at RivTel understands this as well. This means that advertising is a tool to be used when competing for *Potential customers.*

Additionally, advertising quickly <u>decreases</u> in effectiveness as the *potential customers fraction* <u>decreases</u>. By increasing the monthly number of *new customers*, advertising also increases the balancing depletion loop – in fact, for each of the companies, there is one such depletion loop.

However, advertising is not the only way by which NewTel and RivTel have an influence on the purchasing decisions of *Potential customers.* Remember what *effective monthly price* implies. In Chapter 5, you learned that you <u>cannot</u> <u>increase</u> *new customers* by <u>reducing</u> *effective monthly price* below $25.56. This is also true for RivTel. And when the *effective monthly price* of one company <u>becomes larger than</u> $30, the *effect of EMP on demand multiplier* will <u>decrease</u> the *new customers* flow for that company. Other factors such as word-of-mouth and advertising are assumed to be the same. Figure 7.3 allows us to see that a difference between the values of *effective monthly prices* of NewTel and RivTel will lead to differences between their flows of *new customers*:

To reiterate, this means that if you decide to change a decision variable to <u>increase</u> *effective monthly price NewTel*, and RivTel does not do anything comparable, then *effect of EMP on demand multiplier NewTel* is less than the *effect of EMP on demand multiplier RivTel* and, therefore, NewTel will gain <u>less</u> *new customers* than RivTel. And if you <u>increase</u> *advertising spending NewTel* beyond *advertising spending RivTel*, you will be able to gain <u>more</u> of the *total advertising effect* than your rival.

7.2.2 Behaviour

You will now explore the influence of *effective monthly prices* on the *new customers* flow by simulating a simplified model that focuses on competition for *Potential customers* – excluding switching between companies. The first simulation will assume that NewTel and RivTel have identical *effective monthly prices*. Then, two different competitive scenarios will be analysed: rivalry type I price advantage (RIPA) and rivalry type I advertising more (RIAM).

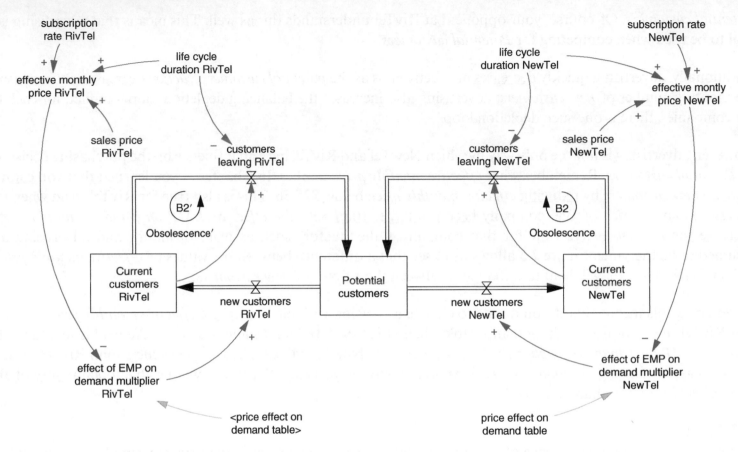

Figure 7.3 The causal structure of *effective monthly price* with rivalry type 1

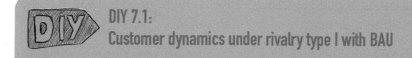
Now it is time for you to build your simulation model for rivalry type 1. One time-saving way to do so is to save a copy of 'C6 Monopoly' and then add 'NewTel' to the names of all variables except *contact rate, conversion fraction WoM, conversion fraction advertising max*, and *price effect on demand table*: By assumption, these are common exogenous variables and will be used for both companies. You can either insert the corresponding RivTel variables or copy-and-paste the NewTel variables and adjust the variable names. Whenever you change a variable name, the software automatically replicates this change in all the equations where this variable is mentioned.

As an alternative to developing this model yourself, you may download the model 'C7 Rivalry type 1' from the companion website.

What are the consequences of having two companies in the same market for your *new customers*?

Use the model and worksheet 7.1 from the companion website to draw a graph of what you expect to be the behaviour of *Current customers NewTel* and *Current customers RivTel*. Explain why you believe this will happen. Then, simulate the model and compare the shape of the graphs (including the inflection point) and the final values.

Recall that in the business as usual (BAU) scenario, *Current customers* followed 'S-shaped growth' behaviour. During the first months, the 'growth engine' loop drove exponential growth; when the *potential customers fraction* <u>decreased</u> enough, the 'depletion' loop became dominant and the behaviour shifted to goal-seeking. The limited *life cycle duration* made repurchases possible, at the cost of not having the entire *population* in the *Current customers* stock. The new model structure contains two 'growth engine' loops and two 'depletion' loops: it is basically the same structure as before. The *contact rate* and the *conversion fraction WoM* apply to both companies, too.

The *price effect on demand table* also applies to both companies. Since NewTel and RivTel will have the same values in their decision variables, *their effective monthly prices* will be identical.

Two hypotheses can be derived from this:

Since the basic causal structure is the same, the shape of behaviour will be 'S-shaped growth' and not all the individuals will be *Current customers* (H 7.1).

Since the same causal structure and the same parameter values apply for NewTel and for RivTel, both companies will have identical *new customers* and *customers leaving* flows. Their *Current customers* curves will therefore be identical (H 7.2).

Now run a simulation with the model 'C7 Rivalry type 1' using *sales price* = $70, *subscription rate* = $26, *life cycle duration* = 18 months, and *advertising spending* = $1 million for each of the first three months both for NewTel and for RivTel. You should encounter the already familiar behaviour mode of S-shaped growth – if you do not then something is wrong with your model.

When there is no difference between the *effective monthly prices* of both companies, there is also no difference in the number of *Current customers* each month; therefore, both lines are superposed in Figure 7.4, which supports both hypotheses (H 7.1 and H 7.2). We are assuming here that individuals pay only attention to the *effective monthly price*, advertising, and the word-of-mouth effect of *Current customers* they meet. Under the circumstances, when the market is mature, the number of *Current customers* for each company is 466 639, which is half of the 933 278 individuals who are not *Potential customers*. The *Accumulated profits* of each company at the end of the year will be $76.1 million, giving a total market value (the sum of both companies' *Accumulated profits*) of $152.2 million. If both companies stick to the default values of their decision variables, there will be 444 195 *Current customers* at the end of the year and each company will close the year with *Accumulated profits* of $44.8 million.

Figure 7.5 allows us to compare *Current customers* in two different runs of the simulation, using different values for the decision variables. The business as usual (BAU) scenario conditions are *sales price* = $50, *subscription rate* = $20, *life cycle*

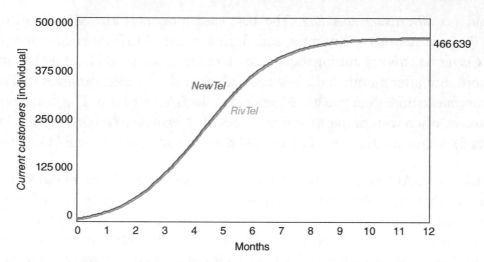

Figure 7.4 Behaviour of *Current customers* of both companies under rivalry type I, BAU scenario

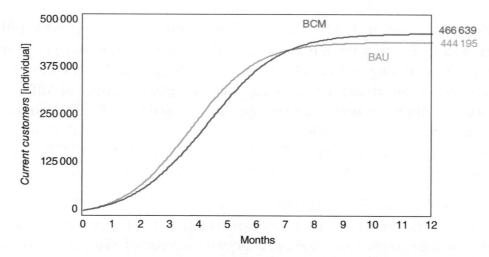

Figure 7.5 *Current customers* graph for the BAU and BCM scenarios

duration=9months, and no *advertising spending*. The best case monopoly (BCM) scenario sets *sales price*=$70, *subscription rate*=$26, *life cycle duration*=18months, and, during months 1 to 3, *advertising spending*=$1 million. There are two differences for *Current customers*: during the first seven months, you would have slightly more *Current customers* under the BAU conditions. But after month 7, the best case values of the decision variables lead to a final situation with about 20 000 *Current customers* more than you would achieve in the BAU scenario. This corresponds to about 5% more *Current customers*. However, when you compare the final values of *Accumulated profits*, the $76.1 million achieved in the BCM scenario (Chapter 6) is almost 70% more than the $44.8 million achieved in the BAU scenario.

Chapter 6 has shown that the BAU results were not good results in terms of *Accumulated profits*. Now comparing the current results – more than 933 000 *Current customers* and total *Accumulated profits* of $152 million – with those from Chapter 6, in which you had no competitor, leads to an intriguing difference. Chapter 6 resulted in a steady-state number of *Current customers* of 931 275 individuals and the corresponding value of *Accumulated profits* was $135 million. How does two companies fighting it out over customers result in <u>more</u> *Current customers* and <u>higher</u> *Accumulated profits*?

The reason for the differences is that the *total amount of advertising spending* in the first month doubles when there are two companies. Since each company has a maximum *monthly advertising spending* of $1 million, going beyond this amount is only possible by adding additional companies. By <u>increasing</u> the *total advertising spending* from $1 to $2 million, the *total effect of advertising* <u>increases</u> and there is a <u>larger</u> number of 'diffusion agents' right from the beginning, thus the total number of *new customers* <u>rises</u> from 19 800 to 29 800 (due to the <u>increased</u> *advertising spending*). This, in turn, <u>decreases</u> the *potential customers fraction* much more than when NewTel is the only company. Therefore, in month 2 there are <u>fewer</u> *Potential customers* and, accordingly, the total number of *new customers* <u>diminishes</u> from more than 60 000 (Chapter 6) to slightly more than 42 000.

7.2.2.1 First scenario for rivalry type I: rivalry I through price advantage (RIPA)

Up to this point, customers have not been able to differentiate between the two companies. But now they can differentiate between the companies using the *effective monthly price*. The question becomes: What are the consequences of adjusting *effective monthly price*? You would expect that if one company is more expensive than its rival, the rival will have a higher flow of *new customers*. 'Rivalry I Price Advantage' (RIPA) would seem to be a convenient name for this scenario. Assuming that neither company engages in advertising, suppose that RivTel sticks to the BCM values of the decision variables and you use the lower default values from the BAU scenario. You would expect that your price advantage and subsequent gain in *new customers* ought to lead to you having more *Current customers* than RivTel. Under these conditions, the *effective monthly price NewTel* is $25.56 and the *effective monthly price RivTel* is $29.89. How will *Current customers* accumulate for each company?

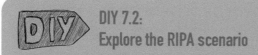

DIY 7.2:
Explore the RIPA scenario

What would happen with the distribution of *Current customers* between NewTel and RivTel if RivTel set its decision variables to *sales price NewTel* = $70, *subscription rate NewTel* = $26, and *life cycle duration* = 18 months but you keep the BAU values *sales price NewTel* = $50, *subscription rate NewTel* = $20, and *life cycle duration* = 9 months?

Sketch the graphs of *net switching from RivTel to NewTel* and the graph of both companies' *Current customers*.

Then use simulation to corroborate your sketch. You can create your own model following the equations described in this section or, alternatively, download the model 'C7 Rivalry type 1' from the companion website.

Since the same causal structure is used, the basic shape of *Current customers* must be an 'S', as before. However, now RivTel has a different *effective monthly price*: in the best case scenario, *effective monthly price* is equal to $29.9, which is higher than the $25.6 of the BAU scenario.

Therefore, *new customers RivTel* should be less than *new customers NewTel*, leading to an <u>increased</u> slope of *Current customers NewTel* (H 7.3).

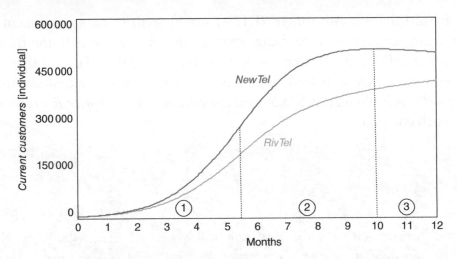

Figure 7.6 Customer dynamics when NewTel implements BAU and RivTel uses the best case values of *sales price*, *subscription rate*, and *life cycle duration*

The behaviour over time shown in Figure 7.6 supports hypothesis H 7.3 that a <u>higher</u> *effective monthly price RivTel* results in NewTel accumulating <u>more</u> *Current customers* than RivTel. The behaviour of *Current customers NewTel* can be separated into three different phases. During phase 1, your *Current customers* <u>grow</u> exponentially, because the reinforcing loops of the two word-of-mouth dynamics dominate. During phase 2, you see goal-seeking <u>growth</u>, which means that the speed of growth <u>diminishes</u> over time. Then, during phase 3, your number of *Current customers* starts to <u>decline</u>. The inflection point, which separates phases 1 and 2, is reached at the same time for you and RivTel. The transition from growth to decline is different for each company: NewTel has this transition at the end of month 10; RivTel has this transition after the first year is over.

The difference between both companies in terms of *Current customers* increases until month 9 but then starts to decrease. The reason for this <u>diminishing advantage</u> becomes clear when you inspect the flows of *new customers* and *customers leaving*.

Figure 7.7 displays the flows of *new customers* in the upper part. It should not come as a surprise that *new customers NewTel* is larger than *new customers RivTel*. You also see that when both variables peak around month 6, the

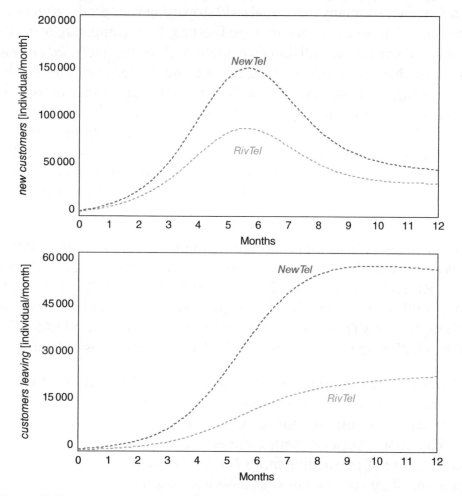

Figure 7.7 *New customers* and *customers leaving* in the RIPA scenario

difference between both flows is much greater than when they begin to stabilize after month 10 or 11. During the same time, *customers leaving NewTel* is larger than *customers leaving RivTel*. This is because your *life cycle duration* is half RivTel's and, therefore, twice as many individuals will stop using your product/service bundle (for an identical number of *Current customers*). And since in a rivalry type I setting, both companies attract *new customers* from the stock of *Potential customers*, some of the individuals coming back to the *Potential customers* stock after leaving NewTel will not actually repurchase NewTel's product, but become RivTel's customers – i.e. join the *new customers RivTel* flow. So RivTel has a <u>smaller</u> *customers leaving* flow and takes advantage of your <u>larger</u> *customers leaving* flow to <u>increase</u> its *new customers* flow: thereby, it is able to achieve a *new customers* flow that is <u>larger than</u> its *customers leaving* flow, and thus experience a slow but more sustained <u>growth</u> in *Current customers*. During that time, your *customers leaving* flow already <u>exceeds</u> your *new customers* flow, which explains the <u>decline</u> of your *Current customers*. If your advantage in *new customers* decreases and your *customers leaving* increase, then your advantage in terms of *Current customers* will diminish over time. Table 7.1 shows the results at the end of the simulation.

Table 7.1 shows the decision variables in the upper section, then the *effective monthly price* and the resulting *effect of EMP on demand multiplier*, followed by the final outcomes in the lower part. According to Table 7.1, NewTel has a substantial advantage over RivTel in terms of the *effective monthly price*: RivTel's *effect of EMP on demand multiplier* is as low as 0.86. Thanks to this you can gain 0.882 million more *Accumulated customer-months* and 0.324 million more *Accumulated purchases* than RivTel. However, RivTel finishes its year with $13.45 million more than you. You finish the year with less than half of the *Accumulated profits*. Hence, the result is not particularly attractive.

Bearing in mind your objective to achieve the highest possible *Accumulated profits* at the end of the year, it would seem that being more competitive on price does not have the desired effect: forgoing $20 for each *new customer* and $8 for each customer-month turns out to outweigh having more *Accumulated customer-months* and more *Accumulated purchases*. This first experience with competition for *Potential customers* suggests that (when you interpret competition in the sense of persuading more *Potential customers* than your competitor) you may indeed achieve an advantage in terms of customers, but still finish with <u>less</u> *Accumulated profits*.

Table 7.1 Results of the RIPA scenario

Decision variables	NewTel	RivTel	Difference
sales price ($)	50	70	−20
subscription rate ($)	20	26	−6
life cycle duration (months)	9	18	−9
advertising spending ($)	0	0	0
Intermediate variables	**NewTel**	**RivTel**	**Difference**
effective monthly price ($)	25.56	29.89	−4.33
effect of EMP on demand multiplier	1.00	0.86	0.14
KPIs	**NewTel**	**RivTel**	**Difference**
Accumulated customer-months (millions)	3.427	2.545	0.882
Accumulated purchases (millions)	0.87	0.546	0.324
Accumulated profits ($ millions)	45.70	59.15	−13.45

7.2.2.2 Second scenario for rivalry type I: Rivalry I by more advertising (RIMA)

A different way to compete might be to attempt to gain an advantage through *advertising spending* instead of reducing the *effective monthly price*. This is considered in the 'Rivalry I Advertising More' (RIMA) scenario. Assume that both companies set the optimal values, i.e. *sales price* = $70, *subscription rate* = $26, and *life cycle duration* = 18 months, but that RivTel will not spend money on advertising, while you spend $1 million in each of the first three months.

By allocating $1 million per month to *advertising spending*, NewTel underlines increases its flow of *new customers*. This leads to a underlined quicker increase of *Current customers NewTel*, which underlined increases the strength of the word-of-mouth dynamics of NewTel. Accordingly, *Current customers NewTel* will grow more than *Current customers RivTel* (H 7.4).

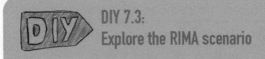

DIY 7.3:
Explore the RIMA scenario

What would happen with the distribution of *Current customers* between NewTel and RivTel if both companies set their respective decision variables *sales price* = $70, *subscription rate* = $26, and *life cycle duration* = 18 months, but NewTel spends $1 million on advertising in months 1, 2 and 3, while RivTel does not allocate resources to *advertising spending*?

Sketch the graphs of what you expect to be the behaviour of *net switching from RivTel to NewTel* and of both companies' *Current customers*. You can use the worksheet from the companion website.

Then, use simulation to corroborate your sketch. You can create your own model following the equations described in this section, or alternatively download the model 'C7 Rivalry type 1' from the companion website. To carry out both simulations, you can use two different simulation variables as described in DIY 2.10. Then, copy the graphs of the simulated behaviours of *net switching from RivTel to NewTel* and of both companies' *Current customers* and compare your expectations to the simulation. If there are differences in behaviour mode or other differences that surprise you, explain why exactly you expected something different and identify the part of the causal structure you did not interpret adequately.

The results is the typical S-shape behaviour in *Current customers* (Figure 7.8), which supports Hypothesis H 7.4.

Both companies' *Current customers* grow exponentially during the first half of the year and then switch to goal-seeking growth. However, it appears that under the conditions of this simulation, *customers RivTel* seeks a steady-state level of 240 000 individuals, whereas *Current customers NewTel* settles at around 695 000 individuals. A total of almost 935 000 individuals use mobile phones by the end of the year, and most of them are your customers.

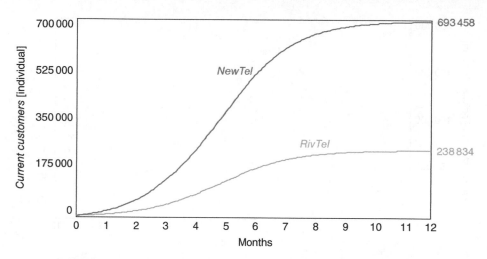

Figure 7.8 Customer dynamics when NewTel and RivTel use the optimal values of *sales price, subscription rate,* and *life cycle duration,* but only NewTel uses advertising

Compared to the previous simulation (Figure 7.6), in which NewTel starts losing *Current customers* in the last months of the year, this time both companies' *Current customers* approach a steady-state level. The loss of *Current customers* in the previous simulation was due to the difference in *life cycle duration* between both companies. In the current simulation, both NewTel and RivTel have a *life cycle duration* of 18 months. Hence, there is no reason for an asymmetric loss of *Current customers*. Now, let us consider how the flows of *new customers* and *customers leaving* behave in this simulation (Figure 7.9).

Turning first to the flow of *new customers* for each company, both flows peak in month 5 and *new customers NewTel* grows to almost 160 000 while *new customers RivTel* does not exceed 55 000 individuals that month. This difference in the growth of *new customers* is the compounded effect of attracting <u>more</u> *new customers* due to *advertising spending* during the first three months. Spending $1 million per month during the first quarter of the year yields 9890 <u>additional</u> *new customers* in the first month, 9662 in the second month, and 9177 in the third month. The

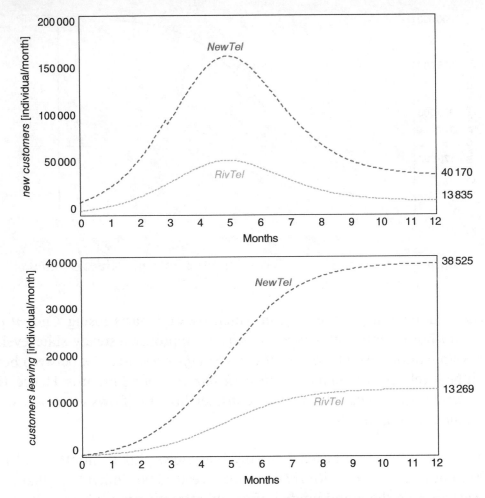

Figure 7.9 *New customers* and *customers leaving* in the RIMA scenario

numbers slightly <u>diminish</u> despite the constant monthly amount because each <u>additional</u> *new customer* <u>increases the depletion</u> of the *Potential customers* stock and, therefore, <u>diminishes</u> the *fraction of potential customers*, which in turn <u>reduces</u> the strength of the *total advertising effect*. At the same time, each <u>additional</u> *new customer* attracts even <u>more</u> *new customers* due to word-of-mouth dynamics. When you stop allocating financial resources to *advertising spending*, NewTel has almost 130 000 *Current customers* and RivTel only about 45 000: you have 85 000 more autonomous promotion agents than RivTel. <u>Stopping</u> *advertising spending* <u>reduces</u> the *purchases from advertising* to zero, and the graph of *new customers NewTel* <u>decreases</u> for a brief period of time at the start of the fourth month (just after the '3' mark on the time axis). However, your 85 000 <u>additional</u> *Current customers* make your word-of-mouth dynamics much stronger than RivTel's, and, after a couple of days, your *new customers* have resumed the quick growth observed before.

Given that *Current customers NewTel* greatly exceeds *Current customers RivTel* and that both companies have identical *life cycle durations*, it follows that *customers leaving NewTel* must be always greater than *customers leaving RivTel*, and the proportions of these flows must correspond to the proportions of the respective *Current customers* stocks. The lower section of Figure 7.9 shows the similarity in behaviour as well as the proportions: when the customer dynamics stabilizes towards the end the year, *customers leaving NewTel* reaches almost 39 000 individuals per month and *customers leaving RivTel* is slightly over 13 000. The monthly numbers of *new customers NewTel* and *customers leaving NewTel* converge towards the end of the year, which is also the case for RivTel. It follows that each company's stock of *Current customers* will remain stable thereafter.

Now turn your attention to the financial results (Table 7.2), which follow from the customer dynamics (remember that in the current scenario there is no *process improvement spending*).

Table 7.2 has the same structure as Table 7.1. In the upper section, the values of the decision variables are shown; the only difference between you and RivTel is that you allocate a total amount of $3 million to *advertising spending* and RivTel does not. Since *sales price*, *subscription rate*, and *life cycle duration* are identical, both companies have the same *effective monthly price*, and, therefore, there is no difference between each company's *effect of EMP on demand multipliers*.

Table 7.2 The results of the RIMA scenario

Decision variable	NewTel	RivTel	Difference
sales price ($)	70	70	0
subscription rate ($)	28	28	0
life cycle duration (months)	18	18	0
advertising spending (months 1–3, millions) ($)	1	0	3
Intermediate variables	**NewTel**	**RivTel**	**Difference**
effective monthly price ($)	29.89	29.89	0
effect of EMP on demand multiplier	0.86	0.86	0
KPIs	**NewTel**	**RivTel**	**Difference**
Accumulated customer-months (millions)	4.917	1.700	3.217
Accumulated purchases (millions)	0.96	0.33	0.63
Accumulated profits ($ millions)	108.34	38.36	69.98

NewTel achieves almost five million *Accumulated customer-months*, which is 3.2 million more than RivTel's *Accumulated customer-months*. When you compare both companies' *Accumulated purchases*, NewTel reaches almost one million and RivTel only one third of that. With such a huge difference in favour of NewTel, and the *sales price* and *subscription rate* being identical, it is clear that NewTel's *Accumulated profits* at the end of the year will be higher than RivTel's in the same proportion; NewTel closes with almost $110 million, whereas RivTel finishes with $38 million. Remembering that in the BAU scenario, both companies closed their years with *Accumulated profits* of about $56 million, this time your *Accumulated profits* have almost doubled, which of course is much better than the outcome in the BAU scenario.

The total value of this market, i.e. the sum of *Accumulated profits*, is only a little bit higher than in the BAU scenario under monopoly because *advertising spending* has sped up the purchasing decisions of *Potential customers*. This means that the steady-state number of *Current customers* and *new customers* has been reached earlier during the year, but the size of the *population* has not grown. Therefore, *advertising spending* has increased the *total revenues* slightly. It follows that your additional *Accumulated profits* resulted in a loss of *Accumulated profits* for RivTel.

As the manager of NewTel you can think that you have won compared to your previous results. You have beaten your competitor; RivTel made less *Accumulated profits* than before and less than you. Of course, this is only a simulation, you cannot seriously believe that your competitor does not understand what *advertising spending* is for and, therefore, you do not really expect them to spend nothing when you have concluded that an initial *advertising spending* would <u>increase</u> your *Accumulated profits*.

Summing up, competing for *Potential customers* is one component of rivalry, and *effective monthly price, life cycle duration*, and *advertising spending* all can be used to compete for *Potential customers*. But they have different effects on customer dynamics and on the accumulation of profits over the year.

> **Management Insight 11 (MI 11): Rivalry type I targets *Potential Customers***
> **Rivalry type I refers to *Potential customers*. Since *Potential customers* are not yet a competitor's *Current customers*, it is less aggressive than trying to win over their *Current customers*. It must be used as long as there are *Potential customers*.**

Reflect for a moment on other ways in which you might win or lose *Current customers* from RivTel. This is discussed next.

7.3 Competing for *Current customers*: rivalry type II
7.3.1 Structure

Competing for *Potential customers* is sensible when there are many individuals who have not yet resolved to purchase. But as *Potential customers* progressively become *Current customers*, and the market saturates, the only way of increasing your own *Current customers* will be to attract individuals who are currently *Current customers RivTel*. Of course, RivTel's manager is in the same situation. This means that there can be a bidirectional monthly flow of individuals between the two stocks:

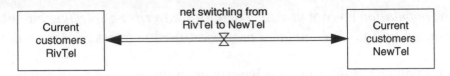

Figure 7.10 Competing for each other's *Current customers* – Rivalry type II

The stock and flow diagram (Figure 7.10) contains a bidirectional flow variable *net switching from RivTel to NewTel*. There is an important difference between flows that have a single direction and bidirectional flows. For instance, *new customers NewTel* is an inflow to *Current customers NewTel*, while *customers leaving NewTel* is an outflow from that stock. Therefore, *new customers NewTel* will not have a negative value at any time during the simulation – after all, adding a negative number of people to a stock is nonsense. *Customers leaving NewTel* will also have only non-negative numbers, and they will be subtracted from the stock. Knowing this, it becomes immediately clear that by subtracting the number of *new customers NewTel* from *Potential customers*, the inflow to *Current customers NewTel* is also an outflow from *Potential customers*. And analogously, *customers leaving NewTel* is an outflow from *Current customers NewTel* and an inflow to *Potential customers*. This flow's value will always be a non-negative number, but it is subtracted from *Current customers NewTel, and* added to *Potential customers*.

A bidirectional flow is different. By definition it can be larger than or smaller than zero. Either company's *Current customers* can switch to the other company, so *net switching from RivTel to NewTel* represents the net effect of some individuals switching from NewTel to RivTel and some individuals switching in the opposite direction. A positive value of the flow adds individuals to *Current customers NewTel* and subtracts them from *Current customers RivTel*. A negative number literally means adding a negative number to *Current customers NewTel*; of course, this is equivalent to subtracting this number from *Current customers NewTel*, and adding them to *Current customers RivTel*.

Representing the switching between companies in one single flow is practical because it avoids adding additional flows, and it is possible because, regardless of the direction of the flow, the switching depends on one factor: the relationship between both companies' *effective monthly prices*. Note that this implies a simplifying assumption: in real life, customers of a mobile telephone company may decide to switch provider for reasons other than price, e.g. service quality. However, as we have detailed in the first chapters of the book, product and service quality are not considered in our models (see Chapter 8 on the limitations). For that reason, customers will not switch providers because of service quality. To keep things as simple as possible, we also assume that *advertising spending* does not have an influence on customer switching.

In Chapter 5, you saw that when the *effective monthly price* <u>increases</u> beyond a critical value of around \$32 per month, *Potential customers* start finding it too expensive and the proportion who decide to become *new customers* because of word-of-mouth dynamics or advertising will <u>decrease</u> – as expressed by the <u>decreasing</u> *effect of EMP on demand multiplier*. You already know that people are sensitive to the *effective monthly price*: they are assumed to follow a policy that is sensitive to the *effective monthly price*. Now you must revise your representation of the customers' policy. Since now there are two companies offering the product service bundle, customers of either company will compare their current *effective monthly price* to the one of the respective other company. Of course, you cannot know how each of them is reasoning in detail and you cannot be sure that all of them reason in the same way either. However, you can approximately represent the logic of how customers behave as a pair of '*if→then*' rules expressing *Current customers*' policy: 'if NewTel is X% cheaper than RivTel in a given month, then Y% of *Current customers* RivTel will switch to NewTel during this month. If RivTel is X% cheaper than NewTel in a given month, then Y% of *Current customers* NewTel will switch to RivTel during this month.

This needs to be considered in the model by a new variable called *relative effective monthly price NewTel* to drive the flow of customers switching between the two companies (Figure 7.11, 'C7 Rivalry type 2').

The *effective monthly price* is calculated in the same way for each company. The *relative effective monthly price NewTel* represents the relationship between the two *effective monthly prices* from the perspective of NewTel. You calculate the value of *relative effective monthly price NewTel* by Equation 7.5:

$$
\begin{aligned}
relative\ effective\ monthly\ price\ NewTel[\text{dimensionless}] = (&effective\ monthly\ price\ RivTel[\$/\text{individual}] - \\
&effective\ monthly\ price\ NewTel[\$/\text{individual}])/(effective\ monthly\ price\ NewTel[\$/\text{individual}] + \\
&effective\ monthly\ price\ RivTel[\$/\text{individual}])
\end{aligned} \tag{7.5}
$$

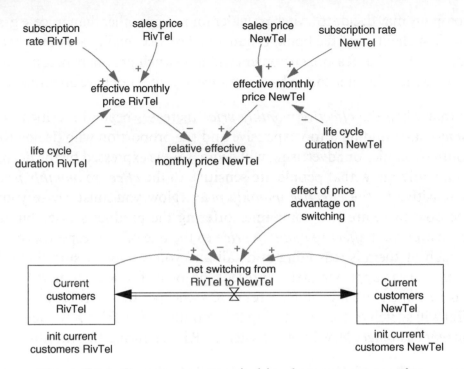

Figure 7.11 Customers net switching between companies

Equation 7.5 looks complicated for the apparently simple purpose of expressing the cost advantage or disadvantage of NewTel. Why not simply divide the difference between both companies' *effective monthly price* and divide it by your *effective monthly price*? Did we not state that we want to keep things as simple as possible? Indeed, this calculation ensures that a given difference between both companies' *effective monthly prices* will always lead to the same absolute value for the relative *effective monthly price*. Consider the examples shown in Table 7.3.

When *effective monthly price NewTel* is $20 and *effective monthly price RivTel* is $30, then the difference is $10, and divided by 50, *relative effective monthly price NewTel* will be $0.2, meaning that NewTel is 20% cheaper than RivTel.

Table 7.3 *Relative monthly effective cost NewTel*

Variable	Example 1	Example 2
effective monthly price NewTel ($)	20	30
effective monthly price RivTel ($)	30	20
relative effective monthly price NewTel	0.2	−0.2

For the opposite situation, the difference is − $10 and, therefore, the *relative effective monthly price NewTel* would be − $0.2: in that case, RivTel is cheaper. This way to compute the comparison treats both possible situations (NewTel is cheaper, NewTel is more expensive) without introducing a bias.

How then does *relative effective monthly price NewTel* drive *net switching from RivTel to NewTel*? If *relative effective monthly price NewTel* >0, then a fraction of *Current customers RivTel* will switch to NewTel. This is the positive sense of the flow. However, if *relative effective monthly price NewTel* <0, then a fraction of *Current customers NewTel* will switch to RivTel. In that case, the flow needs to have a negative number. Since, in each of the two possible cases, a different *population* stock is the basis for calculating the flow, the equation must process both cases. As we want to keep the model free from unnecessary complexity (**Guideline 3**, Chapter 2), we assume that the percentage of *customers* who switch each month is identical to the value of *relative effective monthly price NewTel*: if NewTel is 10% cheaper, 10% of the *Current customers RivTel* will switch to NewTel (and vice versa).

Since for each month of the simulation, the *net switching from RivTel to NewTel* flow depends on either *Current customers RivTel* or *Current customers NewTel*, both stocks are connected to the flow by a causal link. The stocks contain individuals, but you also know that the flow's unit of measure is individual/month. Since the *relative effective monthly price NewTel* is dimensionless, there is one piece missing to have a formulation that respects unit consistency. This piece is the variable *effect of price advantage on switching*: you are sure that this entity does exist in the real situation (Toolbox 1.1) and this effect clearly is 'per month', i.e. its unit is 1/month.

You can say that the monthly effect *net switching from RivTel to NewTel* is equal to the *relative effective monthly price NewTel* multiplied with either *Current customers RivTel* or *Current customers NewTel*:

net switching from RivTel to NewTel $[\text{individual}/\text{month}]$ = *effect of price advantage on switching* $[1/\text{month}]$ *

    relative effective monthly price NewTel $[\text{dimensionless}]$ *

IF THEN ELSE(

    relative effective monthly price NewTel > 0,   (7.6)

    Current customers NewTel $[\text{individual}]$,

    Current customers RivTel $[\text{individual}]$

)

Equation 7.6 uses a conditional part which can distinguish between the two possible situations: Newtel is cheaper than RivTel or vice versa.

7.3.2 Behaviour

Assume that each company has an initial stock of 480 000 *Current customers* and from the BAU values of *sales price* ($50), *subscription rate* ($20), and *life cycle duration* (9 months). The flows between *Potential customers* and each company's *Current customers* stock are not included in this model because you are focusing on the rivalry over *Current customers*.

Both managers know that the BCM values of *sales price* would be $70, the BCM *subscription rate* would be $26, and the BCM *life cycle duration* 18 months. If both companies instantly switched from the BAU values of the decision variables to their respective BCM values, they would maintain identical *effective monthly prices* and, therefore, no customer switching would take place. However, assume that you trust your competitor's manager to do precisely this and, therefore, you decide to do it as well – but surprisingly RivTel's manager chooses to stick to the BAU values. What would this mean for the behaviour of *net switching from RivTel to NewTel* and the two *Current customer* stocks?

DIY 7.4:
The expected effect of *effective monthly price* on *net switching*

What would happen with the distribution of *Current customers* between NewTel and RivTel if both companies start with 480 000 *Current customers* and you set your decision variables to *sales price NewTel* = $70, *subscription rate NewTel* = $26, and *life cycle duration* = 18 months, but RivTel keeps the BAU values? Sketch the graphs of *net switching from RivTel to NewTel* and both companies' *Current customers*.

Then use the simulation model to corroborate your sketch. You can create your own model following the equations described in this section, or alternatively download the model 'C7 Rivalry type 2' from the companion website.

The model 'C7 Rivalry type 2' contains the causal structure discussed so far. The *effective monthly price NewTel* would rise to $28.89 whereas the *effective monthly price RivTel* stays at $25.56. Accordingly, the *relative effective monthly price NewTel* would be $0.0612, which is a *relative cost advantage* for RivTel, not for NewTel. As consequence, there would be no *switching from RivTel to NewTel* but *switching from NewTel to RivTel* and, therefore, *net switching from RivTel to NewTel* is negative (H 7.5).

Since NewTel will <u>lose</u> *Current customers*, the base for *net switching* <u>decreases</u>. This will lead to a <u>decrease</u> in the <u>loss</u> of *Current customers NewTel* over time (H 7.6).

Simulating the model allows both hypotheses to be supported (Figure 7.12):

Values in the graph are negative because NewTel is losing *Current customers* to RivTel. Each time a given number of individuals switches from NewTel to RivTel, the remaining *Current customers NewTel* <u>decreases</u>. In the next time step, the cost disadvantage of NewTel applies to a smaller number of individuals and over

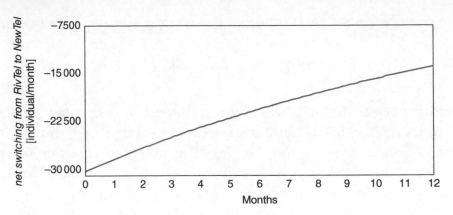

Figure 7.12 *Net switching from RivTel to NewTel* when RivTel uses BAU values and NewTel the BCM values of *sales price, subscription rate* and *life cycle duration*

time the loss of *Current customer* <u>decreases</u>. Figure 7.13 displays how the initial numbers of *Current customers* (both NewTel and RivTel start with 480 000 individuals) change over the course of the year:

In this scenario, approximately 250 000 *Current customers NewTel* decide to become *Current customers RivTel*. At the end of the year, your stock of *Current customers* has decreased from 480 000 individuals to 230 000. You know that *Current customers* are not the only important thing – prices also are important for driving *revenues*. However, the question is whether <u>losing</u> 50% of your *Current customers* will be compensated by <u>increasing</u> the values of the decision variables to their best case levels?

This is a relevant question but to answer it the current model is not sufficient: it is only a partial analysis with only the *net switching from RivTel to NewTel* flow, without the *new customers* flows and everything else, assuming that both companies start with 480 000 *Current customers*. It does not consider the word-of-mouth dynamics, *advertising spending*, and the effects of a limited *life cycle duration* on customer dynamics.

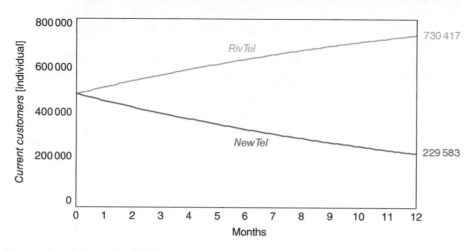

Figure 7.13 The effect of *net switching of Current customers* when NewTel is more expensive than RivTel

Rivalry type II starts becoming important when *Potential customers* have already been depleted and you cannot get additional *Current customers* without 'stealing' them from your competitor. Therefore, it is important to understand this form of rivalry by itself ('ceteris paribus') before going on to analyse the entire situation – which is done here.

The partial results of the effects of *net switching* on the share of your *revenues* that directly depend on the number of *Current customers* are shown in Table 7.4. The first three columns present three model variables. The last column is an indicator that is calculated directly in the table: the accumulated *revenues from subscription* is the result of multiplying the *accumulated customer-months* by the *subscription rate*. The data in the first two rows stem from simulating the model 'C7 Rivalry type 2' with two sets of values: Business as usual (BAU: *sales price* = $50, *subscription rate* = $20 and *life cycle duration* = 9 months) and Best case monopoly (BCM: *sales price* = $70, *subscription rate* = $26 and *life cycle duration* = 18 months). The third row shows the results from maintaining the BAU scenario but <u>decreasing</u> the *subscription rate* from $20 to $14 (this is, $6 cheaper than the BAU value instead of $6 more expensive like in the BCM scenario). RivTel is assumed to use BAU values – if there was no difference between the two companies, talking about rivalry type I and *net switching* is useless:

Table 7.4 Partial effect of rivalry type II on revenues

Scenario	effective monthly price NewTel ($)	relative effective monthly price NewTel	Accumulated customer-months NewTel (millions)	Accumulated revenues from subscription (millions)
Business as usual (BAU)	25.56	0.0000	5.760	115.20
Best case monopoly (BCM)	29.89	0.7816	3.784	98.38
subscription rate = $14	19.56	−0.1330	8.633	120.86

When the values of the decision variables are changed from the BAU to the BCM scenario, the *effective monthly price NewTel* increases from $26.56 to $29.89. Since RivTel did not change its decision variables' values, the *relative effective monthly price NewTel* now rises from 0 to 0.7816: NewTel is much more expensive than RivTel. Accordingly, the *Accumulated customer-months NewTel* decrease from 5.76 million to 3.784 million. Multiplication by the respective value of *subscription rate NewTel* allows us to determine that – assuming only *net switching* takes place – the sum of *revenues from subscription* would decrease from $115.20 million to $98.38 million. This suggests that if only one of the companies becomes more expensive, then the loss of *Current customers* due to *net switching* may weigh more than the increase of the *subscription rate*. When the only change to the BAU values is to decrease the *subscription rate*, then the *effective monthly price NewTel* decreases to $19.56 and the *relative effective monthly price NewTel* sinks to −0.133, expressing the fact that NewTel is now cheaper. In response to the ensuing *net switching*, the *Accumulated customer-months* increase to 8.633 million and multiplication by the *subscription rate* allows us to calculate that the sum of *revenues from subscriptions* would increase to $120.86 million.

Clearly, when you do not have a monopoly any longer, increasing *prices* may *cost* you *customers* and decrease *revenues* – and decreasing *prices* can become a competitive tool to increase *customers* and *revenues*. Be aware: *new customers* also result in an additional stream of *revenues from new customers*. You know that *new customers* will also be affected by changes to the decision variables, but changes in *new customers* and their impact on profits cannot be evaluated with the model 'C7 Rivalry type 2' because it does not contain the corresponding variables.

Systems Insight 12 (SI 12): *relative attractiveness*
When actors must choose between two or more possible alternatives, they compare them. The concept of *relative attractiveness* allows this to be represented in a model.

Management Insight 12 (MI 12): *effective monthly price* influences *relative attractiveness*
The fact that *Current customers* compare attributes such as the *effective monthly price* allows you to adjust them to increase your *relative attractiveness*.

Management Insight 13 (MI 13): Rivalry type II is aggressive
Rivalry type II refers to the competitor's *Current customers*. It is an openly aggressive way to compet, and may trigger an escalation in aggression, which reduces profits – at least in the short term.

7.4 Competing for *Potential* and *Current customers*
7.4.1 The causal structure of diffusion with a competitor
Until now, you have considered the different effects of your decision variables *sales price, subscription rate, life cycle duration, advertising spending*, and *process improvement spending* in isolated ways:

- you know how they affect customer dynamics and the *Accumulated profits* via word-of-mouth and advertising when there is no competitor;
- you understand the interaction between RivTel's and your decision variables when competing for *Potential customers*;
- you also understand how both companies' *effective monthly price*s interact and how this affects rivalry over *Current customers*;
- you know now that *process improvement spending* does not influence the competition because it only <u>increases</u> *monthly profits* by <u>reducing</u> the *Service costs*.

Of course, all these influences occur at the same time, creating a complex decision situation. The structure is represented in detail in the model 'C7 Rivalry' and is mapped out in a simplified manner as causal loop diagram in Figure 7.14.

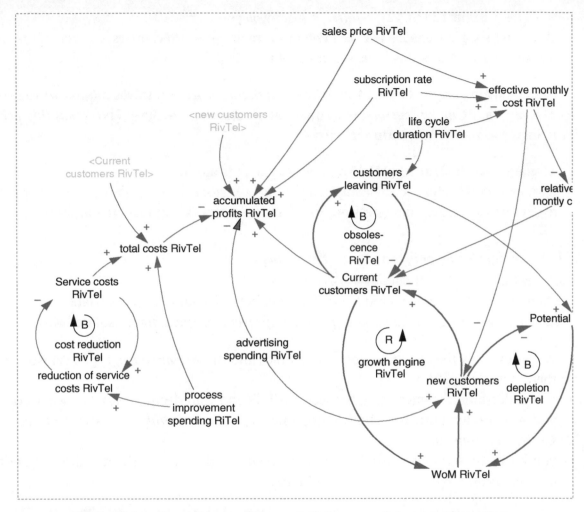

Figure 7.14 Causal loop diagram of the complete causal structure

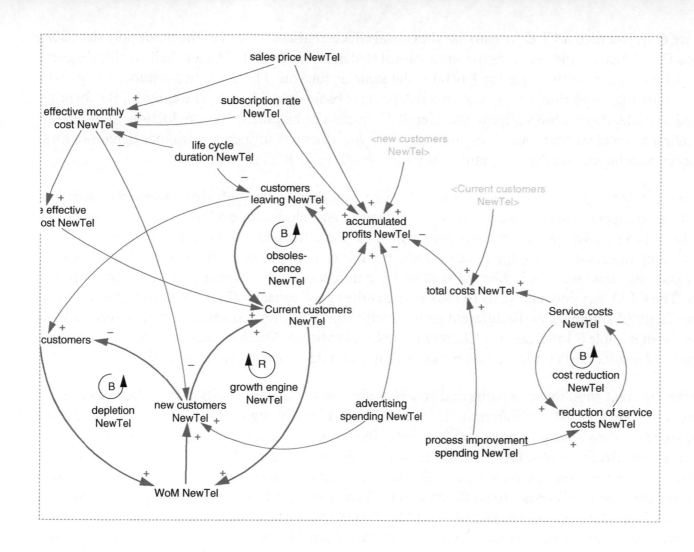

In Chapter 6 (Figure 6.1), you used a CLD to visualize the causal effects that are present in the monopoly situation. Figure 7.14 extends this structure and includes the same causal structure for RivTel. The left half of this diagram is a copy of the right half, because the logic for RivTel is the same as for you. There are two reinforcing 'growth engine' loops, two balancing 'depletion' loops, and two balancing 'obsolescence' loops. The causal links forming these loops are bold to make them more visible in the overall diagram. The balancing 'cost reduction' loops are an exception: the CLD makes it clear that *process improvement spending* does not influence customer dynamics and, therefore, does not have an impact on the competition between NewTel and RivTel.

Both companies interact through *relative effective monthly price NewTel* and through their *advertising spending* (even though this does not appear close to the centre of the diagram). Any change one of the companies decides to make to variables linked to its own *effective monthly price* will affect the other company – in addition to the effects it will have on the company itself. As we have seen before, the *life cycle duration* changes the balance between *Current customers* and *new customers*, and *effective monthly price* influences *new customers*, thereby also affecting *Current customers*. The CLD certainly allows us to look at the entire set of causal influences at once; but it is also a complex diagram. Table 7.5 summarizes the different paths by which each decision variable influences *Accumulated profits*. In addition to what Table 6.1 indicated in Chapter 6, Table 7.5 indicates whether each path from the decision variable to *Accumulated profits* exists under the monopoly situation and/or when a rival is present.

In comparison to the different simultaneous paths that you identified and studied in the monopolistic market, now *sales price*, *subscription rate*, and *life cycle duration* have additional effects brought about by *net switching from RivTel to NewTel*, some of them going in opposite directions. Increasing *sales price* or *subscription rate* leads to negative *net switching from RivTel to NewTel*, while increasing the *life cycle duration* leads to positive *net switching from RivTel to NewTel*. Since *Current customers* are affected in the opposite direction, *Accumulated profits* also change in the opposite direction. Of course, the difference in *Current customers* will later have its own influence on *new customers*, further increasing the complexity of the task of anticipating how a given change in one of these decision variables influences *Accumulated profits*. You also see that *advertising spending* affects customer dynamics under competition, but it will not influence rivalry over *Current customers*. As you already have found out before,

Table 7.5 Multiple influences of the decision variables on *Accumulated profits* under competition

Decision variable	Path from decision variable to *Accumulated profits*	Polarity of influence on *profits*	Market organization	
			Monopoly	Competition
sales price	Direct	+	✓	✓
	effective monthly price → new customers	–	✓	✓
	effective monthly price → relative effective monthly price NewTel → net switching from RivTel to NewTel → Current customers	–		✓
subscription rate	Direct	+	✓	✓
	effective monthly price → new customers	–	✓	✓
	effective monthly price → relative effective monthly price NewTel → net switching from RivTel to NewTel → Current customers	–		✓
life cycle duration	effective monthly price → new customers	–	✓	✓
	customers leaving → Current customers	+	✓	✓
	effective monthly price → relative effective monthly price NewTel → net switching from RivTel to NewTel → Current customers	+		✓
advertising spending	Direct	–	✓	✓
	new customers	+	✓	✓
process improvement	Direct	–	✓	
spending	Service costs	+	✓	

independent of the variables affecting customer dynamics, *process improvement spending* does not affect the competitive situation or its dynamics.

It is clear that any decision concerning *sales price, subscription rate, life cycle duration,* or *advertising spending* by NewTel or RivTel will force the other company to react. For example, if you decide an initial discount and set the *sales price* to zero for the first two months, and RivTel notices your decision and that you are now attracting *Potential customers* that it intended to attract, then it will certainly react (see also the competitive example in Chapter 1). Neither would you tolerate a competitive attack by RivTel, because if it acted in such a way, it would gain a 100% market share, and you would not be able to make the highest possible *Accumulated profits*. The question becomes: how to retaliate without unleashing a price war leading to lower and lower *sales prices* or *subscription rates*. When considering the options available to you, do not forget that any conclusions you reach about the situation are also likely to be those your competitor will come to.

You have several ways into the future, expressed by the following three strategies:

- 'Do not move': leave the decision variables at their default values and hope that things will stay as they are, leaving each company with half of the market.
- 'Compete': attempt to take over the market and drive RivTel out, or at least diminish its market share.
- 'Cooperate': attempt to incentivize cooperative behaviour between NewTel and RivTel.

Consider the strategy 'Do not move', Table 7.6 recalls the final outcomes of the BAU scenario, i.e. the default values for decision variables, versus the best case rivalry scenario (BCR):

If both companies instantly set their respective *sales price*, *subscription rate*, and *life cycle duration* to their optimum values and allocate 1 million to *advertising spending* in months 1 to 3, both NewTel and RivTel can increase their final *Accumulated profits* from $41 million to $73 million, that is, almost twice as much as in the BAU scenario.

Table 7.6 Results of the BAU and BCR scenarios

KPIs (in millions)	BAU		(BCR)	
	NewTel	RivTel	NewTel	RivTel
Accumulated customer-months	3.04	3.04	4.43	4.43
Accumulated purchases	0.78	0.78	0.80	0.80
Accumulated profits ($ million)	40.29	40.29	73.5	73.5
Total *Accumulated profits* ($ million)	80.48		147.00	

Given this opportunity to improve the current situation, the strategy 'do not move' is not attractive, since it implies preferring $41 million over $74 million.

It is reasonable to assume that RivTel's manager also understands that if both companies actually set the BCR values for their respective decision variables, their *Accumulated profits* will also <u>increase</u> by almost 100%. However, can you trust in that RivTel will be satisfied with capturing half of the total market? Are you satisfied with capturing half of the total market?

Of course, if you could get rid of RivTel in a sufficiently short time you could attempt to recover from the necessary losses in the remaining time. And, if you thought you can protect NewTel from the entry of new rivals in the future, then it might become possible to increase your *Accumulated profits* beyond $73 million. But even if you can trust RivTel's manager to understand that <u>increasing</u> its *sales price, subscription rate*, and *life cycle duration* will <u>increase</u> their *Accumulated profits*, by the time you both take your first decisions, how can you know if RivTel plans to share the market or to push you out of it? Of course, RivTel's management team are going to ask themselves the same questions.

Since you have the simulation model, you should use it to explore options open to you to <u>increase</u> A*ccumulated profits* by following the 'Compete' strategy. While doing so, you should assume that RivTel has the same information and understanding as you, and, therefore, it will apply the same policies. This competitive scenario holds the danger of an escalating price war that threatens to ruin at least one of the companies and to reduce the other's *profits* in the first year. Therefore, you should also evaluate the strategy 'cooperate'.

This policy does not promise results as favourable as in the monopolistic scenario but, as you have found out previously, if both companies increase their *effective monthly price*, the *Accumulated profits* can rise well beyond the BAU scenario. The feasibility of the 'Cooperate' strategy S3 depends on whether you can signal your willingness to cooperate with RivTel and if you can find out what its attitude is (Brandenburger and Nalebuff, 1995).

RivTel's decisions can be observed and are your only source of information. You can suppose that *advertising spending* will not be used to compete, since both managers know that, under the given circumstances, they should spend the maximum amount allowed of $1 million in months 1 to 3. Reductions in *Service costs* cannot be observed; anyway, as long as they do not lead to reductions in *sales price* or *subscription rate*, they do not affect *effective monthly price*, which represents the competitive situation between NewTel and RivTel. Therefore, you will use information concerning RivTel's *sales price*, *subscription rate*, and *life cycle duration* to infer their attitude.

You exclude the option of not doing anything, i.e. keeping *sales price, subscription rate*, and *life cycle duration* at their default BAU levels and waiting to see what RivTel does, for this would mean that none of the companies changes any of these variables. Your situation requires you to decide what your first move will be and how RivTel's decisions will influence your own future decisions ('C7 Rivalry policies').

Your aim is to use the simulation model to gain insights concerning how the interaction between both companies might unfold, assuming that both companies have reached the same insights. You, ideally, incorporate each company's decision logic into the model.

You must be able to react to RivTel's moves because they have positive or negative consequences for your *Accumulated profits*. Therefore, you must adjust your own decision variables to account for changing conditions. In addition, since you know that your moves have consequences for RivTel's ability to reach high *Accumulated profits*, you know that you can use your own decisions to send messages to RivTel. If their decisions have hurt you, a punishment (reducing your *effective monthly price* to capture some of its *Current customers*, for example) can tell it not to continue doing so. If its decisions are helpful, a reciprocal helpful move from you could signal to RivTel that it is safe to continue in this cooperative way. If you have previously known the theory of non-cooperative games, this will remind you of the so-called 'tit-for-tat' strategy – in that case, you will find a discussion in Section 7.4. Summing up, each company will take a first decision without knowing how its competitor will behave; from the second month on, decisions will consider the competitor's previous behaviour.

To keep things as simple as possible, you assume that whenever one of the companies reacts to the other company's moves, it will use the same decision variable. For instance, if RivTel change its *life cycle duration* and you react, you will also change the *life cycle duration* and not another decision variable. In principle, you could, of course, respond to a change of RivTel's *sales price* with a change of your *subscription rate*. However, the policies allowing you to decide which variable you chose for your response would be much more complex than the policies allowing you to respond using the same variable. It is also assumed that *advertising spending* is not used as a tool for competition. Both companies know the best way to allocate financial resources to advertising and process improvements. Both managers have the allowance to spend $1 million per month, and they know from when on such spending is not compensated by additional revenues. Since both companies will spend $1 million monthly on advertising during months 1 to 3, and neither company can spend more, *advertising spending* cannot be used as competitive means. And *process improvement spending* does not interact with the customers' dynamics, which renders it useless as a tool for competition.

The initial decision you make concerning *sales price*, *subscription rate*, and *life cycle duration* will be represented by three new exogenous variables in the model: *sales price NewTel impulse*, *subscription rate NewTel impulse*, and *life cycle duration NewTel impulse*. In addition, a constant *impulse time NewTel* represents the month in which NewTel will carry out this move. By default, the three exogenous variables are set to zero, thereby conserving the original model behaviour – unless you decide to apply such an impulse in any given month. The model contains the corresponding exogenous variables for RivTel (Figure 7.15).

When one of the companies detects the rival's move and reacts to it, it can do so more or less intensely. If, for example, you <u>reduce</u> your *sales price* from $50 to $45, then RivTel can <u>reduce</u> its *sales price* by $5, too – but they may prefer to <u>reduce</u> its *sales price* a little more to punish you, or it may rather <u>reduce</u> its *sales price* by less than $5 to signal that it does not want a price war; it might even not react at all. A new variable, *response multiplier*, represents the strength of your responses to RivTel's decisions. Its values will range from 0 to 1.5. If it is exactly one, then your reactions will exactly match the RivTel's previous move. For instance, if RivTel <u>increases</u> its *life cycle duration* by one month, you do the <u>same</u>. However, if your *response multiplier* is less than one, you decide to change the decision variable a bit less than RivTel. And if your *response multiplier* is greater than one, then you change it a bit more. The lower bound is zero, and this value means that you do not react to RivTel's move at all. The upper bound is 1.5 because it appears that responding to a move by RivTel with a move which is 50% stronger should be

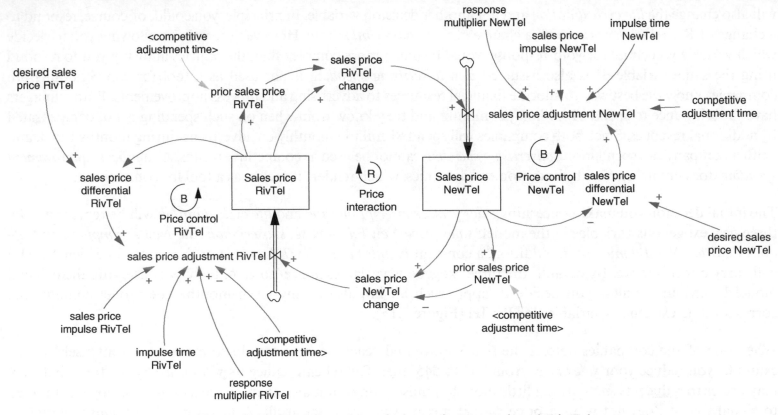

Figure 7.15 Deciding the *sales price* in NewTel and RivTel

sufficient to send powerful messages to your rival. Of course, the model will also have a *response multiplier RivTel*; you assume that it has come to the same conclusion concerning the situation, so it also considers responses of varying strength – however, the model must be able to deal with scenarios in which both companies' *response multipliers* have different values. The values of *response multiplier NewTel* and *response multiplier RivTel* will be set by you for each simulation.

Using the decision variables as tools for competing with your rival may lead to a dilemma: both you and RivTel's manager know that you would have to <u>increase</u> your respective *sales price*, *subscription rate*, and *life cycle duration* to approach the highest possible *Accumulated profits*. But you also need customers, and keeping your *sales price* and *subscription rate* <u>below</u> your rival's ones will <u>increase</u> your *Current customers*. If this leads to any <u>decrease</u> in *sales price* or *subscription rate*, then the need to respond to the rival leads to <u>decreasing</u> *sales price* or *subscription rate*, contradicting the need to <u>increase</u> them towards $70 and $26.

To avoid this dilemma, take it as given that each company wishes its decision variables could approach their ideal values and – if it is possible to get there – would not like to move away from these values. However, the model must respect the bounds defined for each decision variable: for instance, the *sales price* must not become negative or greater than $70. If NewTel detects that RivTel has <u>increased</u> the *subscription rate*, it will do so too, but only until the *subscription rate* reaches the level of $26 (the desired level). And if RivTel has <u>decreased</u> its *subscription rate*, NewTel will to so too, but not below $0. To implement this idea, you will create three new exogenous variables representing the ideal values for the three decision variables: *desired sales price NewTel*, *desired subscription rate NewTel*, and *desired life cycle duration NewTel*. By default, the exogenous variables are set to $70, $26, and 18 months respectively. Then you add three new variables: *sales price differential NewTel*, *subscription rate differential NewTel*, and *life cycle duration differential NewTel*. Each of these variables will represent the difference between the desired value of a decision variable and its current value during the simulation: they will allow the model to decide if the current value is coming close to the desired value, thereby enabling you to block further changes to the decision variable. Of course, the corresponding exogenous variables and variables must be added for RivTel, too.

Consider the stock-and-flow diagram in Figure 7.15, which shows the variables described so far and how they relate to one another:

In the modified model ('C7 Rivalry policies'), the *Sales prices* are represented as stocks: each company can change its *Sales price*, but unless it does so prices do not change. Adjusting *Sales price* is then a flow variable called *sales price adjustment*; it is governed by a decision you and RivTel take based on two aspects – *sales price differential* and *sales price change*. *Sales price differential* represents the difference between *sales price*'s current value and its desired value. *Sales price change* informs you whether the other company has made a change in price in the previous month based on comparing *prior sales price* to the current *sales price*. The simulation model's variable *sales price RivTel* will have a specific value at each time step in the simulation, so it does not show the value it had in the previous time step. Therefore, the first step in performing this comparison is to teach the model how to recall the *sales price* stock's previous value. In other words, you need the model to look back in time over a certain, fixed, delay. The modelling software has a function for doing this:

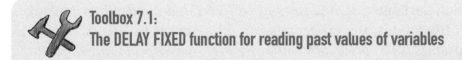

$$\textit{prior sales price}[\$/\text{individual}] = \text{DELAY FIXED}(\textit{Sales price}, \textit{competitive adjustment time}, \textit{Sales price}) \qquad (7.7)$$
$$[\$/\text{individual}]$$

Toolbox 7.1:
The DELAY FIXED function for reading past values of variables

There are situations when one variable affects another variable with a certain delay: a given amount of time between cause and effect. For instance, when a car manufacturer decides to expand production by opening a new production plant, but it takes three years to obtain all the required permits, construct the plant, and have workers and machines ready, then the manufacturer's effective production capacity will go up three years after having taken the decision. Or in the case of a whisky distillery, where the whisky sold today has matured over 12 or 18 years: the number of bottles it can sell this year corresponds to the number of bottles the distillery produced 12 or 18 ago.

The function DELAY FIXED is used to read past values of variables during the simulation. This is sometimes referred to as a 'discrete' delay, as opposed to a 'continuous' delay, in which a change made to one variable progressively shows an effect in another variable. A discrete delay means that after a change in one variable, nothing happens for a certain number of periods, and then suddenly the entire effect of the change impacts on the other variable.

Such a discrete delay requires three parameters: the *delayed variable*, the *delay time*, and an *initial value* for the initial time periods.

Figure 7.16 shows two examples. Each example appears in a table, with the header indicating the delay time as well as the value used as the initial value. The delay times are one and two months, and

Example 1: *Delay time = 1, intial value = x*		
Time period in simulation	Delayed variable	Value returned by DELAY FIXED
Init	10	x
1	10	10
2	20	10
3	20	20
4	20	20

Example 1: *Delay time = 2, intial value = x*		
Time period in simulation	Delayed variable	Value returned by DELAY FIXED
Init	10	x
1	10	x
2	10	10
3	20	10
4	20	10
5	20	20
6	20	30

Figure 7.16 Delay fixed

the *initial value* is equal to x. If, in the production plant example, the new plant was your first one, your initial *production capacity* would indeed be zero; but if you already had a factory, this factory's *production capacity* would be the initial value.

In the first example, the *delay time* is one period of time (according to the time unit chosen for a model). Consider firstly the behaviour of the *delayed variable*. At the beginning of the simulation (Init, which is equivalent to month 0 or the beginning of the first period), the *delayed variable* has the value 10. In period 3, this value increases to 20 and remains there until the end. Consider now the value returned by the function. During the first period it is not possible to read a calculated value of *delayed variable*, because the simulation has not run yet. This is what *initial value* is useful for. But in period 1, when the simulation has already run for a period, the value of 10 is read from *delayed variable*. In period 3, when *delayed variable* increases to 20, the function returns the value of period 2 and, therefore, remains at 10; it will increase to 20 one period later.

In the second example, the *delay time* is two. Accordingly, that *delayed variable* cannot be read during the first two periods, and again *initial value* is used. From time period 2, as the delay function reads the values of *delayed variable* two periods before, each change in decision variable leads to a corresponding change in *delayed value* two periods later.

These examples show that the *initial value* must be defined for *delay time* periods. The initial value should be set to the equilibrium value of whatever the conditions of the system are before the simulated time span starts. In the case of a closed restaurant, this is obviously zero – in other cases it may be different. For instance, if you are managing the whisky distillery from the above example (selling whisky aged 12 or 18 years), if your historic demand was 1000 bottles per year and each of the past 12 or 18 years you have put 1000 bottles into your production line, then the yearly number of bottles becoming available for sale will be 1000 for the next 12 or 18 years.

Once the *prior sales price* has been determined according to Equation (7.7), calculating the *sales price change* is a simple subtraction:

$$sales\ price\ change\left[\$/\text{individual}\right] = Sales\ price\left[\$/\text{individual}\right] - prior\ sales\ price\left[\$/\text{individual}\right] \tag{7.8}$$

The other potential reason for a change in *Sales price* is represented in the *sales price differential*, which is defined as the difference between the *desired sales price* and the current *Sales price*:

$$sales\ price\ differential\left[\$/\text{individual}\right] = desired\ sales\ price\left[\$/\text{individual}\right] - Sales\ price\left[\$/\text{individual}\right] \tag{7.9}$$

During a simulation, you can set the value of the *desired sales price* and the model will compute the *sales price differential*. Why should the model not determine the *desired sales price*, for instance, being equal to the optimum *Sales price*? The first reason for this choice in designing the model is that there are too many ways each company might take such a decision; in an extreme case, it may even not take this difference into account at all, because all attention is focused on the competition. The second reason is that you wish to explore the dynamics of each company's reactions to the other's decisions and, therefore, you would like to be able to make *ad hoc* decisions. If you decided to represent these adjustments endogenously, i.e. expressed by equations in the model, it would have become a goal-seeking feedback loop for each of the decision variables of each company, thus adjustments would be made which diminish the difference between the current and the BCR value.

The *sales price adjustment* is not necessarily equal to the sum of the rival's *sales price change* and your own *sales price differential*; you may choose to spread the adjustment over a given number of months, which is stored in the variable *competitive adjustment time*. By default, *competitive adjustment time* is set to one; however, you can decide to change this and explore the consequences on customer dynamics and *Accumulated profits*.

To enable you to experiment with the model, there are two more variables linked to *sales price adjustment*: the *sales price impulse* is a one-off change in the *Sales price* which can range between −1 and +2, with a default value of zero.

Should you choose to set a different value, this will be applied in one particular month represented by *impulse time*. *Impulse time* has a default value of zero, but you can change it to any integer number from 1 to 12. If, for example, you set *sales price impulse* = 1 and *impulse time* = 1, your *sales price adjustment* of month 1 (*impulse time*) will be increased by 1 (*sales price impulse*).

As mentioned above, both you and RivTel would like to move the current values of the three decision variables closer to their desired values. Our model assumes that when the current values of a decision variable comes close enough to its desired value, then the company stops using it as a tool for rivalry. Since this assumption is made for both companies, there is little risk that you would stick to, say, a high *Sales price* and RivTel would undercut it: both companies ought to behave according to this assumption. How will you decide if the current value of one of these variables is close enough to the desired value to 'freeze' it? The intuitive answer would be: when the current value is equal to the desired value. But consider the following example: if *subscription rate NewTel* is $25.8 and RivTel <u>increased</u> its *subscription rate* $0.5 last month. Assuming that your *response multiplier* = 1, you would now <u>increase</u> your *subscription rate* by $0.5, but then it would be $26.3 and, therefore, further away from the desired value of $26 – *subscription rate differential* would <u>increase</u>. To avoid such undesirable developments, while keeping the model as simple as possible, you use the following policy: 'If the absolute value of *subscription rate differential NewTel* exceeds 0.5, then *subscription rate adjustment NewTel* will be changed by the result of *subscription rate RivTel change* × *response multiplier NewTel;* otherwise *subscription rate adjustment NewTel* = 0, meaning that the subscription rate will not be changed'. Let us go through this step by step.

The absolute value of a variable of the result of an arithmetic operation is obtained by using the function ABS(), which stands for 'absolute value' and ensures that the policy will be applied independently if the *subscription rate NewTel* is approaching desired *subscription rate NewTel* from below or above. An analogous policy will be applied to all decision variables of both companies. Let us provide an example with *sales price*: consider how the different components of the decisions come together as a sequence of calculations. As you go through the diagram, consider an example where *sales price differential NewTel* = 2, *sales price RivTel change* = 1, *response multiplier NewTel* = 1, *impulse time NewTel* and *sales price impulse NewTel* are both = 0, and the *competitive adjustment time* = 1.

Figure 7.17 represents a complex equation that determines the value of *sales price adjustment NewTel*. At the top, you see the policy discussed in the previous paragraph, prescribing how you react to RivTel's changes to its *sales price*. Once this part has been evaluated by the simulation software, the impulse you decide to apply to your *sales price* as your first move is added. The result is then divided by the *competitive adjustment time* to yield the value for *sales price adjustment NewTel*.

In the example, *sales price differential NewTel* is larger than 0.5, and therefore the value of this part of the equation is computed as *sales price RivTel change* × *response multiplier NewTel* = $1 \times 1 = 1$. Then the PULSE part is evaluated and yields 0, which is added to 1. Eventually, 1 is divided by *competitive adjustment time*, and, therefore, *sales price adjustment*

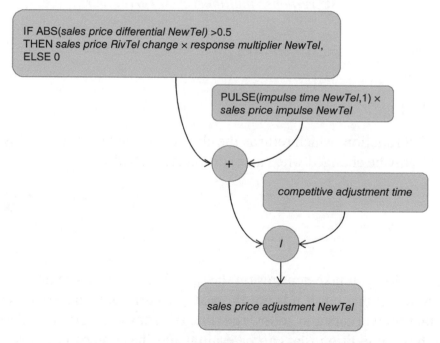

Figure 7.17 Diagram representation of the *sales price adjustment* policy

NewTel=1. If *sales price differential NewTel* was 0.2 (because *sales price NewTel*=25.8 and *desired sales price NewTel*=26), then the first part of the equation would result in 0, and accordingly *sales price adjustment NewTel*=0.

Now consider the complete Equation (7.10):

$$\textit{sales price adjustment NewTel}[\$ / \text{individual}] =$$
$$\text{IF THEN ELSE}$$
$$(\text{ABS}(\textit{sales price differential NewTel}[\$ / \text{individual}]) > 0.5,$$
$$\textit{sales price RivTel change}[\$ / \text{individual}] * \textit{response multiplier NewTel}[\text{dimensionless}],$$
$$0)$$
$$+ \text{PULSE}(\textit{impulse time NewTel}[\text{month}], 1[\text{month}]) *$$
$$\textit{sales price impulse NewTel}[\$ / \text{individual}] /$$
$$\textit{competitive adjustment time}[\text{month}]$$

(7.10)

Equation (7.10) uses the **ABS** function, which returns the absolute value of a number, inside another function that ensures that *sales price* will only be changed when a condition is satisfied.

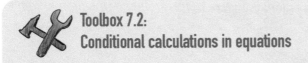

Toolbox 7.2:
Conditional calculations in equations

Sometimes, the action you take depends on the specific circumstance you are facing: if 'something' is the case, you do one thing, but if it is not the case you carry out a different action (or nothing at all). For example, factory workers may follow the rule: IF today is a work day, THEN get up at 6 o'clock. The IF-clause has a condition that can be evaluated; it has one of two possible outcomes: 'true' or 'false'. The THEN part states what happens in case the evaluation is 'true'. In the example, this does not explicitly state what the workers will do on Saturday or Sunday morning, but at least they are not forced to get up at 6 o'clock. 'Doing nothing' can be left without explicitly saying, but if you have to choose between doing one thing or doing another thing, such a rule must be more precise, like for instance: 'IF sales are increasing, THEN increase the price; ELSE decrease the price'. As you see, if you want to have a general way to express conditional rules, it needs to give you the option of stating what must be done if the evaluation of the condition is 'false'. The general shape of a conditional rule will always have the following design:

IF condition THEN action on true ELSE action on false

In Vensim, the function used to describe conditional decisions is 'IF THEN ELSE', and it requires all three parameters: a logical condition, an action to be performed if the condition is true and an action to be performed if the condition is false.

The logical condition is: the absolute value of the *sales price differential* is greater than 0.5. If the condition is true, then the function returns the result of multiplying *sales price RivTel* change by the *response multiplier NewTel*. When the condition is false, the function returns zero. Then the value returned by the IF THEN ELSE function is added to the result of multiplying PULSE (*impulse time NewTel*, 1) by the *sales price impulse NewTel*. The result of this addition is then divided by the *competitive adjustment time*.

Once *sales price adjustment NewTel* has a value, *sales price NewTel* will be updated by the simulation software. The way in which *subscription rate adjustment NewTel* and *life cycle duration adjustment NewTel* are calculated is analogous to the one described for *sales price adjustment NewTel*. Also, *sales price adjustment RivTel*, *subscription rate adjustment RivTel*, and *life cycle duration adjustment RivTel* follow the same logic as three adjustment flows of NewTel.

Taken together, the model represents NewTel's and RivTel's policies concerning their respective *sales price*, *subscription rate*, and *life cycle duration*. These policies depend partially on the other company's previous adjustments decisions. You can directly determine NewTel's first move and the strength of NewTel's responses to RivTel's moves – as well as your assumptions regarding the first move you expect RivTel to make and how strongly RivTel will react to your moves. This is a reinforcing feedback loop. In the beginning of the simulation, both companies have the same *sales price*, and therefore the mutual observation does not yield any information requiring them to perform a *purchase price adjustment*. But if during the year, one of the companies <u>increases</u> or <u>decreases</u> its *sales price*, then the other company's *sales price adjustment* will be in the <u>same direction</u>. This will, in turn, trigger the first company to make one <u>more</u> *sales price adjustment* in the <u>same direction</u>, and the loop is closed. The companies' respective *response multipliers* to each other's *sales price adjustments* are then decisive for the development of the model's sales price dynamics – if the multiplication of the *response multipliers* yields less than one, then each iteration of *sales price adjustment* will be smaller than the previous one, and the effect fades out. If, on the contrary, the multiplication of the *response multipliers* yields a value greater than one, then the *sales price adjustment* will escalate over time. Of course, *sales price adjustments* will have bounds – *Sales price* will not rise above its *desired level* because of the restriction placed on the model (discussed above); neither will the *Sales price* fall below zero.

You can already explicitly see the danger of escalation in this model structure. Should one of the companies somehow decrease its *effective monthly price*, a price war – a 'vicious' cycle – might occur (Toolbox 2.7). Your *Accumulated profits* would suffer in such a case. The same structure could also allow a 'virtuous' cycle of successive increases of both companies' *effective monthly prices*, allowing much higher *Accumulated profits* than in the BAU scenario (which may attract the attention of competition authorities, but since there was no explicit communication between the companies, this could at most be called a tacit collusion). Note that the same structure – a reinforcing feedback loop – can generate both a vicious and a virtuous cycle; it depends on the nature of the initial impulse.

Systems Insight 13 (SI 13): Policies which observe competitors result in loops
Mutual observation amongst rivals in response to the respective rival's decisions configures reinforcing feedback loops. These loops reinforce an initial move with collaborative or competitive intent into sequences of interactions

resembling either a peaceful coexistence, i.e. each rival refrains from aggressive moves or an escalating exchange of aggressive moves.

Model 'C7 Rivalry policies' includes an analogous structure for the *subscription rate* and the *life cycle duration*. In the following section, you will carry out four simulation experiments with this model. Each of these experiments allows you to evaluate a way of implementing one of the strategies 'Compete' or 'Cooperate' which have been discussed previously.

- Experiment COOP 1: Cooperate, NewTel makes a first step towards collaboration to probe whether RivTel complies, increasing *Sales Price, Subscription Rate* and *Life Cycle Duration*.
- Experiment COMP 1: Compete, NewTel attacks reducing the *Sales price*.
- Experiment COMP 2: Compete, NewTel attacks reducing the *Subscription rate*.
- Experiment COOP 2: Cooperate, NewTel and RivTel synchronously increase *Sales price, Subscription rate*, and *Life cycle duration*.

Each of these simulations assumes that both companies have reached an equivalent understanding of the causal structure of the situation and that they will react to each other in the way described above. However, their respective first moves are driven by their own interpretation of the difference between the initial values and the optimum values of the decision variables. Therefore, the first three simulations explore the consequences of initial moves taken by NewTel, before the fourth simulation advances to simultaneous first moves by both companies.

7.4.2 Evaluating four exemplary policies

7.4.2.1 Experiment COOP 1: NewTel collaborates increasing *Sales price, Subscription rate*, and *Life cycle duration*

You want your decision variables to take on their optimum values, which means increasing the *sales price*, the *subscription rate*, and the *life cycle duration*. This is only possible if both companies refrain from competing using the *monthly effective cost* and prefer to collaborate. At the outset, either company knows what the respective rival's first move, the impulse, will be.

You assume that RivTel could adopt a 'wait and see' stance and not change its decision variables unless it has observed your first move. You also assume that both companies will set their response multiplier to one, meaning that they will respond to each other's move by identical moves. In this situation, you decide to <u>increase</u> the *Sales price* and the *Subscription rate* by one dollar and the *Life cycle duration* by one month. This means you will set *sales price impulse NewTel*, *subscription rate impulse NewTel*, *life cycle duration impulse NewTel* and *impulse time NewTel* to one. RivTel's corresponding parameters are kept equal to zero.

DIY 7.5:
The effects of making a fist move of collaboration in the COOP 1 experiment

To explore the dynamics and outcomes of this policy (and the remaining three too) first make sure you have adapted your model.

You need to have created the variables representing RivTel and added 'NewTel' to the variables describing your company. Also, the corresponding causal links between RivTel's variables and the equations need to be in place. If you have started Chapter 7 with the model you had at the end of Chapter 6 and that you have worked through the previous DIY sections in this chapter, you can add the new variables and links from the Rivalry II DIY 7.4 to the model you built for the Rivalry I DIY 7.2.

You then need to create the variables representing the policies described in Section 7.3.1. You can create a new 'view' in the software, using the menu View|New (a pop-up list bottom left of the window allows you to navigate between views), which allows you to diagram the new part of the model in a separate sheet. Since you must replace each company's intermediate variables *sales price*, *subscription rate*, and *life cycle duration* with stocks, you need to work step by step. The software will not allow you to create a stock named '*Sales price NewTel*' as long as there is already an intermediate variable with the same name. One safe way to go about this task is to change the intermediate variable's name into '*Sales price NewTel old*', then create the stock '*Sales price NewTel*' in the new view. Navigate back to the initial view, create a < shadow variable > of the stock *Sales price NewTel*, create the causal links from *Sales price NewTel* to *revenues from sales NewTel* and *effective monthly price NewTel*, and then finally delete *Sales price NewTel old*. You also need to open *revenues from sales NewTel* and *effective monthly price NewTel* with the equation editor to make sure that the equation appropriately reflects the causal links. You may refer to Toolbox 2.1 for explanations concerning causal links.

Of course, the same procedure will be applied to *Sales price, Subscription rate*, and *life cycle duration* of both companies. It is also a good idea to create an additional 'view' in the model file, in which you create the *response multipliers* and the *impulse* exogenous variables of both companies. If you wish to observe more than one variable in a graph during interactive simulation with Synthesim, you will need to create and position so-called 'custom graphs'. To do this, you first need to open the control panel (menu Windows | Control panel), navigate to the sheet 'Graphs' and click the command button 'New…'. A dialog window for setting graph properties will open and you will be required to give your graph a name and a title. The name will be used as internal identifier similar to the variables' names; the title will be displayed on top of the graph. Then you can use the 'Sel' buttons to select the variables you wish to include in the graph. If you want the variables to use the same vertical scale, select the 'Scale' case. Please refer to the tutorial for creating custom graphs from the companion website, if you wish a more detailed instruction. While we recommend going through this process to fully understand the policies, as an alternative you can download the model 'C7 Rivalry policies' from our companion website.

Switch into the Synthesim-mode of Vensim and navigate to the policy view to set NewTel's impulses to this policy's values.

Examine the behaviour of both companies' *Sales price, Subscription rate*, and *Life cycle duration*. Considering the final values of *Accumulated profits, Accumulated customer-months*, and *Accumulated purchases*, explain how the behaviour of the three decision variables creates the difference in the final results.

Even before simulating, one hypothesis can be derived from the model's causal structure. An initial increase in the values of the three decision variables used in this experiment by NewTel leads to a corresponding increase by RivTel, which leads to a corresponding increase by NewTel. Therefore, the prices (*sales price* and *subscription rate*) and the *life cycle duration* of both companies will increase over time, with NewTel's values being greater than RivTel's (H 7.7).

Increasing the *sales price* and the *subscription rate* leads to an increase of the *effective monthly price NewTel*, whereas the *effective monthly price RivTel* remains unchanged. Therefore, the *relative monthly price NewTel* increases, leading to a loss of *Current customers* from net switching. At the same time, the increased *monthly effective price NewTel* will decrease the *new customers NewTel* flow. Both effects lead to NewTel capturing less *Current customers* than RivTel (H 7.8).

NewTel has increased *prices* and decreased *customers*: the combined effect on *total revenues* cannot be indicated without simulation – therefore no hypothesis is formulated concerning *total revenues NewTel*.

Figure 7.18 displays the behaviour of the decision variables over the 12 months. Hypothesis H 7.7 is supported.

Figure 7.18 shows *sales price, subscription rate*, and *life cycle duration* of NewTel and RivTel. After starting with equal values, NewTel's three decision variables increase, while RivTel sticks to the default values. From that moment on, RivTel replicates NewTel's increases and NewTel replicates RivTel's increases. The *subscription rates* reach the optimum value in month 7 and, therefore, stop increasing. The *life cycle durations* increase until month 10, when they reach 18 months and stop increasing because this is the optimum value. As a matter of fact, the optimum *sales price* cannot be reached in 12 increments of one dollar, and for this reason the *sales prices* continue to rise until the end of month 12.

More importantly, NewTel is consistently more expensive than RivTel over the whole year. You know that the differences in *effective monthly price* have consequences for *net switching of customers* between the companies and

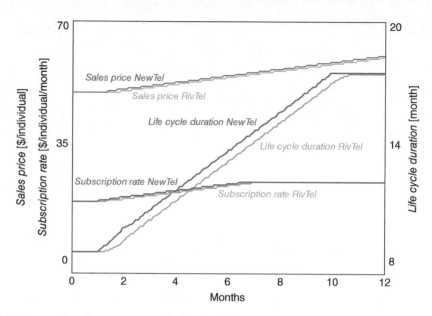

Figure 7.18 Mutual adjustments of the decision variables in the COOP 1 experiment

for each company's flow of *new customers*. Hypothesis H 7.8 is supported. Figure 7.19 shows the behaviour of both companies' stocks of *Current customers*, *new customers* flows, and the *net switching*, which results from the different *effective monthly prices*.

With regard to *Current customers*, NewTel has been defeated in this experiment: more individuals have purchased RivTel's phones. There are two reasons for this. Firstly, NewTel's <u>higher</u> *effective monthly price* <u>reduces</u> the *price effect on demand multiplier*, and therefore NewTel's *new customers* is <u>lower</u> than what it would be for the default *effective monthly price*. Secondly, the *relative effective monthly price NewTel* <u>rises</u>, and therefore *net switching from RivTel to NewTel* <u>becomes negative</u>. In other words: NewTel <u>adds less</u> *new customers* to its *Current customers* stock and <u>loses</u> *Current customers* to RivTel. Both differences lead to a quicker accumulation of *Current customers* by

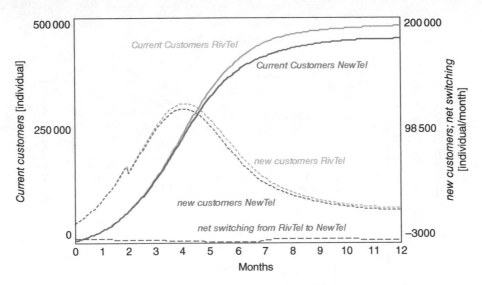

Figure 7.19 Customer dynamics in the COOP 1 experiment

RivTel during the first four months, which appears as a less positive slope in the graph of NewTel's *Current customers*. The *net switching from RivTel to NewTel* becomes <u>more negative</u> during these months, because NewTel has more *Current customers* (i.e. *Current customers NewTel* is higher) to be attracted away by the difference in *effective monthly price*. When, in month seven, the *subscription rates* of both companies equalize, this difference in *effective monthly price* is <u>reduced</u> and, accordingly, the *net switching* becomes <u>less negative</u>; however, during this time *Current customers NewTel* still grows, so the *net switching* does not go to zero. Once all the decision variables have equal values, net switching will fade out – however, this does not happen during the first 12 months.

NewTel has slightly higher prices than RivTel but less *Current customers*. But what does all this mean for final *Accumulated profits*? This can be seen in Table 7.7, which contains the results in terms of *Accumulated customer-months*, *Accumulated purchases*, and *Accumulated profits*, including a comparison between NewTel and RivTel in

Table 7.7 Final KPI outcomes of the COOP 1 experiment

KPI outcomes (millions)	NewTel	RivTel	Difference	
			Absolute	Relative
Accumulated customer-months	3.578	3.783	−0.205	−5.73%
Accumulated purchases	0.697	0.730	−0.033	−4.73%
Accumulated profits ($)	60.97	63.48	−2.51	−4.12%
BAU ratio (%)	147	153		
BCR ratio (%)	42	43		

absolute and relative terms. In addition, both companies' *Accumulated profits* are compared to two benchmark values. The first one is BAU ratio and represents the proportion of the $88.08 million of *Accumulated profits* resulting from both companies carrying out the *advertising spending* and *process improvement spending*, as assumed in this chapter, as compared to the results obtained in the BAU scenario. The second one, the BCR ratio, shows the *Accumulated profits* which would result if both companies instantly adopted the BCR values for *sales price*, *subscription rate*, and *life cycle duration*, thus generating $146.88 million in total.

RivTel has more *Accumulated customers-months* and more *Accumulated purchases*. The *Accumulated profits* of each company are higher than in the BAU scenario, but NewTel has almost $2.5 million less than RivTel. This will probably leave you with mixed feelings; you have certainly increased your own *Accumulated profits* by roughly $20 million, but RivTel's *Accumulated profits* are higher than yours. In a way, by being the first mover company and to increase the values of variables related to the *effective monthly price*, you have not only signalled your readiness for cooperation to RivTel, but you have also created a dynamic in which RivTel performs slightly better than NewTel. You may find this unfair, and in any assessment which will be made of your performance at the end of the year, it might be used against you. In addition, the total value of the market in this experiment suggests that more *Accumulated profit* is possible.

7.4.2.2 Experiment COMP 1: NewTel competes reducing the *Sales price*

For the COMP 1 policy, you will take a competitive stance and reduce the *Sales price* by $1. RivTel will replicate your move, but you will replicate theirs, too. In an analogy to the first experiment, you expect to achieve and maintain a *relative effective monthly price NewTel* less than one and gain an advantage from *net switching from RivTel to NewTel*. You maintain the assumption that both companies' *response multiplier* equals one.

DIY 7.6:
The effects of *reducing* the *Sales price* in the COMP 1 experiment

How would a first move by NewTel that reduces the *Sales price* by $1 play out for customer dynamics over the year? Sketch the graphs of *new customers* and *Current customers*. What would you expect the final outcomes to be in terms of *Accumulated profits*, *Accumulated customer-months*, and *Accumulated purchases* compared to the BAU and the BCR scenarios?

Use the simulation model to simulate the COMP 1 experiment and compare your expectations to the simulation results.

Decreasing the *sales price* will decrease the *effective monthly price NewTel* and trigger *net switching* towards NewTel. However, since the *sales price* is divided by the *life cycle duration* to calculate the *effective monthly price*, the effect is relatively small. Also, decreasing the *effective monthly price* does not increase the *new customers* flow. Therefore, NewTel will have only few more *Current customers* and *new customers* than RivTel (H 7.9).

Note that 12 months are not sufficient to decrease the *sales price* from its default level to zero if it is incrementally decreased by $1 each month. Your *sales price* reaches $39 at the end of the year and *sales price RivTel* descends to $40. Accordingly, NewTel maintains a small advantage in terms of *effective monthly price* over RivTel. This becomes visible in the customer dynamics (Figure 7.20), which supports hypothesis H 7.9.

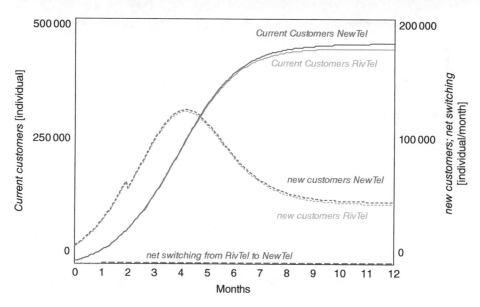

Figure 7.20 Customer dynamics in the COMP 1 experiment

Even though, in general, the behaviour shown in Figure 7.20 is almost identical for both companies, there is a slight and growing advantage for NewTel in terms of *Current customers*. *Net switching from RivTel to NewTel* looks insignificant in this figure; however, a closer look reveals that it is not.

As shown in Figure 7.21, *net switching* rises with a shape that is reminiscent of the one displayed by *Current customers RivTel*. When you remember that the monthly number of net switchers is a proportion of *Current customers RivTel* and that this proportion is given by the relationship between the two *effective monthly prices*, which is constant in this simulation, then you realize that unless both companies reach a *sales price* of $0, this will not change. Therefore, you will win approximately 500 *Current customers* from RivTel, which makes a monthly difference of 1000 *Current customers*. This is what drives the difference in the graphs of *Current customers* (Figure 7.20).

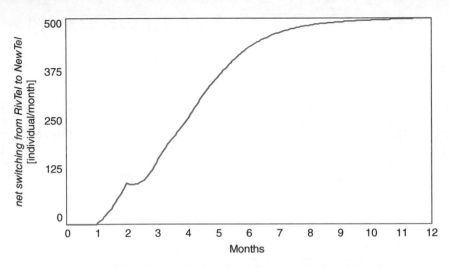

Figure 7.21 *Net switching from RivTel* to NewTel in the COMP 1 experiment

However, having a $1 advantage divided by a *life cycle duration* of nine months does not make a huge difference and, accordingly, the final outcomes of this experiment do not give you a sizable advantage, neither over the BAU scenario nor over RivTel.

Table 7.8 displays discouraging final results. In terms of *Accumulated customer-months* and *Accumulated purchases* you have roughly 1% advantage over RivTel, but your *Accumulated profits* are not even 1% greater than RivTel's and they are $10 million below what you would have achieved in the BAU scenario. But maybe the problem is not that a competitive policy is doomed to fail; possibly changing the *Sales price* has too small an effect on the *relative effective monthly price NewTel*.

7.4.2.3 Experiment COMP 2: NewTel competes reducing the *Subscription rate*

You will, therefore, explore a decrease of $1 (from $20 to $19) in the *subscription rate*, still assuming both companies' *response multiplier* equals one. You expect this to yield a greater effect because the *subscription rate* must be paid entirely each month of the *life cycle duration*.

Table 7.8 Final KPI outcomes of the COMP 1 experiment

KPI outcomes (millions)	NewTel	RivTel	Difference	
			Absolute	Relative
Accumulated customer-months	3.597	3.548	0.049	1.36%
Accumulated purchases	0.840	0.832	0.008	0.95%
Accumulated profits ($)	38.53	38.41	0.12	0.311%
BAU ratio (%)	46	46		
BCR ratio (%)	26	26		

DIY 7.7:
The effects of <u>reducing</u> the *Subscription rate* in the COMP 2 experiment

How would a first move by NewTel of reducing its *Subscription rate* by $1 affect customer dynamics over the year? As before, sketch the graphs of *new customers* and *Current customers*. How would you expect the final outcomes to be in terms of *Accumulated profits*, *Accumulated customer-months*, and *Accumulated purchases* compared to the BAU and the BCR scenarios?

Use the simulation model and compare your expectations to the simulation results.

According to the argumentation for hypothesis H 7.9, the third experiment should show a stronger customers advantage of NewTel over RivTel (H 7.10).

Since the *subscription rate* is paid many more times than the *sales price* (*Accumulated customer-months* > *Accumulated purchases*), decreasing the *subscription rate* will <u>decrease</u> *Accumulated profits* <u>more</u> than <u>decreasing</u> the *sales price* (H 7.11).

Figure 7.22 supports hypothesis 7.10. Now you can attract more *Current customers* than RivTel.

Indeed, the graphs in Figure 7.22 are similar to the **COMP** 1 experiment, but this time the difference between NewTel and RivTel grows faster and continues to grow at least until the end of the year. The $1 difference between the *subscription rates* is not divided by the *life cycle duration* and, therefore, has a much bigger impact on the *effective monthly price* difference between both companies. Therefore, it is not surprising that *net switching* <u>increases</u> more than before, so the difference between *Current customers NewTel* and *Current customers RivTel* <u>grows faster</u>. After month 9, the total outflow of individuals from *Current customers RivTel* – due to *customers leaving RivTel* plus *net switching from RivTel to NewTel* – exceeds *new customers RivTel*, and therefore *Current customers RivTel* starts <u>decreasing</u>.

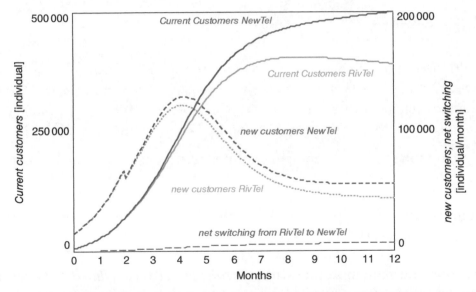

Figure 7.22 Customer dynamics in the COMP 2 experiment

The *subscription rates* of both companies steadily decrease and at the end of the year are $9 and $10 for NewTel and RivTel, respectively. If you remember that *Service costs* are $10 and cannot decreased by more than one dollar over the year, then you expect that competing for customers by <u>cutting</u> the *subscription rates* will <u>reduce</u> *Accumulated profits* (Table 7.9).

Because of the sustained advantage in *effective monthly price*, you have significantly more *Accumulated customer-months* and more of *Accumulated purchases* than RivTel. However, this seemingly impressive advantage comes together with the fact that the *subscription rate* has <u>fallen</u> well below the level where it still has an influence on *monthly profits* before the end of the year: you are foregoing quite a portion of the possible *revenues from subscription* and, since your *Service costs* <u>cannot be reduced</u> at the same pace as you <u>reduce</u> the *subscription rate*, the *monthly profits* must <u>decrease</u> month by month. This shows in the fact that your advantage in terms of *Accumulated customer-months* and *Accumulated purchases* is much bigger than your advantage in *Accumulated profits*. And even if at the end of the year you have beaten RivTel, you finish with almost $30 million less of *Accumulated profits* than in the BAU scenario, supporting hypotheses H 7.10 and H 7.11. Because you are expected to report *Accumulated profits* and not the market-share of *Current customers*, experiment COMP 2 is more of a loss than of a win. Intriguingly, many people intuitively try to beat the competitors rather than focusing on improving their own results. This is, of course, the fundament of many games and sports, but it can also lead to ruinous consequences; you may refer to the well-known Beer game to see how this relates to phenomena like over-ordering (Sterman and Dogan, 2015).

Table 7.9 Final KPI outcomes of the COMP 2 experiment

KPI outcomes (millions)	NewTel	RivTel	Difference	
			Absolute	**Relative**
Accumulated customer-months	3.822	3.324	0.498	13.02%
Accumulated purchases	0.876	0.797	0.079	9.01%
Accumulated profits ($)	20.11	19.75	0.36	1.79%
BAU ratio (%)	24	24		
BCR ratio (%)	14	13		

Until now, the simulation experiments suggest that there is a problem: if you want to signal your cooperative stance by an initial move that <u>increases</u> your *effective monthly price*, then you <u>lose</u> *Current customers* to RivTel and, thereby, <u>diminish</u> your additional *Accumulated profits* below the level reached by them. If you <u>decrease</u> your *effective monthly price*, then you can <u>gain</u> *customer* market share, but the spiralling price <u>decreases</u> (*sales price* and *subscription rate*) will reduce *total revenues* and, therefore, the final *Accumulated profits* will be <u>below</u> the BAU scenario.

This puts your rationality to a test: from an economic standpoint, you should prefer the policy simulated in the first experiment with the <u>increased</u> *Accumulated profits* over the BAU scenario and the competitive policies. But, at the same time, there is an impulse propelling you to make more *Accumulated profits* than RivTel, or at least not less *Accumulated profits*.

How good are the chances that RivTel's manager has carried out similar experiments and has come to the same results and questions? How likely is it that he or she attributes a high likelihood to the possibility that your first decision will be to cooperate? Given all our assumptions and what both you and RivTel know about the market, will cooperating with RivTel achieve a better result? Should your counterpart trust you and increase RivTel's *effective monthly price* from the first month on, without waiting for a signal from your part? You cannot be certain, but you ought to attribute a high likelihood to this possibility.

If both companies reach this conclusion, they can decide to <u>increase</u> their *Sales price, Subscription rate*, and *Life cycle duration*. It is reasonable to assume this will done in small steps. Even if you assign a good likelihood to RivTel's cooperative stance, you cannot be certain; making small steps reduces the possible damage resulting from RivTel taking a competitive first decision. Of course, this argument also holds from RivTel's point of view.

If both companies take the same decisions each month, there will be no difference between *Sales prices, Subscription rates*, and *Life cycle durations* (H 7.12).

Accordingly, the *effective monthly prices* will be identical, and therefore there will be <u>no</u> *net switching* and <u>no increased</u> *new customers flows* (H 7.13).

It follows that both companies will have identical customer dynamics and identical *Accumulated profits* (H 7.14).

Since *sales price* and *subscription rate* steadily <u>increase</u>, the <u>rising</u> *effective monthly prices* <u>decrease</u> the *new customers* flows, leading to <u>fewer</u> *Current customers* when the market is mature. Since the best case values of the decision variables <u>avoid increasing</u> the *effective monthly price* to levels where the *price effect on demand table* returns <u>very small values</u>, it is expected that the combined effect on *net revenues* is positive and that *Accumulated profits* will be <u>much higher</u> than in the previous experiments (H 7.15).

Figure 7.23 displays the behaviours of both companies' *sales prices*, *subscription rates*, and *life cycle durations*. If both NewTel and RivTel make a first move that <u>increases</u> their respective *effective monthly prices*, then each company will respond to the other companies' previous move without producing a difference between their *effective monthly prices*. In other words, there is no difference between your *sales price*, *subscription rate*, and *life cycle duration* and RivTel's (H 7.12 supported). This means that there will be no *net switching* and that the *new customers* flows will be

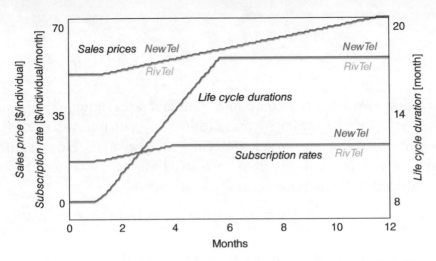

Figure 7.23 Collaborative setting of decision variables in the COOP 2 experiment

equal in the first month. Therefore, the *Current customer* stocks and the *customers leaving* flows will be equal, too (H 7.13 supported):

The behaviours shown in Figure 7.24 remind you of the BAU scenario, were there was no difference between the customer dynamics of both companies. The brief interruption in the growth of *new customers* at the end of month 3 is due to the end of the period in which the companies allocated money to *advertising spending*. But, otherwise, you see the typical S-shaped growth up to a certain steady-state level; not all Plutonians use mobile phones but, in turn, both companies maintain a stable flow of *new customers*. Consequently, both company reach identical final outcomes, which are indicated in Table 7.10 (H 7.14 supported).

The sum of both *Accumulated profits* is $132.5 million – almost as much as the $135.5 million that would result in the monopoly scenario (studied in Chapter 6) if you could set the values of your decision variables to the optimum right away – and quite close to the $146.9 million that would result from both companies jumping to the ideal values of all decision variables instantly. H 7.15 is supported, too.

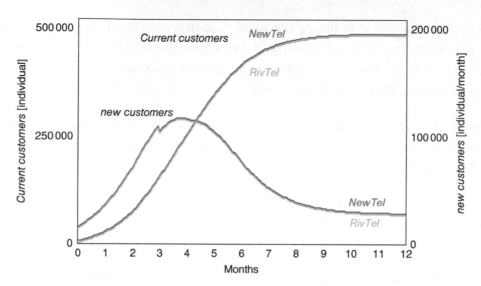

Figure 7.24 Customer dynamics in experiment COOP 2

Table 7.10 Final KPI outcomes of experiment COOP 2

KPI outcomes (millions)	NewTel	RivTel
Accumulated customer-months	3.724	3.724
Accumulated purchases	0.687	0.687
Accumulated profits ($)	66.25	66.25
BAU ratio (%)	80	80
BCR ratio (%)	45	45

There are several differences between the monopoly situation and the competitive situation. The fact that in experiment COOP 2 both companies slowly approached the optimum levels of the decision variables is only one of them. It means that the advantages of the ideal values of the decision variables is only achieved step by step, and therefore the *Accumulated profits* will stay <u>below</u> the ideal case in which total *Accumulated profits* sum up to $146 million. A second difference is because of advertising. As you have seen in the subsection concerning rivalry type I, having both companies allocate $1 million to *advertising spending* during the first three months speeds up the growth of *Current customers* and, therefore, <u>increases</u> the *Accumulated profits*.

When you compare the *Accumulated profits* with the $41 million of the BAU scenario, finishing with $25 million more is apparently a result that comes as close to the Best Case Monopoly result as possible. It is even better than RivTel's *Accumulated profits* in the first experiment.

This takes you back to the question of what your goals are. You can desire to beat RivTel, or you can desire to win compared to the BAU scenario; but you cannot achieve both results in this case.

7.5 Reflecting on rivalry

Customers are necessary for revenues. You remember that rivalry type I – competing for *Potential customers* – can increase your *Current customers* without directly decreasing RivTel's *Current customers*. Rivalry type II is competition for each other's *Current customers*, and what is won by one company is lost by the other. In game theory this is known as zero-sum game. At least in a game with one round, each company sees itself practically forced to look out for itself, thus inflicting losses on its competitor. The situation is represented as a 2×2 matrix; NewTel's possible policies with respect to *effective monthly price* appear as rows and RivTel's possible policies as columns. Each company has the choice between two policies: either it <u>increases</u> *Sales price*, *Subscription rate*, and *Life cycle duration* towards the ideal values, thereby increasing the *effective monthly price*, or it <u>decreases</u> the *effective monthly price* to capture <u>more</u> *new customers*. Each field in the matrix is one of the possible policy combinations. The fields contain a description of the outcomes for each company (the pay-offs). Table 7.11 shows this pay-off matrix.

Based on the pay-off matrix, you can see that the worst possible overall outcome is reached when both companies decrease the *effective monthly price* to achieve customer advantage. However, for you as NewTel's manager, it is unacceptable to imagine that your rival could take advantage of your cooperative stance and capture most *Potential customers*, and you would finish the year with *Accumulated profits* even below the BAU level. Of course, the same

Table 7.11 Pay-off matrix for NewTel and RivTel

		RivTel's actions concerning *effective monthly price*	
		Cooperate: **Increase to approach the Best Case scenario**	**Compete:** **Decrease to achieve customer advantage**
NewTel actions concerning *effective monthly price*	**Cooperate:** Increase to approach the Best Case Rivalry scenario	*Accumulated profits* of both companies come close to the Best Case scenario ($66.25), market shares are equal.	NewTel would not maintain such a policy for long, knowing that it is detrimental.
	Compete: Decrease to achieve customer advantage	RivTel would not maintain such a policy for long, knowing that it is detrimental.	*Current customers* switch back and forth between the companies. *Accumulated profits* of both companies are extremely low (38.53 and 38.41 for COMP1; 20.11and 19.75 for COMP2)

holds for RivTel's manager. In game-theoretic terms: if you want to win against the other company or to be sure that they will not beat you, then you will compete because it assures you that you will not be worse off than your rival, whatever they chose to do. If you have heard of the so-called 'prisoner's dilemma', the situation here will rightfully remind you of that situation which is prominent in game theory. During the past decades, the 'Prisoner's dilemma' has also been used in the behavioural sciences to investigate the decision-making behaviour of individuals.

However, even rivalry type I turns out to be zero-sum. Consider that the *Potential customers* won by RivTel cannot be won by NewTel, and even worse: *Current customers* strengthen the 'growth engine' feedback loop in the word-of-mouth dynamics – which means that *new customers RivTel* in a given month will <u>increase</u> *new customers RivTel* in the future (until *Potential customers* are <u>depleted</u>). Anything undertaken by one company to <u>increase</u> its own *new customers* will be interpreted as a harmful action by the other company – unless it can achieve the same increase in *Current customers* in the same month. But since neither company can know what the other one is deciding before the next month, they only can attempt to anticipate the likely decision from the past decisions. This is possible because you and RivTel are engaged in a repeated game.

In a repeated game, there is a chance that cooperative policies will result and remain. The area of repeated games in non-cooperative situations has been extensively discussed by scientists interested in evolution in the realm of biology, and also of social systems. This is way beyond the scope of this book but it is nevertheless recommended for further exploration. Players in repeated games must be careful to signal their willingness to cooperate and to punish non-cooperative behaviour. The probably best known strategy is called 'tit-for-tat' (Axelrod, 1984) and its policy is as follows: 'start with a cooperative move and then replicate the move made by the other player'. This policy assures that tit-for-tat will cooperate whenever it can but punish (compete) whenever it must (for a theoretical discussion, see Duersch *et al.*, 2014).

If you think back at how the model represents the mutual adjustment of the *Sales prices*, the *Subscription rates*, and the *Life cycle durations*, you recognize that by setting the initial impulse to a rise and then replicating the other company's last move with *response multiplier* = 1, you and RivTel were playing tit-for-tat. But beware: tit-for-tat is not perfect. In situations where information may be distorted or ambiguous, tit-for-tat may reveal itself to be too eager to punish, and 'tit for two tats' may be more successful because it avoids switching from cooperation to competition unnecessarily. This brings you to reflect upon the way the rivals' decisions are recognized and the *response multiplier*.

If there were reasons to think that information may get distorted, the model might use the past two moves of the respective other company to decide if it is cooperating or competing. But you might also consider to use the *response multiplier* in a more sophisticated way. The past four experiments have been carried out under the assumption that each company's *response multiplier* would be constant, that is independent of changes occurring in variables of the model. For instance, the *response multiplier* could be different for two distinct cases. If RivTel cooperates, i.e. its decision variables approach the Best Case values, it can react in a different way to when RivTel competes, i.e. moving a decision variable further away from the ideal value. Also, the value of the *response multiplier* might start low but increase in case RivTel takes a cooperative position. For instance, one competitive move by RivTel might be replicated with *response multiplier* = 0.5, but a second competitive move with *response multiplier* = 1. This would be a smoother way to implement a 'tit for two tats' policy. But even if you had developed a logic for adjusting the *response multiplier*, the *effective monthly price* would still have had different simultaneous effects on customer dynamics and on *Accumulated profits*.

Of course, there are strategies other than tit-for-tat. Some will always cooperate, whereas others may always compete – regardless of what the respective other actor does. If you had reasons to think that RivTel's manager will exclusively focus on competing, you might consider increasing your *response multiplier* to values greater than one. In such a case, if RivTel takes a decision corresponding to strategy S3 ('compete'), your reactions would be like two tits for one tat: a massive response, which increases the price of competing because *Accumulated profits* will become even worse than what they were when the *response multiplier* was equal to one.

One remaining question is if you trust RivTel's manager enough to commit to a tit-for-tat policy. The other remaining question is how much importance you give to the relationship between your own and RivTel's *Accumulated profits*. Of course, you should also wonder how NewTel's board members look upon this: would you be well evaluated for having achieved *Accumulated profits* higher that in the BAU case even if RivTel has as high *Accumulated profits* as NewTel? Surely, the model you have developed does not take these considerations into account – but you should by now know how to articulated the corresponding variables and incorporate them into an extended version of the model.

DIY 7.9:
Try your policy in SellPhone

In Chapter 1, you used the SellPhone simulator to gain experience. The first example was the business as usual (BAU) scenario. You remember that the Compete for Customers (CFC) scenario produced very low *Accumulated profits*, even losses, because NewTel and RivTel entered a price war.

What is your policy now given you have developed your simulation model and evaluated potential policies? If you are not sure that you already have figured out your policy, then perform more policy runs in your simulation model. You can vary the initial impulses (the variable you use to set your first decision in the 'C7 Rivalry policies' model) for *Sales price*, *Subscription rate*, and *Life cycle duration.* One interesting variation may be to set the *impulse time* to a later month (by default, it is set to month 1). Note that RivTel should be taking the same decisions as you do: remember that they have the same information and insights as you. You can also vary the *response multipliers* to find out if the resulting *Accumulated profits* are higher to what your previous policy runs allowed you to achieve. As an exception to the assumption that RivTel knows the same things as you: evaluate what happens if both companies have different values for their respective *response multiplier*.

Then go back to SellPhone (you access it via the book's website), let the computer play RivTel (which means RivTel will replicate your first month decisions and then react to your decisions in the same way you react to theirs (according to your policy).

When it is done, compare the customer dynamics, the decisions (yours as well as RivTel's) and the resulting *Accumulated profits* to the BAU, CFC, and BCR scenarios. Are your *Accumulated profits* in the range between the CFC and the BCR scenarios? Explain this outcome using the policy as driver of the decisions which influence customer dynamics.

7.6 Chapter summary

In this chapter, you have left the assumption that you are a monopoly behind and developed possible policies for a case when you have a competitor. When a decision that you might take has several effects opposing one another, you are in a dynamically complex situation. Whenever you are part of a larger system with actors taking their own decisions, this complexity increases. Since you have articulated all your reasoning as a simulation model, you could simulate it to find out how this complex system behaves using different decision values. As it turned out, if *effective monthly price* is the only differentiating attribute that customers can perceive or pay attention to, then you must decide between cooperative and competitive policies. Since in the case of you being unable to drive your competitor from the market and hence achieve monopoly, the cooperative policies proved to be advantageous in terms of *Accumulated profits* as shown in the pay-off matrix (Table 7.11). Because if the other company is as capable of analysing the situation as you, and under the premise that both companies decide to make a collaborative first decision, it turns out that a tit-for-tat strategy leads to the highest achievable *Accumulated profits*. But keep in mind that this is only the case if both companies' managers trust each other. The necessary trust may be relatively easy to achieve in a case with only two companies; in fact, this specific type of situation is called a duopoly and there is much less competitive pressure than under (almost) perfect competition, with hundreds or even more competitors. Cases involving a higher number of competitors will be discussed in Chapter 8. For the moment, we stick to **Guideline 1** (Chapter 1) and keep our model as simple as possible for studying the relevant aspects.

But customer switching can happen, even if you do not intend to trigger rivalry type II; and you have seen that even rivalry type I will be interpreted as a harmful action by the other company. So almost anything one company can do can lead the other company to feel that it is at a disadvantage and make it switch to competitive policies, unleashing an escalation due to the reinforcing feedback dynamics between the companies.

Systems Insight 14 (SI 14): Cooperation <u>increases</u> *Accumulated profits*
Mutual cooperation <u>increases</u> *Accumulated profits*, but there is always the temptation and the danger of competitive policies.

Management Insight 14 (MI 14): Short time horizons favour competitive policies
In the short run, competitive decisions <u>increase</u> *profits*.

Systems Insight 15 (SI 15): Expected retaliation favours cooperative policies
Your rival's incentives to take competitive decisions depend on how credible your threat of massive response and destruction of potential *profits* is. This reduces the short-term advantages of competitive decisions.

Management Insight 15 (MI 15): Policies should account for past decisions
Your policy needs to be able to recognize when you can take cooperative decisions and when you need to take competitive decisions.

Systems Insight 16 (SI 16): Simulation modelling enables policy design
In highly dynamic situations like the rivalry between companies, simulation modelling helps reduce the uncertainty under which you must develop your business policy.

Despite the simplifying assumptions that were used in this inquiry, where the only remaining mechanisms were word-of-mouth diffusion with a limited *life cycle duration* and the multiple influences of *effective monthly price*, this situation is still complex and justifiable policies are not obvious. In Chapter 8 we will review the simplifications and indicate how they might be relaxed and modified to yield a model which better fits your needs and management situations.

7.7 Epilogue: your debriefing

It is July again – one year has passed. You have avoided a price war with RivTel and both NewTel and RivTel have been able to close their first 12 months in Plutonia with *Accumulated profits* exceeding $ 40 million, which is the base line from the BAU scenario. This part of your endeavour turned out just as you would have expected. But now, some surprising developments have occurred. As it happens your success in Plutonia has attracted the attention of a telecommunication giant: GlobalCom has acquired both NewTel and RivTel; even Samuria Technologies is now under the ownership of GlobalCom.

You remember how surprised you were when this news about GlobalCom reached you the first time. The rivalry with RivTel is over. At last, you have found out who RivTel's manager is: an old fellow student and friend from your MBA days.

Certainly, the mobile telecommunication business in Plutonia will now be dominated by GlobalCom since the government of Plutonia has accepted that there is now a monopoly situation. The government assumes that the coverage with telephone services will be even faster in the future. We can also assume that the mere size of GlobalCom will deter potential market entrants. But this is no longer your or your counterpart's concern because both of you are about to be given a new mission in GlobalCom's strategic analysis and development group. Your initial acquaintance with simulation modelling has awoken your curiosity and it turned out that your former rival also plans to learn more about policy design with simulation-model based management. The year in Plutonia is over, but the story continues: new challenges are waiting for you and new discoveries are to be made.

7.8 Questions and challenges

Questions
1. What is rivalry type I? Give a brief definition.
2. What is rivalry type II? Give a brief definition.
3. If you had to choose between rivalry type I and type II, which one would you prefer? Explain.
4. Can you freely choose between the two types of rivalry, or is your choice restrained by certain conditions? Explain.
5. What is *relative attractiveness*. Explain.
6. How can the *effective monthly price* be used to influence *NewTel's relative attractiveness*?
7. When two rival companies such as NewTel and RivTel take the respective other company's decisions into account to make their own decisions, a feedback loop emerges. What are the possible benefits and threats of such a loop?
8. What are the possible benefits and threats of following a competitive strategy?
9. What are the possible benefits and threats of following a cooperative strategy?
10. If a competitive strategy promises higher *profits* in the short run, but a cooperative strategy leads to higher *profits* in the long run, what can you do to reduce the likelihood of your rival to opt for short term profits?
11. Does simulation modelling help to reduce the uncertainty under which you must develop your business policy? Explain.

Challenges

1. In Toolbox 7.1, the DELAY FIXED function was used to model situations where a fixed amount of time passes between a cause and its effect. The function was used to retrieve a past value of a variable. Now assume that in a car manufacturing plant, each car is painted and then enters an oven to burn the paint. The process takes one hour between a car entering the oven and being finished. Of course, the first car to enter the oven will be the first to finish (and leave the oven). If you

want to know the number of cars leaving the oven 'now', in DELAY FIXED of one hour could be used. Alternatively, the situation can be represented by a stock-and-flow structure. Develop a model which simulates eight hours, calculating in time steps of entire hours. Assume that each hour one car enters the oven, but in the third hour, two cars enter. The flow of cars leaving the oven, therefore, should be zero during the first hour, then equal to one car, except in the fourth hour, when two cars leave the oven. Develop a model that replicates this behaviour. You can compare your model to 'C7 Delay fixed as model' on the companion website.

2. In Toolbox 7.2, conditional calculations have been discussed using the IF THEN ELSE function. Assume you have a store selling mobile phones. You have a certain number of phones in stock. Each hour, there is a certain demand. The number of phones sold cannot exceed the number of phones in stock or the number of phones demanded. This could be expressed as *Phones sold* = IF THEN ELSE (*demand* < *Phones in stock*; *demand*; *Phones in stock*). However, there is a shorter way to obtain an appropriate behaviour, using the function MIN (minimum). MIN requires two values to be passed to the function: MIN(val1, val2) and will return the smaller one of both. Develop a model which uses the MIN function, assuming an initial stock of 100 phones and a demand of 10 phones per hour. Simulate the model over 15 hours and verify that when you are out of stock, no more phones are sold despite the demand. You can compare your model to 'C7 Conditionals' from the companion website.

References

Axelrod, R. 1984. *The Evolution of Cooperation*. Basic Books, New York, NY.

Brandenburger, A.M. and Nalebuff, B.M. 1995. The Right Game: Use Game Theory to Shape Strategy. *Harvard Business Review*, **73**(4): 57–71.

Duersch, P., Oechssler, J. and Schipper, B.C. 2014. When is tit-for-tat unbeatable? *International Journal of Game Theory*, **43**(1): 25–36.

Sterman, J.D. and Dogan, G. 2015. I'm not hoarding, I'm just stocking up before the hoarders get here: Behavioral causes of phantom ordering in supply chains. *Journal of Operations Management*, **39-40**(1): 6–22.

Warren, K. 2008. *Strategic Management Dynamics*. John Wiley & Sons Ltd, Chichester, UK.

RELAXING ASSUMPTIONS AND ADDING RELEVANT ASPECTS OF REALITY

8.1 Introduction

Starting with your briefing in Chapter 1, a series of simplifying assumptions have been used for the case of NewTel. There are good reasons for making such assumptions. Two of the **Guidelines G 3** (Chapter 2) and **G 9** (Chapter 5) have already alluded to at the delicate balance between realism and usefulness:

Guideline 3 (G 3): Model parsimony
When developing and using causal diagrams, make sure that all relevant, and only the relevant, variables and causal links are represented.

Guideline 9 (G 9): Start with only the most important piece of structure
When approaching a complex problem, start modelling with the most fundamental piece of causal structure and incrementally add new pieces of causal structure as you discover the need.

Growth Dynamics in New Markets: Improving Decision Making through Simulation Model-based Management,
First Edition. Martin F.G. Schaffernicht and Stefan N. Groesser.
© 2018 John Wiley & Sons Ltd. Published 2018 by John Wiley & Sons Ltd.
Companion website: www.wiley.com/go/Schaffernicht/growth-dynamics

In other words, we have strived to keep the model as simple as possible in order not to dedicate effortsand time to unnecessary aspects. A model that has only the relevant variables and links also has the appropriate level of simplifications, and it satisfies two criteria related to the model's purpose, which you can use to follow **Guideline 3**.

A model has an appropriate balance between simplification and realism when the following two criteria are satisfied:

1. you cannot take away any variable or link without compromising to achieve of the model purpose;
2. adding more variables or links does not improve the fulfilment of the model's purpose.

If you fail to satisfy the first criterion, you have not worked enough. If you miss the second, you have worked more than necessary. The purpose of the developed models in Chapters 2 to 7 was to understand the principles of diffusion of a new product through the interaction of word-of-mouth dynamics and advertising, and to exploit these principles to achieve your business goals in the presence of a competitor. Other simplifying assumptions have been made along the way.

- The customer *population* in Plutonia is assumed to be constant, which means it cannot be increased by addressing new segments of the *population* living in Plutonia. It can also not be decreased by individuals leaving who do not want to use a mobile phone any longer.
- The *population* is subdivided into only two states: *Potential customers* and a company's *Current customers*. Possible intermediate states between using a mobile phone and not using one are not considered. Moreover, there is no differentiation in loyal customers and other customers who are more prone to switching their service provider. And, finally, the model does not account for disappointed former customers who could be the source for negative word-of-mouth.
- *Potential customers* and *Current customers* are assumed to care only for how much they must pay for having and using a mobile phone, excluding quality, plus the aspects and resources relevant for quality, and customer satisfaction. Note that this simplification has a relationship with the previous two: unsatisfied customers are likely to leave the market or talk negatively about the product and service.

- *Advertising* is assumed to be a homogeneous activity that influences decisions made by *Potential customers* without affecting the word-of-mouth dynamics. Moreover, *advertising* does not influence the switching of *Current customers* between the NewTel and RivTel.
- The mobile phones as physical equipment and the contracts for using them are connected to individuals. There are no prepaid mobile phone services. Also, the contract durations are the same for all contracts. Additionally, the physical life cycle of the equipment and the psychological obsolescence time of individuals are the same for all *Current customers*.
- The frequency of decisions concerning the decision variables is inflexible and relatively long – only one decision every month. The total duration of the simulated operations of NewTel was as short as one year.
- Changes to *life cycle duration* or *subscription rate* are also applied to existing contracts of *Current customers*.
- The number of competitors is limited to RivTel and it is held constant. There are no new entries or exits to the market in Plutonia.
- Nonlinear relationships concerning the reaction of customers to the *effective monthly price* and the option of using *process improvement spending* to reduce *Service costs* have been introduced. They allow the incorporation complex behaviours without including many underlying details into the model (remember **Guideline 3**).
- Resources such as the technical quality of the mobile network, additional functions of the phones, e.g. camera and apps, and customer service quality are not considered, even though in real life they do matter for developing demand and satisfying it.

We made these simplifying assumptions considering the purpose of the model: we want to understand the principles of diffusion of a new product by the interaction of the word-of-mouth dynamics and advertising and to become able to exploit these principles to achieve your business goals in the presence of a competitor. You have achieved this in the past six chapters. The resulting model encapsulates these principles. Now, we have a seed or a prototype that can be adapted to different settings you encounter in reality. The important question becomes: How should the model be changed if one or several of the simplifying assumptions must be relaxed because the situation at hand is not reasonably well represented by the seed model? In the remainder of the chapter, some examples of relaxing assumptions are provided. In most parts, qualitative stock-and-flow models, i.e. without equations, are used. However, in Section 8.8 we use simulation to demonstrate the impact of the change of an assumption.

8.2 The *population* is not constant

You may wish to model fluctuations in the *population* – especially if you are modelling a longer period. There are several reasons for these variations. Both increases in disposable income due to economic growth and changes in habits can move individuals into the *Potential customers* stock who were formerly not able or not interested in paying for your product and service. Also, the depletion of the initial stock of *Potential customers* can suggest that you should deliberately look at different segments of the local or national *population* or even expand your operations into new territories. Similarly, these reasons may work in the opposite direction. Recession, changes in habits or other reasons may reduce your stock of *Potential customers*.

Figure 8.1 shows how the basic stock-and-flow system of customers would be modified by the inflow of *new potential customers* and one outflow from each of the customer stocks. *Potential customers* may be *dropping out* even before they become *Current customers*. Also, *Current customers* may desert. Of course, each of these flows will have a characteristic behaviour according to other *variables* influencing them. The *variables* driving each of these

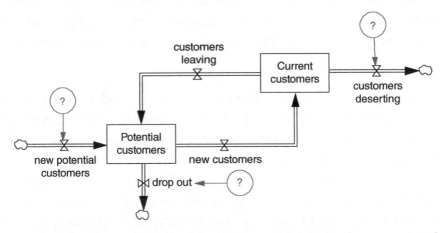

Figure 8.1 Additional flows to make the *population* variable. Unknown *variables* driving the flows are represented by circles with question marks

new flows would need to be understood and incorporated into the modified model. Since they are unknown, in the figure they are shown as circles with question marks linked to the new flows.

8.3 There are not only *Potential customers* and *Current customers*

The simplest way to talk about people is that they are either *Potential customers* or *Current customers*. It may become important to allow your model to deal with more than people knowing or not knowing your product exists. A person might simply not be interested or might be interested but still refrain from buying the product. It is also possible to differentiate between loyal customers and other *Current customers*. Loyal customers, for instance, tend to have longer contracts, drop out less frequently, and would be less likely to switch to RivTel. To represent a finer customer taxonomy, you need to adopt the basic customer stock-and-flow system in a way similar to Figure 8.2.

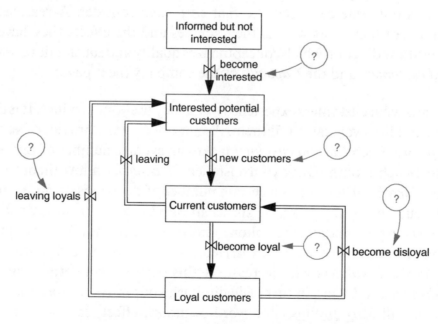

Figure 8.2 Customers go through several states

If we assume there are two statuses for someone who might soon become a customer and if there are different degrees of customer loyalty, additional stocks and a series of new flows are necessary. Customers who are *informed but not interested* turn into *interested Potential customers*, and you would need to figure out how to increase that flow and under which circumstances to allocate resources to this effort. *Interested potential customers* turn into *Current customers*, and again it is your challenge to understand how and when to increase this flow. Thirdly, first-time *Current customers* will become *Loyal customers*. However, *Loyal customers* may become disloyal and leave. A series of causal links with other variables in the model would need to be included – which may require the addition other new variables and resources (stocks) into other parts of your model.

8.4 *Current Customers* care about *Quality*

The *effective monthly price* is only one characteristic that *customers* consider. A real case model would need to account also for quality and satisfaction as well as their sources and the effects they have on flows in the model. Figure 8.3 shows a stock-and-flow diagram which conceptualizes quality and satisfaction, as well as their relationships to the loss of *Disappointed customers* and the *Capacity* of the company (next page).

Quality experienced represents what customers experience when they use your product. It is driven by the relationship between their expectations and how you can fulfil them. As a mobile phone provider, NewTel must have sufficient *IT capacity* and *service capacity*. Each *Current customer* makes an average number of phone calls and uses a certain data volume on the Internet each month. Does your installed *IT capacity* allow them to make all these calls and transfer all this data? Each *Current customer* has a certain number of questions or problems to solve, which require employees to interact with customers. Do you have sufficient *Service capacity* and can it respond in a reasonable time? Your *Current customers* expect seamless telephone and Internet connection and quick responses. How well you fulfil these expectations will influence *quality experienced* by your customers. If the *quality experienced* sinks, the *satisfaction* of your *Current customers* will decrease. If this occurs for a certain time, more of your *Current customers* will be *leaving disappointed*. This, in turn, will diminish your *revenues from Current customers* and reduce your *monthly profits*. But it will also diminish the word-of-mouth effect, so you ought to be careful with the secondary effects of losing *Current customers* because of decreasing *Satisfaction*.

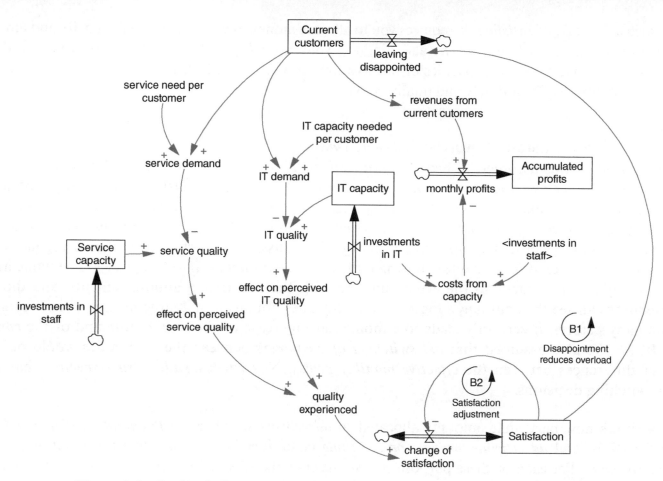

Figure 8.3 *Quality* influences *satisfaction*, which can lead to <u>losing</u> *customers*

Avoiding such a decrease of *satisfaction* requires you to allocate money to *investments in IT* capacity and *investments in staff*. But increasing *costs from capacity* also diminish your *monthly profits*. Therefore, you would need to find out if it is better to invest in your capacities or not to allow your customer base to grow beyond a size that puts a strain on your ability to offer a timely and quality service.

8.5 *Advertising* influences word-of-mouth and *Customers switching*

Advertising spending was assumed to have only one effect: it could persuade *Potential customers* to become *new customers*. *Contact rate* and the *conversion fraction WoM*, which are decisive in the strength of word-of-mouth dynamics, are assumed to be constant. However, some specific forms of *advertising spending* pursue the goal of increasing *contact rate* and the *conversion fraction WoM*. This is the reason why telephone companies – amongst other firms – sponsor, even organize, musical or sports events: they bring many people together and create an emotional context in which the *conversion fraction WoM* increases. The name and logo of the company are associated to the event, starting with the advertising announcements, and during the event, attendees can see the company's logo. Even if this does not mean that large masses of individuals rush to the company's stores, it certainly leads to a momentary increase of the *contact rate* and of the *conversion fraction WoM*. We also assumed that *net switching of customers* between the companies would only occur because of differences between the *effective monthly prices*. Nevertheless, *advertising spending* has also an effect on switching decisions.

Figure 8.4 shows how particular amounts allocated to *advertising spending for Potential customers*, *advertising spending for WoM*, and *advertising spending on switching* come together to constitute the monthly amount of *advertising spending*. For each of these purposes the strength of the effect of $1 spent is supposed to be different. Therefore, the exact shape of the relationship would need to be investigated and used to convert a certain level of spending into a corresponding response in *purchases from advertising, contact rate, conversion fraction WoM*, and *net switching from RivTel to NewTel*.

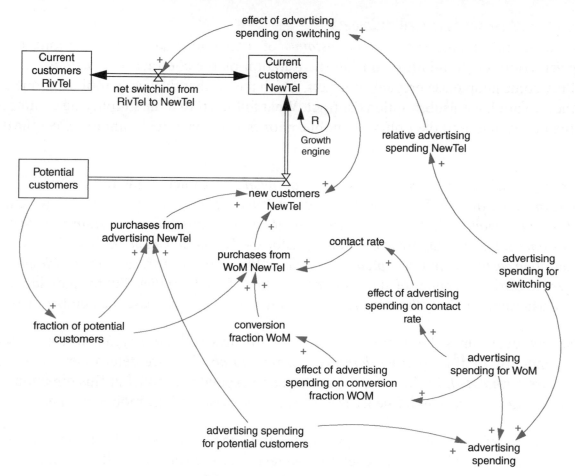

Figure 8.4 Additional effects of *advertising spending*

8.6 Mobile phones are not contracts are not customers

A person can become and remain as a *Current customer* of a telephone company for a longer period than the duration of a given contract. In addition, during the duration of the contract, the *customer* can acquire a new mobile phone. Plus, some people use prepaid contracts, which means that they use a mobile phone and are *Current customers*, but they do not have a subscription contract. What follows is that the simplifying assumption of treating the customers, their contracts, and their physical mobile phones as a single stock cannot reflect the diversity of real situations:

The decision to conceptualize *customers* or *contracts*, and *phones* separately leads to systems of stocks and flows (Figure 8.5). Now, there are three different customer stocks: *Potential customers* are as they were before, but what we represented as *Current customers* in the first seven chapters is split into *Current customers with subscription* and *Current prepay customers*. Besides this, there is now a stock for the *Mobile phones in use*. Two flows lead to adding *new phones*: *new subscription customers* plus *new prepay customers*. Whenever a *Current customer with subscription* changes to the use of a prepaid card, this change of state also means a loss of a *subscription*, but the individual still is a *Current prepay customer*. Customers who switch from prepaid to subscription also increase the number of *subscriptions*.

The *contract duration* determines the fraction of *Current customers with subscription* whose subscription will be *terminated*. Independently of this *contract duration*, the *time to obsolescence* determines the fraction of *mobile phones in use* that are *terminated*. In this way, if you decide to expand the model in this direction, you might also consider that *advertising spending* can influence the *time to obsolescence* of the mobile phones.

You would also need to define the *price* for prepaid cards and connect the *new prepay customers* flow to *revenues from prepaid cards*, which would have to be added to *total revenues*. The *new phones* flow would drive *revenues from new customers*, but maybe the *sales price* would not be the same for *new prepaid customers* as for *new contract customers*; in such a case you would use the *new prepaid customers* and *new contract customers* flows to drive *revenues from new customers*. *Revenues from Current customers* would also depend on both *current contract customers* and *current contracts*.

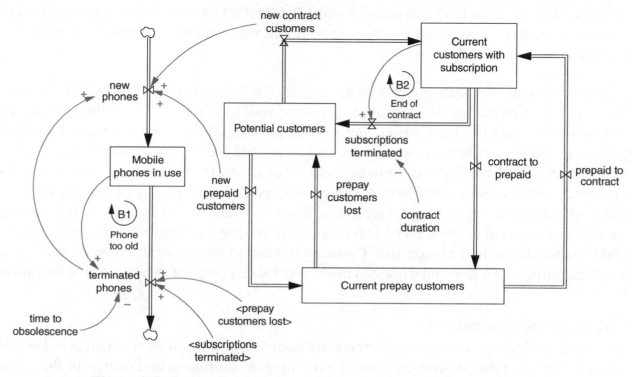

Figure 8.5 Customers, contracts, and telephones as separate stocks

8.7 More frequent decisions and a longer time horizon

You were given one year to achieve the highest possible *Accumulated profits* and could take decisions once a month. Furthermore, when you decided to change the *subscription rate* or the *life cycle duration*, such changes were applied immediately and in a retroactive manner to all existing contracts.

It might be more realistic to say that the *sales price* could be changed more frequently than monthly. In such a case, you would change the 'time step' of the model from month to week. This would have several consequences.

Parameters such as *contact rate* and the *conversion fraction WoM* refer to a month, and you would need to change them to this shorter 'time step'. You would also need to adapt the way you think about *advertising spending*, which happens at the moment on a monthly basis.

Extending the time horizon makes sense because we know that NewTel's business will (hopefully!) not end after one year. Doing this is a case of increasing the number of months of your time horizon to a higher multiple of 12. When considering extending the model's time horizon, you have to consider whether there any processes that influence customer dynamics or the interactions between the companies that become important when a longer time horizon is considered. For instance, during the first year, you were expected to achieve the highest possible *profits*. But what if you had two or three years until the evaluation? Would your boss disapprove your strategy of making losses in the short-term to force RivTel out of the market by <u>reducing</u> *prices*? If you were allowed to make losses for this purpose, after what time would you be expected to break even? This is not relevant when your challenge is limited to one year. But it probably would become relevant in the longer run. Therefore, it is important to note that a model which is appropriate for analysing a given purpose in a given time horizon might become inappropriate when the time horizon is changed.

8.8 Contracts do not change retrospectively

All existing contracts implied by *Current customers* are assumed to adjust instantly to changes in *life cycle duration* or *subscription rate*. This is a practical consequence of amalgamating customers and contracts. But it is different in real life: the existing *contracts* of *Current customers* have a *duration* and a *subscription rate*, and therefore cannot be forced to adjust when changes in *duration* or *subscription rate* of new contracts occur.

However, if the *contract duration* of *Current contracts* must be maintained after deciding to change the *contract duration* of new and future contracts, then you need to make an adjustment in the model structure. Since the stock variable *Current contracts* aggregates all contracts in a single number, the number of *Current contracts* for each month, regardless of differences between specific attributes of these contracts you cannot directly use the stock and the contract duration for calculations that depend on other attributes. Let us think through this: if from a given month on, the contract duration is changed from 9 to 18 months, which number would you apply if there is only one value for contract duration? You can change the value of the variable contract duration from 9 to 18, but then it would be 18 for all the *current contracts*, which is what the model should not do.

There is a way to force your model to consider specific attributes of contracts. For example, different contract types can have different *contract durations*. And it is likely that contracts of different *contract duration* would also have differentiated monthly *subscription rates*. That would mean that for every type of contract there is a specific *contract duration* and a specific *subscription rate*. There are two contract attributes the model should consider. The way to incorporate such a situation into the model structure is to sum up the individual attributes and then average them, as shown in Figure 8.6.

The causal structure in Figure 8.6 includes the *Current contracts* as well as a second stock, *Total contract duration*, and a third stock, *Total subscription rates*. Each time a *new contract* is added, the current number of months in *contract duration* is added to the *total contract duration*. Then the *Total contract duration* is divided by the number of *Current contracts*, yielding the *average contract duration*. In a similar manner, the current *subscription rate* is added to *Total subscription rates* and then divided by *Current contracts* to yield the *average subscription rate*.

This is a way to approximate the fact that after a change of *contract duration* or *subscription rate*, there are two subsets of contracts, each with different *contract durations* and/or *subscription rates*. Customers with older contracts still are there and the commercial conditions of their contract will be maintained while their contracts are valid. These contracts will be progressively replaced by the new contracts. The average *subscription rate* and average *contract duration* will slowly adjust to the changing mix of contracts and, thereby, approximate the real underlying process.

To test if such an aggregate formulation can replicate a process occurring at the disaggregate level, consider how a change in contract duration from 9 to 18 months after the third month would play out over the remainder of a two-year timespan.

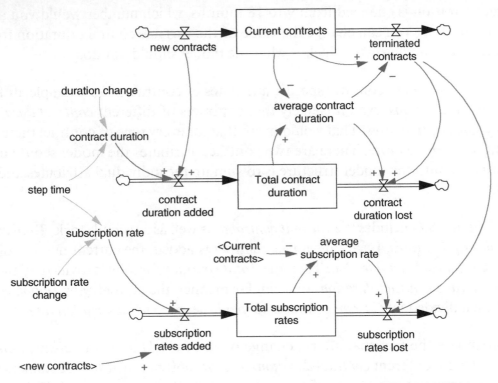

Figure 8.6 Avoiding retroactive changes to *contract duration*

The initial number of *Current contracts* is 90 000, each month they would be 10 000 *new contracts* (this is not shown to save space), and the initial *contract duration* is nine months. This combination of values assures that initially there will be exactly 10 000 *terminated contracts* and, therefore, *Current contracts* will be in equilibrium. Table 8.1 shows this disaggregated data for the contracts with a duration of nine months and the contract with a duration of 18 months. For each type of contract, one column shows the number *of current contracts* and another column shows the number of *terminated contracts*. The last two columns at the right side present the aggregate data, which

Table 8.1 Two different types of *Current contracts* over time

Month	Disaggregated data				Aggregated data	
	Current contracts 9	*terminated contracts 9*	*Current contracts 18*	*terminated contracts 18*	*Current contracts*	*terminated contracts*
1	90 000	10 000	0	0	90 000	10 000
2	90 000	10 000	0	0	90 000	10 000
3	90 000	10 000	0	0	90 000	10 000
4	80 000	8889	10 000	556	90 000	9444
5	71 111	7901	19 444	1080	90 556	8981
6	63 210	7023	28 364	1576	91 574	8599
7	56 187	6243	36 788	2044	92 975	8287
8	49 944	5549	44 745	2486	94 688	8035
9	44 394	4933	52 259	2903	96 653	7836
10	39 462	4385	59 356	3298	98 817	7682
11	35 077	3897	66 058	3670	101 135	7567
12	31 180	3464	72 388	4022	103 568	7486
13	27 715	3079	78 367	4354	106 082	7433
14	24 636	2737	84 013	4667	108 649	7405
15	21 898	2433	89 345	4964	111 244	7397
16	19 465	2163	94 382	5243	113 847	7406
17	17 302	1922	99 138	5508	116 441	7430
18	15 380	1709	103 631	5757	119 011	7466
19	13 671	1519	107 873	5993	121 545	7512
20	12 152	1350	111 880	6216	124 033	7566
21	10 802	1200	115 665	6426	126 467	7626
22	9602	1067	119 239	6624	128 841	7691
23	8535	948	122 615	6812	131 149	7760
24	7586	843	125 803	6989	133 389	7832

are the sum of the two *Current contracts* columns and the sum of the two *terminated contracts* columns. When, in month four, the *contract duration* is <u>increased</u> from 9 to 18 months, the *Current contracts* with a duration of nine months begin to <u>decrease</u> and slowly fade out because from that moment on, all the new contracts have the <u>longer</u> *contract duration*. The reason is that the flow of *terminated contracts* affects always the ninth part of the *current contracts* of this type. This is a goal-seeking behaviour, which slowly approaches the complete depletion of the contracts with nine months duration. During the same time, each month 10 000 new contracts with a duration of 18 months are added to the stock, and 1/18 of them are terminated. Since the outflow of *terminated contracts* is much smaller than the inflow of 10 000 *new contracts*, the number of *Current contracts* with a duration of 18 months <u>increases</u>, progressively approaching a number for which the corresponding outflow will equal the inflow (Figure 8.7).

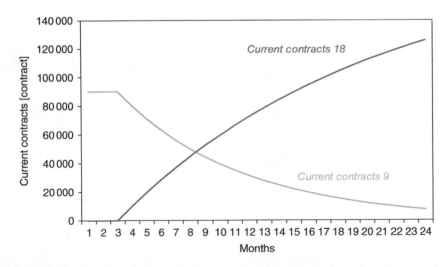

Figure 8.7 Replacement of *Current contracts* from 9 to 18 months

These are the dynamics that the model must replicate, though it cannot directly imitate these two processes because they occur at a lower aggregation level, i.e. more detailed. However, if the number of *Current contracts* and *terminated contracts* simulated by the model is sufficiently similar to the numbers shown at the aggregate level of Table 8.1, then you can consider the model as a sufficiently close replication of reality.

The two graphs in Figure 8.8 display *Current contracts* and *terminated contracts*. The aggregate data from Table 8.1 are used as reference behaviour and printed as a dark blue line; the simulated behaviour appears as light blue line. The *Current contracts* stocks are solid lines, whereas the *terminated contracts* flows are dotted lines.

The simulation shows a behaviour that is similar to the one it strives to replicate. *Current contracts* starts <u>increasing</u> progressively after *contract duration* has been <u>raised</u> from 9 to 18 months after a few months, its slope ceases to increase and slowly <u>decreases</u>. The simulated behaviour starts <u>growing</u> at the same time and stays close to the reference behaviour over the entire simulation. The fit is not perfect, though. The reason for this is that the monthly number of *terminated contracts* <u>decreases</u> more quickly in the simulation than in the reference behaviour (Table 8.1). The difference can be attributed to the fact that the simulation model uses the same contract duration for all contracts, whereas in the spreadsheet (Table 8.1), nine months continues to be applied to the old contracts and 18 months are applied to the new contracts. However, the number of contracts terminated only decreases for a while: in month 15, 7397 contracts are terminated in the reference behaviour, and then their number starts to increase. The simulation yields the minimum value for contracts terminated in month 11 (7342), and their number then also starts increasing. The simulation reaches the minimum earlier, but the minimum value is quite similar to the value calculated in Table 8.1. If the simulated number of *contracts terminated* decreases quicker towards a minimum value, then it is logical that this minimum is reached earlier. During month 14, the two lines cross, and afterwards keep increasing with a similar slope. They may not approach one another but as the number of contracts terminated increases, the relative difference between them, i.e. (simulated − reference) / reference, becomes smaller.

How relevant is this difference for you? Since the simulated number of *Current contracts* is important as a component of *revenues from Current customers*, but the model starts terminating contracts slower due to the increased contract

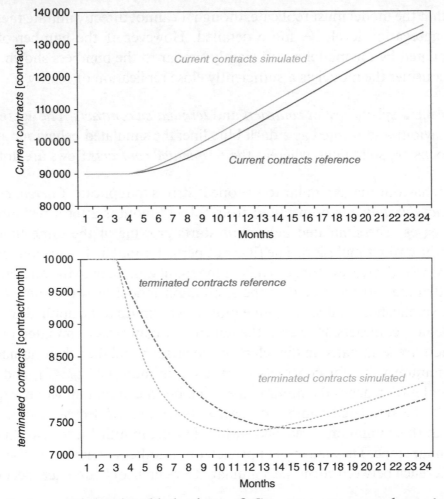

Figure 8.8 Reference and simulated behaviour of *Current contracts* and *terminated contracts*

duration, there will be some simulated *Current contracts* that would not be there in the real situation and, therefore, the simulated *revenues from current customers* is slightly higher than the real one would be. Figure 8.9 shows how the difference (in absolute and relative terms) develops over time. Since the absolute difference shrinks over time, and at the same time the total number of contracts increases, the relative difference (absolute difference / real number of *current contracts*) decreases and is already lower that 2% after 24 months.

More precision in the simulation compared to the reference behaviour could be achieved if it is deemed important but this would require the use of a slightly more advanced modelling feature referred to as 'subscripts'. In the SFD in Figure 8.6, you have one stock to represent the variable *Total contract duration*, one stock for *Current contracts*, and one flow for *terminated contracts*. In this book, you have seen that the simulation software computes one value per time step for each variable and that in the computer variables are not scalars but vectors. Vectors have one dimension – in our simulation, this is dimension is time. Professional modelling software allows you to define additional dimensions and expand these vectors into arrays. Introducing subscripts into a simulation model means

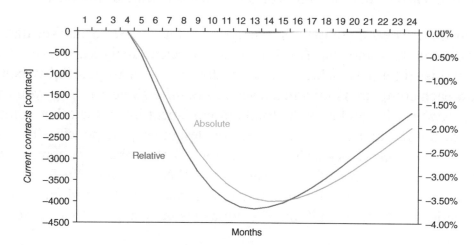

Figure 8.9 Absolute and relative differences between real and simulated *current contracts*

that you disaggregate your model, thereby increasing the number of details you must take care of. Therefore, the choice between representing the different contract types by (i) the average calculations shown in the model of this example or (ii) introducing subscripts into the model must lead to a balance between two aspects: making the model more detailed can increase the accuracy of the numbers created by a simulation, but at the same time it requires more work and makes it difficult for others to understand the model. Accordingly, the relationship between the benefits and the costs implied by making the adjustments to the model will guide your decision. Remember **Guideline 3** and decide if the additional accuracy is relevant to your purpose.

8.9 The number of competitors is higher and varies

In this simulation, RivTel was the only rival. Even though in many countries the total number of companies competing in the mobile telephone market tends to be quite small, it is usually higher than two. If, let us say, there are five companies competing in the market, you would need to take this into account in the model. Luckily for you, this will not necessarily force you to duplicate the variables representing one company for each of the competitors, or possibly introduce subscripts and treat each of the companies of one of the subscripted variables.

The twofold assumption that: (i) each company's management has access to market data and to observations concerning all the other companies and that (ii) it also has sufficient analytical power to understand the same things that you understand is still a reasonable one. Given this, and your responsibility being limited to NewTel, you do not need to know each company's individual level of, say, *advertising spending*, you can just aggregate your competitors' *advertising spending*. If you know the total amount spent by all the other companies taken together, this would be sufficient to use the model in your process of designing your policies. That would mean that you interpret the second *Current customers* stock as 'Current customers of all the other companies' instead of 'RivTel's Current customers', and, in the example of advertising, *advertising spending RivTel* would become *advertising spending rivals*, and of course the total amount of *advertising spending rivals* could increase to the sum implied by each of these rival companies spending $1 million. The same reasoning applies to all other variables, for instance, the *effective monthly price*.

The component of the model where companies observe one another and make adjustments might need a moment of thought concerning the responsiveness and the impulses of the competitors. A single company might be responsive or decide to make a relatively important change to one of their decision variables, but it would be just one of several companies. The strength of the changes and of the reactions of the competitors would probably be a little more moderate than in the two companies case that you have worked through up to and including Chapter 7.

Be aware that this aggregate way of representing all rivals, although simple, does not allow the representation of differentiated strategies or different policies that may be applied by different companies. If you are in a situation where you need to consider such diversity, you might consider representing cooperative companies and competitive companies separately. This would already force you to explicitly include two (groups of) other companies. The case where you need to represent each of the companies as a separate set of variables would certainly increase the number of possibilities to specify detailed policies for each of them. But a simulation model containing, for instance, a total of five companies would be a challenge to build. There would be 20 *net switching* flows between *Current customers* stocks, and each company's *Current customers* would evaluate the *relative effective monthly price* of their current company with four others. And contemplate how complex and detailed your policies would be. Imagine: deciding the *subscription rate* would have to consider what four other companies recently decided concerning their respective *subscription rates*. Not to mention the need to take possible new market entries and market exits into account. Obviously, you would have to evaluate whether you require the additional accuracy so much that it outweighs the effort of building the model.

8.10 Nonlinear relationships replace causal structure

A table function has been used to represent the reaction of *Potential customers* to *effective monthly price*. Using such functions allows you to influence the behaviour of a variable such as *new customers* without requiring you to model all the details of how this behaviour is generated. In a way, it is an economy of work, leaving some parts of the presumable causal structure outside the model boundary, and a table function acts as an interface which incorporates the effects of the structure left out. This idea is shown in Figure 8.10.

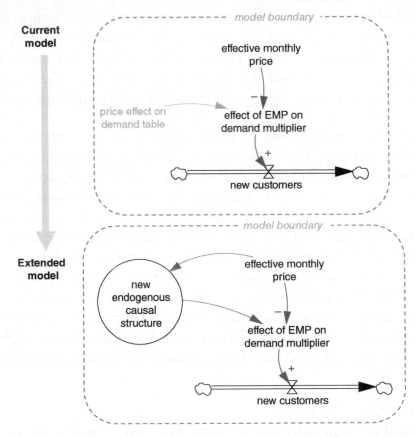

Figure 8.10 Expanding a model's boundary

In the case of this example, you could indeed search psychology and marketing literature to find a detailed model of how individuals react to prices. Maybe the table function cannot represent all the relevant dynamic features of your customers' choice behaviour – after all, once you have defined the data points of a table function, they remain constant over the simulation. You might expand the model boundary and incorporate additional causal structure.

It will be your task to assess if the additional modelling work is compensated by additional relevant dynamics of the model and additional and valuable insights. Here **Guideline 3** becomes relevant once more: put more things into your model only if they are relevant.

The same argument applies to the case of reducing *Service costs* by the way of *process improvement spending*. Of course, you could try to detail what exactly resources are spent on and how they translate into improvements in computer software or other specific aspects impacting *Service costs*. However, this would involve a significant amount of time to work out, and you already know that reducing *Service costs* only makes up a small fraction of the increases in *Accumulated profits*. If there is no reason to doubt that the table functions come reasonably close to the underlying reality, we do not need to replace them by more elaborate causal structures in the model.

Developing table functions usually requires information from existing research or from experts who are able to make informed statements concerning the range of input values, the range of output values, and the shape of the nonlinear function (Sterman, 2000: Chapter 19). However, table functions frequently imply uncertainty. For instance, if the inverted S-shape of the table function used for the reaction to the *effective monthly price* has an exaggerated shape or is not very steep, this may have consequences for the customer dynamics and for *Accumulated profits*. You may not be able to avoid the uncertainty of the situation, but you may test the simulation both with different shapes and values of the table function, if this uncertainty has a relevant effect on *Accumulated profits* or any other important outcome variables. Always remember that you are not trying to develop a model to be as realistic as possible, but a model to be as realistic as necessary. Again, apply **Guideline 3**: investing effort in reducing uncertainty by improving the shape of table functions is only necessary if it reduces relevant shortcomings of the model behaviour.

8.11 The harmonic development of demand and supply capacity: a new book

In Section 8.4, two important resources dealing with your company's capacity to attend to your customers demand have already been mentioned: *Service capacity* and *IT capacity* (Figure 8.3). However, there is more to be said about these capacities and their development. Just like any other company, NewTel constantly has to develop demand

and satisfy it. Developing demand requires marketing capacity; you must find and persuade people to become your *Customers*, and they need to know that your product or service is available and attractive. Your *marketing capacity* will depend on the number of people working in marketing, their skill and experience and the marketing channels you have (as well as the *financial resources* needed). Yes, you also need sufficient *service capacity* and *IT capacity*; otherwise your *Customers* will become increasingly disappointed and eventually desert you. The *network coverage* must be exhaustive and reliable, *response time* must be short and when *Customers* have *Questions* or *Problems*, they expect to be attended to in little time by friendly and competent people. This leads to intermediate and intangible resources such as *Customer satisfaction*. You must recognize that some things you need for your operations (this is the definition of 'resource', as introduced in Box 2.2, Chapter 2) are located outside the company and outside your direct control. You need a high level of *Customer satisfaction*: if it decreases, your efforts to increase or maintain demand would become less effective and fade away (Warren, 2008).

Customer satisfaction can be increased, and it can decrease. Frequently, the speed at which you can increase *Demand* is higher than the speed at which you can command *resources* to satisfy this *Demand*. Also, the speed at which your *Customers* can become frustrated and leave would usually be higher than the speed of capacity build-up. When such differences of speed exist it means that, in some cases (like increasing *Resources* needed to satisfy *Demand*), the causal relationship between variables takes more time to operate; in other words, there is a delay between cause and effect.

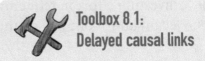

Toolbox 8.1:
Delayed causal links

The methods and tools Box 2.1 (Chapter 2) explained causal links in general. When a causal link is delayed, a special symbol is added to the arrow representing the link in causal loop diagrams, as shown in Figure 8.11.

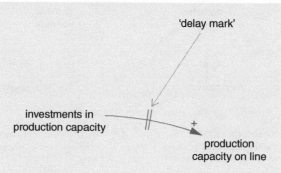

Figure 8.11 A causal link with a delay

The double line crossing the arrow signals the delayed nature of the causal relationship between the two variables connected by the link. Even though this qualitative representation of a delay is easy to set, the underlying stock-and-flow structure will require careful analysis and modelling choices: at the detailed level of quantitative modelling, there are several different types of delay formulations with different behavioural characteristics each. A thorough presentation and discussion of delay formulations can be found in Chapter 11 of Sterman (2000).

But if there is a chance of generating demand and you decide not to because you do not want demand to exceed your *Capacity* to deal with it, then you risk losing this *potential demand* to your competitors. There are two reasons why you could lose demand: firstly, your competitors are better at winning customers or, secondly, your *Capacity* grows slower than your ability to keep your *Customers* satisfied.

Figure 8.12 illustrates the situation in which each company must choose how to allocate *revenues* between developing the *Resources needed to incite demand* and the *Resources needed to satisfy* it. You need to achieve a dynamic balance between inciting demand and satisfying it on one side and a *relative attractiveness* as compared to your competitors on the other side. You can try to grow quickly to prevent your competitors taking over the market, but then again

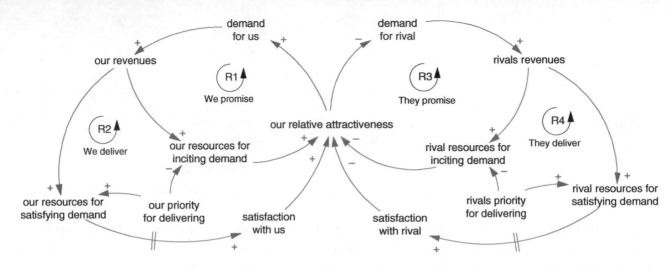

Figure 8.12 The challenges of harmonically developing resources for fostering *Demand* and for *Supply capacity*

growing too quick entails the risk of disappointing your *Customers* and finally collapsing due to a lack of demand. This phenomenon of quick growth being followed by quick decrease is sometimes called 'boom and bust' and otherwise referred to as 'overshoot and collapse' (Paich and Sterman, 1993; Sterman *et al.*, 2007). It is a complex problem implying some additional feedback loops that have not been included and studied in the case of NewTel. Coming to grips with the combined dynamics of word-of-mouth, advertising, and the competition with RivTel already proved to be a task requiring much study, analysis and reflection. The more complex problem affords itself to a different book.

8.12 Chapter summary

This chapter has shown you that many of the simplifying assumptions made in Chapters 1 to 7 can be replaced by developing additional causal structures and, thereby, extending the model. We hope that the relationship between additional realism and additional complexity in the model has now become clear. In fact, if you had to incorporate all these extensions into the original model, the additional effort would be substantial.

However, the responsibility for the outcomes in real-world professional work comes together with the risk of taking poorly informed decisions or devising low performing policies. There is a chain of causation going backwards from results to decisions, to policies and then to your mental model (your understanding of your management situation) and your ability to draw logical inferences from that mental model. Developing a simulation model helps you in different ways. Even a strongly aggregated model can be very useful to gain new insights and understand new principles to enhance your mental model. If you need to experiment with different scenarios and policies to draw inferences, then some more *variables*, links and even some more details may become necessary. And if you must explain your policy to others and maybe even persuade them to buy in on your proposals then you may need to consider many more details and develop a simulation model with a much higher degree of complexity.

By having worked through this book until this point, you have developed enough modelling capability and systemic understanding to adapt the underlying simulation model to a wide range of specific circumstances. 'Systemic' refers to the fact that you recognize your management challenge as an organized set of variables – stocks and flows – in which each decision variable has more than one influence on other variables and where multiple feedback loops create interdependencies. You cannot just focus on a fragment of the 'system' without neglecting the possible side effects. And you cannot take it as a linear input-process-output structure, since the variable's behaviour is generated endogenously, i.e. inside the system.

If your situation requires a much more detailed model, then you should now have sufficient knowledge to work together with a specialized 'Systems Dynamics' analyst or consultant. Years of practice have been spent developing expertise in a methodology of modelling called 'System Dynamics' (Forrester, 1961; Sterman, 2000) of which you have worked through an example of application to one kind of business problem.

As you might imagine already have realized, the same methodology can be applied to a wide variety of other business problems. The inner workings of the model representing such problems will be different, and the insights gained will be different, too, but the construction and simulation will be based on the same principles and guidelines used in this book. Therefore, it is important that you follow through the last step of this book in Chapter 9, which looks back at the work process you have gone through from the methodological perspective of System Dynamics.

References

Forrester, J.W. 1961. *Industrial Dynamics*. Productivity Press, Cambridge, MA.

Paich, M. and Sterman, J.D. 1993. Boom, bust, and failures to learn in experimental markets. *Management Science*, **39**(12): 1439–1458.

Sterman, J.D. 2000. *Business Dynamics: Systems Thinking and Modeling for a Complex World*. McGraw-Hill, Boston, MA.

Sterman, J.D., R Henderson, R., Beinhocker, E.D., and Newman, L.I. 2007. Getting big too fast: strategic dynamics with increasing returns and bounded rationality. *Management Science*, **53**(4): 683–696.

Warren, K. 2008. *Strategic Management Dynamics*, John Wiley & Sons Ltd, Chichester, UK.

SYSTEM DYNAMICS: A METHODOLOGY FOR MODEL-BASED MANAGEMENT

9.1 Introduction

You have gone through six cycles of conceptualizing and modelling causal structures, making these structures operational as part of a simulation model and analysing the simulated behaviour. This gave you an understanding of the system and the dynamics of NewTel's business system in Plutonia.

In this ninth chapter, we systematize the different insights that you have gained during your journey as manager of NewTel and situate them in a more general framework. Firstly, we arrange these insights into a 'big picture' in the context of the nine major insights mentioned at the outset of the book. Secondly, we recount the methodology used throughout the book in more general terms: system dynamics, the development and exploitation of simulation models to design policies (Forrester, 1961; Sterman, 2000). We will outline the skills and knowledge that comprise system dynamics methodology – the system dynamics competence framework. Then, we position the methodological elements, the principles, and the guidelines that you learn in this competence framework. This gives you the opportunity to apply your modelling skills to management or business challenges different to those encountered in this book.

Growth Dynamics in New Markets: Improving Decision Making through Simulation Model-based Management,
First Edition. Martin F.G. Schaffernicht and Stefan N. Groesser.
© 2018 John Wiley & Sons Ltd. Published 2018 by John Wiley & Sons Ltd.
Companion website: www.wiley.com/go/Schaffernicht/growth-dynamics

9.2 Your mental model of growth from diffusion

Throughout the process of successively formulating and evaluating your simulation model, you have developed a mental model of NewTel's business problem and used this to develop a clear understanding of what you can achieve and how to achieve it. In the preface, we looked at nine major insights; consider how these different systems and management insights fit together.

Self-limiting growth: Chapter 2 introduced customers as a strategically important resource and defined what a stock is (**P 1**). It went on to recognize the role of *Current customers* as promotion agents and that *new customers* are a flow (**P 2**). It then elaborated the role of the reinforcing 'growth engine' and the balancing 'depletion' feedback loop in generating the S-shaped *Current customers* growth. We also introduced the principles of feedback loops (**P 3**) and how they drive behaviour (**P 4**). You also found out under which circumstances exponential growth shifts to goal-seeking growth (**P 5**). We saw how increasing growth one moment also leads to its decrease in the future. The relationship between the slope of the *Current customers* stock and the *new customers* flow was introduced and understood as particular manifestation of a fundamental principle (**P 6**).

Obsolescence speeds repurchases: Chapter 3 added an important systems insight into representing the way a limited life cycle duration affects customer dynamics (**SI 1**). You also learned how to model the 'aging' occurring in homogenous stocks: the 'age' of *Current customers* advances from the month of their initial purchase until they eventually flow back to the *Potential customers* stock. Taken together with the previous insights, we could conclude that changes to *life cycle duration* affect *new customers* and *Current customers* in opposite ways (**MI 1**). You recognized that the shift from exponential to goal-seeking growth does not depend on *life cycle duration* (**MI 2**) but on the *potential customers fraction* (**MI 3**). Overall, *life cycle duration* was found <u>not to change</u> the speed of customer growth, but it was recognized as a tool for <u>influencing</u> *Accumulated customer-months* and *Accumulated purchases*, albeit in <u>opposite directions</u> (**MI 4**).

Sell earlier, not more: in Chapter 4 you found out that the effect of *advertising spending* depends on *Potential customers* (**SI 2**), and if *advertising spending* can persuade *Potential customers* to purchase, such gains in *new customers* will reinforce word-of-mouth dynamics (**SI 3**). Therefore, advertising as a tool was recognized to be limited to the initial months of your time frame (**MI 5**). Both advertising and word-of-mouth promotion complement each other, thus increasing *Accumulated customer-months* (**SI 4**), but, due to the reinforced depletion of *Potential customers*, this effect decreases over time (**SI 5**). It was concluded that advertising is only effective for a short span of time (**MI 6**). If the total *population* cannot grow, then advertising does not increase the total number of *Accumulated purchases* (**SI 6**) unless *life cycle duration* is limited and *customers leaving* replenish the *Potential customers* stock (**SI 7**).

Sources of revenue: increasing the *sales price* or the *subscription rate* is a double-edged sword. In Chapter 5, it became clear that increasing the *sales price* or the *subscription rate* would increase the *total revenues*, assuming unchanged numbers of *new customers* and *Current customers* (**SI 8**). However, such changes would increase the *effective monthly price* and, therefore, reduce *new customers* and, thereby, also *Current customers* (**SI 9**). You found that an *effective monthly price* of less than $25 would reduce *total revenues* (**MI 7**), as would an increase over $32 (**MI 8**). *Process improvement spending* was discussed as a means of increasing *monthly profits* by decreasing *Service costs* (**SI 10**). The model turned out to capture the diverse synchronous effects of changing decision variables on *Accumulated profits*, which was selected as your indicator of whether any changes in decision variables have an advantageous total effect or not (**MI 9** and **MI 10**).

Customer net value: in Chapter 6 you experimented with the simulation model to determine the optimum level of your decision variables and the highest possible *Accumulated profits*. The simulation experiments allowed you to confirm the double-edged effect of changes to *sales price* and *subscription rate*, and to determine up to which point the total net effect of *advertising spending* on *Accumulated profits* is positive – you did this by determining the customer net value. The ensuing insight (**SI 11**) was that performance goals should be at the same time feasible and ambitious; you need to evaluate all reasonable combinations of the decision variables. You cannot set achievable high performance goals without finding out how to achieve them at the same time.

Options for rivalry: competition was introduced and analysed in Chapter 7 and you learned about two types of rivalry. The first of them, rivalry type I, refers to competing for *Potential customers* (**MI 11**). You recognized that people compare their possible choices (**SI 12**) and learned to use the concept of relative attractiveness to model the comparison of your offering to those of your competitor (**MI 12**). Relative attractiveness is important for the second type of competition: rivalry type II. This describes attracting a rival's *Current customers* (**MI 13**).

You realized that the mutual observation among competitors form feedback loops that can lead to escalation dynamics (**SI 13**). However, there is a possible risk: even though cooperative policies would <u>increase</u> *profits* (**SI 14**), competitive policies risk triggering a price war (an escalation of <u>reducing</u> *price*) that harm profits, since the short-term benefits of decisions incentivise competitive policies (**MI 14**). To avoid this, you should threaten in a credible way to punish a rival's competitive decisions (**SI 15**). Consequently, your policies must be able to decide when you can cooperate and when you must compete (**MI 15**). Simulation modelling turns out to be helpful in decreasing the uncertainties surrounding multiple feedback loops and interactions between companies through their decisions impact on profits (**SI 16**).

All these insights and principles gradually revealed themselves as we worked through the chapters, with each chapter building on what you had learned in the previous ones. The depth and the solidity of what you have learned depends on how thoroughly you worked through the DIY examples, how much effort you have invested in building your own models, and how critically you have compared your own thoughts concerning the models' behaviour to the explanations provided by the text. In case you did not take advantage of all these opportunities, remember that it is not too late; you can always go back to any chapter or DIY example and work your way through it – more than once, if needed. Figure 9.1 provides the big picture of what you have accomplished during this book. It is organized bottom-up to remind you that the first things you learned were the foundations for later insights and there is one box per chapter (numbers at the left-hand side), thus visualizing the sequence of chapters as a sequence of learning steps. The fact that each chapter box includes the previous ones represents the fact that each chapter not only built upon the previous ones, but also included and made use of their contents.

When you think of the amount of your time spent working through the DIYs, creating, correcting, simulating, and thinking hard to understand the models' behaviour, you should realize that most of these insights are the result of your own modelling activity. The book has only been a guide taking you through the individual steps.

		P	G	SI	MI
	Competition versus cooperation				
7	**Options for rivalry**			12–16	11–15
	Relative attractiveness				
6	**Customer net value**		11–12	11	
5	**Sources of revenue** **Prices – a two-sided sword**		8–10	8–10	7–10
4	**Sell earlier, not more**			2–7	5–6
3	**Obsolescence speeds re-purchases**		7	1	1–4
2	**Self-limiting growth**	1–6	2–6		
1	**SellPhone**		1		

Figure 9.1 Overview of principles, guidelines, systems insights, and management insights

As you progressed, you encountered some important methodological and practical elements of system dynamics methodology as well as principles and guidelines. Together, these have allowed you to learn about system dynamics without losing your focus on the business challenge in front of you. In the following section, we take a methodological perspective and look at what system dynamics is, so that you can see how it can be used in other dynamic business challenges.

The 'system dynamics competence framework' we have developed (Schaffernicht and Groesser, 2016) defines a series of skills that comprise detailed learning outcomes. You will see many elements of system dynamics that you have already learned broken down per the chapter they appeared in.

9.3 System dynamics modelling

In social systems such as companies or markets, nothing remains the same: 'There is nothing permanent except change', said the Greek philosopher Heraclitus. Customers come and go, competitors enter and leave the market, new technologies are developed and others become obsolete. The rate of change depends on many factors; you can control some of them, while others will be out of your reach. Most of the time, different parties influence these factors simultaneously. But whoever wishes to influence a factor needs enough resources to achieve the desired impact. Therefore, managers and decision makers try to generate the resources needed to implement their policies and strategies. Frequently, the different policies are interdependent and unintended feedback dynamics occur. In such complex settings, managers could use a tool which allows them to proceed as car builders and engineers in general: build a prototype and evaluate its quality in crash tests and wind tunnels. They repeat this cycle of modelling–testing–modelling until they are confident that it will work in practice. However, what kind of 'wind tunnels' or laboratories do decision makers have readily available?

System dynamics has been developed to serve exactly this purpose. It is based upon some fundamental assumptions:

- decision makers have deep knowledge of the systems they work in;
- decision makers try to develop resources that build up and decrease into and out of stocks;
- the systems of stocks interact with one another by intended or unintended feedback loops.

The visualization and thinking in stocks and flows allows us to represent the relevant elements of a management situation as well as possible policies, which helps in two simultaneous ways. Firstly, working with visual methods helps to structure our thinking of the underlying situation and, secondly, the simulation results challenge the implications of our frequently inconsistent mental model (Schaffernicht, 2010). When system dynamics is applied to policy design (Forrester, 1994), it provides us with a metaphorical wind tunnel for policies and strategies in a relative brief amount of time (Groesser, 2015). The ability to formulate possible policies and evaluate them in a simulation environment reduces the risks, costs, and time necessary to carry out the design of policies (Sterman, 2001).

9.3.1 The manager as modeller

Figure 9.2 shows how a simulation model influences the work of a decision maker. It shows a generic account of a manager's work process – with and without simulation modelling. Note that the rectangles represent concepts and the arrows denote relationships, given by the labels.

Consider first the circular logic represented by the solid arrows: managers and decision makers have to achieve given objectives, which are built into the policies. An objective variable is defined and a target value set. The situation reveals information concerning the current value of the objective variable; this information feeds into the policy, which results in a decision according to the relationship between the target value and the current value of the objective variable. The decision influences the situation and a circular relationship between the decision maker and the situation emerges from the iterative process of understanding the situation and influencing it. It is important to recognize that the information used is selected according to the manager's mental model and that the policy in place is framed by this the mental model. System dynamicists have since long recognized that the attention of decision makers is selective and that a given mental model makes them pay attention to certain variables but blinds them for other variables (Senge, 1990). At the same time, the information selected can have an influence on the mental model.

Consider now the dotted lines in Figure 9.2. The mental model becomes the foundation for conceptualizing a simulation model. The simulation model reveals and also modifies the structure of the mental model during the

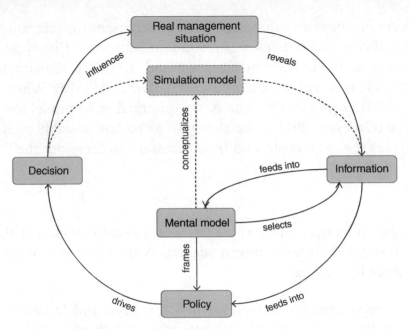

Figure 9.2 Simulation modelling as a process of designing and evaluating policies (based on Sterman, 2000)

modelling process: the visual feedback given by diagrams representing the presumed causal structure of the situation is a new category of information is fed into the mental model. As psychologists say: 'What you see is what there is' (Kahneman, 2011). Then, the simulation model allows the manager to test policies, and the information it reveals about the simulated business situation helps to reject unsuccessful policies and to select well-performing policies. Developing and using a simulation model reduces the risk of not accounting for relevant variables or causal links and of misattributing behaviours to causes which are wrong.

In general, one challenge for managers is to develop their mental model about a complex management problem. In practice, this is achieved in many different ways, ranging from reflecting on and discussing matters with colleagues to more rigorous practices such as model-based management (Groesser *et al.*, 2013; Groesser and Zeier, 2012). Without the help of simulation tools, policies are frequently designed by tradition, by intuition, by negotiation, or using hierarchical power. Of course, the outcomes and information yielded by decisions in the real world can be used to evaluate and perhaps improve or change the decision maker's mental model. But this takes time and thus learning is slow, meaning improved decisions come at high costs. Making substantial changes to policies bears a considerable risk, which means that there are strong incentives not to radically change policies. If competing policies are formulated in a simulation model using the best-known information available, then candidate policies can be evaluated in a comparatively risk-free, quick, and inexpensive manner. This is what is attractive about simulation modelling. The fact that system dynamics accounts for resources such as stocks and directly represents the business system including the respective feedback loops makes it natural to use for this purpose (Dierickx and Cool, 1989).

9.3.2 Basic assumptions of system dynamics

9.3.2.1 Feedback loops as the basic building block of social and natural systems

There are fundamental or root assumptions that define a conceptual framework for the system dynamics methodology. While this book is not the place to discuss them in detail, two of them state basic properties of the world around us:

1. Feedback loops are the basic building block of social and natural systems.
2. Feedback loops consist of resource stocks increasing and decreasing over time.

A manager makes decisions for his or her organization, observing certain variables and trying to influence them according to the organization's objectives. The variables he or she is striving to influence are observed by other agents at the same time and they also try to influence them, even though their objectives may be different. You have dealt with this throughout this book in a business context. But if you think of natural systems, you find the same topic: animal species constitute food chains, take lions and their prey. Lions' prey, i.e. zebras, impala, wildebeest etc., eat grass, and if there is a drought more of them will die of starvation. This reduces the food for lions, and then lions will also starve to death. But when there are less lions, less prey will fall victim to predators and, therefore, the prey population will grow. This, in turn, increases the available food for lions … you can already mentally see the feedback loops.

Assuming that the world we are part of consists of feedback loops, **Guideline 3** (Chapter 2) turns out to be one way to state the 'endogenous' orientation: if a decision you make influences a variable that has an impact on you, you need to have it inside your (mental) model boundary. If you fail to incorporate this variable and the causal links connected to it, your (mental) model will fail to capture the variable's effects and your decisions risk provoking surprising 'side effects' or 'unintended consequences'. These are not side effects, but your model has a blind spot and, as it cannot indicate the variables, its impacts appear to be surprising for you.

However, following **Guideline 1** (Chapter 1) you must also avoid having unnecessary variables inside your model boundary. You must cut off at some point. This leads to the decision that certain variables will not be endogenous, but exogenous or perhaps not considered. The exogenous variables act as interfaces between the endogenous part of your model and the rest of the world. Some of these exogenous variables may be output variables, without causal links back to other variables in the model. Others are input variables, some of which may exhibit behaviour based on external data. Other input variables may be parameters whose values you can modify within certain ranges. Figure 9.3 illustrates how the model boundary separates endogenous from exogenous variables. Think of it again: feedback loops only exist inside the model boundary, i.e. between endogenous variables. If you realize that a currently exogenous variable participates in a loop and this loop is important, then this variable would have at least one causal link pointing at it and one link going out from it. Then, it would be an endogenous variable and you would have inadvertently expanded the model boundary.

One additional thought: we assume that no substance can be created out of nothing or be converted into nothing. This means that the set of flows adding to or draining from a resource in stocks are 'conserved flows': they do not create something out of nothing. For example, in the Plutonia model, the total number of individuals does not change. However, sometimes the model purpose allows it to leave some variables out of the model boundary, as is

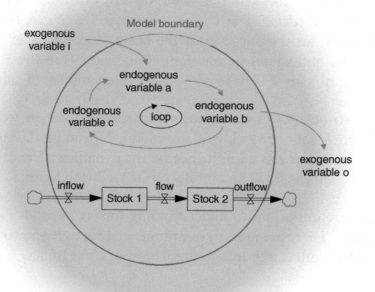

Figure 9.3 The model boundary separates endogenous from exogenous

the case of the customers and the provider's financial resources. In such cases, the 'cloud' symbol at the origin or at the head of the flows represents the amount of this resource 'in the rest of the world'. We acknowledge that this resource does exist before entering our model and after leaving it, but the variables and their dynamics are not relevant enough to be included in the model.

9.3.2.2 Changes over time in interdependent resource stocks

System dynamics models assume that we can safely aggregate individual items into stocks representing certain states of whatever is contained in the stocks. In this book, we have dealt with 'individuals' in a *population* and they were in one of two states: *Potential customer* or *Current customer*. Of course, these individuals are not alike; they differ in many respects. However, for the purposes of the business challenge in Plutonia, we could abstract from these interindividual differences and aggregate one million individuals in these two stocks. As you have seen in Chapter 8, real world situations quickly lead us to consider a higher number of states, that is different sets of stocks.

Whenever there are different sets of stocks, for instance, customers, satisfaction, workforce, and production capacity, the flows adding to or draining from one stock will, in general, depend on the current levels of other stocks. This also means that the level of one stock has an influence on the dynamics of another stock. These relationships of interdependency of the stocks and the flows in a model create feedback loops.

These two root assumptions are important to understanding the endogenous orientation and the principles and guidelines laid out in this book. There are more assumptions and we urge you to read about them in '*Principles of Systems*' (Forrester, 1969), which offers a thorough discussion of these topics.

9.3.3 The system dynamics modelling process

The system dynamics modelling process consists of a sequence of steps that starts with a problem definition (P in Figure 9.4). This definition should state as clearly as possible what the challenge is: Which variable shows a problematic behaviour? What is this behaviour, i.e. the reference mode? How wide should the model boundary be? How long should the time horizon be? Then you start conceptualizing (C), i.e. defining the variables and links which you deem be relevant within the model's bounds. You define the units and then advance to quantification (Q): set parameter ranges and values, formulate equations and, maybe, table functions. The ensuing validation (V) compares the model's structure to what it is supposed to represent, compares the simulated behaviour to the empirical reference mode, and includes other tests, ensuring that behaviour remains reasonable even under extreme parameter values and determines how sensitively the model reacts to uncertainties in parameter values.

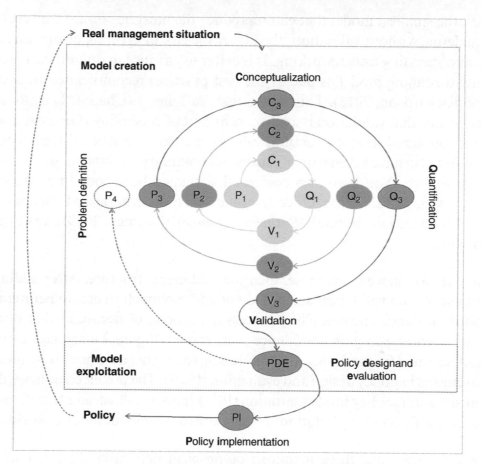

Figure 9.4 The system dynamics modelling process. (P: problem definition; C: conceptualization; Q: quantification; V: validation; PDE: policy design and evaluation; PI: policy implementation; subscript numbers represent different iterations.)

You start this cycle with the smallest model that can reproduce the most important aspects of the reference mode. The more variables you define without validation, the higher the risk of creating errors and, thus, needing to make significant corrections and spending time reworking. It is better to advance to quantification and validation as soon as possible: 'always have a running model' is one of the best practices recommended by system dynamics experts (Martinez-Moyano and Richardson, 2013). This means that **Guideline 1** (Chapter 1) is not applied once but in an iterative process. It also means that validation is a permanent part of modelling (Groesser and Schwaninger, 2012). In this book, you have encountered several structural validation criteria: unit consistency and the need to link each variable to a real entity. You also have taken care of the model boundary, and the model boundary test also belongs to the structural validation tests. You have also compared simulated behaviour to a reference mode; testing the historical fit is part of behavioural validation. Of course, there are more criteria and a set of methods for validation. We motivate you to read Chapter 21 of the book '*Business Dynamics*' (Sterman, 2000) and Groesser and Schwaninger (2012) concerning this topic.

If the model is not yet able to achieve its purpose, then you add more structure. After adding a piece of structure, you go through quantification and validation again. Do not add too much structure per iteration. It is advisable to go through more iterations instead. The modelling process is a process of iterations that bring the model closer to satisfying all the validation criteria to gain confidence in its results. Figure 9.4 represents iterations as subscripts, for instance P_1, P_2, and so on. Upon passing the validation tests, you advance from model creation to model exploitation, where you engage in policy design and evaluation (PDE). The preferred policy will then be implemented in the real management situation: policy implementation (PI). Figure 9.4 illustrates this iterative process and shows the path from model creation through exploitation to using tested policies in the real world.

The process shown in Figure 9.4 has three iterations of problem definition (P_1–P_3), conceptualization (C_1–C_3), quantification (Q_1–Q_3), and validation (V_1–V_3). When looking back to the activities carried out in Chapters 2 to 7, you will recognize this iterative process. Even in each chapter we went through several iterations: each time a new variable was included in the model (C), quantification (Q) and validation (V) were carried out. This sequence has trained you in an important best practice. After several iterations, you found that the model's structure contained a representation of all relevant aspects concerning the decision variables and their influences on customer dynamics and profit accumulation of both companies, and that the model's behaviour replicated the S-shaped growth and maintaining a permanent *population* of *Potential customers* due to the individuals returning from *Current customers* to the stock of *Potential customers*. All this meant we could conclude the model was fit for purpose, allowing us to design and evaluate different candidate policies (PDE) in Chapter 7. Policy design and evaluation can assist in improving your definition of the problem; this is shown as an arrow with dotted line taking your back to an additional iteration starting with P_4. Policy implementation should, if everything runs according to plan, have the desired effect, i.e. allow you to increase the *Accumulated profits* due to the changes to the decision variables' values. If you have done the final DIY in Chapter 7 and went back to the SellPhone simulator, then you have, at least in principle, implemented your policy (PI). Your results in terms of *Accumulated profits* (compared to the business as usual scenario) have revealed how well your policy performs or if you ought to go back to modelling and initiate a new iteration of P, C, Q, and V. Of course, in real life, this will not be the end of the book, but you will move on to the next challenge.

9.4 System dynamics competence

Carrying out all the necessary steps in the different phases of modelling involves several things you must understand and can do. The system dynamics competence framework organizes these into a set of seven skills (Schaffernicht and Groesser, 2016). A skill is the ability to carry out complex activities. The seven system dynamics skills are: system dynamics language (skill 1), dynamic reasoning (skill 2), model analysis (skill 3), project initialization (skill 4), model creation (skill 5), model validation (skill 6), and policy evaluation and design (skill 7). Each of the lower numbered skills prepares for the higher numbered ones. The way they are embedded into one another is represented by Figure 9.5: skill 1 and skill 2 build the foundation for skill 3, which is a prerequisite for skill 5. Together with project initialization (skill 4), they are the basis for model validation (skill 6). Finally, policy evaluation and design (skill 7) encompasses all previous skills.

Skills are acquired progressively. Therefore, the framework also specifies a sequence of competence development stages: beginner, advanced beginner, competent, proficient, expert, and master. The activity of modelling requires the modeller to diagnose his or her current situation and to take appropriate decisions according to this diagnosis.

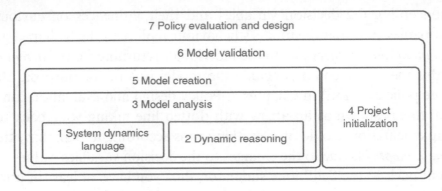

Figure 9.5 The system dynamics skills in the system dynamics competence framework (Schaffernicht and Groesser, 2016)

For example, the modeller must recognize the queues of things such as stocks, flows, feedback loops, and behaviour modes and must know what best to do with them. The beginner has no personal experience; he or she learns abstract definitions and follows abstract rules and guidelines, much comparable to cooking recipes. Carrying out actions such as deciding which part of the situation should be represented as a variable, which type of variable, which equation, and so on, starts a process of accumulating and refining personal experience that enables the learner to develop a personal method of carrying out these activities in a growing number of situations (with increasing complexity). The advanced beginner starts to take his or her own modelling decisions, but frequently needs to recur to the abstract rules. The competent modeller will already have good diagnostic skills but fall back to guidebooks and other sources of rules and guidelines to take an appropriate modelling decision. Proficiency means being able to work in the field, for instance as consultant or analyst. Expertise is reached after at least 10 years of practice (Ericsson *et al.*, 1993, 2007) and means that they intuitively do the right things. Finally, mastery means that a person has conceptualized their expertise and can teach others. Each of these stages is achieved when a specific set of learning outcomes have been reached.

Even though this book focuses on managing a product launch, its diffusion and, hence, elements of strategic management, you have at the same time practiced several system dynamics skills. Skills are not monolithic: they consist of components called learning outcomes. A learning outcome is a description of a directly observable performance that you have learned to carry out (Schaffernicht and Groesser, 2016). After having worked through the book with its models and DIYs, you have achieved the learning outcomes of the beginner stage. You are even halfway through the learning outcomes of the advanced beginner stage. The following sections provide details on which learning outcomes are implied by this book. Of course, there are also other learning outcomes that we have not addressed in this book. You can find a detailed description on our companion website. While reading through these outcomes you should be able to recognize which of the skills you have mastered and which skills need training and practice.

9.4.1 Skill 1: system dynamics language

There are several basic concepts and terms with specific meanings, as well as a set of grammatical rules used to build syntax correct diagrams and models. The skill 'system dynamics language' consists of a series of learning outcomes. The phrases here show those learning outcomes you have dealt with in this book.

- You understand important concepts of system dynamics: policy, reference mode, model boundary, time horizon, units of measure, stock, flow, causality, and polarity.
- You can identify exponential and goal-seeking behaviour in graphs, which are the atomic behaviour patterns – and you can also describe them verbally.
- You can apply the guidelines of good causal loop diagram development: naming the variables as nouns, indicating the polarity of causal links, indicating the relevant feedback loops, naming feedback loops and indicating their polarity.
- You should be able to describe some of the standard formulations for reinforcing feedback loops and the balancing feedback loops, as well as the Bass model for S-shaped growth. This prepares you well for learning about other standard formulations. Standard formulations are like patterns of causal structure that have been tested

and validated in many previous models; therefore, they are safe to use and well known be the community of system dynamics modellers.
- You had at least two situations that required the conversion of diagrams from CLD to SFD, when you constructed a CLD based upon a SFD in Chapters 6 and 7.

You are now well acquainted with many of the concepts and terms of system dynamics. Of course, if you wish to understand the methodology more thoroughly, you need to invest additional time in further reading and application. A comprehensive treatment can be found in Sterman (2000).

9.4.2 Skill 2: dynamic reasoning

Knowing the concepts and the terms is important, but to become useful in practice it must be combined with the ability to account for time and dynamics when analysing a situation. This is what 'dynamic reasoning' is about. In this book, you have acquired some practice and should have achieved the following learning outcomes:

- You have extensively practiced interpreting graphs. And you can describe (and hence understand) the difference and the relationship between stock and flow.
- You also understand feedback loops in CLDs and SFDs. You can identify such feedback loops in CLDs and in SFDs.
- You can associate changing loop dominance to transitions in atomic behaviour patterns. The shift from exponential to goal-seeking growth and the dominance shift from the reinforcing 'growth engine' loop to the balancing 'depletion' loop was introduced in Chapter 2 and has been a reoccurring theme throughout this book.
- This also means that you associate atomic behaviour patterns to fundamental feedback structures (exponential behaviour to positive feedback and goal-seeking behaviour to negative feedback), as well as associating fundamental feedback structures to atomic behaviour patterns (positive feedback to exponential behaviour and negative feedback to goal-seeking behaviour).
- You have also learned how to interpret graphs. Behaviour-over-time graphs were defined in Chapter 1 and used repeatedly in Chapters 1 to 7.

If you want to advance your dynamic reasoning skill, we recommend you to work through the cases discussed in Chapters 4 to 9 of Morecroft (2015), then go through the wealth of examples treated in Warren (2008), and. Eventually. have a go at resolving the challenges posed in Sterman (2000).

9.4.3 Skill 3: model analysis

The first two skills are the foundations upon which application-oriented skills are based. 'Model analysis' is the ability to explore, interpret, and understand a model. Model analysis is to modelling what reading is to writing: how could you write, if you cannot understand what you are writing. Your work in this book helped you to achieve a series of important learning outcomes. In total, model analysis consists of 14 skills. 13 of them require you to 'do' something, not only 'know' something. In such cases, dealing with a simple problem is naturally easier to learn than dealing with a complex problem. Therefore, we distinguish situations of low complexity (1–2 feedback loops), intermediate complexity (3–5 feedback loops), and higher complexity (more than 5 feedback loops). When the complexity of the situation or of the model is relevant, then the respective learning outcome must be achieved for each of the three levels of complexity. Such complexity-dependent learning outcomes count one for each complexity level. Therefore, 13 complexity-dependent learning outcomes makes 39 learning outcomes, plus one which is independent of complexity, leading to a total number of 40 learning outcomes. You have dealt with five of the complexity-dependent learning outcomes:

- You can analyse structural diagrams, mainly interpreting the structure of SFDs and inferring plausible behaviour patterns from SFDs.
- You can reconstruct a description of their content and explain CLDs.
- You can interpret the equations of a stock-and-flow model.
- You know how to experiment with simulation models to assess proposed hypotheses.
- You can explain the structure and the behaviour of stock-and-flow models.

In Chapters 2–7 you have dealt with models of an intermediate level of complexity. You have worked with models ranging from two feedback loops ('growth engine' and 'depletion') to slightly more complex ones, when obsolescence was added and then the competitor became part of the model – for this reason, in the five learning outcomes you have achieved, you have made it to the second complexity level, thus completing 10 items. Accordingly, we count 10 reached learning outcomes. They are all classified as advanced beginner; however, not all aspects of model analysis are part of this book.

9.4.4 Skill 4: project initialization

A modelling project is a practical affair and, consequently, it has not played a major role in this book. There are differences between working through a book and executing a modelling project in real life. One important difference is that in real projects you frequently work to help someone else to come to grips with a situation to be modelled or to design a policy. Accordingly, avoiding misunderstandings and the ensuing overhead work is important.

To give you an overview, there are three groups of learning outcomes: Firstly, to prepare a modelling project means that you establish who are the clients of a project, what the symptoms are that give rise to the project challenge, the reference modes, and if system dynamics is an appropriate methodology. Secondly, to establish the challenge with its logical and temporal scope means that you establish desirable and feared scenarios and a preliminary model boundary, but also that you engage clients and other relevant actors. You also formulate a conceptual model. Thirdly, you establish the purpose of the modelling project, which implies agreement with the clients. Even though a textbook gives you little opportunity to practice project skills, one learning outcome has been dealt with: you established the reference mode, which is part of preparing a modelling project.

9.4.5 Skill 5: model creation

Being able to create a model is the core skill of system dynamics competence. You will have also noticed that there are many aspects to be taken care of, so the number of learning outcomes is high for this skill.

- You know how to define the boundary of the model: you read about it in Toolbox 1.1, then you decided on the initial model boundary in Chapter 2 and expanded it in Chapter 6 and even in Chapter 8.
- You know how to define the time horizon (**Guideline 6**, Chapter 2).

- You can develop the representation of variables:
  - You can discover them in the written text (aided by the fact that they appeared in italics).
  - You can classify them by type (stock, flow, intermediate).
  - You can classify their units of measure.
- You are also able to develop the representation of causal relationships in diagrams and equations:
  - You can discover links implied by the text (the underlined words helped you), discover the link's polarities, and classify the links (with the corresponding polarity sign).
  - You can formulate equations, which were, in part, based on standard formulations (reinforcing feedback loop, balancing feedback loop, Bass model of S-shaped growth, material mixer delay) and, in part, were developed from scratch.
  - You can discover the shape of nonlinear causal relations between variables and incorporate two table functions into the model.
- You can use simulations to improve your understanding:
  - You can use simulations to reproduce reference modes, to formulate structure–behaviour hypotheses, and you experimented with simulation models to assess proposed structure–behaviour hypotheses.
  - You can modify simulation models to assess proposed structure–behaviour hypotheses.
  - You can design policies as part of a simulation model.
    - You can modify your simulation model to incorporate policies.
    - You can experiment with the simulation model to evaluate proposed policies.
- You can design a qualitative model (CLD or SFD) observing the following:
  - You can model processes starting with key stocks, e.g. G., *Customers*, and inferred key variables that had to be endogenous to the model.
  - You know that it is important to strive for an endogenous orientation, so that the necessary variables to have all the causes driving behaviour inside the model boundary, as opposed to exogenous factors. From Chapters 2–5, every extension of the model was the consequence of recognizing that an additional entity had to be represented within the model boundary.
  - You can define the unit of measurement for each variable.

- You are also able to develop a quantitative stock-and-flow model:
  - You can compose logically coherent equations and formulate the simplest possible fragments of structure.
  - You have seen that validation is part of the modelling process. The process in Chapters 2–5 was driven by consistently asking if the factors which were manifest in the SellPhone environment were considered and if the model behaviour is sufficiently close to the reference mode.
  - You can simulate after adding one piece of structure and modified your model to test scenarios or potential policies.
  - You can improve the problem situation according to the purpose of the model.
- You have been guided to determine when to stop modelling and advance to model exploitation. The decision to stop adding more details was justified by explicit arguments and regarding the book's purpose, which needed to be simple enough to serve in a textbook. In a real case, you would have continued adding variables and links to the model. Chapter 8 discussed how the model could be extended from a 'textbook' situation to a real-world application. This introduced you to the need to decide when a model is fit for purpose.

Judging by the number of learning outcomes, you should certainly realize how much you have accomplished by creating the NewTel model and using it to design your policies.

9.4.6 Skill 6: model validation

How you and others gain confidence in a model is of overarching importance to the modelling process. For this reason, 'model validation' is transversal to all modelling-related activities and is treated as a skill. Validation is subdivided into two sets of criteria: structure validation and behaviour validation. Validation, however, does not imply that a model might be totally accurate. Since models are always a simplification of something they represent, to say that a model is valid means that it satisfies a set of standards; these standards may be more or less demanding, depending on the context of the modelling process and the purpose the model serves (Groesser and Schwaninger, 2012).

- You have seen how to validate the model's structure with respect to two criteria (Toolbox 1.1). Firstly, the model's dimensional consistency is assured because you have defined the units in a way which conserves consistency in all equations. Secondly, each variable corresponds to a real entity. For instance, the *contact rate* or the *life cycle duration* were not simply invented to make the model behave as desired, but directly taken out of the problem description. Even the *effective monthly price*, which was not mentioned in the briefing, is justified regarding the way how individuals are thought to take their decisions.

• You know how to do behavioural validation by analysing the fit between the simulation results and the reference mode (business as usual in Chapter 1). Once the model was similar enough to the reference mode and you knew its structure was valid, you decided to cease the validation process.

This means that you have dealt with three of the learning outcomes of this skill. You did not need to evaluate the model's membership of a model family (one aspect of structural validation), neither did you have to test and evaluate extreme condition behaviour, or test and evaluate the sensitivity of the model with respect to uncertain parameters. These activities clearly went beyond the scope of this book.

It is fair to say that aspects such as behaviour under extreme parameter values and sensitivity to uncertainties in parameter values or table functions are rather technical issues and become important only when you are working on real problems. It takes considerable time dedicated to studying and practicing system dynamics proper to really get a feeling for the importance of these validation activities and to develop practice in incorporating them into your set of skills.

9.4.7 Skill 7: policy evaluation and design

If 'model creation' is the core skill of modelling, then 'policy evaluation and design' is its *raison d'être*. You may create a model because you want to understand a phenomenon, because you want to evaluate or design a policy for your own work, or you want to help someone else improve their policies in a problematic situation – in none of these cases is modelling an end: it is always a means.

According to Jay Forrester, the founder of system dynamics, 'one should enter a complex dynamic situation and (be able to) talk about the issues for 20 minutes without contradicting oneself' (Forrester, 2007: 363). He went on to state that a systems dynamics expert should:

a. know the structure causing the problem,
b. know how the problem is created,
c. have discovered a highly effective policy that will alter the behaviour,
d. understand the reasons why the less effective policies will fail,
e. be able to explain how strongly defended policies within the system may be the cause of troubles,
f. be able to argue for better alternative policies.

These are the foundations for defining the learning outcomes of policy design and evaluation. As you may imagine, this last skill requires a relatively advanced development stage in the learning process of the other skills. Out of the six learning outcomes defining skill 7, you have gained some practice with four. You are able to explain the causal structure of a problem or situation, explain how the problem is created by the model structure, explain why one policy has high impact while others fail to do so (at least the four policies evaluated in Chapter 7 –you would also be able to evaluate other ones if required to), and you will be able to argue in favour of better policies in the NewTel case – policies which avoid losing profits for the sake of competing with RivTel.

Four of the six learning outcomes are decomposed by complexity level. As you can imagine, living up to this skill is quite different for a challenge consisting of two feedback loops, five loops or even more. The ability to explain how established policies are the underlying cause of problematic behaviour is a complex task, however reduced the modelled set of feedback loops may be. And being able to communicate effectively with stakeholders about the use of the model does not depend on the model's intrinsic complexity. These two learning outcomes are those that were not covered in this book, because we worked with you on a specifically designed case and without clients. These additional aspects will become relevant when you work in a real setting, where people have developed personal policies over time, and where your communication skills are challenged.

9.4.8 Your stage of competence development
Taken together, you have advanced in most of the seven skills which comprise the system dynamics competence. You have currently left behind the beginner stage and are in the midst of the advanced beginner stage.

Are you an advanced beginner now? You would seem to be well on your way. Congratulations! You have developed a lot of system dynamics knowledge and abilities while you were busy resolving the NewTel management case. If you are interested in advancing, there are several options available for you, as we will discuss next.

9.5 Learning and applying system dynamics

As you are approaching the end of this book, we hope to have shown you that system dynamics has practical value, not only for managing an organization through episodes of growth in new markets but also for other challenging dynamic management situations. Many strategic situations are eminently dynamic in nature, just think of how to keep growing in a mature market, how to develop new products and other innovations and so on. As a manager, you are also responsible for developing your organization's resources (some tangible, others not, some internal to the organization, others external) to develop the demand your organization intends to satisfy and to have sufficient capacity to deliver. Since resources usually grow and decline with different speeds, the pace at which you try to satisfy and create demand can pose dauntingly complex challenges (Paich and Sterman, 1993; Sterman *et al.*, 2007).

It is true that simulation modelling is not a crystal ball or a kind of electronic oracle. But it is immensely helpful in developing your understanding of a situation's causal structure and for designing policies that have at least resisted the crash tests of simulation. For this reason, model-based management has distinctive strengths, and learning more about system dynamics can be not only interesting and personally rewarding but also simply a productive investment of time.

There is a wide range of learning opportunities on offer from a variety of institutions, ranging from short workshops to full PhD programmes. A growing number of undergraduate programmes in business administration incorporate system dynamics modules in more and more countries on every continent. Well established master's level courses and PhD programmes are offered by single universities as well as networks, mostly in the United States of America and in Europe. You will find an overview on the website of the System Dynamics Society at http://www.systemdynamics.org/courses.

In addition, there are proven textbooks for beginners and for advanced modellers. While Morecroft (2007) is a smooth introduction to system dynamics modelling in a number of management situations, Sterman (2000) provides an extensive and detailed reference including more technical aspects.

Finally, the System Dynamics Society offers a social network of specialists to interact with and it edits *System Dynamics Review*, in which methodological advances and the best applications are published several times per year. You will find a detailed description of the system dynamics competence framework there (Schaffernicht and Groesser, 2016). Additionally, you can subscribe to the Society's Facebook page and Twitter, as well as become a member of LinkedIn groups discussing system dynamics topics.

And, finally: Enjoy modelling complex systems to improve the quality of decision making. In the words of Jay Forrester (1985: 134): 'Rather than stressing the single-model concept, it appears that we should stress the process of modelling as a continuing companion to, and tool for, the improvement of judgment and human decision making'.

Let us know about how you are doing. Write to us:

Martin Schaffernicht: martin@utalca.cl

Stefan Groesser: stefan.groesser@bfh.ch

References

Dierickx, I. and Cool, K. 1989. Asset stock accumulation and sustainability of competitive advantage. *Management Science*, **35**(12): 1504–1511.

Ericsson, K.A., Krampe, R.T., and Tesch-Römer, C. 1993. The role of deliberate practice in the acquisition of expert performance. *Psychological Review*, **100**(3): 363.

Ericsson, K.A., Prietula, M.J., and Cokely, E.T. 2007. The making of an expert. *Harvard Business Review*, (**1**): 1–8.

Forrester, J.W. 1961. *Industrial Dynamics*. Productivity Press, Cambridge, MA.

Forrester, J.W. 1969. *Principles of Systems*. Wright-Allen Press, Cambridge, MA.

Forrester, J.W. 1985. The 'model' versus a modeling 'process'. *System Dynamics Review*, **1**(1): 133–143.

Forrester, J.W. 1994. Policies, decisions, and information sources for modeling. In: J.D.W. Morecroft and J.D. Sterman (eds), *Modeling for Learning Organizations*. Productivity Press, Portland, OR, pp. 51–84.

Forrester, J.W. 2007. System dynamics – the next fifty years. *System Dynamics Review*, **23**(2–3): 359–370.

Groesser, S.N. 2015. Lab or Reality: Entwicklung und Analyse von Geschäftsmodellen durch das kybernetische Unternehmensmodell Blue Company©. In S. Jeschke, R. Schmitt, and R. Dröge (eds), *Exploring Cybernetics: Kybernetik im interdisziplinären Diskurs*. Springer, Berlin, pp. 109–135.

Groesser, S.N., and Schwaninger, M. 2012. Contributions to model validation: hierarchy, process, and cessation. *System Dynamics Review*, **28**(2): 157–181.

Groesser, S.N. and Zeier, R (eds). 2012. *Systemic Management for Intelligent Organizations: Concepts, Model-Based Approaches, and Applications*. Springer-Publishing, Heidelberg.

Groesser, S.N., Schwaninger, M., Tilebein, M., *et al.* (eds). 2013. *Modell-basiertes Management*. In M. Tilebein and T. Fischer (eds) *Wirtschaftskybernetik und Systemanalyse*. Drucker & Humblot Verlag, Berlin.

Kahneman, D. 2011. *Thinking Fast and Slow*. Farrar, Straus and Giroux, New York.

Martinez-Moyano, I.J. and Richardson, G.P. 2013. Best practices in system dynamics modeling. *System Dynamics Review*, **29**(2): 102–123.

Morecroft, J.D.W. 2007. *Strategic Modelling and Business Dynamics: A Feedback Systems Approach*. John Wiley & Sons Ltd, Chichester, UK.

Paich, M. and Sterman, J.D. 1993. Boom, bust, and failures to learn in experimental markets. *Management Science*, **39**(12): 1439–1458.

Schaffernicht, M. 2010. Causal loop diagrams between structure and behaviour: A critical analysis of the relationship between polarity, behaviour and events. *Systems Research and Behavioral Science*, **27**(6): 653–666.

Schaffernicht, M. and Groesser, S. 2016. A framework for developing system dynamics competence. *System Dynamics Review*, **32**(1): 52–81.

Senge, P.M. 1990. *The Fifth Discipline: The Art and Practice of the Learning Organization*. Currency & Doubleday, New York, NY.

Sterman, J.D. 2000. *Business Dynamics: Systems Thinking and Modeling for a Complex World*. McGraw-Hill, Boston, MA.

Sterman, J.D. 2001. System dynamics modeling: tools for learning in a complex world. *California Management Review*, **43**(4): 8–24.

Sterman, J.D, Henderson, R., Beinhocker, E.D., and Newman, L.I. 2007. Getting big too fast: strategic dynamics with increasing returns and bounded rationality. *Management Science*, **53**(4): 683–696.

Warren, K. 2008. *Strategic Management Dynamics*, John Wiley & Sons Ltd, Chichester, UK.

ABBREVIATIONS

Context	Abbreviation	Meaning
Scenarios	BAU	Busines as usual
	BCM	Best case monopoly
	BCR	Best case rivalry
	CFC	Compete for customers
	COMP	Simulation experiment based on strategy 'Compete'
	COOP	Simulation experiment based on strategy 'Cooperate'
	RIAM	Rivalry I Advertising More
	RIPA	Rivalry I Price Advantage
Variables	EMP	Effective monthly price
	WoM	Word-of-mouth
Modelling	BOTG	Behaviour-over-time graph
	CLD	Causal loop diagram
	DT	Delta time or time step
	KPI	Key performance indicators
	PI	Policy implementation
	SFD	Stock-and-flow diagram

Growth Dynamics in New Markets: Improving Decision Making through Simulation Model-based Management, First Edition. Martin F.G. Schaffernicht and Stefan N. Groesser.
© 2018 John Wiley & Sons Ltd. Published 2018 by John Wiley & Sons Ltd.
Companion website: www.wiley.com/go/Schaffernicht/growth-dynamics

INDEX OF PRINCIPLES

INDEX OF GUIDELINES

Growth Dynamics in New Markets: Improving Decision Making through Simulation Model-based Management,
First Edition. Martin F.G. Schaffernicht and Stefan N. Groesser.
© 2018 John Wiley & Sons Ltd. Published 2018 by John Wiley & Sons Ltd.
Companion website: www.wiley.com/go/Schaffernicht/growth-dynamics

INDEX OF MANAGEMENT INSIGHTS

Growth Dynamics in New Markets: Improving Decision Making through Simulation Model-based Management,
First Edition. Martin F.G. Schaffernicht and Stefan N. Groesser.
© 2018 John Wiley & Sons Ltd. Published 2018 by John Wiley & Sons Ltd.
Companion website: www.wiley.com/go/Schaffernicht/growth-dynamics

INDEX OF SYSTEMS INSIGHTS

Growth Dynamics in New Markets: Improving Decision Making through Simulation Model-based Management,
First Edition. Martin F.G. Schaffernicht and Stefan N. Groesser.
© 2018 John Wiley & Sons Ltd. Published 2018 by John Wiley & Sons Ltd.
Companion website: www.wiley.com/go/Schaffernicht/growth-dynamics

INDEX OF TOOLBOXES

Growth Dynamics in New Markets: Improving Decision Making through Simulation Model-based Management,
First Edition. Martin F.G. Schaffernicht and Stefan N. Groesser.
© 2018 John Wiley & Sons Ltd. Published 2018 by John Wiley & Sons Ltd.
Companion website: www.wiley.com/go/Schaffernicht/growth-dynamics

INDEX OF DIYS

INDEX

Growth Dynamics in New Markets: Improving Decision Making through Simulation Model-based Management,
First Edition. Martin F.G. Schaffernicht and Stefan N. Groesser.
© 2018 John Wiley & Sons Ltd. Published 2018 by John Wiley & Sons Ltd.
Companion website: www.wiley.com/go/Schaffernicht/growth-dynamics